RESEARCHES IN

INDIAN AND BUDDHIST PHILOSOPHY

FELICITATION COMMITTEE

M. B. EMENEAU

R. N. DANDEKAR

ANDRE BAREAU

MADELEINE BIARDEAU

M.A. DHAKY

MICHAEL HAHN

AKIRA HIRAKAWA

R. V. JOSHI

HAJIME NAKAMURA

ERNST STEINKELLNER

L. N. TIWARI

RAM KARAN SHARMA

Alex Wayman as Professor of Sanskrit at Columbia University in the 1970's.

RESEARCHES IN INDIAN AND BUDDHIST PHILOSOPHY

Essays in Honour of Professor Alex Wayman

Edited by
RAM KARAN SHARMA

MOTILAL BANARSIDASS PUBLISHERS
PRIVATE LIMITED • DELHI

First Edition: Delhi, 1993

ISBN: 81-208-0994-7

Also available at:
MOTILAL BANARSIDASS
41 U.A., Bungalow Road, Jawahar Nagar, Delhi 110 007
120 Royapettah High Road, Mylapore, Madras 600 004
16 St. Mark's Road, Bangalore 560 001
Ashok Rajpath, Patna 800 004
Chowk, Varanasi 221 001

PRINTED IN INDIA
BY JAINENDRA PRAKASH JAIN AT SHRI JAINENDRA PRESS, A-45 NARAINA INDUSTRIAL AREA, PHASE I, NEW DELHI 110 028 AND PUBLISHED BY NARENDRA PRAKASH JAIN FOR MOTILAL BANARSIDASS PUBLISHERS PRIVATE LIMITED, BUNGALOW ROAD, JAWAHAR NAGAR, DELHI 110 007

CONTENTS

Preface vii
Emeneau's Blessings xi
Biographical Sketch of Alex Wayman xiii
Bibliography xxiii

BUDDHIST PHILOSOPHICAL RESEARCHES

A. MISCELLANEOUS

1. The List of the *Asaṃskṛta-dharma* According to Asaṅga ANDRÉ BAREAU 1
2. The Seven Principles of the Vajjian Republic: Their Different Interpretations HAJIME NAKAMURA 7
3. A Difficult Beginning: Comments on an English Translation of Candragomin's *Deśanāstava* MICHAEL HAHN 31
4. A Study of Aspects of *Rāga* N. H. SAMTANI 61

B. KARMA THEORY

5. Principle of Life According to Bhavya SHINJO KAWASAKI 69
6. The Buddhist Doctrine of Karma HARI SHANKAR PRASAD 83
7. A Critical Appraisal of Karmaphalaparīkṣā of Nāgārjuna T. R. SHARMA 97

C. DEPENDENT ORIGINATION

8. The Relationship between *Paṭiccasamuppāda* and *Dhātu* AKIRA HIRAKAWA 105
9. Dependent Origination: Its Elaboration in Early Sarvāstivādin Abhidharma Texts COLLETT COX 119
10. Dependent Origination in Buddhist Tantra GEORGE R. ELDER 143

JAINA PHILOSOPHICAL RESEARCHES

11. *(Kevali)Bhuktivicāra* of Bhāvasena: Text and Translation PADMANABH S. JAINI 163

12. The Earliest Portions of *Daśavaikālika-sūtra*
M.A. DHAKY 179

HINDU PHILOSOPHICAL RESEARCHES

13. Buddhist and Mīmāṃsā Views on Lakṣaṇā
K. KUNJUNNI RAJA 195

14. Grammarians and Philosophers
KAMALESWAR BHATTACHARYA 203

15. Kashmir Śaivism (KS) and the Vedānta of Śaṅkara R.C. DWIVEDI 209

16. Siddhi-s in the Bhāgavata Purāṇa and in the Yogasūtra-s of Patañjali—A Comparison
T. S. RUKMANI 217

17. Language and Metaphor in Indian Stotra Literature R. K. SHARMA 227

18. *Pitta* Versus *Agni*—An Ayurvedic Perspective
BHAGWAN DASH 241

19. The Doctrine of 'Aham-Artha' R.V. JOSHI 247

Contributors 281

PREFACE

It is preeminently fit for the scholarly world to bring out a Felicitation volume to honour Professor Alex Wayman, who has distinguished himself by an outpouring of scholarly works on Buddhism for almost forty years; and who is now Professor of Sanskrit, emeritus, Columbia University, New York.

I am proud of my association with Professor Wayman dating back to 1957 as my distinguished satīrthya when I joined the University of California, Berkeley, as a Fulbright student. There we both studied under Professor Murray Barnson Emeneau, an eminent linguist, classicist and Indologist; and then were awarded our Ph.D.'s the same date in 1959.

Prof. Wayman has been all along a source of inspiration to me. He identifies himself with his studies in an exclusive attention always occupied with scholarly pursuits, finishing one thing, and thinking of his next project. I don't remember if he ever talked of anything other than Indian Philosophy, Buddhism or general Indology.

Prof. Emeneau's kind blessings are found in print in this volume. Those of Prof. R.N. Dandekar and other distinguished members of the Felicitation Committee are also very much there: "punaś ca bhūyo 'pi namo 'stu tebhyaḥ".

I am grateful to the Felicitation Committee and also to the learned contributors for enriching this volume. It is divided into three major sections: Buddhist, Jaina and Hindu Philosophical Researches. In a way this is also the scope of Professor Wayman's researches.

Under the Buddhist researches, the essay by André Bareau, using the Vinaya in Chinese, defends Wayman's position that Asaṅga belonged to the Mahīśāsaka sect. Hajime Nakamura points out differing views, about the seven Vajjian Republic principles; it is nice to have this important set of paragraphs in the present volume. Michael Hahn concerns himself with the famous Buddhist poet Candragomin who might also be the grammarian of that name but hardly the Candragomin who commented on Buddhist Tantras. N.H. Samtani vigorously treats the term *rāga*. After these miscellaneous articles there are two groups of Buddhistic essays. In the group on Karma, Shinjō Kawasaki expounds the views of Bhavya about the differing karma of non-sentient entities and of sentient beings. Hari Shankar Prasad's essay makes the division in terms of when there is lack of agency of presence of agency, especially using Yogācāra sources. The one by T.R. Sharma treats the Mādhyamika position by a chapter of Nāgārjuna's Madhyamaka-kārikā.

There are also three essays on Buddhist Dependent Origination. Akira Hirakawa provides an important article on the relation with dhātu, where this expression is shown to mean a kind of causation. The essay by Collett Cox uses the early Chinese Abhidharma works to show that the present 12-membered formula is taken for granted by such texts, with the divergences consisting in the interpretation of the twelve, sequential, instantaneous, and so forth. George Elder's contribution, while presenting certain features of the Tantric type of Dependent Origination, defends Wayman's translation of certain terms.

While the Jaina section has only two papers, the volume is privileged to have these contributions by Padmanabh S. Jaini and by M.A. Dhaky. Jaini's deals with the theory that an omniscient being can subsist on a subtle kind of food. Dhaky's, while having its main object to ascertain early parts of the *Daśavaikālikasūtra*, also goes into the matter of food.

The section devoted to the Hindu Philosophy is also rich in contributions. While not subdivided as was the Buddhist one, in fact, each essay takes a comparative base. Thus the one by K. Kunjunni Raja compares the Buddhist and Mīmāṃsā views on 'lakṣaṇā', and so deserves to be first. Kamaleswar Bhattacharya speaks of grammarians and philosophers regarding post-Pāṇini grammarians on a certain *anuśāsana*. R.C. Dwivedi makes a comparison between Kashmir Śaivism and Śaṅkara's Vedānta. T.S. Rukmani compares *siddhis* as found in the *Bhāgavata Purāṇa* and in Patañjali's *Yogasūtra*. R.K. Sharma deals with language and with metaphor in two devotional treatises of Śaivism. Then Bhagwan Dash continues the comparisons, this time of Pitta with Agni. Finally, R.V. Joshi, while not explicitly mentioning his comparative base in the essay title, in fact, in this remarkable portrayal of the doctrine of 'aham-artha', is basically comparing the Advaita and the

Vaiṣṇava views of the matter, also bringing in the Sāṃkhya school.

Thus, the work appears to contain solid contributions to the field of Indian Philosophy, sometimes summarizing previously established positions, but usually breaking new ground.

I appreciate the role of the publishing house of Motilal Banarsidass Publishers Private Limited in bringing out this volume; and anticipate an appreciative response from the world Sanskrit community agreeing with my personal view that this volume is interesting and useful for further researches in the great Indian philosophical traditions. And so also a fitting testimonial to Professor Alex Wayman for his unremitting labours to bring these Indian traditions into Western format. We hope he produces more distinguished works: "Śataṃ jīva śarado vardhamānaḥ".

R. K. SHARMA

EMENEAU'S BLESSINGS

January 31, 1991

Dear Ram,

I was so happy to get your card at Christmas, with its greetings and kind wishes. I am so old now that I have stopped sending cards—but believe me, I think of you often.

It is nice to hear that Alex Wayman is to be presented with a volume, to felicitate him on his so distinguished career in Buddhist studies. I wish I had some contribution to make to the volume, but nothing is at hand at the moment nor have I anything in mind that might interest him. All best wishes for your editing what will no doubt be a most distinguished volume.

With all my best wishes.

Affectionately,

M.B. EMENEAU

Professor Ram Karan Sharma
Delhi
INDIA.

A BIOGRAPHICAL SKETCH OF ALEX WAYMAN

Alex Wayman was born January 11, 1921, at Chicago, Illinois, in the United States of America. His father, born near St. Petersburg (later, Leningrad) participated in an aborted Russian revolt of our first decade, and escaped to Paris, where he met and married a lady born in Odessa, Russia, whose family had migrated to Paris. Just before the First World War they shifted to the U.S.A., seeking a 'better life' and both plied the trade of tailoring, first in Chicago. Of four children, one older brother died in a traffic accident in Chicago, another older one years later in a fall. Wayman has one surviving younger sister. When he was eight, his parents moved to Los Angeles, California, where his education continued.

After High School he took stenographic training and passed the Senior Stenographer—Senior Typist exam. of the U.S. Civil Service. During this time and while waiting for an appointment, he spent much time reading in the Philosophy and Religion room of the Los Angeles Public Library. Here he saw for the first time a book on Buddhism—a translation of the *Visuddhimagga*. He also met and learned much from an elderly gentleman, Ramsperger by name, contemporary to Wayman's father, but raised in Switzerland near the German border. His life was an experience of successive deceptions, first the Socialists of that area with their deceived idealism. When a young man the doctors thought he was a 'goner' because of his fevers; but he learned all about the 'nature cure' methods that were circulating in Europe and adopted the 'water cure' of a Father Kneip to control his fevers. Getting alarmed by accounts of a Dutch visionary who saw wolves wandering in the streets of the cities, he and others thought it meant there was going to be a terrible war, and so he left Europe with his son on the eve of the First World War, as the second person to be later important in Wayman's life. He went to Peru and became a shepherd. After the War he moved to Los Angeles, earning a living by minor repair work, including plastering and painting houses. To learn English he attended the free public lectures by the 'occult' groups. There were the Rosicrucians, the Theosophists, Manly Palmer Hall, and other 'break-away' occultists. He acquainted Wayman with those movements, which for Ramsperger were different kinds of deception. Such was going on at the time Wayman was born.

Wayman accepted the first Civil Service job offered, which was in the headquarters office of Death Valley National Monument (a part of the National Park Service), in California bordering the state of Nevada. In those days, the latter part of 1940, gasoline and tire rationing due to the beginning of the Second World War had reduced automobile traffic on the one desert road of Death Valley to about a single car a day. It was very quiet. There was zero humidity. On the floor of Death Valley in the year 1941, trying out a breathing exercise from a little book on Hindu breath control, he soon had a remarkable and terrifying experience; and promptly stopped the exercise. The experience left him with a belief that there was indeed another realm that he was close to, but which had best be left alone. After two and a quarter years here, he was inducted into the U.S. Army. Including overseas service in Australia, the Philippines, and Okinawa, altogether he spent over three years in the army; and was in Australia long enough to complete a course in Metaphysics and Ethics at the University of Queensland in Brisbane.

Returning to Los Angeles he began his university studies early in 1946 at the University of California at Los Angeles (UCLA). There had been virtually no civilian housing built here during the War, so returning veterans found a great housing shortage. Wayman first stayed at the residence of his friend Ramsperger across the city from UCLA. This was on a second floor, on top of a furniture-making shop, at a corner on the edge of the district famous later on by the name of Watt, inhabited by the blacks; and was across from a railroad storage area. At night, despite the bustling character of Los Angeles, this area had an eerie silence. Ramsperger had many close friends among the blacks. He explained to Wayman the 'water cure' for breaking fevers which he had used since he was a young man, but Wayman fortunately was not afflicted with fevers. Since one could not study on the long bus ride across the city, after a few months Wayman found a place not very far from UCLA, where a lady had subdivided an apartment, and she rented the kitchen to Wayman, the 'living room' to someone else, first to a prissy teaching assistant in Architecture, and later to a troubled member of the City Council of Los Angeles. UCLA was still in the trimester system adopted during the War; and Wayman went straight through, never taking a break, thus quickly getting a B.A. (1948) and an M.A. (1949), both degrees in Mathematics. Moving to Berkeley, with a recommendation to continue his mathematic studies, he promptly lost all interest in this discipline of a part of cognition.

He first could find as a place to stay only a crude room behind a restaurant close to the University of California. In the fall, 1949, he took beginning Chinese, Mongolian and Tibetan. Dr. Ferdinand Lessing was the first to introduce the teaching of either Tibetan or Mongolian in an American university, but former students were then teaching these courses because Dr. Lessing was in the hospital recovering from a heart attack. Later on, Wayman found out that when Lessing was in the hospital he took the opportunity to start translating Mkhas-grub-rje's Fundamentals of the Buddhist Tantras. He would clip a folio of the Tibetan (the Labrang edition) on a poster, and on another poster would clip the opened Chinese version by Fa-tsun. Then he would write out his draft translation, leaving a gap if the passage appeared incomprehensible. In this Fall session, also a student Arthur Link had returned from China, probably the last of the Fulbright group to get out with all his possessions. He had brought back the *Lam rim chen mo* by Tsong-kha-pa in the Tashilunpo edition plus the annotation edition called *Mchan 'grel*; also the *Sngags rim* by the same author, because back in Peking he had a mild interest in Tibetan studies; but because now he had no interest at all in Tibetan studies, he traded these books to Wayman in return for some other publications which Wayman gave to him.

When Lessing came out of the hospital, he engaged Wayman as his assistant in his Yung-ho-kung researches on the Lamaist cathedral of Peking. This was also Lessing's last year before retirement; and he was about to embark on his Mongolian-English Dictionary, which would occupy almost the entire decade of the 50's. Lessing became the third person in Wayman's life who had left Europe just before the First World War. This happened because Lessing was one of several advanced students given fellowships by the German government to do research in China. But not long after their arrival there, the First World War broke out, which stopped their research money. Stranded, those researchers sought local jobs; and Lessing got a job teaching German at the University of Mukden, Manchuria. All together, Lessing spent twenty-two years in China. When Lessing published a collaborated work in German on the modern Chinese language he was awarded the doctorate degree at the University of Berlin where he had once studied, and was invited back as a professor arriving about 1931. But then the political situation was increasingly dreadful. So when the University of California, Berkeley, invited Dr. Lessing to take over the Department of Oriental Languages and build it up, he gladly accepted, arriving in 1935.

In that Spring of 1950, Wayman started work on the *Lam rim chen mo*, by transcribing citations on individual sheets, using the manual Royal typewriter he had bought when in Death Valley, but which now was outfitted with diacritics on 'dead' keys. He continued only with Tibetan and Mongolian at the university. Dr. Lessing had a student in the department whose dissertation on Japanese topics he supervised, and who had a big house in Berkeley. He arranged with that student to rent out a room to Wayman, who thus enjoyed a considerable improvement in housing. That summer also the Mongolian Lama Dilowa Hutukhtu visited Berkeley, and Lessing arranged a room for him in the same house so he was staying across the hall from Wayman. Dilowa liked to visit Berkeley, and did it two more times in summers, because the Tibetan collection which Lessing had brought back from China soon after the Second World War on behalf of the East Asiatic library of the university was easily accessible; and there was a sizeable Mongolian collection. In the fall, 1950, Wayman was able to rent a room in the Berkeley hills, and which had a convenient access. It was about this time or a little later that Wayman transcribed the Tibetan of the Mkhas-grub-rje work on one side of a page and facing it Lessing's draft translation, with its gaps. The Dilowa Hutukhtu arranged through his disciple, the Da-lama in Kalimpong, to obtain the collected works of Tsong-kha-pa and of his two main disciples (Mkhas-grub-rje and Rgyal-tshab-rje) in the Lhasa edition. When these collections arrived at the East Asiatic Library, it was possible to figure out any problems with Mkhas-grub-rje's Tibetan text in the Labrang edition; although this still did not solve the bristling problems of a proper translation of the work. Dr. Lessing once relayed to Wayman a kind of prophecy given him by Dilowa. He had told Dr. Lessing that he had been wrong about Wayman—now he believes that Wayman could translate the *Lam rim chen mo*; but had been right about Dr. Lessing—that he could not translate Mkhas-grub-rje's work. It was perhaps for this reason that Dr. Lessing asked Wayman to be his collaborator in the translation of the Mkhas-grub-rje. In a way, the prophecy was fulfilled. The Mkhas-grub-rje treatise was not completed in the 1950's. It was only after the passing of Dr. Lessing that it was possible for Wayman to complete and annotate it (The Hague, 1968). As to the *Lam rim chen mo*, it was only years later that Wayman published the last large section under the title *Calming the Mind and Discerning the Real* (New York, 1978); but now has prepared the Bodhisattva section, to appear in 1991 at Albany, New York. In short, Dr. Lessing introduced Wayman to the world of Buddhist scholarship.

Dilowa Hutukhtu recommended to Takser Rinpoche, the elder brother of the Dalai Lama, that he contact Wayman for English lessons. In the summer of 1951, Wayman gave English lessons to him and his assistant. Takser later adopted the name Thubten Norbu; and was for a number of years a professor at Indiana University.

By 1952 Wayman no longer studied Mongolian. He now took up the study of Sanskrit under Professor Murray Emeneau in the Classics Department of the University of California, Berkeley. Later, Emeneau established the Linguistics Department of that university and moved into it. Professor Emeneau became famous for the collaborated work with T. Burrow, *A Dravidian Etymological Dictionary*. His publications on the Toda language are well-known. His numerous published essays in the area of Sanskrit are characterized by admirable precision and thoroughness. Professor Emeneau set a high scholarly standard for Wayman, a kind of upper limit.

Also in 1952 Wayman began attending the Berkeley Buddhist Church conducted by Rev. and Mrs. Kenmō Imamura, thereby meeting such personages as Alan Watts and Daisetz Suzuki, and later visitors from Japan such as Hajime Nakamura; as well as the poet group of Gary Snyder, Alan Ginsburg, and Jack Kerouac. This attendance presaged the later association with Japanese Buddhist scholars after getting married and visiting Japan several times.

Around 1954 he obtained from the Bihar Research Society, Patna, India, the photographic manuscript of the *Śrāvakabhūmi* which was to be the basis of his doctoral dissertation, and the beginning of extensive readings in Asaṅga's *Yogācārabhūmi*, which was cited for a number of Wayman's essays. This also made it possible for him to translate from Tibetan the *śamatha* section of the *Lam rim chen mo* under the title "Calming the Mind".

In August 1956 Wayman married a Japanese lady Hideko Shimomaki, a native of Japan, graduate of Tsuda College, Tokyo; and who had just completed an M.A. at the University of California, Berkeley, in the topic of child development. She came from a family of lawyers; and her father, an uncle, and her eldest brother were eminent in this field. She added a touch of oriental beauty and refinement. Doubtless, this union made it easier for Wayman to communicate with Japanese professors; and years later when teaching at Columbia University made it possible for him to talk diplomatically with bright female students, several of whose dissertations he sponsored. She collaborated with Wayman in the work *Lion's Roar of Queen Śrīmālā* (New York, 1974; reprinted Delhi, 1990).

As Wayman was finishing his dissertation, a Fulbright student from India was also studying under Professor Emeneau and completing a dissertation on poetry of the Mahābhārata. This was Ram Karan Sharma, and the two were awarded doctorates apparently on the same day in 1959. Dr. Sharma went on to a wonderful career in Sanskrit studies in India, on the aesthetic level with Sanskrit poetry; on the technical level with the valuable translation of the medical text *Carakasaṃhitā*; on the administrative level as Vice-Chancellor of the K. S. D. Sanskrit University, Darbhanga, and Vice-Chancellor of the Sampurnananda Sanskrit University, Varanasi.

Wayman's first academic position after the doctorate was as a visiting lecturer at the University of Michigan at Ann Arbor, during the academic year 1960-61. The regular professor was on leave in Taiwan; he was the same Arthur Link, from whom Wayman had obtained the *Lam rim chen mo,* etc. texts. It was at this time that his first book was being readied for publication, *Analysis of the Śrāvakabhūmi Manuscript* (Berkeley, 1961), stemming from his dissertation.

The flood of federal money in support of certain foreign languages, including those of South Asia, made it possible for the University of Wisconsin to hire Professor Richard Robinson to start a Buddhist studies program, and then to hire Wayman, who was already publishing in the field of Buddhism, to assist him. After joining in fall, 1961, his advancement was steady. Some important events occurred while he was still an Assistant Professor. First was his faculty research in India, Feb. 1963 to Jan. 1964, sponsored by the American Institute of Indian Studies. In cars arranged for by his wife Hideko, they travelled more than 15,000 miles on the floor of India, visiting Hindu and Buddhist monuments, institutes and universities. At Pondicherry they were hosted by the Indologist J. Filliozat. They met such scholars in Sanskrit as Professor R. N. Dandekar of Poona and Professor V. Raghavan of Madras; and secured a good collection of books on Indian culture. The scholars Madeleine Biardeau of Paris and Hidenori Kitagawa of Nagoya, Japan, joined them at meals when the Waymans were stationed at Deccan College, Poona. Later, when they were returning to the U.S. by way of Europe, in Paris Professor Biardeau introduced Wayman to the well-known Sanskritist Louis Renou, the Sinologist Paul Demiéville, and the Buddhologist André Bareau. In Belgium they visited the Buddhologist Étienne Lamotte; and at Leiden they visited J.W. de Jong, joint editor of the *Indo-Iranian Journal.*

After returning to Madison, the site of the University of Wisconsin, Wayman arranged for a Japanese Fulbright student Noritoshi Aramaki to study for a year at the University of Wisconsin; and also arranged for Professor Gadjin M. Nagao to come as a Visiting Professor about the same time. Since both of them were from Kyoto, it became a time to learn something of the Kyoto school of Buddhism. Wayman was promoted to Associate Professor in 1965. In Fall, 1966 he was a Visiting Associate Professor at Columbia in its Department of Religion. He returned to the University of Wisconsin for Spring, 1967, because he was arranging the Tagore Memorial Lectures there, and to be delivered by Dr. Humayan Kabir. From 1967 to June 1991 he has held the position Professor of Sanskrit, Department of Middle East Languages and Cultures, Columbia University. Most of his books and an extensive list of articles have appeared after he joined Columbia University. He has left an indelible stamp on the university because as of his 70th birthday in January 1991 he had sponsored the successful Ph.D. dissertations of seventeen students of the Department of Religion and of five students of the Department of Middle East Languages and Cultures, and is still supervising Ph.D. dissertations in both those departments. Most of those sponsored dissertations were in the field of Buddhism. As of July 1, 1991 he will be Emeritus Professor of Sanskrit.

Wayman's academic career was much affected by his participation in scholarly meetings. Thus, when the congress of the International Association for the History of Religion met at Clairmont, California, in 1965, Wayman gave a talk on the Thirty-five Buddhas of Confession, which led to the invitation to join the Columbia University faculty. In 1972 he attended the Second International Sanskrit Conference in Torino, Italy; and this led to the numerous articles he has written for the annual *Studia Missionalia* published in Rome. Then, while at the 1973 International Congress of Orientalists in Paris, he met Narendra Prakash Jain of Motilal Banarsidass, the famous publishing house of India, and Mr. Jain agreed to publish the *Yoga of the Guhyasamājatantra* (1977). In time this led to a close association with Motilal Banarsidass, eventually to becoming editor of the Buddhist Traditions Series being published by them.

Wayman's list of publications shows that he began writing articles for publication in the year 1952 while he was a graduate student at the University of California, Berkeley; inaugurated his study of Sanskrit, and started attending the Berkeley Buddhist Church. The publication activity continued with regularity. Of course, such early articles he looks upon as somewhat primitive. His essay style gradually evolved, especially to accommodate larger amounts of data. Retirement from Columbia will not dampen his productivity. Indeed, he expects major works to appear in the next several years. First of all, and expectedly in 1991, *The Enlightenment of Vairocana* (study of the *Vairocanābhisaṃbodhitantra*), and *Ethics of Tibet; the Bodhisattva section of Tsong-kha-pa's Lam rim chen mo*. Next, is the collaborated Sanskrit-Tibetan edition of the *Viśvalocana* lexicon with English translation; and twenty-four selected essays under the title *Untying the Knots in Buddhism*. Once these are out of the way, the long-term project *A Millennium of Buddhist Logic* will be put into publishable shape.

Academic Synopsis for Alex Wayman

Education and degrees

University of California, Los Angeles:
Mathematics, 1946-48—B.A. (1948)
University of California, Los Angeles:
Mathematics, 1948-49—M.A. (1949)
University of California, Berkeley:
Sanskrit and Tibetan languages, 1949-59—Ph.D. (1959)
Nalanda University, Bihar, India:
Honorary degree—D.Litt., April, 1978

Professional Employment

1967—June 30, 1991	Professor of Sanskrit, Columbia University, New York
Fall 1966	Visiting Associate Professor, Columbia University, New York
1965—1967	Associate Professor, The University of Wisconsin, Madison, Wisconsin
1961—1965	Assistant Professor, The University of Wisconsin, Madison
1960—1961	Visiting Lecturer in Buddhism and Indic Studies, University of Michigan, Ann Arbor, Michigan

BIBLIOGRAPHY

(Reviews, except for review articles, not included)

1952

1. "Introduction to Tsoṅ-kha-pa's Lam rim chen mo", *Phi Theta Annual* (Oriental Language Honor Soc., Berkeley, Calif.), 3, pp. 51-82.

1954

2. Contributor to *Bibliographie Bouddhique*, XXIV-XXVII (Mai, 1950—Mai, 1954), Paris, Adrien Maisonneuve.

1955

3. "Notes on the three myrobalans", *Phi Theta Annual*, 5, 1954-55, pp. 63-77.
4. "Notes on the Sanskrit Term Jñāna", *Journal of the American Oriental Society*, 75:4, 1955, pp. 253-8.
5. "The Lamp and the Wind in Tibetan Buddhism", *Philosophy East and West*, 5:2, 149-54.

1956

6. "A Report on the Śrāvaka-bhūmi and its author (Asaṅga)", *Journal of the Bihar Research Society*, 42-3-4, pp. 316-29.

1957

7. "Contributions regarding the thirty-two characteristies of the Great Person", *Sino-Indian Studies*: *Liebenthal Festschrift*, Visvabharati, pp. 243-69.
8. "The meaning of unwisdom (*avidyā*)", *Philosophy East and West*, 7:1-2, pp. 21-15.
9. "The concept of poison in Buddhism," *Oriens*, 10:1, pp. 107-09, (in honor of Leonard Olschki).

1958

10. Contributor to *Bibliographie Bouddhique*, XXVIII-XXXI (Mai, 1954—Mai, 1958), Paris, Adrien Maisonneuve.
11. "The rules of debate according to Asaṅga", *JAOS*, 78:1, pp. 29-40.

1959

12. "The Twenty-One Praises of Tārā, a Syncretism of Śaivism and Buddhism", *Journal of the Bihar Research Society*, 45:1-4, pp. 36-43. (A. S. Altekar Memorial Volume).

13. "Studies in Yama and Māra", *Indo-Iranian Journal*, 3:1, pp. 44-75; 3:2, pp. 112-31.

1960

14. "The Sacittikā and Acittikā Bhūmi and the Pratyekabuddhabhūmi (Sanskrit texts)", *Journal of Indian and Buddhist Studies* (Tokyo), 7:1, pp. 375-79.

1961

15. Analysis of the Śrāvakabhūmi Manuscript, University of California Publications in Classical Philology, Vol. 17, Berkeley, California.

16. "Totemic Beliefs in the Buddhist Tantras", *History of Religions*, 1:1, pp. 81-94.

17. "The Buddhist 'Not this, not this' ", *Philosophy East and West*, 11:3, pp. 99-114.

1962

18. "Outline of the Thob Yig Gsal Bahi Me Loṅ", *Indo-Asian Studies*, Vol. I (International Academy of Indian Culture, New Delhi, 1961-62), 109-17.

19. "Analysis of the Tantric Section of the Kanjur correlated to Tanjur Exegesis", *Indo-Asian Studies*, Vol. I, 118-25.

20. "Buddhist Genesis and the Tantric Tradition", *Oriens Extremus*, 9:1, pp. 127-31. (F. D. Lessing memorial issue).

21. "Female Energy and Symbolism in the Buddhist Tantras", *History of Religions*, 2:1, pp. 73-111.

22. "Buddhist Dependent Origination and the Sāmkhya guṇas", *Ethnos*, pp. 14-22. (F. D. Lessing memorial issue).

23. "The Buddha's birthdate, employing new tables of planetary longitudes", (Brief Communication), *JAOS*, 82:3, pp. 374-76.

1963

24. "The Stages of Life according to Varāhamihira", (Brief Communication), *JAOS*, 83.3, pp. 360-61.

1964

25. "Conze on Buddhism and European Parallels", *Philosophy East and West*, 13:4, pp. 361-64.

1965

26. Contributor of ten lecture outlines and bibliographies, to *Civilization of India Syllabus*, Joseph W. Elder, editor (The University of Wisconsin, Madison).

27. "The Buddhism and the Sanskrit of Buddhist Hybrid Sanskrit", *JAOS*, 85:1, pp. 111-15 (Memorial for Franklin Edgerton).

28. "The Five-fold Ritual Symbolism of Passion", *Studies of Esoteric Buddhism* (Koyasan, Japan), pp. 117-44 (Koyasan Temple Anniversary Volume).

29. "Concerning saṃdhā-bhāṣā/saṃdhi-bhāṣā/saṃdhyā bhāṣā", *Mélanges d'indianisme dédiées à la mémoire du Louis Renou* (Paris), pp. 789-96.

30. "The Yogacara Idealism", [a review article] *Philosophy East and West*, 15:1, pp. 65-73.

31. "Climactic Times in Indian Mythology and Religion", *History of Religions*, 4:2, pp. 295-318.

1967

32. "Significance of Dreams in India and Tibet", *History of Religions*, 7:1, pp. 1-12.

33. "The Bodhisattva Practice According to the Lam-rim-chen-mo", *The Tibet Society Newsletter*, 1:2 (The Tibet Society, Inc., Bloomington, Indiana), pp. 85-100.

1968

34. Mkhas grub rje's fundamentals of the Buddhist Tantras, Indo-Iranian Monographs, Vol. VIII (Mouton, The Hague, Paris) (with Ferdinand D. Lessing).

35. "Early Literary History of the Buddhist Tantras, especially the *Guhyasamāja-tantra*", *Annals*, Bhandarkar Research Institute, Poona (Golden Jubilee Volume), pp. 99-110.

36. "The Hindu-Buddhist Rite of Truth—an Interpretation", *Studies in Indian Linguistics* (volume presented to Prof. M. B. Emeneau on his sixtieth birthday year) (Linguistic Society of India, Poona), pp. 365-69.

37. "The Parents of Buddhist Monks", *Bharati*, Vols. 10-11, 1966-68, pp. 25-36.

38. "The Religious Meaning of Possession States", in Raymond Prince, ed., *Trance and Possession States* (R. M. Bucke Memorial Society, Montreal), pp. 167-79.

1969

39. "Contributions to the Mādhyamika School of Buddhism", [a review article] *JAOS*, 89:1, pp. 141-58.

40. "No Time, Great Time, and Profane Time in Buddhism", in Joseph W. Kitagawa, et al, eds. *Myths and Symbols; Studies in Honor of Mircea Eliade* (The University of Chicago Press, Chicago), pp. 47-62.

1970

41. "Guhyasamājatantra; Reflections on the Word and its meaning", *Transactions of the International Conference of Orientalists in Japan*, XV, pp. 34-55.

42. "Preparation of Disciples for Evocation of Deities", *The Tibet Society Newsletter*, Vol. 4-1, pp. 28-34.

43. "The Buddhist Theory of Vision", *Añjali; a Felicitation Volume Presented to Oliver Hector de Alwis Wijesekera on his sixtieth birthday* (University of Ceylon, Peradeniya), pp. 27-32.

44. "Astrology: Indian and Tibetan", *Encyclopaedia Britannica*, pp. 641B-42.

1971

45. "Buddhism" in *Historia Religionum*, Vol. II, Religions of the Present (ed. by C. J. Bleeker and Geo Widengren) (E. J. Brill, Leiden), pp. 372-464.

46. "Contributions on the Symbolism of the Maṇḍala-palace", *Études tibetaines dédiées à la mémoire de Marcelle Lalou* (Paris), pp. 557-66.

47. "A Jotting on the Mirror: Those of Ladies", *Mahfil* 7, pp. 209-13.

48. "The Mirror-like Knowledge in Mahāyāna Buddhist Literature", *Asiatische Studien* 25, pp. 353-63 (Paul Horsch Memorial issue).

49. "Buddhist Dependent Origination", *History of Religions*, 10:3, pp. 185-203.

1972

50. "Observations on Translation from the Classical Tibetan Language into European Languages", *Indo-Iranian Journal,* 14:3/4, pp. 161-92.

1973

51. The Buddhist Tantras; Light on Indo-Tibetan Esotericism (Samuel Weiser, Inc., New York).

52. "Buddhist Tantric Medicine Theory on Behalf of Oneself and Others", *Kailash,* I:2, pp. 153-58.

1974

53. The Lion's Roar of Queen Śrīmālā; A Buddhist Scripture on the Tathāgatagarbha Theory, translated and annotated (with Hideko Wayman) Columbia University Press, New York).

54. "Buddhist Sanskrit and the Sāṃkhyakārikā", *Journal of Indian Philosophy,* Vol. 2, Nos. 3/4, pp. 344-354.

55. "Two Traditions of India—Truth and Silence", *Philosophy East and West,* Vol. 24:4, pp. 389-403.

56. "The Ritual in Tantric Buddhism of the Disciple's Entrance into the Maṇḍala", *Studia Missionalia,* Vol. XXIII, pp. 41-57.

57. "The Intermediate-State Dispute in Buddhism", *Buddhist Studies in Honour of I.B. Horner,* ed. by L. Cousins, et al (D. Reidel Publishing Company, Dordrecht), pp. 227-39.

58. "The Mirror as a Pan-Buddhist Metaphor-Simile", *History of Religions,* 13:4, pp. 251-69.

1975

59. "Tibetan Buddhism—an Historical Survey", appeared in Spanish, "Budismo tibetano, un bosquejo histórico", *Estudios de Asia y Africa,* X:2, pp. 155-72 (EI Colegio de Mexico).

60. "The Significance of Mantras, from the Veda down to Buddhist Tantric Practice", *Brahmavidyā*; *Adyar Library Bulletin,* XXXIX (The Theosophical Society Centenary), pp. 65-69.

61. "Purification of Sin in Buddhism by Vision and Confession", in G.H. Sasaki, ed., *A Study of Kleśa* (Tokyo), pp. (58)-(79).

62. "Notes on Mirror Words and Entities in the Area of India", *Ural-Altaische Jahrbücher,* Band 47, pp. 204-06 (Karl H. Menges Festschrift).

1976

63. "Regarding the Translation of the Buddhist Terms saññā/saṃjñā, viññāṇa/vijñāna", *Malalasekera Commemoration Volume* (Colombo), pp. 325-35.

64. "Buddhist Sanskrit—an Appraisal", *Proceedings of the First International Sanskrit Conference*, Vol. II, Part II, ed. by V. Raghavan (New Delhi), pp. 20-30.

65. "Buddhism in Malaysia", in Heinrich Dumoulin and John C. Maraldo, eds., *Buddhism in the Modern World* (Collier Macmillan Publishers, New York), pp. 194-201.

66. "Aspects of Hindu and Buddhist Tantra", *The Tibet Journal* (Newark Museum Symposium on Tibet), pp. 32-44.

67. "Meditation in Theravāda and Mahīśāsaka", *Studia Missionalia*, Vol. 25, pp. 1-28.

1977

68. Yoga of the Guhyasamājatantra; The Arcane Lore of Forty Verses (Motilal Banarsidass, Delhi).

69. "Doctrinal Disputes and the Debate of Bsam Yas", *Central Asiatic Journal*, XXI:2, pp. 139-44 (honoring Prof. Helmut Hoffmann's 65th birthday).

70. "The Goddess Sarasvatī—from India to Tibet", *Kailash; a Journal of Himalayan Studies*, V:3, pp. 245-51.

71. "The Significance of Mantras, from the Veda down to Buddhist Tantric Practice", *Indologica Taurinensia*, III-IV, Torino, 483-97 [has slight alterations from the article, no. 60, above].

72. "Secret of the Heart Sūtra", in *Prajñāpāramitā and Related Systems; Studies in honor of Edward Conze*, L. Lancaster, ed. (Berkeley Buddhist Studies Series, Berkeley), pp. 135-52.

73. "Who understands the four alternatives of the Buddhist texts?" *Philosophy East and West*, 27:1, pp. 3-21.

74. "Reflections on the Study of Buddhist Logic", *Indologica Taurinensia*, Vol. V, pp. 289-308.

1978

75. Calming the Mind and Discerning the Real; Buddhist Meditation and the Middle View, from the *Lam rim chen mo* of Tsoṅ-kha-pa (Columbia University Press, New York).

76. Introduction to the Buddhist Tantric Systems, by F. D.

Lessing and Alex Wayman (Motilal Banarsidass, Delhi) [same as no. 34, above, but with a new introduction by A. Wayman].

77. "The Mahāsāṅghika and the Tathāgatagarbha (Buddhist Doctrinal History, Study 1)", *The Journal of the International Association of Buddhist Studies*, 1:1, pp. 35-50.

78. "Indian Buddhism" [a review article], *Journal of Indian Philosophy* 6, pp. 305-18.

79. "A Reconsideration of Dharmakīrti's 'Deviation' from Dignāga on Pratyakṣābhāsa", *Annals*, Bhandarkar Oriental Research Institute (Diamond Jubilee Volume), 1977-78, pp. 387-96.

80. "'The Role of Art among the Buddhist Religieux", in Kenneth K. Inada, ed. *East-West Dialogues in Aesthetics* (State University of New York at Buffalo), pp. 2-15.

1979

81. Calming the Mind and Discerning the Real; Buddhist Meditation and the Middle View, from the *Lam rim chen mo* of Tsoṅ-kha-pa (Motilal Banarsidass, Delhi) [Indian edition of no. 75, above].

82. "Ancient Buddhist Monasticism", *Studia Missionalia*, Vol. 28, pp. 193-230.

83. "The twenty reifying views (*sakkāyadiṭṭhi*)", *Studies in Pali and Buddhism* (a homage volume to the memory of Bhikkhu Jagdish Kashyap), ed. by A.K. Narain (B.R. Publishing Corp., Delhi), pp. 375-80.

84. "Yogacara and the Buddhist Logicians", *The Journal of the International Association of Buddhist Studies*, II:1, pp. 65-78.

1980

85. "Similes for the Four Elements from Buddhist Literature", *Indologica Taurinensia*, Vol. VII (Sternbach Volume), pp. 393-99.

86. "The samādhi lists of the *Akṣayamatinirdeśasūtra* and the *Mahāvyutpatti*", *Acta Orientalia Academiae Scientiarum Hung.*, Tomus XXXIV (1-3), pp. 305-18.

87. "Observations on the History and Influence of the Tantra in Tibet", *Studies in History of Buddhism*, ed. by A.K. Narain (B.R. Publishing Corp., Delhi), pp. 359-63.

88. "A Report on the *Akṣayamatinirdeśa-sūtra* (Buddhist Doctrinal History, Study 2)", *Studies in Indo-Asian Art and*

Culture, Vol. 6. ed. by Lokesh Chandra (International Academy of Indian Culture, New Delhi), pp. 211-32.

89. "Some Accords with the Sāṃkhya Theory of Tanmātra", *A Corpus of Indian Studies*; *Essays in Honour of Professor Gaurinath Sastri* (Sanskrit Pustak Bhandar, Calcutta), pp. 115-22.

90. "Buddha as Savior", *Studia Missionalia*, Vol. 29, pp. 191-207.

91. "Nescience and insight according to Asaṅga's Yogācārabhūmi", *Buddhist Studies in honour of Walpola Rahula* (Gordon Frazer, London), pp. 251-66.

92. "The Sixteen Aspects of the Four Noble Truths and Their Opposites", *The Journal of the International Association of Buddhist Studies*, Vol. 3, No. 2, pp. 67-76.

93. "Dependent Origination—the Indo-Tibetan Tradition", *Journal of Chinese Philosophy* 7, pp. 275-300.

1981

94. "Aśoka and Upagupta-Moggalliputta", *K. P. Jayaswal Commemoration Volume*, ed. by J. S. Jha (K. P. Jayaswal Research Institute, Patna), pp. 300-07.

95. "Reflections on the Theory of Barabudur as a Maṇḍala", in *Barabudur: History and Significance of a Buddhist Monument*, ed. by Luis Gomez and Hiram W. Woodward, Jr. (Berkeley Buddhist Studies Series, Berkeley), pp. 139-72.

96. "The Title and Textual Affiliation of the Guhyagarbhatantra", *Daijō Bukkyo kara Mikkyō e* (From Mahāyāna Buddhism to Tantra); Honorary Volume for Dr. Shunkyō Katsumata (Shunjusha, Tokyo); pp. 1320-34 (Japanese order), pp. (1)-(15) (English order).

97. "Notes on Metaphoric Transfer", *Brahmavidyā*; *Adyar Library Bulletin*, Vols. 44-45, 1980-81 (Dr. K. Kunjunni Raja Felicitation Volume), pp. 275-85.

1982

98. "Is it a crow (P. *dhamka*) or a nurse (S. *dhātrī*)?" (Brief communication), *JAOS*, 102:3, pp. 515-6.

99. "A Study of the Vedāntic and Buddhist Theory of Nāmarūpa", *Indological and Buddhist Studies*, Volume in honour of Professor J. W. de Jong on his sixtieth birthday (Faculty of Asian Studies, Canberra), pp. 617-42.

100. "Notes on the *phur-bu*", *The Journal of the Tibet Society*, Vol. I, pp. 79-85.

101. "The religious meaning of concrete death in Buddhism", *Studia Missionalia*, Vol. 31, pp. 273-95.

102. "The Human Body as Microcosm in India, Greek Cosmogony, and Sixteenth Century Europe", *History of Religions*, 22:2, pp. 172-90.

1983

103. "Eschatology in Buddhism", *Studia Missionalia*, Vol. 32, pp. 71-94.

104. "Three Tanjur Commentators—Buddhaguhya, Ratnākaraśānti, and Smṛtijñānakīrti", *The Tibet Journal*, VIII.3, pp. 24-36.

105. "Male, Female, and Androgyne, per Buddhist Tantra, Jacob Boehme, and the Greek and Taoist Mysteries", *Tantric and Taoist Studies in Honour of R. A. Stein*, ed. by M. Strickmann, Vol. Two (Institut Belge des Hautes Etudes Chinoises, Bruxelles), pp. 592-631.

1984

106. Buddhist Insight; Essays by Alex Wayman, edited and introduced by George E. Elder, Religions of Asia Series, No. 5 (eds. Lewis W. Lancaster and J. L. Shastri); Motilal Banarsidass, Delhi.

107. "The Sarvarahasyatantra", in *Studies of Mysticism in Honor of the* 1150*th Anniversary of Kōbō-daishi's Nirvanam*, Acta Indologica, Vol. VI, pp. 521-69 (published by Naritasan Shinshoji, Japan).

108. "The Metaphysics of Cooking in the Satyartha Prakash and in the Indian Tradition", *World Perspectives on Swami Dayananda Saraswati* by Ganga Ram Garg (Concept Publishing Company, New Delhi), pp. 288-97.

109. "The Interlineary-type Commentary in Tibetan", in *Tibetan and Buddhist Studies*, commemorating the 200th anniversary of the birth of Alexander Csoma de Körös, ed. by Louis Legeti, Vol. 2 (Akademiai Kiado, Budapest), pp. 367-79.

110. "The Mahāvairocanasūtra and the Kriyā-Samgraha", *Kōbōdaishi to Gendai* [The Chizan-Ma's volume for 1150th anniversary of Kōbodaishi] (Chikuma Shobō, Tokyo), pp. (23)-(34).

111. "Śākyamuni, Founder of Buddhism", *Studia Missionalia,* Vol. 33, pp. 65-99.

1985

112. Chanting the Names of Mañjuśrī, translation and study of the *Mañjuśrī-nāma-saṃgīti* (Shambhala Publications, Inc., Boston).

113. "The Gait (*gati*) and the (*mārga*)—Reflections on the Horizontal", *JAOS*, 105.3, pp. 579-88 (the Daniel H. H. Ingalls issue).

114. "Imperatives in the Buddhist Tantra Mantras", *Berliner Indologische Studien* Band 1, pp. 35-40.

115. "Nāgārjuna: Moralist Reformer of Buddhism", *Studia Missionalia,* Vol. 34, pp. 63-95.

116. "The Disputed Authorship of Tibetan Canonical Commentaries on the Sarvadurgatipariśodhana-tantra", from *Buddhism and its Relation to Other Religions*; *Essays in Honour of Dr. Shozen Kumoi on His Seventieth Birthday* (Kyoto), pp. 201-13.

117. "Some observations on dualistic mirror symbolism in Western Philosophy and in the Upaniṣads", *Aligarh Journal of Oriental Studies* II,1-2, pp. 113-16 (Ram Suresh Tripathi Commemoration Volume).

118. "Bhartṛhari citations in Kamalaśīla's commentary on Tattvasamgraha", *Proceedings of the Fifth World Sanskrit Conference* held at Varanasi, Oct. 1981 (Rashtriya Sanskrit Sansthan, New Delhi), pp. 699-705.

119. "Ratnākaraśānti's *Antarvyāptisamarthana*", *Journal of the Asiatic Society* (Calcutta), XXVII:2, pp. 31-44 [Insert page for that missing between p. 32 and 33 is available from the author, A. Wayman].

1986

120. "The Vedic Three Worlds in Early and Later Times", *Adyar Library Bulletin,* Vol. 50, pp. 373-87 (Adyar Library Centenary).

1987

121. Acharya Dharmananda Kosambi Memorial Lectures (Second Series): *Delvings in Logic*: "The term *guṇa*—a problem

in communication"; "The controversy over Dharmakīrti's 'uncaused destruction' (*ahetuvināśa*)". Bhandarkar Oriental Research Institute, Poona.

122. Contributor to *The Encyclopedia of Religion* (Mircea Eliade, ed., New York); "Buddhist Esotericism" (6000 words), "Buddhist Soteriology", and the term *vijñāna*.

123. "The causes of an utterance per rival grammatical *śikṣā* traditions", *Philosophical Essays; Professor Anantalal Thakur Felicitation Volume* (Sanskrit Pustak Bhandar, Calcutta), pp. 81-87.

124. "A Prajñāpāramitā Scripture Within a Tantra", *Śramaṇa Vidyā*; Prof. Jagannath Upadhyaya Commemoration Volume (Central Institute of Higher Tibetan Studies, Sarnath, Varanasi), pp. 287-303.

125. "The Guru in Buddhism", *Studia Missionalia*, Vol. 36, 195-213.

126. "Researches on Poison, Garuḍa-birds, and Nāga-serpents based on the *Sgrub thabs kun btus*", *Silver on Lapis; Tibetan Literary Culture and History*, ed. by Christopher J. Beckwith (The Tibet Society, Bloomington), pp. 63-77.

127. "O, that Liṅga", Ramakrishna Gopal Bhandarkar 150th Birth Anniversary, *Annals of the Bhandarkar Oriental Research Institute*, Poona, pp. 15-54.

1988

128. "The Tathāgata chapter of Nāgārjuna's Mūla-Madhyamaka-kārikā", *Philosophy East and West*, XXXVIII:1, pp. 47-57.

129. "The Tibetan negatives *med* and *ma yin* and the *Mañjuśrī-nāma-saṃgīti*, VI, 19 commentaries", *Studia Tibetica, Band II; Tibetan Studies*, ed. by Helga Uebach and Jampal Panglung (München), pp. 551-58.

130. "Vasubandhu—Teacher Extraordinary", *Studia Missionalia*, Vol. 37, pp. 245-81.

131. "The Mathurā Set of Aṣṭamaṅgala (Eight Auspicious Symbols) in Early and Later Times", *Mathurā; The Cultural Heritage*, general edito Doris Meth Srinivasan (American Institute of Indian Studies, New Delhi), pp. 236-46.

1989

132. "Doctrinal Affiliation of the Buddhist Master Asaṅga

(Buddhist Doctrinal History, Study 3)", *Amalā Prajñā; Aspects of Buddhist Studies* (Prof. P. V. Bapat Felicitation Volume), ed. by N. H. Samtani and H. S. Prasad (Delhi), pp. 201-21.

133. "Aśoka and Peace", *Studia Missionalia,* Vol. 38, pp. 265-82.

134. "The Dreṣkāna Chapter of Bṛhat-Jātaka", *Studies in Indology; Prof. Rasik Vihari Joshi Felicitation Volume* (Shree Publishing House, New Delhi), pp. 5-14.

1990

135. "Messengers, What Bring Ye?" *Indo-Tibetan Studies* (Prof. David L. Snellgrove Honorary Volume), ed. by Tadeusz Skorupski (The Institute of Buddhist Studies, Tring, U.K.), pp. 305-22.

136. "Human Rights in Buddhism", *Studia Missionalia,* Vol. 39, pp. 341-58.

137. "The negative a/-an- prefix in Sanskrit", *Sanskrit and Related Studies,* ed. by B. K. Matilal and P. Bilimoria (Delhi), pp. 15-23.

138. The Lion's Roar of Queen Śrīmālā: A Buddhist Scripture on the Tathāgatagarbha Theory (Motilal Banarsidass, Delhi) [Indian edition of no. 53, above]. With a new foreword by Alex Wayman.

139. The Buddhist Tantras; Light on Indo-Tibetan Esotericism (Motilal Banarsidass, Delhi) [Indian edition of no. 51, above]. With a foreword by Alex Wayman and a new frontispiece.

140 "Report on the partial MS Viśvalocana", *The Journal of the Asiatic Society, Calcutta,* Vol. XXXII, nos. 1 & 2, pp. 10-28.

141. "Varāhamihira's Nakṣatra Chapter", (Prof. Ram Murti Sharma Felicitation Volume), ed. by S. G. Kantawala, Priti Sharma (Eastern Book Linkers, Delhi, India), pp. 365-73.

142. "The Rise of Mahāyāna Buddhism and Inscriptional Evidence at Nāgārjunakoṇḍa" (with Elizabeth Rosen), *The Indian Journal of Buddhist Studies* (Varanasi), Vol. II, No. 1. pp. 49-65.

1991

143. Ethics of Tibet; Bodhisattva Section of Tsong-Kha-Pa's Lam Rim Chen Mo, translated from the Tibetan original with a Foreword by the Dalai Lama (State University of New York, Albany).

144. Yoga of the Guhyasamājatantra; The Arcane Lore of Forty Verses (Motilal Banarsidass, Delhi) [Reprint edition of no. 68, above]. With a new foreword by Alex Wayman.

145. "The Position of Women in Buddhism", *Studia Missionalia*, Vol. 40, pp. 259-85.

146. "A problem of 'synonyms' in the Tibetan language: *bsgom pa* and *goms pa*", *The Journal of the Tibet Society*, Vol. 7 (Bloomington, 1987) [released in 1991, with Tibetan citations omitted by mistake, to be printed in an appendix to next issue of the Journal], pp. 51-6.

147. "Buddhist Tantra and Lexical Meaning", *Current Advances in Semantic Theory*, ed. by Maxim Stamenov (John Benjamins Publishing Company, Amsterdam), pp. 467-80.

148. "Dharmakīrti and the Yogācāra Theory of *bīja*" in *Studies in the Buddhist Epistemological Tradition*, ed. by Ernst Steinkellner (Osterreichischen Akademie der Wissenschaften, Wien), pp. 419-30.

1992

149. The Enlightenment of Vairocana; Book One: Study of the Vairocanābhisambodhi Tantra, by Alex Wayman; Book Two: Study of the Mahavairocanasūtra, by R. Tajima (Motilal Banarsidass, Delhi).

1 THE LIST OF THE *ASAMSKṚTA-DHARMA* ACCORDING TO ASAṄGA

ANDRÉ BAREAU

In a recent article, Professor Alex Wayman gives several good reasons supporting the theory that Asaṅga had belonged to the old school of the Mahīśāsaka before becoming an adept of Mahāyāna Buddhism.[1]

One other argument strengthens his viewpoint and seems rather important. It concerns the list of the various *asaṃskṛta-dharma*, which is found in some parts of the very large doctrinal work written by Asaṅga.

The schools (*nikāya*) of early Indian Buddhism, generally called Hīnayāna, had different ideas about the nature (*dharma*) that they considered to be *asaṃskṛta*. The term *asaṃṣkṛta* had the meaning 'non-composed', that is to say, 'lacking condition' (*apratyaya*), existing without having been brought forth by a concatenation of various causes. Thus, it is what has no origin, no beginning, no production; and consequently what will have neither end our cessation. In other words, any *asaṃskṛta* does not depend upon the universal law of impermanence (*anityatā*)—a basic tenent of Buddhism.

That is the reason why the first nature which the old Buddhists named *asaṃskṛta* was *nirvāṇa*.[2] That is also the reason why *nirvāṇa* was the only *asaṃskṛta* which was admitted by several of these early schools, particularly by the Theravādin, the Vātsīputriyā, and the Sammitīya.[3]

About the beginning of our era, they formulated their *Abhidharma-piṭaka*, voluminous collections of canonical texts where the doctrine attributed to the Buddha and transmitted by his sermons (*sūtra*) had been explained and completed by successive generations of his disciples and expounded in a rational order. By this time, most of the ancient schools had added several other *asaṃskṛta* to the *nirvāṇa* one. They probably began by dividing *nirvāṇa* into two 'cessations' (*nirodha*): the cessation by a discriminative knowledge (*pratisaṃkhyā-nirodha*) and the cessation without a discriminative knowledge (*apratisaṃkhyā-nirodha*). The first one is the *nirvāṇa* of the earliest Buddhist conceptions, and the second one is the non-existence of future things, lives, passions, and so on, which will not be brought forth, since the causes of their production have been destroyed. Soon afterwards, a third *asaṃskṛta* was admitted: empty space (*ākāśa*), where any substantial composed (*saṃskṛta*) natures appear, move, change, and disappear. Some sects, especially the Sarvāstivādin one, which was indeed important, established a list consisting of only these three *asaṃskṛta*,[4] and they refused to add other natures to their list. In contrast, some longer lists were formulated by other schools, by the addition of various new *asaṃskṛta* to the *nirvāṇa* one, or more usually to the two cessations (*nirodha*), and often to the space (*ākāśa*) one.

As the notion of *asaṃskṛta* was closely connected with some very important aspects of Buddhist doctrine, the progressive formulation of these lists gave rise to numerous and lively controversies between the old schools. This is proved by several chapters of the Theravādin *Kathāvatthu*[5] and by various paragraphs of the Sarvāstivādin *Mahāvibhāṣā*[6] and the *Abhidharmakośaśāstra.*[7] Consequently, the lists of *asaṃskṛta* can be regarded as characteristic signs of the different ancient sects. We have the complete lists of the Theravādin, Sarvāstivādin, Vātsīputrīya, Sammitīya, Mahīśāsaka, Mahāsāṃghika, and probably the Dharmaguptaka,[8] but the lists of some other schools, like the Pūrvaśailya,[9] are only partially known by us. This is the reason why we can definitely declare that a certain given treatise cannot belong to the Theravādin or to the Sarvāstivādin, because its list of *asaṃskṛta* contains more than three elements, but we cannot precisely determine what was the school which in fact produced it.

Luckily, the problem set by Asaṅga is clearer, for this master draws up a list of eight *asaṃskṛta*, of which he gives the definitions in several places of his works. As his list contains eight elements, it is evident that Asaṅga's ideas on these important points of Buddhist doctrine were rather different from the conceptions of the schools whose list of *asaṃskṛta* was shorter, having one or three elements only, that is to say, the Theravādin, Vātsīputrīya, Sammitīya, and Sarvāstivādin. Therefore, it is certain that the young Asaṅga was not a monk of these sects—in particular, not a Sarvāstivādin—before he became converted to the Mahāyāna.

According to Asaṅga, there are eight *asaṃskṛta-dharmas*:[10] (1) space (*ākāśa*); (2) cessation by a discriminative knowledge (*pratisaṃkhyā-nirodha*); (3) the motionless (*āneñjya*), obtained by the fourth meditation (*dhyāna*); (5) cessation of sensations and perceptions (*saṃjña-vedayita-nirodha*), obtained by the attainment of cessation (*nirodha-samāpatti*); (6) thusness (*tathatā*) of virtuous natures (*kuśala-dharma*); (7) thusness of unvirtuous natures (*akuśala-dharma*); (8) thusness of neutral natures (*avyākṛta-dharma*). In a paragraph of the voluminous *Yogācārabhūmi-śāstra*, this list is given as having eight or six elements, according as the three thusnesses (*tathatā*) of the virtuous, unvirtuous, and neutral natures are reckoned separately or not.[11]

We do not know of other lists having eight or six *asaṃskṛta-dharma*, but we do know of three lists containing nine elements. One of them is found in the *Śāriputra-abhidharma-śāstra*, and the other two in Vasumitra's *Samayabhedacanacakra-śāstra*.

In fact, the big work named *Śāriputra-abhidharma-śāstra*, only preserved by its Chinese translation, is the complete *Abhidharma-piṭaka* of a school whose identity has been unfortunately lost, but the work probably belonged to the Ḍharmaguptaka. Here is its list of *asaṃskṛta-dharma*:[12] (1) cessation by discriminative knowledge (*pratisaṃkhyā-nirodha*); (2) cessation without discriminate knowledge (*apratisaṃkhya-nirodha*); (3) fixity (*niyāma*) on the Path (*mārga*) leading to Deliverance (*vimukti*); (4) stability of natures (*dharmasthitatā*), which keeps them to their own nature; (5) production by mutual relations (*pratītya-samutpāda*); (6) attainment of the domain of the infinity of space (*ākāśānantyāyatana*); (7) attainment of the domain of the infinity of consciousness (*vijñānānantyāyatana*); (8) attainment of the domain of nothingness (*ākiñcanyāyatana*); (9) attainment of the domain without perception or non-perception (*naivasaṃjñānāsaṃjñāyatana*).

The *Samayabhedacanacakra* is a little work attributed to a certain Vasumitra, perhaps a Sarvāstivādin, who baldly enunciates numerous doctrinal theses held by the savants of the various schools of early Buddhism at the beginning of our era, but without explaining or commenting upon them. That this small book was well-known is proved by its three different Chinese translations and its Tibetan translation, which have been preserved up to present times. Also, it is one of the main sources of our knowledge about the various opinions of these ancient schools, among which most of their doctrinal literature disappeared long ago. However, this treatise cannot by any means take the place of this lost literature, which was certainly very large, because the Vasumitra work is very short and we cannot trust it as much as would be necessary. It gives us two complete lists of nine *asaṃskṛta-dharma*, which it respectively attributes to the Mahāsāṃghika and the Mahīśāsaka.

The list of the Mahāsāṃghika[13] would have consisted of: (1) cessation by discriminative knowledge (*pratisaṃkhyā-nirodha*); (2) cessation without discriminative knowledge (*apratisaṃkhyā-nirodha*); (3) space (*ākāśa*); (4) domain of the infinity of space (*ākāśānantyāyatana*); (5) domain of the infinity of consciousness (*vijñānānantyāyatana*); (6) domain of nothingness (*ākiñcanyāyatana*); (7) domain without perception or non-perception (*naivasamjñānāsaṃjñāyatana*); (8) own-nature (*svabhāva*) of the twelve members (*aṅga*) of the production by mutual relations (*pratītya-samutpāda*); (9) own-nature (*svabhāva*) of the eight members of the noble Path (*ārya-mārga*).

According to Vasumitra, the Mahīśāsaka taught that the following *dharmas* are *asaṃskṛta*:[14] (1) cessation by discriminative knowledge (*pratisaṃkhyā-nirodha*); (2) cessation without discriminative knowledge (*apratisaṃkhyā-nirodha*); (3) space (*ākāśa*); (4) motionlessness (*āneñjya*); (5) thusness (*tathatā*) of virtuous natures (*kuśala-dharma*); (6) thusness of unvirtuous natures (*akuśala-dharma*); (7) thusness of neutral natures (*avyākṛta-dharma*); (8) thusness of the Path (*mārga*); (9) thusness of production by mutual relations (*pratītya-samutpāda*).

The commentary (*atthakathā*) of the *Kathāvatthu* attributes to the Mahīśāsaka these theses: the two cessations (*nirodha*), space (*ākāśa*), and the production by mutual relations (*pratītya-samutpāda*), are uncomposed (*asaṅkhata*).[15] The *Abhidharmakośaśāstra* written by the famous master Vasubandhu confirms that the Mahīśāsaka regarded the production by mutual relations as an *asaṃskṛta*.[16]

We can therefore see that the list drawn up by Asaṅga is closer to this Mahīśāsaka one than to the Mahāsāṃghika and the *Śāriputra-abhidharma-śāstra* ones. The first two lists have the same following elements: the two cessations, space, the three thusnesses of the virtuous, unvirtuous, and neutral natures, and motionlessness. They differ only because Asaṅga's list includes the attainment of the cessation of sensations and perceptions (*saṃjñā-vedayita-nirodha*) as an *asaṃskṛta*, but includes neither the thusness of the production by mutual relations nor the thusness of the Path, whereas these last two elements are present in the Mahīśāsaka list. However, we may theorize that Asaṅga omitted these two thusnesses from his list because the *tathatā* of *pratītya-samutpāda* can be considered equivalent to the one of unvirtuous *dharmas*, and the *tathatā* of *mārga* can be considered equivalent to the one of virtuous *dharmas*, in such a way that their inclusion in his list could be regarded as needless repetitions. By a similar reasoning, Asaṅga has shortened his list from eight to six elements in the *Yogācārabhūmi-śāstra* by putting the three thusnesses together in only one element, as we have noticed above.

The differences are much greater between Asaṅga's list and the other two lists, which belonged to the Mahāsāṃghika and to the *Śāriputra-abhidharma-śāstra*. On the one hand, these two last ones include the four attainments (*samāpatti*) called 'immaterial' (*ārūpya*) as *asaṃskṛta*, whereas neither Asaṅga's list nor the Mahīsāsaka list admit these attainments among the 'non-composed' natures. On the other hand, neither the Mahāsāṃghika nor the *Śāriputra-abhidharma-śāstra* regard motionlessness (*āneñjya*) and the three thusnesses (*tathatā*) as *asaṃskṛta*. The list of the *Śāriputra-abhidharma-śāstra* is obviously closer to the one of the Mahāsāṃghika than to the lists of Asaṅga and the Mahīśāsaka, although the first two named ones are not identical. However, the *Śāriputra-abhidharma-śāstra* probably belonged to the Dharmaguptaka school, which was closely allied to the Mahīśāsaka.[17] The foregoing facts show that the bonds which connected Asaṅga with the Mahīsāsaka were much tighter than were the relations which associated this latter school with the Dharmaguptaka.

It is therefore sufficiently obvious that Asaṅga had been a Mahīśāsaka when he was a young monk, and that he incorporated a large part of the doctrinal opinions proper to this school within his own work after he became a great master of the Mahāyāna, when he made up what can be considered as a new and Mahāyānist *Abhidharma-piṭaka*.

Consequently, the examination of the list of *asaṃskṛta-dharmas* established by Asaṅga brings forward a good argument in support of the thesis held by Professor Alex Wayman on the very close relations of this great Buddhist savant with the old school of the Mahīśāsaka.

References

1. Alex Wayman, "Doctrinal Affiliation of the Buddhist Master Asaṅga (Buddhist Doctrinal History, Study 2)", *Amalā Prajñā*; *Aspects of Buddhist Studies* (Prof. P.V. Bapat Felicitation Volume), ed. by N.H. Samtani and H.S. Prasad (Delhi), pp. 201-21.

2. Louis de la Vallée-Poussin, *Nirvāṇa*, Paris, 1925, pp. 180-87.

3. André Bareau, *Les Sectes bouddhiques du Petit Véhicule*, Ecole française d'Extrême-Orient, Saigon, 1955, chap. XXIX, XV, XVI. *Kathāvatthu*, chap. II, 11; VI, 1; VI, 2; VI, 3; VI, 4; VI, 5; VI, 6; XIX, 3; XIX, 4; XIX, 5. *Abhidharmakośa-śāstra*, trad. Louis de la Vallée-Poussin, chap. I, p. 7, n. 2; IX, p. 234, p. 237. *Sammitīya-nikāya-śāstra*, chinese trad., Taishô Issaikyô Edition (=T.S.) n° 1649, p. 464c.

4. *Abhidharma-mahāvibhāṣā*, T.S. n° 1545, p. 65a.

5. Chap. II, 11; chap. VI, 1, 2, 3, 4, 5, 6; chap. XIX, 3, 4, 5.

6. *Mahāvibhāṣā*, n° 1545, p. 919a, 116c, 65b, 190a, etc. *Abhidharmakośa-śāstra*, trad. la Vallée-Poussin, chap. III, p. 77 sq.

7. Missing.

8. A. Bareau, *Ibid.*, chap. XXVI.

9. *Ibid.*, p. 100.

10. *Āryaśāsanaprakaraṇa*(?), chinese trad. T.S. n° 1602, p. 484b.

11. *Yogācāryabhūmi*, T.S. n° 1579, p. 293c.

12. *Śāriputra-abhidharma*, T.S. n° 1548, p. 526c, 535a.

13. *Samayabhedacanacakra*, T.S. n° 2031, p. 15c; T.S. n° 2032, p. 18c; T.S. n° 2033, p. 20c.

14. *Ibid.* T.S. n° 2030, p. 16c; T.S. n° 2032, p. 19b; T.S. n° 2033, p. 22a.

15. *Kathāvatthu-atthakathā*, chap. II, 11; VI, 2, 6.

16. *Abhidharmakośa*, trad. la Vallée-Poussin, chap. III, p. 77, n. 1.

17. A. Bareau, *Les Sectes...*, p. 190.

2 THE SEVEN PRINCIPLES OF THE VAJJIAN REPUBLIC
Their Different Interpretations

HAJIME NAKAMURA
(Professor Emeritus, University of Tokyo.
Founder-Director, The Eastern Institute, Inc.)

In the beginning of the *Mahāparinibbāna-suttanta* the seven principles which were observed by the Vajjian republic are mentioned. The Sanskrit, Pali and Tibetan versions and a German translation of I-tsing's Chinese translation of a Sanskrit Vinaya text of the Mūlasarvāstivādins were published by the late Ernst Waldschmidt.* The corresponding passages run as follows:

**Das Mahāparinirvānasūtra. Text in Sanskrit und Tibetisch, Verglichen mit dem Pāli nebst einer Übersetzung der Chinesischen Entsprechung im Vinaya der Mūlasarvāstivādins* auf Grund von Turfan-Handschriften herausgegeben und bearbeitet von Ernst Waldschmidt, Akademie Verlag Berlin, 1951, S. 108-18.

Sanskrit	Dīghanikāya XVI
16 (tena khalu samayenāyuṣmān ānando bhagavataḥ pṛṣṭhataḥ sthito bha)-gavantaṃ vījayamānaḥ / tatra bhaga(vān āyuṣmantam ānandam āmantrayate /)	1,4 tena kho pana samayena āyasmā ānando bhagavato piṭṭhito ṭhito hoti bhagavantaṃ vījamāno / atha kho bhagavā āyasmantaṃ ānandaṃ āmantesi /
[Principle I]	
17 (kiṃ nu tvayānanda śrutaṃ vṛjayo 'bhīkṣṇasannipātā abhīkṣṇaṃ sannipātabahulā viharanti /)	kin ti te ānanda sutaṃ vajjī abhiṇhaṃsannipātā sannipātabahulā ti /
18 (śrutaṃ me bhadanta vṛjayo 'bhīkṣṇasannipātā abhīkṣṇaṃ sannipātabahulā viharanti /)	sutaṃ me taṃ bhante vajjī abhiṇhaṃsannipātā sannipātabahulā ti /
19 (yāvac ca varṣākāra vṛjayo 'bhīkṣṇasannipātā abhīkṣṇaṃ sannipātabahulā vihariṣyanti vṛddhir eva vṛjīnāṃ pratikāṃkṣitavyā kuśalānāṃ dharmāṇāṃ na parihāṇiḥ /)	yāvakīvañ co ānanda vajjī abhiṇhaṃsannipātā sannipātabahulā bhavissanti vuddhi yeva ānanda vajjīnaṃ pāṭikaṅkhā no parihāni /
[Principle II]	
20 (kiṃ nu tvayānanda śrutaṃ vṛjayaḥ samagrāḥ sannipatanti samagrā vyuttiṣṭhanti samagrā vṛjikaraṇīyāni kurvanti /)	kin ti te ānanda vajjī sutaṃ vajjī samaggā sannipatanti samaggā vuṭṭhahanti samaggā vajjikaraṇīyāni karontīti /
21 (śrutaṃ me bha) danta vṛjayaḥ sama-(grāḥ sannipatanti samagrā vyutthiṣṭhanti samagrā vṛjikaraṇīyāni kurvanti /)	sutaṃ me taṃ bhante vajjī samaggā sannipatanti samaggā vuṭṭhahanti samaggā vajjīkaraṇīyāni karontīti /

Vinaya. Tibetisch	Vinaya. Chinesisch
16 de-nas yaṅ dei tshe bcom-ldan-'adas-kyi snam-logs-na tshe-daṅ-ldan-pa kun-dga-bo bsil-yab thogs-te / bcom-ldan-'adas-la gyobciṅ 'adug-go / de-nas bcom-ldan-'adas-kyis tshe-daṅ-ldan-pa kun-dga-bo-la bka-stsalpa /	Damals stand der ehrwürdige Ānanda hinter dem Buddha, hielt einen Fächer in der Hand und fächelte (ihm) Kühlung zu. Der Buddha sprach zu Ānanda:
17 (1) ci kun-dga-bo yul-spoṅ-byed-pa-rnams yaṅ daṅ yaṅ-du 'adu-žiṅ / yaṅ daṅ yaṅ-du 'adu-ba-las riṅ-du gnas-par thos sam /	„Hast du wohl gehört und weißt du, ob das Volk im Lande der Vṛji sich häufig versammelt, um die Bedeutung der Gesetze zu erörtern?“
18 btsun-pa bdag-gis ni thos lags-te / yul-spoṅ-byed-pa-rnams yaṅ daṅ yaṅ-du 'adužiṅ / yaṅ daṅ yaṅ-du 'adu-ba-las riṅ-du gnas lags-so /	„Ehrwürdiger, ich habe gehört, daß die Leute jenes Landes sich viel versammeln, um die Bedeutung der Gesetze zu erörtern.“
19 dbyar-byed ji-srid-du yul-spoṅ-byed-pa-rnams yaṅ daṅ yaṅ-du 'adu-žiṅ riṅ-du gnas-pa-las / yul-spoṅ-byed-pa-rnams-kyi dge-bai chos-rnams ñams-par mi 'agyur-žiṅ rgyas-par 'agyur-bar śes-par byao /	Der Buddha sprach zu dem Brahmanen: „Wenn die Leute in jenem Lande sich viel versammeln um die Bedeutung der Gesetze zu erörtern, muß man wissen, daß jenes Land von Tag zu Tag wächst und daß die *kuśala dharmas* kein Abnehmen erfahren.“ (1)
20 (2) ci kun-dga-bo yul-spoṅ-byed-pa-rnams 'athun-par 'adug-ciṅ 'athun-par 'agro 'am / yul-spoṅ-byed-pa-rnams-kyi dgos-pa daṅ /bya-ba 'athun-par byed-par thos sam/	„Ānanda, hast du wohl gehört und weißt du, ob die Leute im Lande der Vṛjis sehr einträchtig sind, (ob sie) gemeinsam sich erheben und gemeinsam sich setzen, um die Angelegenheiten des Landes zu erörtern?“
21 btsun-pa bdag-gis thos lags-te / yul-spoṅ-byed-pa-rnams 'athun lags-so žes bya-bai bar goṅ-ma bžin-duo /	Er antwortete: „Ich habe es gehört.“... ausführlicher Wortlaut wie oben.

Sanskrit	Dīghanikāya XVI
1.22 (yāvac ca varṣākāra vṛjayaḥ samagrāḥ sannipatiṣyanti sama) grā vyutthāsyanti (samagrā vṛjikaraṇīyāni kariṣyanti vṛddhir eva vṛjīnāṃ pratikāṃkṣitavyākuśalānāṃ dharmāṇāṃ na parihāṇiḥ /)	yāvakīvañ ca ānanda vajjī samaggā sannipatissanti samaggā vuṭṭhahissanti samaggā vajjikaraṇīyāni karissanti vuddhi yeva ānanda vajjīnaṃ pāṭikaṅkhā no parihāni /

[Principle III]

23 (kiṃ nu tvayānanda śrutaṃ vṛjayo 'pra)-ṇihitaṃ na praṇi(dadhati praṇihitaṃ ca na samucchindanti yathāprājñaptaṃ vṛjidharmaṃ samādāya vartante /)	kin ti te ānanda sutaṃ vajjī appaññattaṃ na paññāpenti paññattaṃ na samucchindanti yathā paññatte porāṇe vajjidhamme samādāya vattantīti /
24 (śrutaṃ me bhadanta vṛjayo 'praṇihitaṃ na praṇidadhati praṇihi) taṃ ca na samucchin(da)n(ti yathāprajñaptaṃ vṛjidharmaṃ samādāya vartante /)	sutaṃ me taṃ bhante vajjī appaññattaṃ na paññāpenti paññattaṃ na samucchindanti yathā paññatte porāṇe vajjidhamme samādāya vattantīti /
25 (yāvac ca varṣākāra vṛjayo 'praṇihitaṃ na praṇidhāsyanti praṇihitaṃ ca na samucchetsyanti yathāprajñaptaṃ) vṛijidharmaṃ samādā (ya vartiṣyante vṛddhir eva vṛjīnāṃ pratikāṃkṣitavyā kuśalānāṃ dharmāṇāṃ na parihāṇiḥ /)	yāvakīvañ ca ānanda vajjī appaññattaṃ na paññāpessanti paññattaṃ na samucchindissanti yathā paññatte porāṇe vajjidhamme samādāya vattissanti vuddhi yeva ānanda vajjīnaṃ pāṭikaṅkhā no parihāni /

	Vinaya. Tibetisch	Vinaya. Chinesisch
1.22	dbyar-byed ji-srid-du yul-spoṅ-byed-pa-rnams 'athun-par 'adug-ciṅ 'athun-par 'agro-ba daṅ / yul-spoṅ-byed-pa-rnams-kyi dgos-pa daṅ bya-ba 'athun-par byas-pa-las / yul-spoṅ-byed-pa-rnams-kyi dge-bai chos-rnams ñams-par mi 'agyur-ži̇ṅ rgyas-par 'agyur-bar śes-par byao /	(*S.* 383_a) Der Buddha sprach zu dem Brahmanen:...auch ganz wie oben im Wortlaut, bis: ,,und daß die *kuśala dharmas* kein Abnehmen erfahren. "(2)
23	(3) ci kun-dga-bo yul-spoṅ-byed-pa-rnams-smon-pa ma yin-pa-la ni smon-par mi byed / smon-pa ni kun-tu 'ador-bar mi byed-ciṅ / ji-ltar yul-spoṅ-byed-pa-rnams-kyis khrims bcas-pa bži̇n yaṅ-dag-par blaṅs-nas spyod do žes thos sam /	„Ānanda, hast du wohl gehört und weißt, ob die Leute jenes Landes Angelegenheiten, nach denen man nicht trachten soll, auch nicht erstreben, ob sie nicht Angelegenheiten, die man erreichen müßte, zum Abbruch bringen, ob sie den Gesetzen des Landes beständig und gern nachkommen?"
24	btsun-pa bdag-gis thos lags-te / yul-spoṅ-byed-pa-rnams smon-pa ma yin-pa-la ni smon-par mi bgyid/smon-pa ni kun-tu 'ador-bar mi bgyid-ciṅ / ji-ltar yul-spoṅ-byed-pa-rnams-kyis khrims bcas-pa bži̇n yaṅ-dagpar blaṅsnas spyod lags-so /	Er antwortete: „Ich habe es gehört." . . . ausführlicher Wortlaut wie oben.
25	dbyar-byed ji-srid-du yul-spoṅ-byed-pa-rnams smon-pa ma yin-pa-la ni smon-par mi byed / smon-pa ni kun-tu 'ador-bar mi byed-ciṅ / ji-ltar yul-spoṅ-byed-pa-rnams-kyis khrims-su bcas-pa bži̇n yaṅ-dag-par kun-tu	Der Buddha sprach zu dem Brahmanen: . . . auch ganz so wie oben im Wortlaut, bis: „und daß die *kuśala dharmas* kein Abnehmen erfahren."(3)

Sanskrit	Dīghanikāya XVI
[Principle IV] 26 (kiṃ nu tvayānanda śrutaṃ yās tā vṛjīnāṃ vṛjiprajāpatyo vṛjikumārikāś ca pitṛrakṣitā mātṛrakṣitā bhrātṛrakṣitā bhaginīrakṣitāḥ śvaśurarakṣitāḥ śvaśrurakṣitā jñātirakṣitā gotrarakṣitāḥ saparidaṇḍāḥ sasvāmikāḥ kan) yāḥ paraparigṛ(hītā antaśo mālāguṇaparikṣiptā api tadrūpāsu) na sa(hasā cāritram āpadyante /)	 kin ti te ānanda sutaṃ vajjī yā tā kulitthiyo kulakumāriyo tā na okkassa pasayha vāsentīti /
1.27 (śrutaṃ me bhadanta vṛjayo yā) tā vṛjīnāṃ vṛji (p)r(ajāpatyo vṛjikumārikāś ca pitṛrakṣitā mātṛrakṣitāḥ pūrvavad yāvad antaśo mālāguṇaparikṣiptā a) pi tad-rūpā(su na sahasā) cāritram āpadya(nte /)	sutaṃ me taṃ bhante vajjī yā tā kulitthiyo kulakumāriyo tā na okkassa pasayha vāsentīti /

	Vinaya. Tibetisch	Vinaya. Chinesisch
	spyod-pa-las / yul-spoṅ-byed-pa-rnams-kyi dge-bai chos-rnams ñams-par mi 'agyur-žiṅ rgyas-par 'agyur-bar śes-par byao /	
26	(4) ci kun-dga-bo khyod-kyis yul-spoṅ-byed-pa-rnams-kyis / spoṅ-byed-kyi bud-med-rnams daṅ / spoṅ-byed-kyi gžon-nu-ma gaṅ-dag yin-pa 'adi-lta ste / phas bsruṅs-pa / mas bsruṅs-pa / miṅ-pos bsruṅs-pa / phu-nu-mos bsruṅs-pa / sgyug-mos bsruṅs-pa / gyos-pos bs-ruṅs-pa / ñe-dus bsruṅs-pa / rus-kyis bsruṅs-pa / chad-pa daṅ bcas-pas / sgrib-pa daṅ bcas-pa / gžan-gyi chuṅ-ma gžan-gyis yoṅs-su gzuṅ-ba-dag daṅ / chuṅ-ṅu-na me-tog-gi phreṅ-ba bor-ba de-lta-bu-dag-la yaṅ yul-spoṅ-byed-pa-rnams 'aphral-la khyaddu bsad-nas / mthus 'adod-pakun tu-mi spyod-par thos sam /	„Ananda, hast du wohl gehört und weißt du, ob die Frauen und Jungfrauen jenes Landes behütet werden von den Müttern, behütet werden von den Vätern oder von den Brüdern, den Schwestern, den Schwiegereltern oder der Verwandtschaft behütet werden; ob diese (Verwandten) sie, wenn sie Übertretungen begangen haben, ermahnen und strafen; ob (die Frauen und Jungfrauen,) wenn sie Frauen order Nebenfrauen eines anderen (d.h. Mannes) geworden sind und sogar durch Blumenüberreichung deren Ehefrauen zu werden gestattet haben, nicht mit diesen übereilt unsittliche Dinge treiben?"
1.27	btsun-pa bdag-gis thos lags-te / yul spoṅ-byed-pa-rnams spoṅ-byed-kyi bud-med-rnams daṅ / spoṅ-byed-kyi gžon-nu-ma gaṅ-dag yin-pa 'adi-lta ste / phas bsruṅs-pa daṅ / mas bsruṅs-pa žes bya-ba-nās / chuṅ-ṅu-na me- tog-gi phreṅ- ba bor-ba delta-bu-dag-la yaṅ / yul-spoṅ-byed-pa-rna-	Er antwortete: „Ich habe gehört"... ausführlicher Wortlaut wie oben.

Sanskrit	Dīghanikāya XVI
28 (yāvad ca varṣākāra vṛjayo yās tā) v(ṛ)jīnāṃ vṛji (prajāpatyo vṛjikumārikāś ca pūrvavad yāvad antaśo mālāguṇaparikṣiptā api) tadrūpā su na sa (hasā cāritram āpatsyante vṛddhir eva) vṛjīnāṃ (pratikāṃkṣitavyā kuśalānāṃ dharmāṇāṃ na parihāṇiḥ /)	yāvakīvañ ca ānanda vajjī yā tā kulitthiyo kulakumāriyo tā na okkassa pasayha vāsessanti vuddhi yeva ānanda vajjīnaṃ pāṭikaṅkhā no parihāni /
[Principle V]	
29 (kiṃ nu tvayānanda śrutaṃ vṛjayo ye) te vṛjīnāṃ vṛjimah (allakās tān satkurvanti gurukurvanti mānayanti pūjayanti teṣāṃ vaca naṃ śrotavyaṃ manyante /)	kin ti te ānanda sutaṃ vajjī ye te vajjīnaṃ vajjimahallakā te sakkaronti garukaronti mānenti pūjenti tesañ ca sotabbaṃ maññantīti /
30 (śrutaṃ me bhadanta vṛja) yo ye te vṛ(jīnāṃ vṛjima hallakās tān satkurvanti gurukurvanti mānayanti pūjayanti teṣāṃ vacanaṃ śrotavyaṃ manyante /)	sutaṃ me taṃ bhante vajjī ye te vajjīnaṃ vajjimahallakā te sakkaronti garukaronti mānenti pūjenti tesañ ca sotabbaṃ maññantīti /

Vinaya. Tibetisch

ms 'aphral-la khyad-du bsa-d-nas / mthus 'adod-pa kun-tu mi spyod lags-so žes bya-ba goṅ-ma bžin-no /

28 dbyar-byed ji-srid-du yul-spoṅ-byed-pa-rnams-kyis spoṅ-byed-kyi bud-med-rn-ams daṅ / spoṅ-byed-kyi gž-on-nu-ma gaṅ-dag ces bya-ba-nas / chuṅ-ṅu-na me-tog-gi phreṅ-ba bor-ba de-lta-bu dag-la yaṅ / yul-spoṅ-byed -pa-rnams 'aphral-la /khyad du bsad-nas / mthus 'adod-pa kun-tu mi spyod-pa-las yul-spoṅ-byed-pa-rnamskyi ge-bai chosrnamsñams-par mi 'agyur-žiṅ rgyas-par 'agyur-bar śespar byao /

29 (5) ci kun-dga-bo khyod-kyis yul-spoṅ-byed-pa-rnams sp-oṅ-byed-kyi rgan-rabs-rna-ms daṅ / ya-rabs-rnams daṅ / pha-mai rgyud gaṅ-dag-la yul-spoṅ-byed-pa-rnams-ky-is bkur-sti byed / bla-mar byed / ri-mor byed / mchod-par byed-ciṅ / de-dag-gi tsh-ig-la dad-pas ñan-par byed/ sems-par byed-par thos sam/

30 btsun-pa bdag-gis thos lags-te / yul-spoṅ-byed-pa-rnams yul-spoṅ-byed-kyi rgan-ra-bs-rnams daṅ / ya-rabs-rna-ms daṅ / pha-mai rgyud gaṅ-dag-la yul-spoṅ-byed-pa de-dag bkur-sti bgyid /

Vinaya. Chinesisch

(28) Der Buddha sprach zu dem Brahmanen: ... auch ganz so wie oben im Wortlaut, bis: „und daß die *kuśala dharmas* kein Abnehmen erfahren." (4)

(29) „Ānanda, hast du wohl gehört und weißt du, ob die Leute jenes Landes ihren Eltern und Vorg-esetzten gegenüber Achtung und Verehrung zeigen, (ob sie deren) Unterweisungen folgen, (und ob ihre) Gefühle (gegen dieselben) ohne Widersetzlich-keit und Unlust sind?"

(30) Er antwortete: „Ich habe gehö-rt." ... ausführlicher Wortlaut wie oben.

Sanskrit	Dīghanikāya XVI
1.31 (yāvac ca varṣākāra vṛjayo ye te vṛjīnāṃ vṛjimahallakās tān satkariṣyanti gurukariṣyanti mānayiṣyanti pūjayiṣyanti teṣāṃ vacanaṃ śrota) vyaṃ ma(ṃ)sy(ante) v(ṛ)ddhir eva vṛjīnāṃ prati-(kāṃ kṣitavyā kuśalānāṃ dharmāṇāṃ na parihāṇiḥ /)	yāvakīvañ ca ānanda vajjī ye te vajjīnaṃ vajjimahallakā te sakkarissanti garukarissanti mānessanti pūjessanti tesañ ca sotabbaṃ maññissanti vuddhi yeva ānanda vajjīnaṃ pāṭikaṅkhā no parihāni /

[Principle VI]

32 (kiṃ nu tvayānanda śrutaṃ vṛjayo ye te vṛjīnāṃ caturdikṣu vṛjicaityās tān satkurvanti gurukurvan) ti mānayanti pūjayanti teṣāṃ ca pau(rāṇaṃ cihnavṛttaṃ na samucchindanti /)	kin ti te ānanda sutaṃ vajjī yāni tāni vajjīnaṃ vajjicetiyāni abbhantarāni c'eva bāhirāni ca tāni sakkaronti garukaronti mānenti pūjenti tesañ ca dinnapubbaṃ katapubbaṃ dhammikaṃ baliṃ no parihāpentīti /
33 (śrutaṃ me bhadanta vṛjayo ye te vṛjīnāṃ caturdikṣu vṛjicaityās tān satkurvanti gurukurvanti mānayanti pūjayan) ti teṣāṃ ca paurāṇaṃ cih(n)avṛttaṃ (na samucchindanti /)	sutaṃ me taṃ bhante vajjī yāni tāni vajjīnaṃ vajjicetiyāni abbhantarāni c'eva bāhirāni ca tāni sakkaronti garukaronti mānenti pūjenti tesañ ca dinnapubbaṃ katapubbaṃ dhammikaṃ baliṃ no parihāpentīti /

Vinaya. Tibetisch	Vinaya. Chinesisch
bla-mar bgyid / rimor bg-yid / mchod-par bgyid-ciṅ / de-dag-gi tshig- la dad-pas ñan-par bgyid / sems-par bgyid lags-so /	
1.31 dbyar-byed ji-srid-du yul-spoṅ-byed-pa-rnams yul-sp-oṅ-byed-kyi rgan-rabs-rna-ms daṅ /ya-rabs-rnams daṅ/ pha-mai rgyud gaṅ-dag-la yul-spoṅ-byed-pa de-dag bk-ursti byed / bla-mar byed / ri-mor byed / mchod-par byed-ciṅ / de-dag-gi tshig-la dad-pas ñan-par byed / sems-par byed-pa-las / yul-spoṅ-byed-pa-rnams-kyi dge-bai chos-rnams ñams-par mi 'agyur-ẑiṅ rgyas-par 'agyur-bar śes-par byao /	Der Buddha sprach zu dem Brahmanen: . . . auch ganz so wie oben im Wortlaut, bis: „und daß die *kuśala dharmas* kein Abnehmen erfahren.“ (5)
32 (6) ci kun-dga-bo khyod-kyis yul-spoṅ-byed-kyi ph-yogs bẑi-po gaṅdag-na / yul spoṅ-byed-kyi mchod-rten de-dag-la yulspoṅ-byed-pa-rnams bkursti byed / bla-mar byed / ri-mor byed / mchod-par byed-ciṅ / de-dag-gis sṅongyi mtshan-mar bzuṅ-ba mi 'ador-bar thos sam /	„Ānanda, hast du wohl gehört und weißt du, ob die Leute jenes Landes den Caityas ständing Verehrung darzubringen pflegen und ob sie die vorhandenen, alten, ehrenwerten gesetzlichen Vorschriften nicht außer acht geraten lassen?“
33 btsun-pa bdag-gis thos lags-te / yul-spoṅ-byed-kyi phy-ogs bẑi-po gaṅ-dag-na / yul-spoṅ-byed-kyi mchod-rten de-dag-la / yul-spoṅ-byed-pa-rnams bkur-sti byed bla-mar byed / ri-mor byed / mchod-par byed-ciṅ / de-	Ausführlicher Wortlaut bis: „und daß die *kuśala dharmas* kein Abnehmen erfahren.“(6)

Sanskrit	Dīghanikāya XVI
34 (yāvac ca varṣākāra vṛjayo ye te vṛjīnāṃ caturdikṣu vṛjicaityās tān satkari)-(181.1)ṣyanti gurukariṣyanti mānayiṣyanti pūjayiṣyanti teṣāṃ ca paurāṇaṃ cihnavṛttaṃ na samu(cchet) sya-(n)ti vṛddhir eva vṛjīnāṃ pratikāṃkṣitavyā kuśalānāṃ dharmāṇā(ṃ) na parihāṇi(ḥ) /	yāvakīvañ ca ānanda vajjī yāni tāni vajjīnaṃ vajjicetiyāni abbhantarāni c'eva bāhirāni ca tāni sakkarissanti garukarissanti mānessanti pūjessanti tesañ ca dinnapubbaṃ katapubbaṃ dhammikaṃ baliṃ no parihāpessanti vuddhi yeva ānanda vajjīnaṃ pāṭikaṅkhā no parihāni /

[Principle VII]

Sanskrit	Dīghanikāya XVI
35 (kiṃ nu tvayānanda) śrutaṃ vṛjīnām arhatā(m anti)ke tīvracetasa ārakṣāsmṛtiḥ pratyupasthitā kaccid anāgatāś cārhanta āgaccheyur āgatāś cābhirameraṃs te ca na vihanyerañ cīvarapiṇḍapā (taśayanāsanaglā) napratyayabhai-ṣajyapariṣkāraiḥ /	kin ti te ānanda sutaṃ vajjīnaṃ arahantesu dhammikārakkhāvaraṇagutti susaṃvihitā kin ti anāgatā ca arahanto vijitaṃ āgacchey yuṃ āgatā ca arahanto vijite phāsuṃ vihareyyun ti /

Vinaya. Tibetisch

dag-gis sṅon-gyi mtshan-
mar bzuṅ-ba mi 'ador-bar
lags-so /

34 dbyar-byed ji-srid-du yul-
spoṅ-byed-kyi phyogs bži-
po gaṅ-dag-na / yul-spoṅ-
byed-kyi mchod-rten de-
dag-la / yul-spoṅ-byed-pa-
rnams bkur-sti byed / bla-
mar byed / ri-mor byed /
mchod-par byed-ciṅ / de-
dag-gis sṅon-gyi mtshan-
mar bzuṅ-ba mi 'ador-ba-
las / yul-spoṅ-byed-pa-rna-
ms-kyi dge-bai chos-rnams
ñams-par mi 'agyur-žiṅ rgyas-par 'agyur-bar śes-par
byao /

35 (7) ci kun-dga-bo khyod-kyis yul-spoṅ-byed-pa-rnams
dgra-bcom-pa-rnams-la dad-
pa drag-pos kun-tu bsru-
ṅs-pa dran-pa ñe-bar gn-
as-te / dgra-bcom-pa ma
byon-pa-rnams ni spyan-
'adren-par byed / byon-pa-
dag-la mṅon-par dga-bar
byed-ciṅ / de-dagla chos-gos
daṅ / bsod-sñomsdaṅ / mal-
stan daṅ / nadgsos-kyi rkyen-
sman daṅ / yo-byad-rnams-
kyis mi brelbar byed-pa tho
s sam /

Vinaya. Chinesisch

„Ānanda, hast du wohl gehört und weißt du, ob die Leute jenes Landes den Arhats gegenüber, in ehrerbietiger Gesinnung und eifrig, (auch) beständig die rechte Erinnerung her-vorbringen: Diejenigen von ihnen, die (noch) nicht gekommen sind, mögen (doch) alle hierher kommen; diejenigen von ihnen, die schon gekommen sind, sollen einen fried-lichen, zurückgezogenen Aufenthalt errei-chen; Kleider, Trinken und Essen, Lager-stätten und Arzneien, die notwendigen Besitztümer, (wollen wir) vollzählig spenden, so daß kein Mangel eintritt?'

	Sanskrit	Dīghanikāya XVI
1.36	śrutaṃ me bhadanta vṛjī nām arhatām an tike tīvracetasa āra kṣāsmṛtiḥ pratyupasthitā kaccid anāgatāś cārhanta āga(ccheyur āgatāś cā) bhirameraṃs te ca na vihanyerañ cīvarapiṇḍapātaśayanāsanaglānapratyayabhaiṣajyapariṣkāraiḥ /	sutaṃ me taṃ bhante vajjīnaṃ arahan tesu dhammikārakkhāvaraṇagutti susaṃ-vihitā kin ti anāgatā ca arahanto vijitaṃ āgaccheyyuṃ āgatā ca arahanto vijite phā suṃ vihareyyun ti /
37	yāvac ca varṣākāra vṛ(jī)nām arhatām an-tike tīvra cetasa (ārakṣāsmṛtiḥ) pratyupasthitā bhaviṣyati kaccid anāgatāś cārhanta āgaccheyur āgatāś cābhiramera(ṃ)s te ca na vihanyerañ cīvara piṇḍapātaśayanāsanaglānapratyayabhai-ṣajyapariṣkā (rair vṛddhir eva vṛjī) nāṃ pratikāṃkṣitavyā kuśalānāṃ dharmānāṃ na parihāṇiḥ /	yāvakīvañ ca ānanda vajjīnaṃ arahantesu dhammikārakkhāvaraṇagutti susaṃvihitā bhavissati kin ti anāgatā ca arahanto vijitaṃ āgaccheyyuṃ āgatā ca arahanto vijite phā suṃ vihareyyun ti vuḍḍhi yeva ānanda vajjīnaṃ pāṭikaṅkhā no parihānīti /

[Conclusion]

38	yāvac ca varṣākāra vṛjaya imān saptāparihāṇīyān dharmānsamādāya vartiṣyan	1.5 yāvakīvañ ca brāhmaṇa ime satta aparihāniyā dhammā vajjīsu ṭhassanti imesu ca sattasu

	Vinaya. Tibetisch	Vinaya. Chinesisch
I.36	btsun-pa bdag-gis thos lags-te / yul-spoṅ-byed-pa-rnams dgra-bcom-pa-rnams-la dad-pai sems drag-pos kun-tu bsruṅs-pa dran-pa ñe-bar gnas-te / dgra-bcom-pa ma byon-pa-dag ni spyan-'adren-par bgyid / byon-pa-dag-la ni mṅon-par dga-bar bgyid-de / de-dag-la chos-gos daṅ / bsod-sñoms daṅ / mal-stan daṅ / nad-gsos-kyi rkyen-sman daṅ / yo-byad-rnams-kyiṣ mi brel-bar bgyid lags-so /	
37	dbyar-byed ji-srid-du yul-spoṅ-byed-pa-rnams dgra-bcom-pa-rnams-la dad-pai sems drag-pos / kun-tu bsruṅs-pa dran-pa ñe-bar gnas-par gyur-ciṅ / gaṅ dgra-bcom-pa ma 'oṅs-pa-dag ni spyan-'adren-par byed-pa / 'oṅs-pa-dag-la ni mṅon-par dga-bar byed-ciṅ / de-dag-la chos-gos daṅ / bsod-sñoms daṅ / mal-stan daṅ / nad-gsos-kyi rkyen-sman daṅ / yo-byad-rnams-kyis mi brel-bar byed-pa-las / yul-spoṅ-byed-pa-rnams-kyi dge-bai chos-rnams ñams-par mi 'agyur-žiṅ rgyas-par 'agyur-bar śes-par byao /	Ausführlicher Wortlaut bis: „und daß die *kuśala dharmas* kein Abnehmen erfahren."(7)
38	dbyar-byed ji-srid-du yul-spoṅ-byed-pa-rnams ñams-par mi 'agyur-bai chos 'adi	Der Buddha sprach zu dem Brahmanen: „Falls nur die Leute jenes Landes in diesen sie-

	Sanskrit	Dīghanikāya XVI
	te vṛjiṣu ca saptā parihā(ṇīyā dharmāḥ sandrakṣyan) te vṛddhir eva vṛjīnāṃ pratikāṃkṣi tavyā kuśalānāṃ dharmāṇāṃ na parihāṇiḥ /	aparihāniyesu dhammesu vajjī sandissanti vuddhi yeva brāhmaṇa vajjīnaṃ pāṭikaṅkhā no parihānīti /
39		evaṃ vutte vassakāro brāhmaṇo magadha-mahāmatto bhagavantaṃ etad avoca /
1.40	ekaikena tāvad bho gautamāṅgena samanvāgatā vṛja yo 'gamanīyāḥ syū rājño māga(dhasyājātaśa) tror vai dehīputrasya kaḥ punar vādaḥ sarvaiḥ /	ekamekena pi bho gotama aparihāniyena dhammena samannāgatānaṃ vajjīnaṃ vuddhi yeva pāṭikaṅkhā no parihāni ko pana vādo sattahi aparihāniyehi dhammehi / akaraṇīyā va bho gotama vajjī raññā māgadhena ajātasattunā vedehiputtena yadidaṃ yuddhassa aññatra upalāpanāya aññatra mithubhedā /
41	hanta bho gautama gamiṣyāmo bahukṛtyāḥ smo bahukaraṇīyāḥ /	handa ca dāni mayaṃ bho gotama gacchāma bahukiccā mayaṃ bahukaraṇīyā ti /
42	yasyedānīṃ varṣākāra kāla(ṃ) ma nyase /	yassa dāni tvaṃ brāhmaṇa kālaṃ maññasīti /
43	atha varṣākāro brāhmaṇa magadhamahāmātro bhaga vato bhāṣitam abhinandyānumodya bhagavato 'ntikāt prakrāntaḥ /	atha kho vassakāro brāhmaṇo magadhamahāmatto bhagavato bhāsitaṃ abhinanditvā anumoditvā uṭṭhāy' āsanā pakkāmi /

Vinaya. Tibetisch	Vinaya. Chinesisch
bdun yaṅ-dag-par blaṅs-nas/ kun-tu spyod-ciṅ / yul-spoṅ-byed-pa-rnams-la ñams-par mi 'agyur-bai chos 'adi bd-un kun-tu snaṅ-ba-las yul-spoṅ-byed-pa-rnams-kyi d-ge-bai chos-rnams ñams-par mi 'agyurẑiṅ rgyas-par 'ag-yur-bar	ben Bedingungen des Nichtniederganges sich üben und sie befolgen, muβ man wissen, daβ jenes Land beständig Wachstum erfährt, daβ es kein Abnehmen gibt und daβ die *kuśala dharmas* aufblühen."
śes-par byao /	Der Brahmane sprach:
1.40 kye gau-ta-ma re-śig yul-spoṅ-byed-pa-rnams yan-lag 'adi gcig daṅ ldan-na yaṅ / lus-'aphags-mai bu yul-ma-ga-dhai rgyal-po ma-skyes-dgras thub-par mi 'agyur-na / thams-cad daṅ ldan-pa lta smos kyaṅ ci 'atshal-bas /	„Ehrwürdiger, wenn die Leute jenes Landes auch (nur) eine unter den sieben Bedingungen erfüllen, darf sich der König Ajātaśatru nicht daran machen, sie zu strafen. Um wieviel mehr (darf er das nicht, wenn sie) die sieben Bedingungen allesamt erfüllen."
41 kye gau-ta-ma bdag-la bgyi-ba maṅ-ba daṅ / bgyi-bar 'agyur-ba maṅ-bas da mchi-bar 'atshal-lo /	Der Brahmane sprach (weiterhin): "Ehrwürdiger Gautama, ich habe viele Verpflich-tungen und möchte (daher) Abschied nehmen und fortgehen."
42 dbyar-byed dei dus-la bab-par śes-na soṅ-śig /	Der Buddha sprach: „Handle ganz nach Gefallen!"
43 de-nas yul-ma-ga-dhai [sna] chen-po-la gtogs-pa bram-ze dbyar-byed bcom-ldan-'adas-kyis gsuṅs-pa rjes-su yi-raṅ-nas mṅon-par dga-ste / bcom-ldan-'adas-kyi s-pyan-sṅa-nas laṅs-ste soṅ-ṅo /	Damals hörte der Brahmane die Predigt des Buddha, freute sich und handelte danach.

The Pali version was translated by T.W. and C.A.F. Rhys Davids, which runs as follows:*

1. "Thus have I heard. The Exalted One was once dwelling in Râjagaha, on the hill called the Vulture's Peak. Now at that time Ajâtasattu, the son of the queen-consort of the Videha clan, the king of Magadha, had made up his mind to attack the Vajjians; and he said to himself, 'I will strike at these Vajjians, mighty and powerful though they be, I will root out these Vajjians, I will destroy these Vajjians, I will bring these Vajjians to utter ruin!'

2. So he spake to the brahmin Vessakâra (the Rain-maker), prime-minister of Magadha, and said:

'Come now, brahmin, do you go to the Exalted One, and bow down in adoration at his feet on my behalf, and inquire in my name whether he is free from illness and suffering, and in the enjoyment of ease and comfort and vigorous health. Then tell him that Ajâtasattu, son of the Vedehî, the king of Magadha, in his eagerness to attack the Vajjians, has resolved, "I will strike at these Vajjians, mighty and powerful though they be, I will root out these Vajjians, I will destroy these Vajjians, I will bring these Vajjians to utter ruin!" And bear carefully in mind whatever the Exalted One may predict, and repeat it to me. For the Buddhas speak nothing untrue!'

3. Then the brahmin Vassakâra, the Rain-maker, hearkened to the words of the king, saying, 'Be it as you say.' And ordering a number of state carriages to be made ready, he mounted one of them, left Râjagaha with his train, and went to the Vulture's Peak, riding as far as the ground was passable for carriages and then alighting and proceeding on foot to the place where the Exalted One was. On arriving there he exchanged with the Exalted One the greetings and compliments of politeness and courtesy, sat down respectfully by his side (and then delivered to him the message even as the king had commanded).

[Principle I]

4. Now at that time the venerable Ânanda was standing behind the Exalted One, and fanning him. And the Blessed One said to

**Dīgha-Nikāya* XVI, 1-5 vol. II, pp. 72-76.

Dialogues of the Buddha, Part II: *Translated from the Pāli of the Dīgha Nikāya* by T.W. and C.A.F. Rhys Davids. Published for the Pali Text Society by Luzac & Company, London, 1951, pp. 78-81.

him: 'Have you heard, Ânanda, that the Vajjians foregather often and frequent the public meetings of their clan?'

'Lord, so I have heard', replied he.

'So long, Ânanda', rejoined the Blessed One, 'as the Vajjians foregather thus often, and frequent the public meetings of their clan; so long may they be expected not to decline, but to prosper.'

(And in like manner questioning Ânanda, and receiving a similar reply, the Exalted One declared as follows the other conditions which would ensure the welfare of the Vajjian confederacy.)

[Principle II]

'So long, Ânanda, as the Vajjians meet together in concord, and rise in concord, and carry out their undertakings in concord—

[Principle III]

so long as they enact nothing not already established, abrogate nothing that has been already enacted, and act in accordance with the ancient institutions of the Vajjians, as established in former days—

[Principle IV]

so long as they honour and esteem and revere and support the Vajjian elders, and hold it a point of duty to hearken to their words—

[Principle V]

so long as no women or girls belonging to their clans are detained among them by force or abduction—

[Principle VI]

so long as they honour and esteem and revere and support the Vajjian shrines in town or country, and allow not the proper offerings and rites, as formerly given and performed, to fall into desuetude—

[Principle VII]

so long as the rightful protection, defence, and support shall be fully provided for the Arahants among them, so that Arahants from a distance may enter the realm, and the Arahants therein may live at ease—

[Conclusion]

so long may the Vajjians be expected not to decline, but to prosper.'

5. Then the Exalted One addressed Vassakâra the brahmin and said:

'When I was once staying, O brahmin, at Vesâlî at the Sârandada Shrine, I taught the Vajjians these conditions of welfare; and so long as these conditions shall continue to exist among the Vajjians, so long as the Vajjians shall be well instructed in those conditions, so long may we expect them not to decline, but to prosper.'

'We may expect then', answered the brahmin, 'the welfare and not the decline of the Vajjians when they are possessed of any one of these conditions of welfare, how much more so when they are possessed of all the seven. So, Gotama, the Vajjians cannot be overcome by the king of Magadha; that is not in battle, without diplomacy or breaking up their alliance. And now, Gotama, we must go; we are busy and have much to do.'

'Whatever you think most fitting, O brahmin', was the reply. And the brahmin Vassakâra, the Rain-maker, delighted and pleased with the words of the Exalted One, rose from his seat, and went his way."

In the Chinese version of the *Madhyamāgama,* chuan 35 a sūtra entitled *Yu-shi-ching* (probably its Sanskrit title must have been *Varṣakārasūtra*) is included. (*Taisho Tripitaka*, vol. I, p. 648a-650b.) This was translated into Chinese by the Kashmerean monk Gudon Sogyadaiba (=Gautama Saṅghadeva) in the years 397-98 A.D. Its contents are more or less the same as the passages relevant to Varṣakāra in the Pāli and Sanskrit versions which are extant.

However, the Seven Principles of the Vajjian republic as are mentioned in other Chinese versions of the Mahāparinirvāṇasūtra are fairly different from those which are unanimously mentioned in the Pali, Sanskrit, Tibetan versions and in the Chinese versions by Saṅghadeva and by I-tsing.

The other Chinese versions of this sūtra are as follows:

Version A: *Hatsu-nai-on-gyō (Pan-ni-yüan-ching).* (*Taisho Tripiṭaka,* No. 6, vol. I, pp. 176a- 191a.) Its translator is anonymous.

The date of its translation is not known. Which school in India was its compiler, is not known, either. The posthumous manuscript of the Late Dr. Hakuju Ui's study on this sūtra was published (*Yakukyōshi Kenkyū,* Tokyo, 1971, pp. 517-23). His conclusion is that its translator was Shiken (Tche K'ien). His reasons for this conclusion is: (1) The Chinese technical terms used in this version are those which are peculiarly used in Tche K'ien's translations. (2) When we examine earlier Sūtra-Catalogues, we are led to the same conclusions. (Tche K'ien was a "Laic né d'une famille d'orig. indo-scythe établie en Chine dès 168-89. ..... Dès 220 rés. à Nankin où trav. 220-52." Paul Demiéville, Hubert Durt et Anna Seidel: *Fascicule annexe du* Hōbōgirin, Maison Franco-Japonaise, 1978, p. 275.)

If this text is proved to be a translation by Tche K'ien, we must think that this must be one of the earliest text among Chinese versions of Buddhist scriptures. Even if this conjecture is disapproved, we cannot doubt that this version is a very old one. This text, as a whole, tinged and modified by Confucian thought.

Version B: *Butsu-hatsu-nai-on-gyō* (*Fo-pan-ni-yüan-ching*). Translated by Haku-hosso (or Byaku-hō-so, Po-fa-tsou). "Orig. prince royal de Koutcha. Trav. *Lo yang* 259. P. Demiéville: op.cit. p. 253. This was translated into Chinese in 290-306 A.D. (*Taisho Tripiṭaka,* N. 5, vol. I, pp. 160 b-175.) With regard to its content, this sūtra is close to Version A.

Version C: chuans 2-4 of the Chinese version of the Dīrghāgama-sūtra translated by Buddhayaśas and Buddhasmṛti in the years beginning with 399 A.D. (*Taisho Tripiṭaka,* vol. I, pp. 11a- 30b.) With regard to its content, it substantially corresponds with the Sanskrit text of the *Mahāparinirvāṇa-sūtra.*

Version D: *Dai-hatsu-ne-han-gyō* (*Ta-pan-nieh-p'an-ching*). Translated by Fa-hien in 416-18 A.D. (*Taisho Tripiṭaka,* No. 7, vol. I, pp. 191b-207c.) This lacks the former portion of the story of the last journey of Śākyamuni. It does not refer to the sermon at the summit of the Gṛdhrakūṭa, but in the sermon addressed to the Licchavis the Seven Principles of the Republic are taught in modified forms (*Taisho Tripiṭaka*, vol. I, p. 193c). So this sūtra is still useful for comparison in this context.

Version E: *Kom-pon-setsu-is-sai-u-bu-bi-naya-zō-ji* (*Kên-pên-shuo-i-ch'ieh-yu-pu-p'i-na-yeh-tsa-shih*), chuans 35-40. (*Taisho Tripiṭaka*, No. 1451, vol. 24, pp. 382b-411c.) Translated by I-tsing in 710 A.D.

This Chinese text corresponds to the Tibetan *Ḥdul-ba phran-tshegs kyi gshi* (Skt. Vinayakṣudrakavastu). This Chinese text fairly corresponds to the Sanskrit text of the *Mahāparinirvāṇa-sutra*, so the late E. Waldschmidt translated it into German, as is mentioned above. In comparison with the Pali version the grade of hyperbolization of description and the deification of Śākya-muni are more advanced.

Version F.: *Hō-dō-hatsu-nai-on-gyō* (*Fang-têng-pan-ni-yüan-ching*). Translated by Dharmarakṣa in 269 A.D. (*Taisho Tripiṭaka*, No. 378, vol. 12, pp. 912-28c.) This text depicts only the last scene of the passing away of the Buddha. Its content is mahāyānistic. So, this text is out of scope for comparison.

In addition to them there exist two Chinese versions of the (Mahāyāna) *Mahāparinirvāṇasūtra*, and some fragments of the Sanskrit original have been found. However, these texts also should be out of scope for comparison in this case.

[Some Sanskrit fragments have been preserved at the cathedral of Kōyasan in Japan. Other fragments were edited and published by Prof. Bongard-Levin of Russia.]

In the following we shall compare passages in Chinese versions relevant to the Seven Principles of the Vajjian Confederacy. We shall examine one by one succeedingly.

Principle I:

The republican character of the Vajjian Confederacy is still expressed in versions A, B, C. In versions A and B the phrase "to defend themselves" is inserted. In version D the translation runs: "People are in concord joyfully. They are not in conflict with each other." Here the republican character of the Vajjian Confederacy in the Indian original is completely wiped out.

Principle II:

The Chinese versions A, B, C have the phrase: "Monarchs and subjects are peacefully in concord". Versions A and B add the phrase: "Appointed officials are loyal (to the kings) and useful mutually". These facts mean that Chinese translators wanted to conceal the republican character of the Indian original and tried to adapt this Buddhist teaching to the traditional monarchical social order of China.

Principle III:

Versions C and D interpret this principle with the traditional Chinese term *li*.

Principle IV:

In the Indian original the virtue of respecting the elders alone is taught. But in Chinese versions A and B it is said: "Between men and women there should be discrimination". In versions C and D this phrase is inserted: "One should be reverential to one's father and mother". Here filial piety, the traditional virtue of the Chinese, is emphasized.

Principle V:

Versions A and B run as follows: "One is filial to father and mother; one is obeisant to elders; one obeys to their instructions." Version D is completely different, saying, "Relatives should be harmoniously in concord. They should be obeisant to each other." It is only version C that conveys some sex-ethical implications, saying: "One should be righteous in terms of sexual behaviour. One should be pure. Even if one should get into smile and laughter, one should not say anything indecent." Why was it that such a drastic change of the phrase of the Indian text was made? I think it is due to the traditional attitude of the Chinese to avoid referring to sexual affairs explicitly.

Principle VI:

In Versions A and B the phrase was altered in such a way as would conform to Chinese ways of thinking, as "One should conform oneself to Heaven and Earth; one should revere ancestral shrines of one's own. One should do things in accordance to the change of the Four Seasons."

Principle VII:

The Indian originals enjoin to revere and protect arhats regardless the difference of religions. The term "arhat" was used not only by Buddhists but also by Jains and followers of other religions. Principle VII should be applied universally. But version D limits the scope of its application to Buddhism alone. It says, "One should observe Bauddha-dharma. Heartfully revere bhikkhus and bhikkhunis. Protect lovingly upāsakas and upāsikās." This alteration may not be due to Chinese influence, but due to the alteration of the Indian original text. In earlier days, Buddhists were rather tolerant to other religions. But with the lapse of time the Buddhist orders came to be conscious of, and sensitive to, the distinction between the Buddhist order of their own and the orders of other religions.

The fact that so many alterations were made when the Seven Principles of the Vajjian Republic were conveyed to Chinese reveals the necessity of their adaptations to the traditional Chinese ways of thinking to lessen the objections and frictions from the side of the native Chinese. When the Sanskrit original of version E was translated, the work was done in the reign of the Tang dynasty which was of highly international character and which supported Buddhism. There was no need of twisted interpretation or alteration of the text. That is why version E is so close to the Indian original, as is represented by Waldschmidt's German translation.

When we examine twisted interpretations or insertions carefully in the light of social or ideological context, we come to know that they were made, not arbitrarily, but due to some reasons.

3 A DIFFICULT BEGINNING
Comments on an English translation of Candragomin's *Deśanāstava*

MICHAEL HAHN, MARBURG

A. Introduction: Candragomin, his works and his time

Between 1976 and 1985, Mark Tatz published two papers and two books dealing with various aspects of the life and literary activities of the erstwhile famous Buddhist poet Candragomin. The four publications are:

(1) "On the Date of Chandragomin", *Buddhism and Jainism*, ed. by Harish Chandra Das, Chittaranjan Das, Satya Ranjan Pal, Orissa 1976 (Institute of Oriental and Orissan Studies), pp. 281-97.

(2) "The Life of Candragomin in Tibetan Historical Tradition", *The Tibet Journal*, Vol. VII, No. 3 (1982), pp. 1-22.

(3) *Candragomin's Twenty Verses on the Bodhisattva Vow and its Commentary by Sakya Dragpa Gyaltsen.* Transl. with an introduction by Mark Tatz, Dharamsala 1982, 74, pp.

(4) *Difficult Beginnings. Three Works on the Bodhisattva Path. Candragomin.* Translated, with commentary by Mark Tatz, Boston & London 1985.

The last-mentioned work, a beautifully produced book, goes back to the author's unpublished Ph.D. thesis *Candragomin and the Bodhisattva Vow*, University of British Columbia, 1978, "which can be obtained in microfiche from the National Library of Canada, Ottawa K1A 0N4 (Canadian Theses Divisions, No. 40796)."[1]

In at least two points the publications of Tatz touch upon issues which were also dealt with in my previous publications on Candragomin.[2] The two points are:

(1) the date of Candragomin;
(2) works attributed to a certain Candragomin which might have been written by the same Candragomin who also wrote the *Lokānanda* and the *Śiṣyalekha.*

Although my own research work was and is focused mainly

on Candragomin's two most important literary compositions, the drama "Joy for the World" (*Lokānanda*) and the "Letter to a Disciple" (*Śiṣyalekha*), I have also given a short list of all the works attributed to Candragomin in the Tibetan Tanjur (Peking Edition) and in this connection expressed my opinion that there are among them four works which by their literary quality point to an author of the stature of Candragomin. They are:

(a) *Deśanāstava*: Hymn in [Form of a] Confession,
(b) *Bhagavadāryamañjuśrīsādhiṣṭhānastuti*: Praise of the Noble Mañjuśrī, Accompanied by a Firm Resolve,
(c) *Manoharapāpavidāraṇanāmalokanāthastotra*: Hymn to the Protector of the World called 'The Splitting of Enticing Sins',
(d) *Śrīmahātārastotra*: Hymn to the Glorious Great Tāra.[2a]

The first of these four works is contained in Tatz's book and the evaluation of his English translation will form the main part of this paper. First, however, I would like to summarize the contents of the two papers on the date and the historical tradition about Candragomin by Tatz and then present my own opinion about this topic.

In the paper on the date of Candragomin, Tatz starts with a delineation of the issues (A), collects the evidence which points to a seventh century date (B), tries to describe Candra as grammarian according to the Tibetan and Indian traditions (C), and finally presents his conclusion (D). On the whole, the paper is characterized by the laudable attempt to collect in one place all the known direct and indirect references to the life and works of Candragomin and also to take into account what modern scholarship has written on this issue. Tatz's judgment is particularly careful and sober with regard to the relevance of Tibetan historical materials. Let us summarize his main arguments and conclusions.

In the first part of his paper, Tatz rightly states that the Tibetan sources are by themselves not reliable as they were composed 600 or more years after the events with which they deal, that some of these traditions can be regarded basically as pious legends, and that we have to reckon with the possibility that two authors bearing the same name were assimilated to one another. One can easily agree with what Tatz states. He then turns to the testimony of the works themselves which are attributed to

Candragomin in the Tibetan Tanjur. The most important among them are those works which contain direct reference to their author. For example, in the *Lokānanda* Candra(gomin) is mentioned in the prologue and at the end of each act; in the *Śiṣyalekha* there is mention of the moon (*candra*) in the concluding stanza[3] and the text is also attributed to Candragomin in Vairocanarakṣita's commentary *Śiṣyalekhaṭippaṇa*;[4] in the last stanza of the Deśanāstava the moon is also mentioned.[5] Tatz thinks that "in general, translations of his [=Candragomin's] works into Tibetan during the 'early spread' of the Dharma (eighth to ninth centuries) may also be attributed with confidence to him."[6] They include the *Bodhisaṃvaraviṃśaka*, several stotras and minor works like the *Nyāyasiddhyāloka*.[7]

Tatz then discusses I-ching's references to Candragomin. He admits that I-ching's record contains inaccuracies but thinks that they concern only persons who had already passed away at the time of I-ching. He mentions the case of Bhartṛhari who, according to I-ching, died around 650 A.D. whereas modern scholarship places him between 450 and 510 A.D. Tatz is convinced that I-ching would not have committed such a blunder in regard of a contemporary. But there is enough evidence that not everything that I-ching related with regard to Candragomin is correct, be it I-ching's fault or that of his informant. The first instance of such a doubtful passage is a stanza which I-ching attributes to Candragomin. Translated directly from the Chinese it runs:

> The difference between poisonous herbs
> and poisonous sense-objects
> Is indeed very great.
> Poisonous herbs harm only when they are swallowed
> But poisonous sense-objects burn
> (as soon as you) think of them.[8]

Although the Sanskrit original of this stanza[9] is indeed attributed to a certain Candragopin (no doubt a corruption of Candragomin) in Vallabhadeva's medieval collection of Sanskrit verses called *Subhāṣitāvalī* one has to be somewhat cautious about this attribution. The stanza also occurs in the old Nepalese manuscript[10] of the *Śiṣyalekha* between stanzas 75 and 76 (my counting). However, it can be shown easily that the stanza is a later addition, not belonging to the original *Śiṣyalekha*. First, it is not contained in the Tibetan translation of the 'Letter to a Disciple' which was done in the beginning of the ninth century A.D. Second, the stanza is written in the Anuṣṭubh metre which is used nowhere else in the *Śiṣyalekha*. Third, it is a poor repetition of what was already stated in a much more elaborate and elegant way in the two preceding stanzas and moreover it disturbs the internal connection between those two stanzas and the following stanza 76. I would like to illustrate this by quoting fully the relevant passage.[11]

āpātamātramadhurā viṣayā viṣaṃ ca
ghorā vipākakaṭukā viṣayā viṣaṃ ca/
mohāndhakāragahanā viṣayā viṣaṃ ca
durvāravegacapalā viṣayā viṣaṃ ca//74//

kāmaṃ viṣaṃ ca visayāś ca nirūpyamāṇāḥ
śreyo viṣaṃ na viṣayā viṣamasvabhāvāḥ/
ekatra janmani viṣaṃ viṣatāṃ prayāti
janmāntare 'pi viṣayā viṣatāṃ prayānti//75//

[*viṣasya viṣayāṇāṃ ca dūram atyantagocaram/*
upayuktaṃ viṣaṃ hanti viṣayāḥ smaraṇād api//75a//]

saṃsṛṣṭaṃ vrajanti viṣaṃ viṣeṇa śāntiṃ
sanmantrair agadadharaiś ca sādhyamānam/
yuktaṃ vā bhavati viṣaṃ hitāya nṛṇāṃ
na tv evaṃ viṣayamahāviṣaṃ kadā cit//76//

74. Both the objects of the senses and poison
are sweet only when first encountered;
both the objects of the senses and poison
are terrible and sharp when digested;
both the objects of the senses and poison
share the great darkness of unconsciousness;
both the objects of the senses and poison
are incalculable in their vehemence,
so difficult to restrain.

75. Should one, however, take a closer look
at poison and the objects of the senses,
then poison would prove to be the better thing
when weighed against the objects of the senses
with their dangerous nature.
For poison's bane is perilous

but in a single round of existence,
while sensual pleasures will poison a being
in the incarnation to come as well.

76. Poison when mixed with poison
is rendered ineffective
and also when subdued by good spells
carrying the power of an antidote;
moreover, properly used,
poison even becomes beneficial to beings—
never, however, does this strong poison
"objects of the senses" behave in such a way.

Every attentive reader of these three stanzas will notice that they form a logical and stylistical unity which would be destroyed by the insertion of the Anuṣṭubh stanza 75a. Moreover I am somewhat doubtful that Candragomin, after having composed the two stanzas *Śiṣyalekha* 74 and 75 on the relationship between 'poison' (*viṣa*) and 'objects of the senses' (*viṣaya*), would have expressed the same idea in the much less polished form of the spurious Anuṣṭubh stanza. In my opinion it is no coincidence that the *Lokānanda* contains *Śiṣyalekha* 74 and 75,[12] but not 75a. I think, it is much more likely that somebody else summarized Candragomin's pair of verses in the Anuṣṭubh stanza quoted above and that the attribution to Candragomin is meant only to give full credit to the inventor of the idea and the pun (*viṣa-viṣaya*) belonging to it.

The second instance of I-ching's inaccuracy with regard to Candragomin is his description of the play. According to I-ching, the name of the hero is P'i-yu [read: shu]-an-ta-lo (Skr. Viśvantara), whereas it is actually Maṇicūḍa. As stated already earlier,[13] we can safely assume that this error is due to the similarity between the Viśvantara and Maṇicūḍa legends.

During his long stay in India, I-ching must have read about or heard thousands of facts of all kinds. It is therefore plausible that some of them were mixed up or not properly recalled when after more than 25 years he set out to incorporate them into his record. It suffices to point to I-ching's inacceptable dating of Bhartṛhari mentioned above. From the way I-ching writes about Candragomin it seems likely that he did not meet him in person but only heard about him. We have to reckon with the possibility that the Candra about whom he heard could have been either a figure of the past or a namesake closer in time to I-ching.

Tatz next dwells on the form of the name 'Candradāsa' in the prologue (verse 4) of the *Lokānanda* without giving a convincing explanation why it may have been used instead of Candra or Candragomin. In my opinion there were two reasons for the use of *(*Candra*)-*dāsena*. The first of them could have been the metre of the stanza, Anuṣṭubh, that does not allow the sequence – U – for the syllables 7 to 9 of the first and third lines. I assume that the first line began with the words *prabaddhaṃ* 'composed by.'[14] The continuation *Candragominā* would have been the proscribed sequence – U – at the end of the first line. By using *Candradāsena* Candragomin could establish the correct metrical structure and at the same time could express humbleness towards the audience. There might have been even a third, additional motive for using °*dāsa* instead of °*gomin*. As I will show later, there is good reason to assume that Candragomin was not only a younger contemporary of Kālidāsa but also one of his admirers, and hence °*dāsena* might contain a reference, maybe even an expression of respect towards the famous dramatist.

The following passage from Tatz's paper should not be left uncontradicted because of the serious misjudgments and factual errors contained in it:

> "A comparison of the dramas of Harṣa (whether composed by the monarch himself or a member of his court) with that of CG [=Candragomin] also indicates that CG came later. Both major plays are based on Jatakas and are found in the section of the Tanjur bearing that title, along with the Jataka-mala of Arya-sura, who is probably of the seventh century as well. This seems to have been an age for elaboration of bodhisattva birth stories. I-Tsing discusses the three works together, and the two plays may have appeared together in eighth century Japan."[14a]

Tatz commits the same mistake as did Sylvain Lévy forty years before him, that is, he assesses a difficult and complex literary composition of which he could not have and did not have more than a superficial knowledge. Tatz's only source of information on the *Lokānanda* was Ratna Handurukande's inadequate transliteration and synopsis.[15] Only the critical edition and annotated translation of the drama which appeared in 1974[16] would have enabled Tatz to get an understanding of the details of the play, but it is obvious from his paper that this publication was not accessible to him at the time he wrote his paper. Moreover an intimate knowledge of the Tibetan *Lokānanda* would be just one precondition for an opinion about the mutual relationship between the *Lokānanda* and the *Nāgānanda*, the other one being a thorough familiarity with the classical Sanskrit drama, its theory, its development and the linguistic and stylistic peculiarities of the various authors. Tatz's views concerning the date of Āryaśūra and the introduction of poetic elements into the Buddhist narrative literature are also not tenable. No serious scholar has ever placed Āryaśūra as late as the seventh century A.D.[17] and the beginnings of Buddhist narrative literature written in an elaborate style can be traced down to the second century A.D., the most likely time of Kumāralāta, who wrote the *Kalpanāmaṇḍitikā Dṛṣṭāntapaṅkti*, a well-known work of the Buddhist narrative literature.[18]

In the last section of his paper Tatz discusses Candra the grammarian. He tries to distinguish between Candra, the name used for the grammarian, and Candragomin, the name used for the poet. He also tries to diminish the historical value of the often-quoted example from the commentary on *Cāndravyākaraṇasūtra* 1.2.81, *ajayaj jarto hūṇān*, by questioning Candragomin's authorship of the *Vṛtti* and attributing it to a certain Dharmadāsa.[19] This is a rather controversial issue. The German scholar Birwé held that at least the *Vṛtti* on the first four chapters of the *Vyākaraṇasūtra* was Candragomin's own work.[20] Afterwards, this was refuted by several other scholars,[21] but recently J. Bronkhorst has again defended Candragomin's authorship of the *Vṛtti*.[22] However, this point is without any importance for Tatz's main argument because in the end he accepts that the grammarian can by no means be a contemporary of I-ching. The main conclusion at which he arrives is the solution already proposed by Ratna Handurukande in her book on the *Maṇicūḍāvadāna*, namely to distinguish between the grammarian Candra who lived in or before the sixth century A.D. and the Yogācārin and poet Candragomin who lived in the latter three quarters of the seventh century. Being left with one important piece of counter-evidence, namely stanza 6 of the first act of the *Lokānanda* which mentions the grammar composed by the author of the drama, he also follows Handurukande in declaring it an interpolation. This is hardly possible. In stanza 4 the poet's name is mentioned, in stanza 5 his family, and in stanza 6 his literary merits are praised. Having devoted two full stanzas to the factual details about the author and then leaving aside the central topic, the self-appraisal of the poet through the mouth of the stage-director, would be rather unusual in any case and even more so in the case of Candragomin. The five act-concluding stanzas of the *Lokānanda* in which he refers to himself as well as the concluding stanzas of the *Śiṣyalekha* and *Deśanāstava* which also contain the word *candra* 'moon' clearly prove that Candragomin would never have missed a chance to speak about his literary accomplishments. One could argue that the very passage about the grammar was forged; however, who would have dared to do that and to what end? Moreover the assumed forgerer must have been a very learned person to be able to include in this passage the three attributes—*laghu*, *vispaṣṭa* and *saṃpūrṇa*—which characterize the grammar of Candragomin. I shall not dwell longer on this passage and its implications because I have discussed it at some length in my previous publications,[23] however I would like to point out two other implications:

(1) To declare that either the relevant passage in stanza 6, the whole stanza or even the whole prologue is an interpolation[24] on the ground that it does not go with I-ching's statement that the playwright Candra(gomin) was still alive in the second half of the seventh century would mean to discard one of the few, and therefore, precious passages in early classical Sanskrit literature in which an author discloses information about his person and work. There is no internal reason whatsoever to doubt the authenticity of this passage, and the external reason is not a cogent one, as stated above.

(2) In a paper to be published shortly,[25] I have tried to give an indirect proof for my claim that the complete prologue of the *Lokānanda* is genuine by pointing to some of the improbable, if not absurd, consequences which follow from the assumption that the whole prologue or some of its parts were forged. These consequences were not taken into account by those scholars who hold this view.

Despite his intensive study of the available source materials which are basically the same that were used by his predecessors

Tatz was not able to put forward a new theory. His paper which has its own value as a new presentation of the known facts and their interpretation and which is characterized by a sober assessment of the value of the Tibetan source materials (which have at times been overestimated) suffers from one major deficiency: Tatz's insufficient familiarity with the *Lokānanda* and its place in Indian literature. This could have been avoided, at least partially, if Tatz had had access to my publications on Candragomin of 1970, 1971 and 1974. This makes his article basically a repetition of what had already been stated more briefly by me and moreover he was not aware of the different solution proposed by me with regard to the contradictory statements of I-ching and the *Lokānanda*, stanza 6, that is to cast doubt on the correctness of I-ching's statement that Candragomin, the author of the drama, was still alive in the last quarter of the seventh century.[26]

I have dwelt on this question at some length because even after carefully reconsidering the arguments proposed by Tatz[27] I still feel that the available evidence overwhelmingly supports the identity of the grammarian and the playwright and hence an earlier date for the *Lokānanda*. At least in one respect the decision about Candragomin's date is extremely crucial, in establishing the correct relationship between the *Lokānanda* and Harṣadeva's *Nāgānanda*. The close affinity between them is undisputable,[28] the question is only one of asking which was the model and which one the 'copy'.[29] The detailed comparison between the two plays is still to be written; however, I have contended already earlier that it is most unlikely (1) that the Hindu writer Harṣadeva who was clearly influenced by Kālidāsa in his two other plays, *Ratnāvalī* and *Priyadarśikā*, would have been more original in his play on a Buddhist topic and (2) that Candragomin, a dyed-in-the-wool Buddhist, would have taken the composition of a Hindu as his direct model. Moreover, Candragomin's claim that he had composed a 'brand-new' play[30] would have become ridiculous if the *Nāgānanda* were older by several decades and therefore known to all the spectators of the *Lokānanda*.

I believe that Candragomin was influenced by a Hindu poet, Kālidāsa, but in a more general way. In an unpublished lecture which I delivered on the occasion of the Silver Jubilee of the Kālidāsa Academy in Ujjain in November 1982 I collected as many as fifteen passages in which Candragomin uses both elements of action and dramaturgical devices also to be found in Kālidāsa's *Abhijñānaśakuntala*.[31] I concluded that Candragomin was so much impressed by Kālidāsa's ingenuity in handling the form of drama that he tried to include at least some of his inventions in a suitably adapted form in a Buddhist drama. I have the strong feeling (which is difficult to substantiate) that Kālidāsa's play was comparatively new when Candragomin came to know of it. Moreover I assume that the *Śiṣyalekha* also might be a response to another of Kālidāsa's work, the *Meghadūta*. Admittedly there is no similarity in content; however, there is a striking one as far as form is concerned. Both works are *Khaṇḍakāvyas*, devoted to a single topic and of approximately the same length.[32] There is a difference in the usage of metres: Kālidāsa uses only the one metre, Mandākrāntā, which is quite appropriate to the elegiac tone of his poem; in contrast, the *Śiṣyalekha* contains as many as nine different metres.[33] This might have been a deliberate alteration on the part of Candragomin who was too much an original writer to follow slavishly the pattern created by Kālidāsa. If my impression that both the *Lokānanda* and the *Śiṣyalekha* were written under the influence of the two works by Kālidāsa is correct, this would be fully in accordance with the dates proposed for the Hindu poet (fl. c. 400 A.D.) and the Buddhist grammarian (fl. c. 450 A.D.).

Tatz deserves our gratitude for having made accessible in his book *Difficult Beginnings* three more works attributed to Candragomin: 'Candragomin's Resolve' (*Candragomipraṇidhāna*), the 'Twenty Verses on the Bodhisattva Vow' (*Bodhisattvasaṃvaraviṃśaka*), and the 'Praise in Confession, (*Deśanāstava*). I will deal here only with one of them, the 'Hymn in (Form of a) Confession'. While reading the translation I felt justified with regard to my former claim, based only on a rapid perusal of the Tibetan text, that the author of this work might be the same poet who also wrote the *Lokānanda* and the *Śiṣyalekha*. Apart from the elegant style of the *Deśanāstava*, there are two indicators which point to the author of the two afore-mentioned compositions. The first one is the use of 'moon'[34] in the concluding stanza which reminds us of the same practice found in "Joy for the World' (the five act-concluding stanzas contain the name Candra 'Moon') and the 'Letter to a Disciple' (the first and the last stanza contain the word 'moon'). The second one is the actual stanzas 4 through 6 of the 'Hymn in (Form of a) Confession':

[4] "To pacify the scorching fire of aversion,
Even if I develop the lotus pond of *love*,
There, wishing happiness for all people,
The mind ends in the mire of attachment.
[5] To purify the stains of the mire of attachment
If I cleanse it with the water of *even-mindedness*,
There even the World-protector's *compassion*,
Which dispels the distress of all creatures, would decay.
[6] O Chieftain, if I cultivate compassion,
Great sorrow is generated in me;
If I rely on *gladness* to pacify this,
The distracted mind grows excited."[35]

Here Candragomin uses the four 'infinitudes' (*apramāṇa*), 'love' (Skt. *maitrī*, Tib. *byams pa*), 'joy' (Skt. *muditā*, Tib. *dga' ba*), 'compassion' (Skt. *karuṇā*, Tib. *snying rje*), and 'equanimity' (Skt. *upekṣā*, Tib. *btang snyoms*) as his structural principle. In a very similar, yet even more ingenuous way Candragomin has squeezed the same four technical terms together with their general designation into one stanza in the opening portion of the 'Joy for the World' (benedictory stanza 2):

[I.2] "O you whose loving (*maitrī*) character is vast
beyond all measure (*apramāṇa*),
you who were once so blissfully (*muditā*)
embraced by your wife Yaśodharā—
in your great compassion (*karuṇā*)
should you also not show
toward us a similar equanimity (*upekṣā*)?
But we of course must not behave as did
the noble mistress Yaśodharā!"
O, may you gain the knowledge of the Buddha
who was so addressed by the envy-drunk daughters of
Māra, the god of desire!

I believe that these two indicators, together with the name of the author of the 'Hymn in (Form of a) Confession', sufficiently prove the common authorship of the *Lokānanda*, the *Śiṣyalekha*, and the *Deśanāstava*. The blend of the form of a hymn with that of a confession of sins is also quite remarkable and worthy of an author of the stature of Candragomin.

Tatz has translated not only Candragomin's hymn but also Buddhaśānti's commentary which is available only in its Tibetan rendering in the Tanjur. This is valuable from several points of view: it is the oldest and at the same time the only extant Indian explanation of the poem and it is another example for the study of Indian commentaries in Tibetan translation. It is also of great importance for textual criticism as the whole text of the *Deśanāstava* is incorporated into it. Thereby it helps to select the correct reading in more than one case and it also throws light on some of the ambiguous constructions in the rendering of the basic text. The translation of such a work is by no means an easy task as it presupposes a great familiarity with the Indian commentarial literature and their renderings into Tibetan. Unfortunately only few of these works have been studied so far.[36]

While reading Tatz's translations of the *Deśanāstava* and its *Vṛtti* I came to an appreciation of the work he has accomplished; however, in several places I felt dissatisfied with his interpretation. In the portion that follows I have collected my notes in the hope that this will further the correct understanding of both works. I was primarily concerned with Tatz's translation of the 'Hymn in (Form of a) Confession' and I have checked his rendering of Buddhaśānti's commentary mainly in those places which were helpful for a better understanding of difficult or doubtful passages in the basic text. While preparing these notes (in June of 1987) I did not have access to Tatz's critical edition of the two Tibetan texts. My quotations of original passages were entirely based on the Japanese reprint of the Peking edition of the Tibetan Tripiṭaka (Tokyo, Kyoto 1957). Recently (March 1991) Dr. Mark Tatz was so kind as to send me a xerox-copy of the relevant portion of his unpublished thesis (pp. 469-544) which enabled me to compare my quotations with his critical texts. Wherever necessary, I quote the readings from his critical edition.[37]

As a whole the two Tibetan translations[38] are very good pieces of work, and moreover they seem to be well preserved. This is especially so with regard to the 'Hymn in (Form of a) Confession' which is available not only as an independent text but also as a text embedded in the commentary which quotes all its lines. This makes it mandatory that the English version of this interesting work, composed by one of the finest poets of Mahāyāna Buddhism, is also presented in its best possible form. I hope that by the following remarks we will get a little closer to this goal.[39]

B. Corrections of Tatz's Translation of Candragomin's Deśanāstava

2b: *sordid discursive preoccupation.* The Tibetan has **rtog daṅ dpyod pa ṅan pa'i**; one should accordingly translate this as dvandva.

3a: *Tossed by the great waves.* The Tibetan has **dba' rlabs cher 'khrugs tshe.** [In his edition of the *Vṛtti,* Tatz reads **che.**] **cher** (not **ches**) points to an adverbial expression: *greatly tossed by the waves.* Tatz's translation, however, can be justified by the *Vṛtti*: ***dba' rlabs*** **ni de daṅ ldan pa'i rnam par rtog pa** ***du ma*** **ste/des** [!] ***'khrugs*** **pa . . . .**

3b: *If I rely on the vessel as unclean* (**gal te mi gtsaṅ gziṅs la brten gsur na**). I prefer the simple translation "If I rely on an unclean vessel."

4cd: *There, wishing happiness for all people*
The mind ends in the mire of attachment.

/ **der ni skye bo thams cad bder 'dod pa'i** /
/ **chags pa'i 'dam gyis yid ni zin par gyur** /

One would think that the term ending **'dod pa'i** should refer to **chags pa'i**: *there the mind ends in the mire of attachment which is the wish for happiness for all people,* however the *Vṛtti* obviously explains it in such a way that it indeed refers to *yid* as Tatz translates it: **bde bar 'dod ciṅ gnod pa daṅ bral bar dga' ba'i sems so.** The construction is very unusual from the point of view of Tibetan syntax. It can be explained only as a kind of syntactical Sanskritism which I have not found very frequently in translations done in collaboration with Rin chen bzaṅ po.

7b: *Helplessly* (**dbaṅ med; raṅ dbaṅ med par** in the *Vṛtti*). The underlying Sanskrit word **avaśyam** usually means 'necessarily, inevitably'.

8a: *I cultivate all-emptiness, the antidote to that* (***de yi gñen por thams cad ston ñid sgom***). Because of the terminative **gñen por** I prefer to translate "[If] I cultivate all-emptiness **as** the antidote to that."

8d: *There the wish for wealth is born* (**der yid nor gyi bsam pa skye bar 'gyur**). Because of **yid** one should add 'in the mind' to the translation. **der yid** is not explained in the *Vṛtti*.

9d: *Higher aims*. This is the translation of **mṅon 'dod** which simply renders Sanskrit **abhimata** 'desired, wished, cherished (things)". Tatz here seems to translate one part of the explanation of the *Vṛtti*: **mṅon par mtho ba daṅ ṅes par legs pa'i rgyur gyur pa'i *mṅon* par *'dod* pa'i don *thams cad bcom* źiṅ brlag par *'gyur* ro.**

10d: *For a long time after I regret it* (**de tshe yun riṅ dus su rjes su 'gyod**). 'After' is absolutely superfluous because **rjes su 'gyod** is nothing but a mechanical rendering of Sanskrit **paścāttāpa** 'repentence, contrition, regret'.

11a: *In a future reward.* This seems to render **slar yaṅ** which in my opinion simply means 'again'. **slar yaṅ** is not explained in the *Vṛtti*.

15a: *The regret to follow* (**rjes 'gyod**). Cf. the note on 10d.

15b: *Rebirth would be suffering unendurable* (skye ba sdug bsṅal 'gyur ba mi bzad lags). If I am not mistaken *would* (*be*) seems to translate **'gyur ba** which, of course, is absolutely impossible from the point of view of Tibetan syntax. **'gyur ba** can have a potential function, however in this case this would require a sentence like **skye ba sdug bsṅal mi bzad 'gyur.** The line is not easy to understand, as far as its construction is concerned, however the *Vṛtti* sheds some light on what the author and the translators seem to have intended. First the two expressions **skye ba** *birth* (Skr. **jāti**) and **sdug bsṅal** *suffering* (Skr. **duḥkha**) are explained individually, then together, like a compound: **skye ba sdug bsṅal ni skye ba sdug bsṅal te** which even Tatz translates in the following way: *'Rebirth...suffering' refers to the suffering of rebirth.* This contradicts his own translation of the basic text. The *Vṛtti* suggests that something like a Karmadhāraya was intended: *the suffering which is rebirth, the suffering of rebirth.* Usually this would require a genitive **skye ba'i** in Tibetan, but the translators might have been influenced by the Indian resolution of a Karmadhāraya compound into two nominatives: **jātir eva duḥkhaṃ jātiduḥkham.** As for **'gyur ba,** it is difficult to decide whether it refers to **sdug bsṅal** or to **mi bzad. I** suggest the following compromise: *The suffering of rebirth with its* (*frequent*) *changes is unendurable*. Cf. the explanation of the *Vṛtti*: *produces and lets experience the suffering of change*.

15d: *I myself course the same way* (**de ltar na yaṅ de la raṅ ñid spyod**). Leaving aside the not so felicitous translation "to course" for Tibetan **spyod pa** we should add 'even so' as translation of **de ltar na yaṅ.**

16: *When I turn away from harming others,*
Which acts as the cause of the various sufferings,
Having become an enemy to the blameless wretched crowd,
I shake at it with violence like the edge of a sword.

/ **gal te sna tshogs sdug bsṅal rgyur gyur pa'i** /
/ **gźan la gnod byed pa las bzlog pa na** /
/ **skye bo ṅan pa ñes med dgrar gyur pa** /
/ **ral gri'i so ltar gdug pas de 'khrug byed** /

I cannot see how any reader of the translation of the stanza can arrive at a sensible and coherent meaning out of its two contradictory halves, even when consulting Tatz's translation of the *Vṛtti*. In my opinion we have to change just two points of the translation in order to achieve a perfectly logical meaning for the stanza: we have to take **de** as the (grammatical) subject of the whole sentence and **ñes med dgrar gyur pa** as one expression referring to **skye bo ṅan pa**. The whole stanza then reads:

When (my heart or mind) turns away from harming others,
Which acts as the cause of the various sufferings,
Then bad people, who have become the enemy of the blameless
And are as dangerous as the edge of a sword, will shake it (i.e. my heart).

This interpretation is fully corroborated by the *Vṛtti*. The explanation of the last two lines runs as follows: . . . . **ces bya ba smos te /bzod par mi nus kyi blo 'khrug ('khrugs D) ciṅ sems kyi rgyun rñog pa can du byed do/ /gaṅ gis źe na/** ***skye bo ṅan pa ñes med dgrar gyur pa/ /ral gri'i so ltar gdug pas*** (D adds: **de 'khrug byed**) **źes bya ba skye bo'i tshogs tshul khrims daṅ bzod pa la sogs pa dam pa'i spyod pa daṅ bral ba raṅ bzin ṅan par gyur pa rnams ni bdag gis gnod pa (par D) byas pa'i ñes pa gźi med par yaṅ rgyu med pa'i dgra bor gyur ciṅ rjes su sdaṅ bar gyur pa rnams kyi spyod pa ral gri'i so ltar gdug ciṅ źe gcod par byed pas**

bdag gi ***sems 'khrug*** **par** ***byed*** **do/** *While unable to tolerate* (*it*), (*they*) *agitate the mind and pollute the flow of mind. Who* (*agitates and pollutes*)? "*The bad people, who have become the enemy of the blameless and are as dangerous as the edge of a sword*", *that is, the host of bad people who are lacking good conduct, i.e. morality, patience and so forth, who have become of wretched nature, who without reason—that is even when faults in the form of harmful deeds committed by myself do not exist as a basis—have become enemies, and who in their conduct of hating people are as dangerous as the edge of a sword and practice harshness; they shake my heart.*

17. *Even when I wish to make myself patient*
It is tied by their binding misconduct;
Terribly blocked and tied by that,
The fire of aversion dries me of all sympathy.

/gaṅ tshe bdag yid bzod byed 'dod na yaṅ/
/de tshe de yi *ñer spyod 'chiṅ bas bsdams/
/de ni bkag ciṅ yoṅs bsdams drag po yi/
/źe sdaṅ me yis yoṅs bskems brtse daṅ bral/

The stanza continues the idea of verse 16. Tatz has not translated **yid** in 16a which is referred to by **de** in line c. The reading **ñes spyod** of the main text is to be corrected as ***ñer spyod** (Skr. **upacāra**, cd. Lokesh Chandra, *Tibetan-Sanskrit Dictionary*, pp. 865, 869) in accordance with the *Vṛtti* which reads **ñe bar spyod pa, ñer spyod** and again **ñe bar spyod pa.** I prefer the following, more coherent translation:

Even when I wish to make my heart patient
I am tied by the fetter of their (*bad*) *conduct;*
Blocked, tied and completely dried up
By the fierce fire of aversion, it is without sympathy.

18. *Just as vipers, unbearable to see,*
Dwelling within a tree repel the wise
So concealing a course of hatred,
My attitude repels virtue.

/ji ltar mi bzad lta ba'i dug can dag/
/naṅ gnas śiṅ ni mkhas rnams spoṅ bar byed/
/de bźin khoṅ khro'i spyod pa sbed pa yi/
/bdag gi bsam pa dge ba rnams spoṅ byed/

In this stanza, Tatz has completely missed the point. Most probably influenced by the order of words in the original Sanskrit and in the *Vṛtti*, the objects of the sentences are not placed before the verbs but at the beginning of the respective phrases and the subjects have taken the places which are normally occupied by the objects. Hence it is not the vipers who repel the wise but the wise who repel (or shun) the trees inhabited by snakes, and likewise it is not Candragomin's attitude which repels virtue but the virtues which repel Candragomin's attitude. Compared to this, it is only a minor blunder that Tatz did not recognize that **lta ba'i dug can** is nothing but a literal rendering of Sanskrit **dṛṣṭiviṣa** '*(the animal) whose gaze is poisonous*', *serpent*. This is also the explanation of the *Vṛtti*: **mi bzad lta ba'i dug can dag ces pa sbrul gaṅ bltas pa tsam gyis gsod par nus śiṅ /dug can gyi dbugs kyis brgyal bar byed nus pa'o/** **viṣamo dṛṣṭiviṣaḥ—refers to serpents which are able to kill by their mere gaze and to make one faint by their breath.* The correct translation of the whole stanza would run as follows:

> *Just as the wise avoid a tree*
> *Whose inner parts are inhabited by dangerous serpents*
> *So virtues completely shun my inner dispositions*
> *In which actions of hatred are hidden.*

20. *My own unbearable suffering uninvestigated,*
Someone as such tries to do me a favor,
Who helps me with forbearance and generosity,
That, O World-protector, I am unable to bear.

/raṅ gi sdug bsṅal mi bzad ma dpyad pas/
/gaṅ źig bdag la phan brtson lta bur ni/
/bzod daṅ sbyin pas mchog tu phan 'dogs pa/
/'jig rten mgon de'aṅ [or: **'di'aṅ**] **bdag gis bzod mi nus/**

From his translation I cannot see whether Tatz has correctly understood the grammatical construction of the stanza. He seems to translate **gaṅ źig . . . lta bur** as 'someone as such', cf. his rendering ' "Someone such as" yourself' of the passage **khyed lta bu gaṅ źig** in the *Vṛtti* which simply means 'someone like you'. The **lta bu** before **gaṅ źig** has, of course, nothing to do with the **lta bur ni** at the end of this line. **gaṅ zig** is an indefinite pronoun which is taken up by **de'aṅ** 'even him' in line d. The *Vṛtti* correctly informs us that the relative construction refers to the addressee, the world-protector, the Buddha. **lta bur (ni)** at the end of the second line goes back to Sanskrit **iva**, and the *Vṛtti* enlightens us about the two possible interpretations of this word. First, it can here have its ordinary meaning 'like', and second, it can be understood in the sense of **eva**, expressing a restriction or limitation **(avadhāraṇa**, Tib. **ṅes par gzuṅ ba)**: *'Someone' like you who has become 'like' a friend who tries to help me and wards off what is harmful*; *or else iva (Tib.* ***lta bur****), not functioning as a particle of comparison, may also be used to denote a restriction 'only (****ñid****, Skt. eva) trying to help me', (meaning) 'having reached the state in which his only concern is to help me.'* . . .**khyed lta bu** ***gaṅ zig bdag la phan*** **par** ***brtson*** **źiṅ gnod pa las bzlog pa'i mdza' bśes** ***lta bur*** **gyur pa 'am/** ***lta bu*** **źes bya ba dper mi draṅ bar gaṅ źig bdag la phan par brtson pa ñid ces ṅes par gzuṅ bar draṅ du yaṅ ruṅ ste bdag la phan par brtson pa ñid du gyur pa'o//**

The mechanical rendering of **iva** by **lta bur** and of **eva** by **ñid** greatly obscures the meaning of this passage for all those readers who know only Tibetan. There is still another possibility for the translation of **iva**; it also means *in a certain manner, in some measure, somehow*'; cf. *I feel somehow cold* in English.

gaṅ gis źe na which introduces the quotation and explanation of lines cd in the *Vṛtti* is not *How*? as Tatz translates but simply *Who*? because it refers to **de'aṅ** in line d.

Bearing in mind what has just been stated I propose the following slightly changed translation of the stanza which in my opinion expresses more clearly what Candragomin said:

> *Because (I) have not (properly) analyzed*
> *(my) own unbearable suffering,*
> *I can stand not even him, O World-protector,*
> *who, somehow (or: only) trying to do me a favor,*
> *helps me much with forbearance and generosity.*

The second part of that sentence in the *Vṛtti* which explains the lines 20cd is, in my opinion, not correctly translated by Tatz. The Tibetan text runs: **de dag gis** [**gi** Tatz] **mchog tu phan 'dogs śiṇ dgos pa sgrub par byed pa'i ṅaṅ tshul can yin pa las de dag rjes su ston par mdzad pa na/ bdag gis bzod ciṅ bsten par mi nus so źes bya ba'i don to//**. Tatz translates: *The sense is that there are, among the best of them,* [*some*] *with the disposition to help and fulfill one's needs. But when they exhibit those two* [*traits*], *he cannot* *bear it, he cannot rely upon it.* The use of the honorific **mdzad pa** clearly indicates that it is not 'some' who 'exhibit' but the Buddha who is addressed in this stanza. Moreover, the use of the particle **dag** strongly suggests that **de** refers to the two perfections *forbearance* and *generosity* which were explained immediately before. Hence I propose to translate the passage in the following way: *When, because (you, i.e. the Buddha) have the nature of someone who by these two (perfections) renders the greatest help and procures what is necessary, (you) exhibit these two (perfections), then (I) am not able to bear (it) and adhere to (them)—this is the meaning.*

22. *Even having gone to request it, it is hard to find;*
At a time for patience, the best, the great medicine,
If I am not patient with a patient disposition,
What other occasion for patience will I have?

/soṅ ste gsol ba btab kyaṅ rñed dka' ziṅ/
/bzod pa'i dus su sman chen mchog gyur pa/
/bzod pa'i ṅaṅ tshul gal te mi bzod na/
/bzod pa'i rgyu gzan bdag la ci żig mchis/

The literalness and sticking to the order of lines in the Tibetan text obscures the understanding of the meaning of this stanza. In my opinion we should render the verse in the following way:

If I do not 'tolerate' (i.e. adhere to) a patient disposition
difficult to obtain even when one has gone to request (it)
and the most excellent (and) powerful medicine
at a time for patience (i.e. when patience is needed),
what other occasion for patience will I have?

The first line could also be translated in a different way: *Which even by prayers is difficult to find after it has gone.* This is, however, not supported by the commentary.

23d. *Aversion is born* **(bdag sdaṅ ñid skye'i). bdag** (paraphrased in the *Vṛtti* as **bdag gi sems la ni)** and **ñid** are unnecessarily omitted in the translation which should hence read: *only aversion is born in me.*

25c. *I count patience a blessed quality in another,*
But for this I am not patient—here's the wonder!

/bzod pa yon tan phun [sum] tshogs gźan mchis kyaṅ/
/gaṅ phyir mi bzod de 'dir ṅo mtshar che/

The translation of **gźan** as *in another* is slightly misleading. It is, however, correct if we take it as a free rendering of the *Vṛtti's* alternative interpretation *the blessed quality of another's patience.* This clearly indicates that the Sanskrit equivalent of **gźan** was the first part of a compound which could be understood both as a Tatpuruṣa and a Karmadhāraya compound. **gaṅ phyir** in line d is certainly not 'for this' but the translation of the consecutive conjunction **yad** *that.* Hence the translation of the two lines should rather read:

> *Although patience is another blessed quality*
> (*or*: *a blessed quality of others*),
> *That I don't tolerate* (*it*)—*herein lies a great wonder*!

27c. *Smoke* (**rab rib**) is an unnecessary deviation from the literal meaning of the Tibetan word which is *mist, dimness, glimmer; darkness, dimness, faintness.* Its standard Sanskrit equivalent is **timira** *darkness. Smoke* would be **du ba** in Tibetan. As for **bdo ba** I am not sure whether the translation 'spread' (although given in the dictionaries) is correct in the context of this line. First, the wording **bdo gyur pas** points rather to an adjective than to a noun. Second, I would like to refer to another famous poem by Candragomin, the **Śiṣyalekha,** where the word **ulbaṇa** can be found thrice, in 20c, 27b and 37b. In 20c, its Tibetan equivalent is **bod de,** and in 27b the Tibetan version of the **Śiṣyalekha-ṭippaṇa** explains it as ***bdo ba ste.** Skt. **ulbaṇa** means *thick, clotted, copious, abundant; much, excessive, intense; strong, powerful, great.* Third, it seems to me that the *Vṛtti* explains **bdo ba** in exactly this way:/ **de bdo ba ni śugs drag par 'byuṅ bas sems gsal ba zil gyis gnon par nus pa'o**/ *It* (*the darkness*) *is bdo ba means it has the ability to overshadow a clear mind* (*or*: *mental clarity*) *because it arises with fierce power.* Hence I propose to translate line a **gñid daṅ rmugs pa'i rab rib bdo gyur pas** by *because the darkness of drowsiness and languor have become powerful.*"

27d. I would like to suggest a minor change in the translation of the *Vṛtti* which yields a slightly better meaning. Instead of *thoughts that desire by any means to lie in a comfortable bed* (**mal stan bde mo [ma Tatz] dag la ñal bar 'dod pa'i sems**) I propose *the desire to rest on a comfortable bed*; cf. *Bodhicaryāvatāra* 1.28a where **'dod sems** renders Skt. **āśā.** Why did the translators use **bde mo** (or **ma**) instead of **bde ba?**

29d. *I circle through the lower range of Māra.* (**dman pa bdud kyi spyod yul dag na 'khyam).** Syntax of Tibetan as well as the explanation of the *Vṛtti* make it clear beyond doubt that **dman pa** refers to the subject of the sentence, not to **bdud kyi spyod yul dag na,** in which case the genitive **dman pa'i** would be required. Hence we have to translate *(I), being mean, wander through the sphere of Māra.*

30. *Whatever, however I envisage for the calm state,*
Focusing, refocusing the mind there upon it,
From this the noose of defilement
Drags me helpless toward objects with the rope of attachment.

/ji lta ji ltar źi gnas la dmigs śiṅ/
/de daṅ der yid yaṅ yaṅ gtad pa na/
/de daṅ de las ñon moṅs źags pa ni/
/yul la chags pa'i thag pas dbaṅ med draṅs/

From Tatz's translation of the stanza and the *Vṛtti* it seems as if he has split up **ji lta ji ltar** into two different words: the object *whatever* (**ji lta**) and the adverb *however, in whatever manner* (**ji ltar**). This is, of course, impossible. As in **Bodhicaryāvatāra** 8.174, **ji lta ji ltar** may go back to Sanskrit **yathā yathā** *as much as* (in that case usually followed by **tathā tathā**) or else to **yathā kathaṃ cit** *anyhow, somehow or other.* In the latter case iteration is used to express indefiniteness. This is also the function of the iteration of **daṅ de** in lines b and c which is not expressed in Tatz's translation. For the sake of preciseness I prefer the following translation:

If (I), somehow envisaging the state of calmness,
Repeatedly focus my mind on this and that (object),
(Then) the noose of defilement drags me helplessly away
From this and that (object) with the rope of attachment to the sense-objects.

31d. *What shall I do for my agitated mind?* (**bdag gi sems dkrugs pa ni ji ltar bgyi).** This is an unnecessary deviation from the literal rendering *what shall my agitated mind do?*" which is fully corroborated by the explanation of the *Vṛtti.*

32d. Cf. the note on 31d.

33d. Cf. the note on 31d.

34d. I find the expression *in advance* **(mdun na)** very irritating in the context of the line. As **mdun na** renders Sanskrit **puraḥ** *before, in front* (hardly *in advance*) I suspect that the translators might have used a manuscript in which **puraḥ** is nothing but a corruption of **punaḥ (na** and **ra** resembling each other very much in many of the older scripts of India and Nepal) *again*. There is at least one half of a proof of this hypothesis; when explaining the simile contained in this line the Tibetan *Vṛtti* writes **slar skye bar daṅ 'dra bar.** Here **slar** obviously reflects Sanskrit **punaḥ.** However, in the second half of the explanation we find **mdun na gnas pa'i tshul du mṅon du skye bar 'gyur ro,** where **mdun na gnas pa'i** is a paraphrase of **mdun na.** Hence the issue is as yet undecided.

35c. *Do they not eliminate even the flow of thought?* **(sems kyi rgyun kyaṅ spoṅ bar byed mod kyi).** This can hardly be correct as **kyi** is not an interrogative particle but an adversative particle. Moreover, the emphasis expressed by **mod** should not be neglect-ed. I propose to translate "One may *actually eliminate even the flow of thought, but...*"

36. Although it is not directly wrong, Tatz's translation of the stanza obscures the grammatical and logical relations between its parts. A very literal translation would run: *The flow of thought of the 'guardians'* (***tāyin,*** *Arhats*), which *is regardless of the whole world* because *they are free only from attachment, has entered the nirvāṇa in which the remaining aggregates are consumed, like a lamp whose cause* (*for burning, that is oil*; cf. the *Vṛtti*) *is exhaust-ed.* The stanza seems to make use of (or at least alludes to) a well-known pun in Indian literature, the two meanings of Skt. **sneha** 'love, attachment' and 'oil'. It is perhaps no coincidence that we can find a similar idea in a stanza in Candragomin's **Lokānan-danāṭaka,** act II, verse 17:

All human beings are heir and subject
to constant flux and change.
They come into being moment after moment
like lamps of oil
and soon perish once again
due to a lack of the oil of love.
Only those escape suffering
for whom rebirth is no more.

36b. In his translation of the *Vṛtti,* Tatz has, as already earlier in a similar case, failed to understand the nature of the phrase **'gro ba yaṅ yin la kun kyaṅ yin pas 'gro ba kun te** which he translates in the following way: *Whatever the world may be, and however many be all those in all of it, so "all the world"*. In fact this is nothing but the common Tibetan rendering of the usual Indian explanation of a Karmadhāraya compound which is characterized by the grammatical congruence of its two constituents: *it is 'all' and it is 'the world', hence the (compound) 'all-world'* (**sarvaś ca lokaś ceti sarvalokaḥ**). In the Tibetan translation the order of the two constituents of the compound had to be inverted because the attribute always follows the referent; only **'gro ba kun** is permitted, not ***kun 'gro ba; kun gyi 'gro ba** would be a different syntagma!

37ab. *Whatever dispels the distress of all the world—*
The thought of awakening: ambrosia, elixir—
/gaṅ yaṅ 'gro kun ñam thag sel byed pa/
/byaṅ chub sems ni bdud rtsi bcud kyis len/

From his translation of the *Vṛtti* we can see that Tatz has correctly understood both the meaning and construction of these two lines. For an ordinary reader, however, the following translation should be more intelligible than Tatz's anacoluthon:

That which dispels the distress of all the world,
The thought of awakening, (is like) ambrosia (or) elixir;

37d. The translation of the commentary contains a serious blunder. *The term 'only' (eva) indicates independence of other modes* renders **kho na źes bya ba'i sgras ni tshul gźan las raṅ dgar ba ste.** Obviously Tatz's translation 'independence' for **raṅ dgar ba** goes back to the entry **raṅ dga' ba** *free, independent* in the dictionary of Sarat Chandra Das. As **ba** is hardly possible after the terminative particle **-r** I think that **(raṅ) dgar ba** here describes the separative function of Skt. **eva. dgar ba** is quite well known as a grammatical term from Tibetan works on grammar. The underlying Sanskrit term is **avaccheda.**

39cd. The translation of the commentary is again misleading. Tatz has: *The immeasurable things that may be thus cherished and prized...Or, a particular antidote path congenial with the perfections...While discursively preoccupied with whatever that path may be, "it becomes at first only [a source of] frustration and anxiety*". *In short, the sense is that: "Whatever antidote I may rely upon to defeat the host of defilements is, by reason of its impotence, overwhelmed by negative alternatives.*" The Tibetan text runs: **'di ltar *gces* śiṅ sñiṅ por bya ba'i dṅos po tshad med *pa* 'am/ pha rol tu phyin pa rnams daṅ rjes su mthun pa'i gñen po'i lam *gaṅ daṅ gaṅ rtog* ciṅ dpyod par gnas *pa* na lam *de daṅ de ñid daṅ po* kho na*r rnam par ñams* śiṅ 'jig[s] par 'gyur ro zes pa ste/ don du na ñon moṅs pa'i tshogs gźom pa'i phyir gñen po gaṅ la brten kyaṅ de ñam chuṅ bas mi mthun pa'i phyogs kyis zil gyis gnon par 'gyur ro źes bya ba'i don to/**

This is not, as Tatz's translation suggests, a series of unconnected anacolutha but one coherent sentence which explains, by way of quotation and expansion, the lines 39cd

> **/bdag ni gces pa gañ daṅ gaṅ rtog pa/**
> **/de daṅ de ñid daṅ por rnam par ñams/**
> *Whatever important (thing) I examine,*
> *That very (thing) will be completely damaged*
> *(right) in the beginning.*

Which the exception of **bdag ni**, all the words of 39cd appear in the *Vṛtti*, here marked in italics. I propose to translate the commentary in the following way which maintains the original structure of its analysis:

> *"When, in such a manner, (I) am engaged in* ***examining****, that is investigating,* ***whatever is important****, i.e. a matter which is to be regarded as (absolutely) essential, namely the way which is an antidote (to those defilements and which consists) of either the (four) immeasurable (things) or what is congenial with the perfections, then* ***exactly that*** *way* ***will be completely damaged*** *right* ***in the beginning****, that is (it) will be destroyed;" the actual (true) meaning (of these two lines, explained in this manner), is: Even if (I), in order to defeat the host of defilements, rely on a certain (means), it will, because of (my) weakness, be overcome by elements adverse (to it).*

40ab. In his translation of the *Vṛtti*, Tatz does not seem to have recognized the etymological explanation of Skt. **bhagavant.** The Tibetan text and Tatz's translation: **bcom ldan 'das ni bdud bźi bcom pa 'am /dbaṅ phyug la sogs pa'i yon tan drug daṅ ldan**

pa ste saṅs rgyas so/ *'The Lord' is the conqueror of the four Māras,* [*'the Lord' because he*] *possesses the qualities of the Ruler and other* [*gods*]. *The Buddha is at issue.* In Nils Simonsson's book *Indo-tibetische Studien*, Uppsala 1957, which until today has lost nothing of its value, we can see that the passage quoted above is more or less an abbreviation of the explanation of **bhagavant** as contained in the ***Madhyavyutpatti**, the **Sgra sbyor bam po gñis pa**. Its first part runs as follows (Simonsson, pp. 266):

> **bha ga bā na źes bya ba gcig tu na / bha ga na mā ra ca tuṣṭa patva dva bha ga bān / zes bya ste bdud bźi bcom pas na bcom pa la bya / yaṅ rnam pa gcig tu na bha ga ni legs pa rnam drug gi miṅ ste/ gzugs daṅ / grags pa daṅ/ dbaṅ phyug daṅ /dpṅ daṅ/ śes rab daṅ /brtson pa ste 'di drug gi spyi la bya/**
>
> ***bhagavān**, on one hand,* [*can be analysed as*]: ***bhagnamāra-catuṣṭayatvād bhagavān** 'because he has conquered the four Māras he is called "the Conqueror";' or, in another manner, the word **bhaga*** [*contained in **bhagavān***], *is a word for the sixfold good, it is a general term for the* [*following*] *six* [*things*]: ***rūpa** 'beauty', **yaśas** 'fame', **aiśvarya** 'sovereignty', **śrī** 'glory', **prajñā** 'wisdom', and **vīrya** 'striving'.*

Simonsson gives all the important references to canonical and lexicographical works which contain this and similar explanations of the term **bhagavant.**

From this quotation we can easily see that **dbaṅ phyug** here renders not Skt. **īśvara** 'ruler' but **aiśvarya** 'sovereignty' and that the short passage in the *Vṛtti* actually means:

[*The term*] ***bhagavant*** [*etymologically means*]: *the one who has conquered ('broken') the four Māras, or, the one who is endowed with the six virtues, sovereignty etc.*; [*it refers to*] *the Buddha.*

41. I prefer a slightly altered translation because the subject of the stanza is not 'I' (not contained in the verse or in the *Vṛtti*) but 'a leper' (**mdze can**):

> *Of what use is it for a leper,*
> *having relied for a long time*
> *on what is the basis for his disease,*
> *his mind constantly infatuated with it*
> *and his hands* [*already*] *cut off,*
> *to rely on medicine* [*only*] *for a certain period of time?*

The first sentence of the *Vṛtti* is not correctly translated by Tatz: "*As medicine at the end is not a suitable treatment for the disease of leprosy, what can I do?*" *should be added.* **mdze'i nad gsor mi ruṅ bas zin pa la sman gyis ci bgyir mchis źes bya bar sbyar ro/**. *At the end* seems to be a translation of **zin pa la**. The actual meaning of the sentence is however: [*The rest of the sentence*] *is to be connected with "As the disease of leprosy is incurable, what is the use of medicine for him who is 'seized' (infected) [by it]?*"

In the following sentence the expression **dkon mchog gi rten bśig [gśig CN] pa la sogs pa** is left untranslated.

42a. The *Vṛtti* contains a resolution and etymological explanation of the compound ***anādikālaḥ** (Tib. **thog ma med dus can**) neither of which has been recognized by Tatz. What he translates as *Time is that which has no beginning, so "beginningless ages of time". "Ages of time" refers to its delimitation by sun, moon, planets, stars and so forth...* **(thog ma med pa yaṅ yin la dus kyaṅ yin pas *thog ma med dus can* /*dus can* ni ñi ma daṅ zla ba daṅ gza' daṅ skar ma la sogs pas yoṅs su bcad pa la bya ba la/**. The correct translation runs: *Because it is both 'beginningless' and 'time' it is '**endowed with (the attribute) beginningless time**'; it is called **endowed with (the attribute) time (kāla)** because it is 'limited' **(parikalita)** by sun, moon, planets, stars and so forth...*

42b. Instead of *fostered* read *stained* or *infected* or *defiled* **(bsgos pa)**. What Tatz translates is the explanation of the *Vṛtti* **(de lta bu'i khu bas brlan pas bskyed ciṅ 'phel bar bya ba yin la)**, however it is not at all certain that **bskyed ciṅ 'phel bar bya ba** paraphrases **bsgos pa**.

43. *My mind has all the faults by its very nature;*
Great wonder should awakening become the philosopher's stone!
Even as I apply myself to just that quality,
I continue to be the very substance of fault.

/bdag yid ñes pa kun gyi raṅ bźin ñid/
/byaṅ chub gser bsgyur rtsir gyur ṅo mtshar che/
/yon tan de daṅ de ñid la sbyar nas/
/ñes pa'i dṅos po ñid du gyur te gnas/

Perhaps the stanza should better be translated in the following way which follows the explanation of the *Vṛtti*:

(Even) after having brought into contact
My mind, which has the nature of all the faults,
With this or that quality of enlightenment,
The most wonderful gold-transforming potion,
It (i.e. my mind) continues to remain in the state of faultiness.

The close relationship of this stanza with **Bodhicaryāvatāra** 1.10 is very important as it may provide another upper limit for the determination of the date of the author of the **Deśanāstava.**

44, 45. *Relevancy* and *relevant* are not so fortunate translations of **rigs pa** *propriety, correctness, suitability.*

45c. *Being in my mind* is a very misleading translation of **bdag sems na** *if I reflect, consider (like this).* The *Vṛtti* makes it absolutely clear, that **sems** is a verb, not a noun.

48. *Your body blazing with marks of beauty,*
As I see the presence before me,
So I come to hear the nectar drunk by ear;
The seeds of defilement are entirely destroyed.

/khyed sku mdzes pa'i mtshan gyis 'bar gyur pa/
/de yaṅ mdun na bźugs pa mthoṅ ba daṅ/
/rna bas btuṅ ba'i bdud rtsi'aṅ thos gyur pa'i/
/ñon moṅs sa bon ma lus rnam par 'jig/

'aṅ in line c is certainly not "so" but "also". Apart from this I would like to propose a slightly altered construction which corresponds more faithfully with that of the original.

Your body blazing with the marks of beauty,
Who has seen it directly before his eyes
And who has also heard the nectar to be drunk by the ears,
For him the seeds of defilement are entirely destroyed.

The reading **thos gyur pa'i** is fully confirmed by the explanation of the *Vṛtti* which reads: **de lta bu'i sku mthoṅ ba daṅ /gsuṅ thos pa'i skyes bu'i ñon moṅs pa**. . .It entails the construction as given above. Tatz reads **gyur pa** both in the main text (no variant reading given) and in the text of the *Vṛtti* where he mentions that all the editions actually read **gyur pa'i.**[40]

References

1. *Difficult Beginnings*, p. 20.

2. So far I have written on Candragomin in the following books and papers: "Ist ein Vers der Nāndī in Harṣadevas Drama Nāgānanda verlorengegangen?", *Wiener Zeitschrift für die Kunde Süd- und Ostasiens*, Band XIV (1970), pp. 39-45. "Some Remarks Concerning an Edition of the Tibetan Translation of the Drama *Lokānanda* by Candragomin," *Indo-Iranian Journal*, Vol. XIII (1971), pp. 104-112. "Der Autor Candragomin und sein Werk," *Zeitschrift der Deutschen Morgenländischen Gesellschaft*, Supplement II, XVIII. Deutscher Orientalistentag, 1974, pp. 331-355. *Candragomins Lokānandanāṭaka.* Nach dem tibetischen Tanjur herausgegeben und übersetzt. Ein Beitrag zur klassischen indischen Schauspieldichtung, Wiesbaden 1974 (*Asiatische Forschuegen.* 39.) "Strophen des Candragomin in der indischen Spruchliteratur," *Indo-Iranian Journal*, Vol. XIX (1977), pp. 21-30. "The Play *Lokānandanāṭaka* by Candragomin," *Kailash*, Vol. VII (1979), pp. 51-67. "Eine Anleihe Gopadattas bei Candragomin," *Wiener Zeitschrift für die Kunde Südaisiens*, Band XXVIII (1984), pp. 67-72. *Joy for the World.* A Buddhist Play by Candragomin. Berkeley, 1987. "Über den indirekten Beweis bei literaturhistorischen Fragestellungen" (forthcoming) [A refutation of Oberlies's view that the grammarian Candragomin and the playwright Candragomin might be two different persons; cf. fn. 21.].

2a. Only after the completion of this paper I found the time for a detailed study of the three hymns mentioned under (b), (c) and (d). I discovered that the **Manoharapāpavidāruṇanāmalokanāthastotra* attributed to Candragomin is nothing else but the first of three independent Tibetan translations of Carpaṭi's *Avalokiteśvarastotra* (alias *Lokanāthastotra*) which is still available in its original Sanskrit. It was edited by the Russian scholar I. Minaev in his paper "Buddijskija molitvij. I.", *Zapiski vostočnago otdelenija imperatorskago archeoločeskago obščestva* 2 (1887), pp. 125-136. The form and style of the work (26 Mātrāsamaka stanzas making use of rhyme throughout) as well as its ascription to Carpaṭi(pāda) in the Sanskrit manuscripts and in the two other Tibetan translations positively prove that it can no longer be counted among the works of Candragomin.

3. Also in the opening stanza: Even nowadays the forests of lotuses, being the faces of Māra's daughters, shrink, as if hit by the rays of the moon (*candrakiraṇair iva*), when the beautiful goddesses and Kinnaras, the musicians of the heaven, sing of the most difficult deeds which He did in the exploits of His former lives.

4. Cf. Hahn (1974a), p. 340 n. 42.

5. "Bright like a beautiful moon" (*zla mdzes ltar dkar*).

6. Tatz 1976, p. 283.

7. On this work cf. Ernst Steinkellner's paper, "Miszellen zur erkenntnistheoretisch-logischen Schule des Buddhismus. IV. Candragomin, der Autor des *Nyāyasiddhyāloka*", *Wiener Zeitschrift für die Kunde Südasiens* XXVIII (1984), pp. 177-8.

8. *Taishō Tripiṭaka*, vol. LIV, 229c7-8.

9. *viṣasya viṣayāṇāṃ ca dūram atyantam antaram /*
upabhuktaṃ viṣaṃ hanti viṣayāḥ smaraṇād api //
Subhāṣitāvalī 3368 and a spurious verse between stanzas 75 and 76 of the *Śiṣyalekha.*

10. On this manuscript cf. Cecil Bendall, *Catalogue of the Buddhist Sanskrit Manuscripts in the University Library, Cambridge*, Cambridge 1883, pp. 31-2.

11. Quotations from my as yet unpublished edition and translation of the *Śiṣyalekha.*

12. As stanzas 19 and 20 of Act II.

13. Cf. Hahn 1971, p. 106.

14. Cf. my reconstruction of the line as given in Hahn 1979, p. 51:
prabaddhaṃ Candradāsena kavināpūrvanāṭakam /
darśayāmi sabhām adya tal lokānandanāṭakam //
There are, however, many other possibilities to reconstruct the Sanskrit wording of / *sñan ṅag tsandra dā sa yis* [*śa yā* CDNP!] / / *zlos gar 'jig rten kun tu dga'* / / *sṅon med zlos gar rab sbyar bas* / / *de riṅ tshogs la bdag gis ston* / "As the poet Candradāsa has composed a brand-new play—the play 'Joy for the World' (or: a play which is a joy for the world)—I will now present it to the audience."

14a. *Op cit.*, p. 286.

15. Ratna Handurukande, *Maṇicūḍāvadāna. Being a translation and edition. And Lokānanda. A translation and synopsis*, London 1967. (*Sacred Books of Buddhists*, Vol. XXIV). Cf. fn. 2 for my review of the section containing the transliteration of the *Lokānanda.*

16. Cf. note 2.

17. The date of Āryaśūra is a difficult, not yet satisfactorily solved question. Usually 434 A.D. was an accepted *terminus ante quem*, based on the assumption that the **Karmaphalanirdeśasūtra* (*Taishō* 723), attributed to him and translated into Chinese by Saṅghavarman 434 A.D., was composed by the author of the *Jātakamālā*. This is, however, by no means certain. The second argument used for dating Āryaśūra is the verses from his Jātakamālā discovered at the bottom of several paintings in the Ajaṇṭā caves. From the paleographical point of view these inscriptions are not later than the sixth century A.D. Again this argument is not an absolute proof as the date entirely depends on the expertise of the paleographists. A third argument is provided by my recent dating of Haribhaṭṭa (before 445 A.D.); cf. my paper 'Das Datum des Haribhaṭṭa', *Studien zum Jainismus und Buddhismus. Gedenkschrift für Ludwig Alsdorf*, Wiesbaden 1981 (*Alt- und Neu-Indische Studien*. 23). If this is correct then we would have the first safe upper limit for the time of Āryaśūra because Haribhaṭṭa mentions Āryaśūra as his model in the introduction to his own *Jātakamālā*. A full discussion of the problem of the date of Āryaśūra with all the bibliographical references can be found in the introduction of Carol Meadows' book *Ārya-Śūra's Compendium of the Perfections*, Bonn 1986 (*Indica et Tibetica*. 8).

18. Cf. the well-known monograph by Heinrich Lüders, *Bruchstücke der Kalpanāmaṇḍitikā des Kumāralāta*, Berlin 1926; recently reprinted in *Monographien zur Indischen Archäologie, Kunst und Philologie*. Band 1, Wiesbaden 1979, pp. 117-375.

19. This name is actually mentioned in the manuscript used by Bruno Liebich for his edition. The sentence is however written by a different hand. Cf. also the reference in the following note.

20. Cf. Richard Birwé, "Ist Candragomin der Verfasser der Candravṛtti?", *Mélanges d'indianisme à la mémoire de Louis Renou*, Paris 1968, pp. 127-48.

21. For the last printed discussion cf. T. Oberlies, *Studie zum Cāndravyākaraṇa*. Eine kritische Bearbeitung von Candra IV.4.52 und V.2, Stuttgart 1989 (Alt-und Neu-Indische Studien. 38.), paragraph 1.2.6.

22. Personal communication in a letter dated January 5, 1991.

23. Cf. especially Hahn 1971, 1974a and 1974b.

24. All these possibilities have been proposed; cf. the book by T. Oberlies on Candragomin's grammar mentioned in fn. 21.

25. "Über den indirekten Beweis bei literaturhistorischen Fragestellungen."

26. Cf. Hahn 1974a, pp. 334-37, and Hahn 1974b, pp. 3-9.

27. Likewise the cruder approach to the same issue by Oberlies, cf. fn. 21.

28. In my previous publications, especially in the notes to my German translation of the *Lokānanda*, I have pointed to several of the related passages.

29. This is not to be taken literally as in both plays we find enough scope for originality, despite the general agreement with regard to the underlying story and the structure of the plays.

30. Cf. stanza 4 as quoted in fn. 14.

31. I did not find any striking parallels between the *Lokānanda* and Kālidāsa's other two plays, the *Mālavikāgnimitra* and the *Vikramorvaśīya*.

32. According to my counting the *Śiṣyalekha* consists of 116 stanzas. I exclude the Anuṣṭubh stanza 75a, cf. above; hoewever, I include two stanzas (64 and 71) which are available only in their Tibetan translation.

33. There is one basic metṛe, Vasantatilakā, which is interspersed with eight other metres: Viyoginī (23-33), Pṛthvī (54-8), Śikhariṇī (71-2), Praharṣiṇī (76, 84-5), Mandākrāntā (86-9), Puṣpitāgrā (105-6), Mālinī (107-8), and Hariṇī (109-16).

34. *zla ba* in Tibetan, *candra* in Sanskrit.

35. Translation quoted from Mark Tatz, *Difficult Beginnings*, pp. 39-40.

36. A recent thorough and copiously annotated critical edition of the Tibetan translation of a Sanskrit commentary is the book by Yukihiro Okada, *Die Ratnāvalīṭīkā des Ajitamitra*, herausgegeben und erläutert, Bonn 1990 (=*Nāgārjuna's Ratnāvalī, Vol.* 2) (*Indica et Tibetica*, 19).

37. It seems highly desirable that these editions should be published as they are carefully done and well organized.

38. The *Deśanāstava* was translated by Buddhākaravarman and Rin chen bzaṅ po, the *Vṛtti* by its author Buddha(śrī)śānti and Rin chen bzaṅ po.

39. It would be rewarding to compare the *Deśanāstava* with the other extant texts of this genre and also to study its reception in indigenous Tibetan literature. Cf the two volumes of translations from Tsongkhapa's *Lam rim chen mo* by Alex Wayman, *Calming the Mind and Discerning the Real*, New York 1978, and *Ethics of Tibet*, New York 1991, in which several quotations from the *Deśanāstava* can be found.

40. I have to thank my friend and colleague Peof. Dr. Leslie Kawamura, University of Calgary, for reading this paper and making nemerous valuable suggestions.

4 A STUDY OF ASPECTS OF *RĀGA*

N. H. SAMTANI

The first *pāda* of the second verse of the *Uragasutta* in the *Suttanipāta*,[1] one of the earliest collections of Buddhist poems in the Theravāda Canon, significantly focuses attention on the eradication of *rāga* (lust or passion)[2] for the final emancipation.

The Pali verse is as follows:

yo rāgam udacchidā asesaṃ,
bhisapupphaṃ va saroruhaṃ vigayha/
so bhikkhu jahāti orapāraṃ,
urago jiṇṇam ivattacaṃ purāṇaṃ//

(Tr. One who has entirely uprooted lust (*rāga*) as one cuts off a lotus flower grown in a lake after diving (into the water), that monk leaves this and the further shore (*orapāraṃ*) as a snake (leaves) its old worn out skin.)

Suttanipāta, Uragavagga, v. 2

It is significant to note that in the initial four verses in the *Uragasutta*, the place of *rāga* (lust) as one of the defilements or hindrances in the deliverance from the cycle of death and birth is next only to *kodha* (anger, Skt. *krodha*) followed by *taṇhā* (craving, Skt. *tṛṣṇā*) and *māna* (conceit). The order of these defilements (*kleśas*) is worth noting although it cannot be said that the Buddha had fixed that order when speaking about defilements and hindrances. In fact there is no definite order as it is in the three *akuśalamūlas* (roots of demerit), where *lobha* (greed), which includes *rāga*, is placed first followed by *dveṣa* (Pali *dosa*, hatred) which includes *krodha*, the third being *moha* (infatuation). In fact *lobha* and *rāga* are interchangeably used[3] in the Buddhist texts. Verily, the Buddha preaches in different contexts with a view to the particular person or persons to be trained (*vineyāśayapekṣayā*).[4] It is difficult to say whether in the order of intensity *lobha* (or *rāga*) is a more serious defilement which is to be abandoned first.

But the stress on the eradication of *rāga* is more pronounced in the Buddhist texts.

This small paper concentrates on the concept of *rāga* and its various aspects as well as employment of the word in different contexts. And the inspiration for writing this article for the volume in honor of Professor Alex Wayman is the first *pāda* of the *Suttanipāta*, verse 2.

The *Dhammapada*, the most quoted work among the early Buddhist texts (*Suttanipāta* is probably the second in that order) uses the word *rāga* in the very first chapter (*Yamakavagga*) as follows:

> *yathā agāram ducchannaṃ, vuṭṭhi samativijjhati/*
> *evam abhāvitaṃ cittaṃ, rāgo samativijjhati//*
> *yathā agāram succhannaṃ, vuṭṭhi na samativijjhati/*
> *evaṃ subhāvitaṃ cittaṃ, rāgo na samativijjhati//*
>
> (Tr. Just as rain penetrates an ill-thatched house, so does lust penetrate an uncultivated mind. Just as rain does not penetrate a well-thatched house, so does lust not penetrate a well cultivated mind.)
>
> *Dhammapada*, vs. 13-14

Thus *rāga* is a great impediment in the development or cultivation of mind which is the path towards attainment of wisdom (*prajñā*) or final emancipation (*nirvāṇa*).

Now let us briefly review the definition of *rāga* in Buddhist texts. *Rāga* is explained in the *Dhammasaṅgaṇi* under the category of *lobha*:

> *tattha katamo lobho? yo rāgo sārāgo anunayo anurodho nandī nandirāgo cittassa sārāgo icchā mucchā ajjhosānaṃ gedho paligedho saṅgo paṅko ejā māyā ianikā sañjananī sibbanī jālinī saritā visattikā*[5]...
>
> (Tr. What is greed? That which is lust, intense lust, affection, compliance, taking delight in, taking passionate delight in, intense lust of mind, longing, infatuation, strong attachment, greediness, omnivorous greed, attachment, mire, seduction, trickery, that which gives birth (in the cycle of death and birth), that which gives rebirth, that which sews or joins (to rebirth), ensnarement, the river,[6] that which is poisonous (etc.)...[7]

Aṭṭhasālini, a commentary on the *Dhammasaṅgaṇi*, explains the various terms given above in the Pali quotation which defines *lobha*. *Rāga* is explained as *rañjanavasena rāgo* "that which finds pleasure or excitement is *rāga*." Literally, the root *rañj* means 'to colour', 'to dye'. Thus *rāga* colours, stains the mind and therefore it is a defilement. It is used in the sense of 'attachment', 'enamouring of'.[8]

According to the *Mahāniddesa*[9] an *arhat* is neither attached nor detached (*arahā neva rajjati no virajjati*) and he is without any kind of attachment (*viratta*) because his attachment or lust is eradicated (*khayā rāgassa*), he being free from attachment (*vīta-rāga*). In the *Vibhaṅga* of the *Abhidhamma Piṭaka*, *rāga* is explained as one of the synonyms of *taṇhā*.

> What is craving (*taṇhā*) conditioned by feeling (*vedanā*)? That which is lust, affection, compliance, taking delight in, taking passionate delight in, intense lust of mind. This is called craving conditioned by feeling.[10]

In the *Abhidharmakośa-Vyākhya*, the difference between *chanda* and *rāga* is explained. *Chanda* is a future desire (*anāgate'rthe prārthanā*) and *rāga* is attachment (*adhyavasānaṃ*)[11] to what one possesses.[12]

In the *Arthaviniścaya-Nibandhana* in the section of the four noble truths (*catvāry āryasatyāni*), while explaining the second truth viz. *samudayasatya* (the truth of arising of suffering), the commentator gives a good comment on *nandīrāga*. He explains *nandī* (delight) as a defiled happiness (*kliṣṭa-saumanasya*) and *rāga* as a characteristic of attachment (*saktilakṣaṇa*).[13] Also it is said that *nandī* and *rāga* are present alternatively (*paryāyeṇa*) when craving (*tṛṣṇā*) is endowed with *nandī* and *rāga* (*nandīrāga-sahagatā*).[14]

The *Abhidharmakośa-bhāṣya* mentions *rāga* of the four types: (1) Lust for colour (*varṇarāga*); (2) Lust for shape (*saṃsthānarāga*); (3) Lust for a tangible or contact (*sparśarāga*); (4) Lust for immediate vicinity or neighbourhood (*upacārarāga*)[15] and explains the removal of them by visualising opposite entities (*pratipakṣas*). In a general way, visualisation of skeleton (lit. chain of bones= *śaṅkalā*) removes the lust of lustful beings (*rāgin-s*).[16]

The *Aṅguttarainkāya*[17] speaks of ten dharmas leading to the taming of *rāga*, *dosa* (Skt. *dveṣa*) and *moha*, viz. all the constituents of the Eightfold Path plus the right knowledge (*sammāñāṇa*) and the right deliverance (*sammāvimutti*). The text says that these ten dharmas are not found elsewhere except in the discipline (*vinaya*) of the Sugata (=Buddha).[18]

Nirvāṇa is also explained as the eradication of *rāga, dosa* (*dveṣa*) and *moha.* In a reply to a recluse (*pabbajita*), Sāriputta answers that *nibbāna* is the eradication of lust, ill-will and infatuation (or delusion).

> *'nibbānaṃ', 'nibbānaṃ' ti, āvuso, Sāriputta, vuccati. katamaṃ nu kho, āvuso, nibbānaṃ ti?*
> *yo kho, āvuso, rāgakkhayo dosakkhayo mohakkhayo—idaṃ vuccati nibbānaṃ ti.*[19]

In the *Dhammapada* there is one significant *gātha* which says that by cutting off lust (*rāga*) and ill-will (*dosa*), one reaches *nibbāna* (*chetvā rāgaṃ ca dosaṃ ca tato nibbānam ehisi*).[20] The *gātha* compares one's personality like a boat in which *rāga* and *dosa* (*dveṣa*) are an extra burden and a boat can sail swiftly if the water of *rāga* and *dveṣa* is baled out. Thus when the boat is emptied of these vices (*rāga, dveṣa*) in the form of extra water it can safely reach the destination of *nibbāna.*[21]

Rāga is also like a fire (*Dhammapada* verses 202, 251). *Natthi rāgasamo aggi, natthi dosasamo kali* (There is no fire like lust; there is no evil like ill-will (hatred)). The *Arthaviniścaya-sūtra* mentions two kinds of persons who are by nature (1) of intense lust (*tīvra-rāga*) and (2) of little lust (*alparāga*) and how the path of meditation is difficult for a person of intense lust to enter into *samādhi* and easy for one who has little lust.[22] The person of intense lust is one who is dominated by lust (*adhimātra-rāgacarita*).[23] Among the persons dominated by lust (*tīvra-rāga*), the name of Ārya Sundarānanda is given in the *Arthaviniścaya-Nibandhana* in the explanation of an epithet of Buddha, viz. *anuttarapuruṣadamyasārathi* (the incomparable charioteer of persons to be tamed).[24]

Ragā (vl. *Rāgā*) is one of the daughters of Māra,[25] the great tempter. The other two daughters are *Taṇhā* and *Arati.* They are the personifications of the three of the ten forces in Māra's army as given in the *Padhānasutta.*[26]

The opposite of *rāga* is *virāga* or *vairāgya. Vairāgya* is mentioned in Sanskrit Buddhist texts in different aspects. There are many references in the *Abhidharmakośa-Bhāṣya*.[27] *Virāga* is one of the characters of *nirvāṇa*, other being *nirodha, upaśama, tṛṣṇā-kṣaya, pratiniḥsarga, vyantībhāva*, etc.[28] It is one of the best among the dharmas (*virāgo seṭṭho dhammānaṃ*).[29] The word *vītarāga* is frequently used for *arahats* and those who have eradicated *rāga*. In *Dhammapada* (v. 356) it is said that *rāga* (lust) spoils all beings. Therefore *dāna* (giving) to those free from lust (*vītarāga*) yields great benefit.[30]

There is another term associated with *rāga* which is often used in Buddhist texts viz. *kāmarāga*. This term embraces lust for objects of enjoyment (*kāmaguṇa*) and various other kinds of lust (*rāga*).

There is a *samādhibhāvanā* mentioned in the *Arthaviniścaya-sūtra* which is particularly practiced to remove the lust for objects of enjoyment (*kāmarāga-prahāṇāya*).[31] In this *samādhibhāvanā*, a monk reflects on the impurities of the body in which nails, teeth, bones, bladder, sweat, phlegm, pus, blood etc. are included.[32]

Thus we see that *rāga* (lust, passion, attachment), a most important term—being at the root of demerit (*akuśalamūla*)—has been discussed in the Buddhist texts from various aspects. Freedom from *rāga* along with the freedom from ill-will (*dosa* Skt. *dveṣa*) and delusion (*moha*) is the attainment of *nirvāṇa*. Hence the Buddha has rightly stressed the complete uprooting of lust in the second verse of the *Uraggasutta* in the *Suttanipāta* with which we commenced this article.

References

1. Cf. Bhikkhu J. Kashyap (ed.) *Khuddanikāya*, Vol. 1, *Suttanipāta*, (Nalanda, 1959) verse 2, p. 269.

2. *Rāga* has been variously rendered, viz. attachment, lust, passion, desire, craving, etc. However, I have come to the conclusion that 'lust' is the better rendering, although in different contexts it can be rendered as 'passion' and 'attachment' also. Cf. also Alex Wayman, *Yoga of the Guhyasmājatantra* (Delhi, 1980), *rāgadharma*='doctrine of lust', p. 114.

3. They are generally used synonymously. Cf. *rāga*, *Buddhist Dictionary* ed. Nyanatiloka, (Kandy, 1980), p. 182. See also, *PED*, p. 567.

4. *Arthaviniścayasūtra-Nibandhana* (*AVSN*) ed. N. H. Samtani (Patna, 1971), pp. 128, 273. Also cf. *vineyarucibheda, ibid.* p. 112. See also *Abhidharmakośa-bhāṣya*, ed. P. Pradhana, (Patna, 1967), I.20, p. 14.

5. Cf. *Dhammasaṅgaṇi*, ed. P. V. Bapat and R. D. Vadekar (Poona 1940)

§1059, pp. 240-41. There are many other words to explain *lobha*. See the text for further words.

6. 'River' is here used in the sense of a 'stream' lubricated with craving. Cf. *Dhammapada*, verse 341. Cf. also *Aṭṭhasālini*, ed. P. V. Bapat and R. D. Vadekar, (Poona, 1942), V. §48, p. 289.

7. Cf. C.A.F. Rhys Davids, *A Buddhist Manual of Psychological Ethics* (Tr. of *Dhammasaṅgaṇi*) §1059, p. 276. I have changed translation of some terms.

8. Cf. *rañjati*, *PED*, p. 562. For *rāga*=attachment, see R. C. Childers, *A Dictionary of Pali Language* (Kyoto, 1976), p. 397.

9. Cf. *Mahāniddesa*, ed. J. Kashyap, (Nalanda, 1960), p. 198.

10. Cf. *Vibhaṅga* (Nalanda, 1960), p. 182.

11. Cf. *Abhidharmakośa* with *Sphuṭārthā* Commentary, ed. D. Shastri (Varanasi, 1970), p. 323. Cf. also Pali *ajjhosāna*=attachment, PED, p. 12.

12. *Prāpte 'rthe 'dhyavasānaṃ.*, *Sphuṭārthā*, *Ibid.*

13. Cf. *AVSN*, p. 162.

14. *Ibid.*, p. 163.

15. Cf. *upacāra*, *PED*, p. 140. Could it be rendered as 'honour'? *Abhidharma-Kośabhāṣyam* (Eng. Trans. from Poussin's French Trans. by L. M. Pruden, Berkeley, 1989) renders 'craving for honours', p. 917. *PED* gives one of meanings, 'civility, polite behaviour', p. 140.

16. Cf. *Abhidharmakośa*, ed. P. Pradhan (Patna, 1967), VI.9, p. 337.

17. Cf. *Aṅguttaranikāya* (Nalanda, 1960), iv, p. 294.

18. *Nāññtrasugatavinayā*, *Ibid.*

19. *Saṃyuttanikāya* (Nalanda, 1959), IV, p. 223.

20. Cf. *siñca bhikkhu imaṃ nāvaṃ sittā te lahum essati |*
chetvā rāgaṃ ca dosaṃ ca tato nibbānam ehisi ||
Dhammapada, v. 369

21. Cf. *Dhammapada*, *Ibid.*

22. Cf. the Section of the four *pratipads*, *AVS*, p. 21.

23. Cf. *AVSN*, p. 200.

24. *Ibid.*, pp. 245-46.

25. Cf. *Māradhitu-Sutta*, *Saṃyuttanikāya* (Nalanda 1959), I, p. 123.

26. Cf. *Padhānasutta*, *Suttanipāta* (Nalanda, 1959), pp. 331-32. Cf. also 'Māra' in G. P. Malalasekera, *Dictionary of Pali Proper Names* (London, 1960), Vol. II, p. 616.

27. Cf. *Abhidharmakośa-bhāṣya*, ed. P. Pradhan (Patna, 1967) for possession of Buddha's qualities which were obtained through *vairāgya*, pp. 70, 421; cf. also *vairāgyamārga* in meditation, p. 448, etc.

28. Cf. *AVS*, p. 15. In the Pali canonical texts we have *cāga* (Skt. *tyāga*), *mutti* (*mukti*), *anālaya* replacing some words found in Skt. Buddhist texts. Cf. *Dighanikāya* (Nalanda, 1958) II, p. 231.

29. Cf. *Dhammapada*, verse 273.

30. *Ibid.*, verse 356.

31. Cf. *AVS*, p. 22. The Pali version of this *samādhibhāvanā* replaces *kāma-rāga-prahāṇāya* by *āsavānaṃ khayāya*. Cf. *Dighanikāya*, III, p. 175. The explanation is also different.

32. There are 36 items of impurities of body. Cf. *AVS*, pp. 23-24. See also *ibid.*, nt. 9, p. 23.

ABBREVIATIONS

AVS	=	*Arthaviniścayasūtra*, ed. N. H. Samtani (Patna, 1971).
AVSN	=	*Atthaviniścayasūtra-Nibandhana*, ed. N. H. Samtani (Patna, 1971). (Both the above texts edited in the same Volume)
PED	=	Pali Text Society's *Pali-English Dictionary*, ed. by T. W. Rhys Davids and William Stede (London, 1959).

5 PRINCIPLE OF LIFE ACCORDING TO BHAVYA[1]

SHINJO KAWASAKI
University of Tsukuba, Japan

How did the Indian Buddhists of the sixth century think about the principle of life in the humanities and other sentient beings?[2] On the basis of the Sanskrit fragments of the Ninth Chapter of the *Madhyamaka-hṛdaya-kārikā* and its commentary *Tarkajvālā* (extant only in the Tibetan translation, *rtog ge ḥbar ba*) of Bhavya (Bhāvaviveka or Bhāviveka[3]), the present writer would like to discuss some details of the Buddhist standpoints on the principle of life.

The *Abhidharma-kośa-bhāṣya*, in the Second Chapter which deals with the faculties (indriya-nirdeśa), briefly denies the sentience in plants, classifying them, together with earth and water as sādhāraṇa-karma-saṃbhūtatva (the arising fact of shared karma). It reads just as follows: "Why are the non-sentient beings, which are the products of Karman, not to be understood as a fruitful maturity (vipāka)? By reason of their being shared in common. Others, too, can enjoy them just the same. Lesults of a fruitful maturity, on the other hand, cannot be shared; none, other than oneself, can experience the fruit of the act done by oneself. Why, then, can the dominant fruition (adhipati-phala) be shared in experience in common? By reason of their being the product of the Karmic force shared in common. (kasmād asattvâkhyo 'rthaḥ karmajo na vipākaḥ/ sādhāraṇatvāt/ anyo 'pi hi tat tathaiva paribhoktuṃ samarthaḥ/ asādhāraṇas tu vipākaḥ/ na hy anyakṛtasya karmaṇo 'nyo vipākaṃ pratisaṃvedayate/ adhipati-phalaṃ kasmāt pratisaṃvedayate/ sādhāraṇa-karma-saṃbhūtatvāt/ Pradhan ed.: *Abhidharmakośabhāṣya* p. 95).

According to the Abhidharma view, there are two kinds of the Karmic results. One, shared, which can be experienced in common by others. They are the non-sentient beings (asattva) in the surrounding world (bhājana-loka). The other, peculiar and unique, which are living (sattva) and multiplying themselves in the course of their lives, cannot be shared in experience by others.

Plants, together with rocks and waters, are classified in the former group.

In the Ninth Chapter of his *Madhyamaka-hṛdaya-kārikā* and *Tarkajvālā*, following this traditional Buddhist standpoint proclaimed in the *Abhidharmakośa-bhāṣya*, Bhavya answers the Mīmāṃsaka's assertions in the following five verses:

acetaneṣu caitanyaṃ sthāvareṣu prakalpitam (/)
dṛṣṭyā durvihitaṃ trayyā yuktaṃ yat tyajyate trayī//
/sems med pa yi brtan pa laḥaṅ/
/sems ni yod par rtogs byed paḥi/
/ñes bstan gsum la mthoṅ bas na/
/gsum po ḥdi ni spaṅ baḥi rigs/

(*MHK* IX, 139)

sacittakā hi taravo na catur-yony-asaṃgrahāt/
madhya-cchede 'pi vâspandāj jāḍyatve sati loṣṭavat//
/ljon śiṅ sems daṅ bcas pa min/
/skye gnas bshir ni ma bsdus phyir/
/dkyil du bcad kyaṅ bzod paḥi phyir/
/phag dum bshin du bems po yin/

(*MHK* IX, 140)

sparśato yadi saṃkocād yathā maṇḍala-kārikā (/)
sacittake tathâbhīṣṭe sa[maṅgâñ]jala-kārike//
/gal te srog chags rkaṅ brgya ltar/
reg na ḥkhums par ḥgyur bas na/
/sa ma ga daṅ thal sbyar ni/
/sems daṅ bcas par ḥdod ce na/

(*MHK* IX, 141)

vahni-saṃspṛṣṭa-keśâdau syād dhetor vyabhicāritā(/)
cūrṇṇa-pārata-saṃsṛṣṭa-keśair vâpi viśeṣataḥ//
/me yis reg paḥi skra sogs daṅ/
/skra la ḥtshal phyes blugs pa yi/
/khyad par de dag ñid kyis kyaṅ/
/ḥdi ni ma ṅes pa ñid yin/

(*MHK* IX, 142)

cikitsyatvān na taravo yujyante hi sacittakāḥ(/)
vinaṣṭasyâpi madyâdeḥ pratyāpatteś ca saṃśayaḥ//

/gso ba yod pas śiṅ rnams ni/
/sems daṅ bcas par mi ḥgrub ste/
/chaṅ la sogs pa ñams pa dag/
/ldog pa yod par the tshom ḥgyur/

(*MHK* IX, 143)

samāna-prasavād vṛddher dohadāc ca sacittakāḥ(/)
ṛtu-janāt tathā svāpān nâpīṣṭās turagâdivat//
/mthun pa las skyes ḥphel ḥgyur daṅ/
/sdaṅ sems dus ldan skye baḥi phyir/
/de bshin gñid log smyo baḥi phyir/
/sems yod rta sogs bshin du ḥdod/

(*MHK* IX, 144)

In the above-mentioned six verses, Bhavya tries to analyze the reasons for denying sentience in plants, dividing them in ten categories just as follows:

(i) In Verse 139, there is introduced the view of those who hold the Three Vedas (trayī) as the authority and who acknowledge the intelligence (caitanya) in the insentient stable plants (acetaneṣu sthāvareṣu). From the *Tarkajvālā* we can learn that their form of reasoning is as follows: "The plants have their mind. Because they have the sensible faculties (indriya). Like a human being."

To prove this, there are mentioned the cases of a sun-flower (helianthus) and a passion-flower which follow the movement of the sun as the evidences of plant's faculty of seeing. The case of a Mātuluṅga tree which bear good fruit with dogs barking around its stem as the evidence of a plant's ability of hearing. The case of an olive tree which produces sweet fruit by milk poured close at its base as the evidence of a plant's ability of tasting. An Aśoka tree may bloom and have fruit by a touch of a lovely woman and a (flowerless) Bakula tree puts forth flowers and fruit by a young girl's breathing of liquor; these are the evidence of plants' mental faculty. (Bhavya seems to be well-acquainted with Dohada in the Kavi-samaya or the Indian poetic conventions.)

Against those Trayī-Vedic assertions, Bhavya denies the existence of mind in plants, saying that the reason: ⟨Because they have the sensible faculties (indriya)⟩ is uncertain (anaikāntika). And as evidences in disproof of the Mīmāṃsaka's statement, Bhavya produces the case of iron attracted by a magnet. It does not necessarily prove iron's faculty of seeing things. Resonance of a bronze pot does not necessarily prove a pot's faculty of hearing sounds. Rat poison prevails in the rainy season though it has no mental faculty of knowing seasons.

(ii) *caturyony-asaṃgrahāt*: In the Buddhist way of classification of living beings in four categories by the forms of birth, namely, aṇḍa-ja, jarāyu-ja, sveda-ja and upapāduka, there is no place for the birth of plants, making a clear-cut contrast to the Brahmanical idea of udbhij-ja (birth in the form of a bud) as is mentioned in the *Manu-smṛti* I, 46. (*MHK* 140)

(iii) *madhya-cchede 'pi vâspandāt*: A plant may be cut in the middle of its body, as it is insensible and can stand the pain of being cut in the middle. (*MHK* 140)

(iv) *sparśato yadi saṃkocāt*: Plants like mimosa, Samaṅga and Añjala-kārikā would shrink and curl themselves when touched by a finger. But they do not have a mind, just as a human hair has no mind though it is frizzled by a touch by fire or by quick silver. (*MHK* 141-42)

(v) *cikitsyatvāt*: Plants work as a remedy for an illness, as if they have their mind to sympathize with. This Hetu also remains uncertain, in the light of alcohol, musk-deer's musk, or a surgeon's knife for operation, working as a remedy for an illness. (*MHK* 143)

(vi) *samāna-prasavāt*: Plants multiply themselves, keeping their generic distinctions, just as wheat as wheat, rice as rice. Again, this reason, too, is not effective since germ and efflorescence spread themselves while keeping their generic classes. (*MHK* 144)

(vii) *vṛddheḥ*: Plants grow, from a state of seed to a state of bud, to a state of shooting, and to a state of a big trunk. Again this reason for the plants' mind is not effective, as human hair, nail, claw, and coral are not understood to have their own mind. (*MHK* 144)

(viii) *dohadāt*: Some plants are noxious as if they have a mind and will to give harm to humanity. But, the same can be said about the germ of a disease. (*MHK* IX.144) (In spite of Bhavya's good understanding of the Indian Kavi-samaya, he uses dohada here, rather literally—to mean having a morbid desire, and not in a technical way to apply to the context).[4]

(ix) *ṛtu-janāt*: Plants have their own particular seasons of blooming and fruition. (*MHK* 144)

(x) *svāpāt*: Plants have cycles of hibernation and active operation. Again, the cases of influenza, small pox, and hepatitis as having their own seasons of diffusion may be mentioned as nullifying the reason's universal validity. (*MHK* 144)

All these reasons for the possibilities of plants' sentience and sensibility (*MHK* IX, 139; 140; 141; 143; and 144) are refuted as uncertain (anaikāntika) by Bhavya. And, in the *Tarkajvālā* which we can find only in the Tibetan translation, to verify his standpoint Bhavya quotes as the supporting authority the opinion of some Pūrvācāryas as follows:

(a) "A thing in which the characteristics such as the duration of vitality (āyus), warmth (ūṣman), intelligence (vijñāna), and actions (kāya-ceṣṭā) are acknowledged can be called vital (prāṇin)."

(D315b5) sṅon gyi slob dpon dag gis ḥdi skad du/
/tshe daṅ drod daṅ rnam śes daṅ/
/g'yo ba shes bya so soḥi shiṅ/
/chos ḥdi gaṅ la dmigs gyur pa/
/de la ḥtsho ba shes byaḥo/

(b) "One without warmth, without actions, having no faculties like hearing, and without any reaction to the sounds, such a one is not a living being (sattva), but a stationary being."

/drod med g'yo ba med ñid daṅ/
/thos la sogs par mi ḥgyur daṅ/
/sgra la sogs pa rtogs med ni/
/sems can ma yin brtan pa ñid/

(c) "As the good and bad Karmic activities are the matters concerned only with the beings which have their mind, they do not to do with the inanimate stationary things (sthāvareṣu). For this reason, there is no mind in plants."

/dge ba daṅ ni mi dgeḥi las/
/sems yod rnams la ḥbyuṅ ḥgyur gyi/
/brtan pa rnams la de med pas/
/des na śiṅ rnams sems med yin/

(d) "They are apart from desires and anger, knowing no fatigue in their body, without care for the reasonable or the unreasonable. For this reason, there is no mental activities in plants."

/ḥdod daṅ she sdaṅ daṅ bral shiṅ/ /lus la dam pa med pa daṅ/
/rigs daṅ mi rigs las grol bas/ /des na śiṅ la sems pa med/

(e) "In a living being, there are bodily outer activities like birth, coming, doing and winking. These cannot be observed in a case of the stationary things. For this reason, there are no mental activities in plants."

/srog ni ḥbyuṅ ḥjug bye btsums sogs/
/lus kyi phyi rol bya ba rnams/
/brtan pa rnams la ma mthoṅ bas/
/de nas śiṅ la sems pa med/

/ces bya ba la sogs pa ḥbyuṅ ba yin no/ (*bstan pa* here is changed to be read *brtan pa* on the basis of the Tibetan translations of *MHK* IX, 139).

We cannot identify who were the Pūrvācāryas to whom Bhavya referred here in the *Tarkajvālā*. But, in the *Abhidharmakośa,* we can find the similar statements quoting a scriptural authority as follows:

(f) "When the duration of vitality, warmth and intelligence leave the body, it will be thrown down to the ground just senseless as decayed wood."

/āyur ūṣmā 'tha vijñānaṃ yadā kāyaṃ jahaty amī/
/apaviddhas tadā śete yathā kāṣṭham acetana iti/
Abhidharmakośa-bhāṣya ad II, 45ab (Pradhan ed., p. 73)

Here, intelligence or mentality is counted as one of the indispensable conditions for the principle of life—vitality: (a), (b) and (f). (Mentality, however, is not vitality itself. Here, the English translation 'sentient being' for the Sanskrit word 'sattva', which literally means 'being', leads us to confusion.) The peculiar Karmic force (asādhāraṇa-karman) is an evidence of mentality: (c). Consciousness of desire, anger, fatigue, and rationality is a proof for mentality: (d). Bodily movements are understood as another sign for mentality: (e).

In fact, a plant holds the marginal position in the distinction of the living beings on the one hand and what is not on the other. Bhavya's idea of denying sentience and intelligence (caitanyatva and vijñāna) in plants shows in a very clear-cut way, and in a subtle marginal way, how the old Indian Buddhists thought about the principle of life.

Meat-eating is a sin of taking an other's life. But, if a plant is acknowledged as living, taking grains and seeds and eating the blades and leaves of a plant also means an act of taking an other's life. Bhavya extends his discussions on harming and taking an other's life (hiṃsā), in answer to the Mīmāṃsaka's idea of Yajña and in reference to the Buddhist idea of Tri-koṭi-śuddha-māṃsa and Māṃsa-bhakṣaṇa (*MHK* IX, 132-36). The early Buddhists exceptionally admitted the act of meat-eating only on the understanding that the killing of an animal is not observed, heard or suspected (tikoṭi-parisuddha). But, Bhavya's interpretation of the purity (śuddhi) seems to differ from what Dr. Alsdorf puts it in the following way: "Since all food—whether animal or vegetal—is ⟨killed⟩ when it is prepared for consumption, ⟨the essential criterion was that it should not have been specifically prepared for the monk⟩ (Alsdorf, p. 7)." Bhavya examines the reasons prohibiting the act of meat-eating, and concludes in a very realistic way that the act does not necessarily form a sin. In this context, the following six verses in the Ninth Chapter of his *MHK* should be examined.

na mānsa-bhakṣaṇaṃ bhoktuṃ bhujyate 'pāpa-kāraṇāt/
kṣut-pratīkāra-hetutvād yad-ṛcchāgata-bhaktavat//
/gaṅ yaṅ śa ni zos pa yis/
/sdig paḥi rgyur ni mi ḥgyur te/
/bkres pa zlog paḥi rgyu yin phyir/
/ma blaṅs byin paḥi zas skom bshin/

(*MHK* IX, 133)

aśucitvād abhakṣyaṃ cen mānsaṃ kāyo 'pi cintyatām(/)
bīja-sthānād upastambhād aśuci-viṭkrimir yathā/
/śa ni mi bzaḥ ba yin phyir/
/mi za she na lus la rtogs/
/sa bon daṅ ni brten byed pa/
/mi gtsaṅ mi gtsaṅ srin bu bshin/

(*MHK* IX, 134)

śukrâdi-sambhav[ād eva matsya-mānsaṃ vigarhitam/]
taṃ ghṛta-kṣīrâdir hetoḥ syād evaṃ vyabhicāritā//
/khu ba sogs las byuṅ baḥi phyir/ /ña śa sogs ni smad ce na/
/mar daṅ ḥo sogs rgyu yin pas/ /ḥdi ni ma ṅes pa ñid yin/

(*MHK* IX, 135)

mānsâdaḥ prāṇi-ghātī cet tan-nimittatvato mataḥ(/)
ajinâdi-dharair hetoḥ syād evaṃ vyabhicāritā//
/śa za srog gcod ñid yin te/
/de yi rgyu mtshan phyir she na/
/lbags sogs thogs pas gtan tshigs ni/
/ma ṅes pa ñid yin par ḥgyur/

(*MHK* IX, 136)

na mānsa-bhakṣaṇaṃ duṣṭaṃ tadānīṃ prāṇy-aduḥkhanāt(/)
muktā-barhi-kalāpâdi taṇḍūlâṃbûpayogavat//
/śa za ba ni skyon bcas min/
/de tshe srog chags gnod min phyir/
/mu tig rma byaḥi sgro sogs daṅ/
/ḥbras daṅ chu yi dgos pa bshin/

(*MHK* IX, 137)

saṃkalpa-jatvād rāgasya na hetur [mānsa-bhakṣaṇam/]
[tad-]vinâpi tad-utpatter gavām iva tṛṇâśinām//
/ḥdod chags kun rtog las byuṅ phyir/
/śa zos de yi rgyu ma yin/
/de ma zos laḥaṅ de ḥbyuṅ ste/
/rtvsa zan ba laṅ la sogs bshin/

(*MHK* IX, 138)

In the above-mentioned verses, Bhavya examines the reasons for the meat-prohibition in the following six aspects:

(i) The act of meat-eating as a means of nutrition, a remedy from an illness, and a cure for hunger does not form a sin.

(*MHK* 133)

(ii) The prohibition against meat-eating by reason of impurity is not sustainable. Our body is by itself born impure and retained impure, no matter whether one takes meat or not. The human body is innately impure, like a worm in a dung mound.

(*MHK* 134)

(iii) The prohibition against fish-eating by reason of a fish's constituency from the union of semen and blood is again unsustainable. When a fish is prohibited from the taking, why should not the clarified butter and milk, which are after all a product of the union of semen and blood, be prohibited? (*MHK* 135)

(iv) The prohibition against meat-eating by reason of taking animal's life is not sustainable. If an ascetic did not wear the fur and hide for his pants, a Śarabha deer might survive. An animal's life has been taken, not simply for the purpose of eating its flesh. (*MHK* 136)

(v) The prohibition against meat-eating by reason of creature's agony and sufferings is not sustainable. When eaten, the beast is already stunned to death. The act of meat-eating is not sinful just as the acts of grain-taking or water-drinking is not. The creatures may not be tormented by the act of their flesh eaten, just as a peacock does not suffer from the act of taking his train. Just as an elephant does not die from his ivory extracted. Just as a mother-shell does not suffer to death from the act of removal of pearls. If it is sinful, why is not the cremation of a dead body? (*MHK* 137)

(vi) The prohibition against meat-eating by reason of its enhancing human sexual desire is not sustainable. Though being a grass-eating (hervivorous) creature, an ox or a hare is known to have a strong sexual inclination. (*MHK* 138)

Thus, Bhavya refutes all the reasons for the prohibition against meat-eating, and allows the Buddhists to take Tri-koṭi-śuddha-māṃsa, though not positively encouraging the habit.

The scriptural authorities Bhavya mentioned in the *Tarkajvālā* are the *Hastikakṣya-sūtra*,[5] the *Mahāmegha-sūtra*,[6] the *Laṅkāvatāra-sūtra*,[7] and the *Aṅgulimālīya-sūtra*.[8] At the first glance it seems that much of his assertion is based on, and agrees with, the Māṃsa-bhakṣaṇa Chapter of the *Laṅkāvatāra-sūtra*. But when we examine closely and in details, we can see his standpoint differs from that of the *Laṅkāvātara-sūtra*.

Some of the reasons, though employed by the both sides, lead to the contrary conclusions; conditional admission in Bhavya and total prohibition of meat-eating in the *Laṅkāvatāra-sūtra*.

The spirit of sympathy and pity (maitrī-karuṇā), expressed so explicitly in those *Mahāyāna-sūtras* are not emphasized in Bhavya's case. The *Aṅgulimālīya-sūtra* states, side by side with the idea that all sentient beings are interrelated in the frame of infinite Saṃsāra, the idea that "the element (dhātu) of the Sattvas is in fact the Dharma-dhātu itself. This consciousness of the ultimate oneness of the two Dhātus have made the Buddhas abstaining from flesh and fish". (sems can thams cad kyi dbyiṅs ni chos kyi dbyiṅs te/ dbyiṅs gcig tu gyur paḥi śa za bar ḥgyur bas/ saṅs rgyas rnams śa mi gsol lo/ See Ruegg, p. 236.) Though mentioning the name of the *Aṅgulimālīya-sūtra* as the authority, Bhavya seems to have actually ignored what is discussed in the *Sūtra*.

And Bhavya's standpoint is so distant from what the Chinese and the Japanese Buddhists have taken for granted. Traditionally these Buddhists of the later Mahāyāna development have held the idea of Issai-shujō-shitsuu-busshō (the possession of the Buddha-nature by all sentient beings). Sometimes they go to an extreme to express an animistic idea of Sōmoku-kokudo-shikkai-jōbutsu (Plant-earth's Attainment of Buddhahood). In the Vijñapti-mātratā theory, the Ālayavijñāna is the root-cause, not only of living beings (sattva-loka), producing their material sense-faculties and bodies, but also of the things in the external world (bhājana-loka). (See Schmithausen: *Ālayavijñāna*, p. 203) So, the difference between sentient (sattva) and insentient (asattva) is no longer a matter of the crucial or substantial importance.

Under the influence of such ways of thinking, the Chinese and the Japanese Buddhists claim that not only the beings in the Sattva-loka, but also the things in the Bhājana-loka could be acknowledged to have the Buddha-nature—sentience—potentiality to be the Buddha. And their source of authority for proclaiming their standpoint is the (*Mahāyānist*) *Mahāparinirvāṇa-sūtra*. This *Mahāparinirvāṇa-sūtra* was already clearly mentioned in the *Laṅkāvātara-sūtra* as its source for the prohibition of meat-eating. Intentionally or not, however, Bhavya excluded the name of this *Mahāparinirvāṇa-sūtra* from his own list of enumeration of the sources.

The philosophy of Tathāgatagarbha or Hongaku (Innate Enlightenment) seems to be not a matter of a great interest and attraction for Bhavya. Seemingly, logical consistency on the basis of the Abhidharma traditional interpretation of the existing things is a stronger concern for this sixth century Indian Buddhist, at least in his *Tarkajvālā*.

BIBLIOGRAPHY

E.W. Hopkins: "The Buddhistic Rule against Eating Meat",

Journal of the American Oriental Society, Vol. 27, 1906, pp. 455-464.

Yukio Sakamoto: "On the Existence or Non-existence of the Buddha-nature in Non-sentient Beings—Cases of Chan-jan and Ch'eng-kuan (in Japanese)", *Journal of the Japanese Association of Indian and Buddhist Studies,* Vol. VII, No. 2 (March 1959), pp. 416-25; (repr. 1980), pp. 384-96.

——"The Japanese Development of the Concept of Plant-earth's Attainment of Buddhahood (in Japanese)", *The Essays Dedicated to Prof. Gisho Nakano* (1960), pp. 303-21; (repr. 1980), pp. 397-412.

Shōson Miyamoto: "On the Cultural Meaning of the Buddhist Motto: 'Earth, Herbs and Trees, All Attain Buddhahood', and its Author (in Japanese)", *Journal of the Japanese Association of Indian and Buddhist Studies,* Vol. IX, No. 2 (March 1961), pp. 262-91; (repr. 1985), pp. 469-504.

L. Alsdorf: "Beitrage zur Geschichte von Vegetarismus und Rinderverehrung in Indien", (*Akademie der Wissenschaften und der Literatur, Abhandlungen der geistes-und sozialwissenschaftlichen Klasse,* Jahrgang 1961, Nr. 6, Wiesbaden, 1962) pp. 559-625.

Sōchū Kamei: "Concepts of Plant-earth's Attainment of Buddhahood in the Shingon Buddhism—Man-witness the Immediate Attainment of Buddhahood (in Japanese)", *Journal of the Nippon Buddhist Research Association,* Vol. XXXI (March 1966), pp. 181-95.

H.P. Schmidt: "The Origin of Ahiṃsā", *Mélanges d'Indianisme à la mémoire de L. Renou* (Paris, 1968), pp. 625-55.

P.V. Kane: *History of Dharmaśāstra,* Vol. 2, Part 2, (Poona, 1974), pp. 757-800.

Shinjō Kawasaki: "A Reference to Maga in the *Tarkajvālā*", *Journal of the Japanese Association of Indian and Buddhist Studies,* Vol. XXIII, No. 2, (March 1975), pp. 1-7.

C.S. Prasad: "Meat-Eating and the Rule of Tikoṭiparisuddha, Studies in Pali and Buddhism", in A.K. Narain, ed.: *A Memorial Volume in Honor of Bhikkhu Jagdish Kashyap,* (Delhi, 1979), pp. 289-95.

D.S. Ruegg: "Ahiṃsā and Vegitarianism in the History of Buddhism", *Buddhist Studies in Honor of Walpola Rahula,* (London, 1980), pp. 235-41.

W. Halbfass: *Studies in Kumārila and Śaṅkara* (Reinbek, 1983), 14p. 140p.

J.C. Heesterman: "Non-violence and Sacrifice", *Indologica Taurinensia*, Vol. XII, (Torino, 1984), pp. 119-26.

Minoru Hara: "A Note on the Pāśupata Concept of Ahiṃsā", *Ṛtam* (*Shri Gopal Chandra Shinha Commemoration Volume*), Vol. XVIII, (Lucknow, 1984-86), pp. 145-54.

Shinjō Kawasaki: "Meat-eating and Bhāvaviveka (in Japanese)", *Tōhō* (*The East*), No. 1 (April 1985), pp. 174-84.

——"Mind in a Plant?—Concept of Sentient Being according to Bhāvaviveka (in Japanese)", *Memoirs of the Society for the Busan Study*, No. 14, (1986), pp. 1-15.

Lambert Schmithausen: *Ālayavijñāna*; *On the Origin and the Early Development of a Central Concept of Yogācāra Philosophy*, *Studia Philologica Buddhica* IV, (the International Institute for Buddhist Studies, Tokyo, 1987), in 2 Parts, 701p.

Masahiro Shimoda: "Tri-koṭi-pariśuddha-māṃsa, Reconsidered (in Japanese)", in *Bukkyo Bunka*, Vol. 22, (Tokyo, 1989), pp. 1-21.

Noriaki Hakamaya: *Hongakushisō-hihan* (*Criticism on the Idea of Innate Enlightenment*, in Japanese), (Daizo-shuppan, 1989).

Masaki Furuya: *Shokubutsuteki-seimeizō* (*Botanical Idea of Life*, in Japanese), (Kodan-sha, June 1990), 243p.

Yoshirō Tamura: "On the Innate Enlightenment (Hongakushisōron, in Japanese)", *The Collected Works of Yoshirō Tamura* I, (Shunju-sha, 1990).

Fumihiko Sueki: "Medieval Tendai and the Idea of Innate Enlightenment (in Japanese)", *Āgama* No. 118 (February 1991), pp. 42-73.

Lambert Schmithausen: "Buddhism and Nature", pp. 22-38, International Symposium on the Occasion of the International Garden and Greenery Exposition, 1990, Osaka.

——"Buddhism and Environmental Ethics", pp. 1-39; "Plants as Sentient Beings in Earliest Buddhism?", mimeograph copies for his lectures at the International Institute for the Buddhist Studies, and the University of Tokyo, Tokyo, October, 1990.

References

1. This study is based on Rev. Rāhula Sāṃkṛtyāyana's hand-written copy of the Sanskrit *MHK* offered by Prof. V. V. Gokhale of Poona and Late

Prof. G. Tucci's photo-copy of the same text made available by Prof. Gokhale. The present writer remains thankful to Prof. Gokhale's kind guidance and his generous permission for the use and publication of the material. The complete Sanskrit and Tibetan texts of the IXth Chapter of *MHK* were published by the present writer. See Shinjō Kawasaki ed.: "The Mīmāṃsā Chapter of Bhavya's *Madhyamaka-hṛdaya-kārikā*—Text and Translation—(1) Pūrva-pakṣa", *Studies* 1976, Institute of Philosophy, University of Tsukuba (September 1977), pp. 1-15; (2) "Uttara-pakṣa", *Studies* No. 12, (March 1987), pp. 1-23; (3) "Uttara-pakṣa (II) with the Sarvajña Chapter", *Studies* No. 13 (March 1988), pp. 1-42.

2. Since Hindu and Jain traditions have prohibitions of meat eating, they have a literature on this topic. The present essay cannot go into their theories since it would take too much space, and would not serve the purpose of exposing Bhavya's standpoint.

3. There are several possibilities to name the author of *MHK*. Dr. Y. Ejima recently suggests a reading "Bhāviveka". See *Journal of the Japanese Society of Indian and Buddhist Studies*, Vol. 38, No. 2 (March 1990). The present writer follows the Tibetan naming Bhavya, mentioned in the end of the Tibetan translation of the works (DK40b6; DV329b2).

4. The Buddhist logicians seem to be interested in this term *dohada*. We can find a reference in Ratnakīrti's *Sarvajña-siddhi*: "paryante tu sarva-sarvajña-dohadam apy apaneṣyāmaḥ, (*Ratnakīrti-nibandhāvalī*, Thakur ed. p. 1, 1.18).

5. *Peking Tibetan Tripiṭaka* No. 873, *glaṅ poḥi rtsal*; *Taishō Tripiṭaka* No. 816, Vol. 17, 787a.

6. *Peking Tibetan Tripiṭaka* No. 898, *sprin chen po*; *Taisho Tripiṭaka* Vol. 12, 1099b.

7. Bunyū Nanjiō ed.: *The Laṅkāvatāra Sūtra, Bibliotheca Otaniensis*, Vol. I, (Kyoto, 1923; repr. 1953), N.244-N. 259; P. L. Vaidya ed.: *Saddharmalaṅkāvatārasūtram, Buddhist Sanskrit Texts* No. 3, (Darbhanga, 1963), V. 100-105; *Peking Tibetan Tripiṭaka* No. 775: *laṅ kar gśegs paḥi theg pa chen poḥi mdo*, Vol. 29, pp. 68-71; *Taishō Tripiṭaka* Vol. 16, pp. 513b-514b; 561a-564c; 622c-624c.

8. *Peking Tibetan Tripiṭaka* No. 879: *sor moḥi phreṅ ba la phan pa* (Vol. 34, p. 336); *Taishō Tripiṭaka* No. 120, Vol. 2, 540c-541a.

The first draft of this paper was read in the presence of Prof. Alex Wayman at the VIIIth World Sanskrit Conference, Vienna, August-September 1990.

6 THE BUDDHIST DOCTRINE OF KARMA

HARI SHANKAR PRASAD
Department of Philosophy, University of Delhi

I

The doctrine of karma is one of the central themes of Buddhism. It has metaphysical, epistemological, ethical, religious, cultural and social implications, so much so that all kinds of activity, becoming, happening, creativity and temporal processes are denoted by the word 'karma'. Karmas can broadly be classified into two groups:

(1) All those karmas in which agency of any kind, human or non-human, is absent. I call such karma *karma-without-agency.* Under this category comes the dynamic nature of reality, a necessary factor for developing the Buddhist world-view, according to which man as well as the world (*saṃsāra*) is epistemic manifestation of such reality. All this is a contingent matter. This kind of karma is essential and blind, for example, the internal bodily processes, the causal efficiency (e.g., burning) of fire, etc.

(2) All those karmas in which agency of a sentient being is involved. But here I shall focus on human agency only. I call such karma *karma-by-human-agency* which is the basis of the popular doctrine of karma and its retribution (*vipāka*). This kind of karma is essentially ethical and causal in nature, and morally praiseworthy or blameworthy.

The understanding of *karma-without-agency,* I think, is a prerequisite of the understanding of *karma-by-human-agency.* In that case, I am supposed to explain, albeit in brief, the whole evolution and devolution of the phenomenon according to Buddhism. For this purpose, I am taking the philosophic paradigm of the idealistic school of Buddhism, the Yogācāra-Vijñānavāda, according to which the whole phenomenal show is attributed to the functioning of consciousness (*citta-vṛtti*).

The relevant issues which the concept of karma anticipates for comprehensive treatment are:

(1) Nature of essential reality which constitutes man and his world.
(2) Nature and purpose of *karma-by-human-agency* and other activities.
(3) Spatio-temporal continuity of man's body in the present life and that of his mind (*citta*=consciousness) in the three times: past, present and future, so that his personal identity is maintained in some specific sense, which is at the base of the issue of his survival after death.
(4) The memory criterion to prove man's personal identity.
(5) Causal explanation and continuity of his karma and its retribution.
(6) The process of transformation of karma into *phala*.
(7) Man's exercise of his free will in doing actions so as to assign responsibility for his own actions.
(8) Types of karma and types of *phala*.

The scope of present study is mainly confined to the Yogācāra-Vijñānavāda school of Buddhism. But I shall also survey in brief the earlier discussions of karma in Pali sources and the Sanskrit Abhidharma. In early Buddhism, the duality of mind (*citta*) and matter (*rūpa*) is maintained, but in the Yogācāra-Vijñānavāda, matter is explained away (?) and the sole ontological reality of *citta* is established. In Yogācāra-Vijñānavāda itself there is a gradual shift from the ontological plurality (or individuality) of *citta*-s to the one universal *citta*. In the former, each person-based individual *citta* has its own world (*saṃsāra*) in which it performs deeds and bears the responsibility for the same, and accordingly experiences pleasure and pain. Its actions may even bring to it liberation (*nirvāṇa*), which is its *summum bonum*, from worldly sufferings. In the latter development, the universal *citta* (cf. *cittamātratā, vijñaptimātratā, vijñānamātratā* and *prajñaptimātratā*) is propounded on the basis of the culmination of the epistemological analysis of illusory experiences as discussed in the *Viṃśatikā* of Vasubandhu.

After a sketchy discussion of the paradigmatic features of the Yogācāra-Vijñānavāda school, without touching upon the historical issues of its divergent thought developments, I shall take up selected passages of the Buddhist texts and interpret them so as to address myself to the issues raised above.

The basic assumption of the Yogācāra-Vijñānavāda is that *citta* is essentially of creative nature. This is in accordance with the general Buddhist view of reality as ever dynamic. The Buddhist sources are replete with such references. The *citta* in its original state, even if creative by nature, remains in its apparently latent form. Somehow at some stage, there is a stir in it. The cause of this first stage of evolution is not discussed in any Buddhist text. It is only said that this kind of inherent potency is beginningless or atemporal (*anādikāla*) in the sense that it is impossible to think of a state in which *citta* is without potency. Once the evolution begins, other forces generated by its activities, such as epistemic appearances of objective phenomena, keep accumulating in it. Then it becomes the womb of the whole phenomena (*saṃsāra*). It is also called the seed of everything and is therefore a receptacle of all kinds of *vijñānas* (cf. *sarvabījakam ālayavijñānam*).[1]

Since *citta* is ever dynamic, its forms or states are in perpetual flux like the waves of ocean (*udadhitaraṅga*). In this sense it is momentary (*kṣaṇika*). But its essence is eternal (*nitya*) which is the substratum of these wave-like changes. This *citta* is the principle of phenomenal reality. In other words, the cause of all kinds of evolution (=*saṃsārapravṛtti*) is *citta*. Once the functioning of the *citta* (*cittavṛtti*) has started, it is said that it has its relation with all the three time epochs: past, present and future, corresponding to its quiescent, actualised and potential states respectively. Because of the forces generated by its past activities (*atītakarmavāsanā*) it continues its present activities, which produce similar forces (*vāsanā*) to take it to the future ones. Thus the phenomenal process keeps going, till there is a deliberate and systematic attempt by man at degenerating the *karmavāsanā* to achieve a state of tranquillity (*nirvāṇa*) which is also a state of bliss (*sukha*). This explains the causal link between any two states of *citta*. The so-called original *citta* free from all activities is an explanatory presupposition based on speculation. As a matter of fact, the starting point of the whole philosophic enterprise in Yogācāra-Vijñānavāda is *ālayavijñāna*, which is taken "as the basic principle of pollution (*saṃkleśa*),. . .as the seat or sum of Badness (*dauṣṭhulya*), and. . .as constituting, or having the nature of it, ultimate unsatisfactoriness (*saṃskāraduḥkhatā*) or the Truth of Suffering (*duḥkha-satya*)."[2]

The most important issue in the present study is: How do the activities of *ālayavijñāna* become an issue of ethical concern. *Prima facie* they appear to be mechanical and non-human. But the Yogācāra-Vijñānavāda shows that the *karma-by-human-agency* is the root cause of the whole functioning of the *ālaya-vijñāna*. The issue is not merely individual, but it has social implications also. It is in this sense that an individual is responsible for his actions which are good (*kuśala*), bad (*kliṣṭa* or *akuśala*) or indeterminate (*avyākṛta*). The activities mature according to their respective nature in the individual *ālaya-vijñānas*, which in turn regulate the individual conducts. In this sense, *ālayavijñāna* is nothing but accumulation of the forces resulting from the maturation of *phala* (*vipākasaṃgṛhīta*).

In the Yogācāra-Vijñānavāda, there is a clear tendency of shift from the plurality of individual *ālayavijñānas* to the oneness and universality of the *ālayavijñāna* leading to idealistic absolutism. Another tendency of shift is from the duality of matter (*rūpa*) and mind (*citta*) to monism of consciousness. In this scheme, an individual is assimilated into the Absolute. On the contrary, the individuality and plurality of *ālayavijñāna* makes a man responsible for his karma, and he is thus inspired and motivated to regenerate or transform himself by carving out the path for his spiritual growth. In this way, he rises above the phenomenal evils (*dauṣṭhulya, saṃkleśa*). This is reflected in the spiritual career of an Arhat, who has suspended the activities of his *ālayavijñāna* from generating evil forces (*vāsanā*) any more. This he has achieved by practising spiritual virtues (*kuśalakarma*). The Arhat's case shows the individual's freedom of action.

Further, an individual's reason, belief, desire and purpose are motivations of moral actions. All these elements are person-based and thus internal to man himself. These factors determine the type and course of action he wants to perform. Moreover, man has certain control over these factors, for he is free to train/culture his mind and interpret a particular situation in such a way that his existing belief, desire, etc. change radically. In this sense, he has control over these elements and freedom in exercising his choice of action. But in certain cases, where there is external force, for example, when somebody is attacking him, or in the case of internal bodily mechanism, which are beyond his control, he is not free to act according to his own desire. He has no other option but to undergo these activities.

A careful analysis of human circumstances shows that it is very difficult to conceive of a situation when man has complete freedom of choosing his actions. In each case where we say that a man is free to take a decision, there are some factors like desire, reason, belief, etc. which influence his so-called freedom of choice and are thus determining factors. But in the same case, it is very much possible for him to change his mind and thus the very rationale on certain other grounds in choosing another type of action instead. This kind of freedom with some kind of determinism is *deterministic freedom* where man has freedom to change the very determining factors of his freedom (cf. *cittena ciyate karmaḥ*).[3] This means absolute freedom is not possible. It is always related to certain conditions.

An important point in exercising our freedom is the correct understanding (*samyagjñāna*) of the nature of action, its means, its ethical consequences and social implications. Thus right cognition of things is a necessary condition for the realisation of values (cf. *samyagjñānapūrvikā puruṣārthasiddhiḥ—Nyāyabindu*, I.1).

In Yogācāra-Vijñānavāda, evolution of *citta* (=*vijñānapariṇāma*) is broadly classified into two categories, viz., subjectivity (*ātman*) and objectivity (*dharma*). The source of this duality is our *ālayavijñāna*. All sorts of our behaviour—mental, bodily and linguistic—are guided by this apparent duality. The subjectivity of *citta* and its logical implications establish Absolutism in which oneness and universality of *citta* is maintained by explaining away the ontological plurality of mind and matter, and their manifestations. This makes it impossible to account for the responsibility of actions performed by man whose individuality is explained away together with the phenomenal plurality.

In Buddhism, an individual is a cluster of psycho-physical organism (*pañcaskandha*) possessing both mind (*citta*) and body (*rūpa*). For any *karma-phala* process in an ethical sense, one's personal identity, one's continuity in the present life with the same mind and body and one's continuity from the past life when one's body was different, and the same in the future when one will have a different body, have to be maintained. The continuity with regard to one's body in spatio-temporal terms is established only in one's present life-span. The ethical doctrine of karma demands that an individual continues during one's transition from one time-epoch to another and since a body cannot maintain continuity in this respect, the only explanation left with us is that it is mind or consciousness (*citta*) which retains its continuity. The memory criterion of personal identity also can be explained in terms of *citta*. This means that an individual which is construed in terms of pure consciousness can be said to survive after the death of one's body (cf. *janmāntara-pravṛtti*).

The Buddhist theory that the past karmas mature in the present and the present ones in the future explains the suffering or happy life of a person in the present for which, to the best of one's knowledge, one has not done any karma. The fact of inequality among human beings is also explained on this line. It is needless to say that the karma doctrine shows that it is not at all necessary to posit the existence of God. The Buddhist karmic discipline aims at inculcating highest univeral moral values on secular lines. A Bodhisattva is, thus, motivated to doing actions for the welfare of others, maintaining total passivity towards one's own interest. This is one's social morality, which is an ideal to be pursued by every individual in order to make the world worth living.

A Buddhist will generally subscribe to a karma theory which endorses retributive justice and assignment of responsibility to the agent. He opposes any kind of fate (*niyati, vidhi*) theory, according to which a man is not responsible for his action, rather he is simply a puppet in the hands of external determining factors. The postulation of the theories of *saṃsāra* and rebirth (*punarbhava, janmāntara, punarjanma*) by the Buddhists are logically consistent with their theory of karma and karma-phala. In this direction, the Buddhist doctrine of the transference of merit (*pariṇāmanā*) as seen in the case of a Bodhisattva is the climax of the Buddhist moral and spiritual discipline. Although this doctrine seems to be logically inappropriate, psychologically it is a great inspiring force towards creating social harmony and mutual concern among human beings.

It is not my purpose here to give an elaborate exposition of all sorts of evolution (*pariṇāma*) or functioning (*karma, vṛtti*) of *citta* or *vijñāna*. I have only tried to show the place of the individual in the philosophic scheme of Yogācāra-Vijñānavāda. I have argued that the doctrine of karma requires a consistent theory of knowledge, ontology and ethics. When a Bodhisattva performs karma with a view to eradicating the suffering of one's fellow beings (*jagadduḥkhaparitrāṇāya*), one is guided by these theories and in that very act one is elevated to the highest level of consciousness.

II

The following textual passages from Pali as well as Buddhist Sanskrit sources and their interpretations throw light on the issues involved in the preceding discussion.

(1) The Buddha, in his sermons, talks of the ethical consequences of one's actions, Man's present condition, such as being inferior or superior, beautiful or ugly, and of good or bad nature, is attributed to one's past actions.

The correlation between one's moral and immoral actions on the one hand, and one's experience of pleasure and pain spanning throughout the three time-epochs is discussed by the Buddha. Again, the cause of human condition is said to be one's own karmas; unethical karma reaps an unhappy life and ethical karma reaps a happy life:

> *so dibbena cakkhunā visuddhena atikkanta-mānusakena satte passati cavamāne upapajjamāne, hīne paṇīte suvaṇṇe dubbaṇṇe sugate duggate yathā-kammūpage satte pajānāti: "ime vaṭa bhonto sattā kāya-duccaritena samannāgatā vācī-duccaritena samannāgatā mano-duccaritena samannāgatā ariyāṇaṃ upavādakā micchā-diṭṭhikā micchā-diṭṭhi-kammasamādānā. te kāyassa bhedā paraṃ maraṇā apāyaṃ duggatiṃ vinipātaṃ nirayaṃ upapannā. ime vā pana bhonto sattā kāya-sucaritena samannāgatā vācī-sucaritena samannāgatā mano-sucaritena samannāgatā ariyāṇaṃ anupavādakā sammā-diṭṭhikāsammā-diṭṭhi-kamma-samādānā. te kāyassa bhedā paraṃ maraṇā sugatiṃ saggaṃ lokaṃ upapannā ti."*
>
> —*Dīghanikāya*, I, p. 82. 22-38. (P.T.S. edition)

(2) The causal correlation between one's actions—mental, bodily and linguistic—and the results of their maturation is called the law of karma (Pali *kamma*). This assigns the responsibility of an action to the agent himself. Therefore, every human being is advised by the Buddha to reflect upon this inexorable law:

kammassako 'mhi kammadāyādo kammayoni kammabandhu kammapaṭisaraṇo, yaṃ kammaṃ karissāmi kalyāṇaṃ vā pāpakaṃ vā, tassa dāyādo bhavissāmī ti abhiṇhaṃ paccavekkhitabbaṃ itthiyā vā purisena-vā gahaṭṭhena vā pabbajitena vā. —*Aṅguttaranikāya*, III, p. 72.1-6. (P.T.S. edition)

(3) Here the Buddhist assumption is that karma and its result are casually correlated. There is no relenting of this relationship. This explains the inequality among human beings in all respects, their differing psychological, biological, economic and social conditions; that is, karma makes a man low-class or high-class according to its nature:

kammassakā, māṇava, sattā kammadāyāda kammayonī kammabandhu kammapaṭisaraṇā. kammaṃ satte vibhajati yadidaṃ hīnappaṇītatāyati.

—*Majjhimanikāya* III, p. 203.4-6. (P.T.S. edition)

(4) Further, the law of karma also explains the present human condition for which one thinks one is not responsible, simply because one does not remember or know that one did anything in the past which has brought about this present condition. The ethical argument of the Buddhists is that in such cases the rational explanation is that the person's present condition is because of one's past karmas. But the epistemological question in this connection is: How do we know that the person had his life in the past, has survived in the present and will survive in the future also after one's death? The only answer the Buddhists give is that the Buddha himself perceived through his clairvoyant vision (*dibbacakkhu*) the whole process of man's existence in the past, one's actions and their consequent maturation, and one's survival in the present. One can develop one's own clairvoyant vision (*dibbacakkhu*) and see the whole *karma-phala* process oneself:

sattānaṃ cutuppāto bhikkhave cakkhunā sacchikaraṇīyo.

—*Aṅguttaranikāya* II, p. 183.11. (P.T.S. edition)

(5) We may not believe the Buddhist account of the *karma-phala* process and the Buddha's possessing clairvoyant vision (*dibbacakkhu*), but it has certainly ethical bearings on man and his social order. Some philosophers may regard these issues as transcendental and thus meaningless or nonsensical, but for the Buddhists they are not worthless and unimportant. It is here that

they transcend the extreme form of rationality. They firmly believe that the efficacy of karma never fails to produce results:

> *na hi nassati kassaci kammam*
> *eti ha tam, labhat' eva suvāmī*
> *dukkhaṃ mando paraloke*
> *attani passati kibbisakārī.*
>
> —*Suttanipāta, Gāthā* 666, p. 128.11-14. (P.T.S. edition)

(6) The Buddhist categorisation of human beings is done in two ways: One, on the basis of their karmas as found in the early sources, and the other, on the basis of the levels of their spirituality (=*gotra*) as found in the Mahāyāna sources (cf. *The Uttaratantra of Maitreya*).[5] These two factors are not exclusive. They are found together. The only difference between them is that the early Buddhism lays maximum emphasis on the individual moral action, while the Mahāyāna on the spiritual growth of man in general. In the latter, the perfection in moral virtues such as *dāna, maitrī, karuṇā* and *muditā*, and the extension of the field of karma universally is demonstrated in the Bodhisattva's activities towards the eradication of human suffering (*jagadduḥkhaparitrāṇa*). All this is practically possible. This shows that morality is not trascendental or a meaningless enterprise. However, a Bodhisattva is not interested in purposeless speculative metaphysical thinking.

The Buddhists primarily aim at the cultivation and promotion of the culture of mind, a mind which is enlightened (*bodhicitta*) and shows concern for the welfare of human beings. Such a mind is pre-requisite for all our conduct—mental, bodily and speech. The human agent is free to choose and act (*karma*) in the sense that one can have control over one's volitional capers, such as desire, urge and motivation, which are technically called *cetanā*. *Cetanā* is said to be the root cause of behaviour (=*karma*) in general. That is why the Buddhists define *karma* as *cetanā*:

> *cetanā 'haṃ bhikkhave kammaṃ vadāmi; cetayitvā kammaṃ karoti kāyena vācāya manasā.*
>
> —*Aṅguttaranikāya* III, p. 415.7-8. (P.T.S. edition)

(7) If our volitional capers are not controlled and guided according to our moral needs, they will generate our behaviour in such a way that there will be widespread perpetuation of evils:

imesaṃ kho ahaṃ tapassi tiṇṇaṃ kammānaṃ evaṃ paṭivibhattānaṃ evaṃ paṭivisiṭṭhānaṃ manokammaṃ mahāsāvajjataraṃ paññāpemi pāpassa kammassa kiriyāya pāpassa kammassa pavattiyā, no tathā kāyakammaṃ no tathā vacīkammaṃ. —*Majjhimanikāya* I, 373. (P.T.S. edition)

(8) The Buddhists maintain that because of such volition-loaded behaviour (*sañcetanikaṃ kammaṃ*) a man experiences pain:

sañcetanikam, āvuso Pāṭaliputta, kammaṃ katvā kāyena vācāya manasā, dukkhaṃ so vediyatīti.

—*Majjhimanikāya* III, p. 207.26-27. (P.T.S. edition)

(9) A morally cultivated mind is developed by suppressing and eliminating volitional capers, the very root of our immoral behaviour. These capers are: *rāga, dosa* and *moha*:

tīṇ' imāni bhikkhave nidānāni kammānaṃ samudayāya. katamāni tīṇi? lobho nidānaṃ kammānaṃ samudayāya, doso nidānaṃ kammānaṃ samudayāya, moho nidānaṃ kammānaṃ samudayāya.

—*Aṅguttaranikāya* I, p. 134.15-18. (P.T.S. edition)

(10) *Cetanā* forms our habits and attitudes. It dictates to the contents and influences their cognition. *Cetanā* is a polluted form of *citta.* Its main function is to co-ordinate its own epistemic states which are grasped as phenomenal objects. Its another function is to conate, urge or motivate in the moral realm guiding our moral karmas. *Cetanā* is thus a very powerful drive[4] for action (*karma*):

cetayatī ti cetanā. saddhiṃ attanā sampayuttadhamme ārammaṇe abhisandahatī ti attho. sā cetayitalakkhaṇā, cetanābhāvalakkhaṇā ti attho. ayūhanarasā. . .ayūhanarasā pana kusalākusalesu eva hoti. kusalākusalakammāyūhanaṭṭhānaṃ hi patvā sesasampayuttadhammānaṃ ekadesaṃ attakaṃ eva, kiñccaṃ hoti. cetanā pana atireka-ussāhā atirekavāyāmā, diguṇa-ussāhā diguṇavāyāmā.

—*Aṭṭhasālinī*, p. 91.26-31, (ed. P.V. Bapat and R.D. Vadekar, Poona, 1942)

(11) *Cetanā* is essentially a mental driving force, a mental activity, towards phenomena:

cetanā mānasaṃ karma.—*Abhidharmakośa*, IV.lc.
cetanā cittābhisaṃskāro mānaskarma.

—*Abhidharmakośa-bhāṣya* on II.24.

cetanā cittābhisaṃskāro manasaś ceṣṭā yasyāṃ satyām ālambanaṃ prati cetasaḥ praspanda iva bhavati.—Sthiramati's *bhāṣya* on *Triṃśikā*, 3, p. 48. 4-5. (See note 1)

cettābhisaṃskāramanaskarmalakṣaṇā cetanā ceti.—*Madhyamakakārikā-vṛtti*, p. 134.16 (ed. P.L. Vaidya, Darbhanga, 1960).

cetanā=cittābhisaṃskāra=manasceṣṭā=karma.

(12) The essential character of *cetanā* is effected in three kinds of karma: (1) ethical deeds (*puṇya-karma*) which result in happiness (*sukha*), (2) unethical deeds (*apuṇya-karma*) which mature to painful experience (*duḥkhavedanīya*), and (3) such deeds which mature neither to pleasant experience nor to painful one (*aduḥkha-asukha-vedanīya*), but to a new series of individual *ālayavijñāna* for the next life. The *cetanā*-generated karma—mental, bodily and speech—and the illusion of duality of subject and object (=*grāhya-dvaya*) created by the subjectivity of *vijñāna* or *citta*, further generate a force (=*vāsanā*) which is accumulated in the individual's *ālayavijñāna* for further maturation:

sukhavedanīyaṃ karma yat puṇyam, tridhyānavedanīyaṃ cāniñjyam. duḥkhavedanīyaṃ karma yad apuṇyam. aduḥkha-sukhavedanīyaṃ karma yat sarvatrālayavijñānavaipākyaṃ karma, caturthāc ca dhyānād ūrdhvam āniñjyam.

—*Yogācārabhūmi*, p. 192.6-9 (ed. V. Bhattacharya, University of Calcutta, 1957)

karmaṇo vāsanā grahādvayavāsanayā saha |
kṣīṇe pūrvavipāke 'nyad vipākaṃ janayanti tat ||

—Vasubandhu's *Triṃśikā* 19 and *bhāṣya* thereon (See note 1)

(13) The inherent evil tendency of *citta* when it is in the form of *ālayavijñāna*—with respect to *kleśāvaraṇa* and *jñeyāvaraṇa*—and the follow-up karmas are the root cause of the whole phenomenon. *Kleśas* are further considered as the primary cause of all creations. Under the influence of *kleśas*, an individual's karmas mature to a new existence (*punarbhava*). Again, this karma in the form of new existence comes under the influence of *kleśas* till the latter are exhausted by following virtuous path (*aṣṭāṅga-mārga*).

saṃsārasya hi karma kleśās ca kāraṇaṃ tayoś ca kleśāḥ pradhānam. tathā hi kleśādhipatyatvāt karma punarbhavākṣepasamarthaṃ bhavati nānyathā. tathā ākṣiptapunarbhavam api karmakleśādhipatyād eva punarbhavo bhavati nānyathā. evaṃ ca kleśā eva saṃsārapravṛtteḥ pradhānatvān mūlam. atas teṣu prahīṇeṣu saṃsāro vinivartate nānyathā.

—Sthiramati on *Triṃśikā* 19, p. 61.24-27 (See note 1)

Sthiramati's *Bhāṣya* on the *Triṃśikā* (19, 29 and 30) discusses the remedy and the process of elimination of *kleśas* which generate evil karmas. The Buddhists, therefore, advise one to rise above the level of *kleśas* and to work for the universal good of all sentient beings. The basic pre-requisite of all this is realisation of the oneness of the cosmic principle (*dharmakāyādvayajñānabhāva*):

āśrayasya parāvṛttir iti. āśrayo 'tra sarvabījakam ālayavijñānam. tasya parāvṛttir yā dauṣṭhulyavipākadvayavāsanābhāvena nivṛttau satyāṃ karmaṇyatādharma-kāyādvayajñānabhāvena parāvṛttiḥ.

—*Ibid.*, p. 69.3-5

This cosmic principle transcends all discursive thought (*acintya*), logic (*tarka-agocara*), and analogy (*dṛṣṭānta-abhāva*). It is known only through realisation (*pratyātmavedya*). It is the foundation of spirituality (*āryadharmahetu*), free from defilements (*anāsrava*), immutable (*dhruva, nitya*), indestructible (*akṣaya*) and ultimately blissful (*sukha*):

anāsravo dhātur iti sa evāśrayaparāvṛttirūpaḥ. anāsravo dhātur ity ucyate. nirdauṣṭhulyatvāt sa tv āsravavigata ity anāsravaḥ. āryadharmahetutvād dhātuḥ. hetv artho hy atra dhātuśabdaḥ. acintyas tarkāgocaratvāt pratyātmavedyatvāt. dṛṣṭāntābhāvāc ca. kuśalo viśuddhālambanatvāt kṣematvāt anāsravadharmamayatvāc ca. dhruvo nityatvāt. akṣayatayā. sukho nityatvād eva yad anityaṃ tad duḥkham ayaṃ ca nitya iti. asmāt sukhaḥ. kleśāvaraṇaprahāṇāt śrāvakāṇāṃ vimuktikāyaḥ...

—*Ibid.*, p. 69.14-19

All this is the result of our analytical thinking and interpretation of our experiences which change fundamentally the attitude of those individuals who are engaged in pursuing selfish good only. Thus, an individual transcends himself and works for the welfare of entire humanity. This is the highest karma of man in general.

The Buddhists classify and discuss the types of karma in two ways: (1) *kuśala, akuśala* and *avyākṛta*, and (2) *vijñapti* and *avijñapti*. I have above discussed the former in brief. The latter is discussed in detail by Vasubandhu in his *Abhidharmakośa* and *Karmasiddhiprakaraṇa*. Some modern scholars have taken up this issue including the transformation of *karma* into *phala*, and their types and correlates. A discussion on them goes outside the purview of this study and I need not go into them here.

References

1. *Bhāṣya* on *Triṃśikā* 29 (See A.K. Chatterjee, *Readings on Yogācāra Buddhism*, Banaras Hindu University, 1971, p. 69.3-4).

2. Lambert Schmithausen, *Ālayavijñāna* (On the Origin and the Early Development of a Central Concept of Yogācāra Philosophy), 2 Parts, Tokyo, The International Institute for Buddhist Studies, 1987, p. 6.

3. *Laṅkāvatārasūtra*, ed. P.L. Vaidya, Darbhanga, 1963, p. 64.22.

4. H.V. Guenther (*Philosophy and Psychology in the Abhidharma*, Delhi, Motilal Banarsidass, 1974, p. 41) rightly translates *cetanā* as stimulus, motive and drive.

5. See H.S. Prasad, *The Uttaratantra of Maitreya*, containing Introduction, E.H. Johnston's Sanskrit Text and E. Obermiller's English translation, Delhi, Indian Books Centre, 1991.

7 A CRITICAL APPRAISAL OF KARMA-PHALAPARĪKṢĀ OF NĀGĀRJUNA*

DR. T.R. SHARMA
Reader in Sanskrit, S.G.T.B. Khalsa College, Delhi University, Delhi-110 007

The doctrine of action (*karma*) is pivotal to Indian culture. In all the philosophical systems of India the doctrine of action plays a very important role and in a way it can be said that this doctrine is the very back-bone of Indian philosophy in general. Likewise, in Buddhist philosophy also *karma* occupies an important position. As far as the principle of karmic continuity and fruition in Buddhism is concerned; Thomas L. Dowling says, "The centrality of the principle of karmic continuity and fruition to Indian Buddhism is such that one can easily understand the concern for formulating an intelligible and constant explanation of this principle in the sectarian literature."[1] With regard to the usage of this word it may be said that in the pre-Buddhist literature it was used in the sense of either religious or social functions and the duties of man. The *Īśopaniṣad* (2) uses the word *karma* in the latter sense. This meaning has survived in the Buddhist texts where *karma* is used in plural to denote the various professions or occupations of man. Nāgārjuna in the chapter known as *Karmaphalaparīkṣā* critically examines this doctrine from the Mādhyamika stand point and in the end repudiates the tenability of this doctrine. The object of this paper is to show how Nāgārjuna tries to cross-examine the different schools' viewpoints on the karmic continuity and fruition.

The seventeenth chapter of the *Madhyamakaśāstra* known as *Karmaphalaparīkṣā* is divided into thirtythree *kārikās*. First of all, theories of ancient Buddhism with regard to reality and transmigration, thought acts, cause of *karma*, two kinds of acts, three kinds of acts and seven kinds of acts have been described (*kārikās* 4-5). Then the theories of the Sautrāntikas and the refu-

*This paper was read in the 32nd International Congress of Asian and North African Studies, Hamburg, West Germany, July, 1986.

tation of the theories of the Vijñānavādins have been discussed (*kārikā* 6). Afterwards the theories of the germination of act have been discussed (*kārikās* 7-10) along with ten paths of acts. Then the theories of the *Sammitīyas* and the refutation of the Sautrāntrikas have been given in detail (*kārikās* 10-12). Then the nature of the *dharma* as *avipraṇāśa* (non-perishing) has been discussed (*kārikās* 13-20). After this the Madhyamaka position of *karma*, the non-existence of the sensual acts (*kārikās* 28-30) and the efficacy of non-substantial *karma* (*kārikās* 31-33) have been discussed.

Right in the beginning Nāgārjuna distinguishes between two: the world (*saṁsāra*) and the relation between *karma* and its fruition (*karmaphalasaṁbandha*), then he refers to a position according to which, on account of non-breakage of the continuity (*santāna*), there is a series of birth and death and there is also a cause and effect relation (*hetu-phala-bhāva*).[2] Here a tacit approval is given to the continuity (*santāna*) of the impressions (*saṁskāra*) or the self (*ātman*). Here it appears that the commentator Candrakīrti is referring to the position of the Sammitīya school which believes in the existence of *pudgala*. Subsequently he observes that there is no world (*saṁsāra*); consciousness (*citta*) is also perishable just after its emergence, thus there is a complete absence of the relation between action and its retribution (*karmaphasaṁbandha*).[3] He further observes that if world (*saṁsāra*) is accepted; the retribution of the action should also be accepted. As far as consciousness (*cetaḥ*) is concerned; it is further sub-divided into three categories: (1) self-controlling consciousness (*ātmasamyamakaṃ cetaḥ*); (2) consciousness controlled by another (*parānugrāhakaṃ cetaḥ*); and (3) friendly consciousness (*maitra cetaḥ*).[4] The primary function of a mind is to regulate the good and the bad actions and consciousness (*citta*), mind (*manaḥ*) and *vijñāna* are all synonyms.[5] In this context Guenther remarks, "The importance of the *citta*-attitude—whether it tends to become involved in *saṁsāra* or whether it tends to find its fulfilment and expression in *nirvāṇa*, is the key to Buddhist philosophy and psychology."[6] Actions (*karmas*) are divided into two: (1) volitional (*cetanā*) and (2) acts according to volition (*cetayitvā karma*). Volitional actions (*cetanā*) are those mental deeds that are performed by the mind consciousness. *Cetayitvā* actions are those deeds that are performed according to consciousness (*citta*) and are put into actions by the body and speech. After describing the different types of actions Nāgārjuna[7] raises a question whether actions continue to exist up to their retribution or not. If the former, then we have to accept them as eternal. In other words we might say that if actions are destroyed just after their birth; then they are not in a position to produce their retribution on account of non-existence of their self-being (*svabhāva*) of their own.[8] To justify his argument Nāgārjuna gives another example to make his position clear. According to him there are three things: (1) seed (*bīja*); (2) sprout (*aṅkura*) and (3) the conducive elements for the seed. The seed is a series of moments (*santāna*). The seed itself is momentary but it has the capacity to produce the sprout if it is accompanied by the conducive elements. As far as the *bīja* theory is concerned, it may be said that Vasubandhu's *Abhidharmakośabhāṣya* and the *Sphutārtha Abhidharmakośavyākhyā* of Yaśomitra contain several references to the theory of *bīja*. To this *bīja* theory Nāgārjuna has added a new dimension of sprout (*aṅkura*) in order to make his point more explicit. According to the *Abhidharmakośa* *bīja* is a *nāma-rūpa*, i.e. either the complex of five *skandhas* capable of producing a fruit, either immediately or mediately by means of a *pariṇāma-viśeṣa* of the *santati*.[9] As a matter of fact the Sautrāntikas developed this *bīja* theory in their own way. The Vaibhāṣika school raised all sorts of objections against this *bīja* theory and they (Vaibhāṣikas) developed *dharmas* known as possession (*prāpti*) and non-possesion (*aprāpti*). It appears that the theory of *bīja* was employed by the Sautrāntikas primarily to replace the Vaibhāṣika *dharma* called *prāpti* in explaining the phenomenon of immediate succession (*samanatarotpāda*) between the two consciousness (cittas) of heterogenous nature, and secondarily to reconcile the abiding nature of the *santati* (continuity) with the momentary flashes of *dharma*. According to Edward Conze[10] possession (*prāpti*) is not a separate *dharma* but a state (*avasthā*) capable of producing such and such effect. Thus seed (*bīja*) itself is the cause of sprout, but the seed is not able to produce the fruit due to some opposite factors like fire etc. and it is destroyed before giving rise to sprout. In this way we have to accept the extinction of the seed. And if the seed is not destroyed and is able to produce the sprout in the form of continuity (*santāna*), then we have to accept the continuity of the seed. But we find that both exist in the seed.[11] Nāgārjuna applies the same reductio ad absurdum argument to the *karma* theory and proves the impossibility of the *karma*, its series and retribution.

Thus as in the model of *bīja* theory where there is neither extinction of the *bīja* nor the continuity (*santāna*) of it; similarly in the consciousness also there is no extinction of action (*karma*) and its continuity also is not there. According to P.S. Jaini this power of producing a new consciousness (*citta*) is what is called a *bīja*. It is an independent entity but only a nominal thing (*prajñā-mātra*).[12] Before going further into the details of the working of consciousness (*citta*) and seed (*bīja*) and their bearing upon the object (*phala*); it is of some interest to consider the whole situation from the points of matter and mind. As far as matter is concerned; we can have its perceptual view and its conceptual view. When we are talking of *bīja* theory, it means we are having first its perceptual view, in so far as the material seed (*bīja*) is concerned; along with its perceptual view we are also having the conceptual view in so far as our mind is concerned. In other words we may say that matter and mind have two fields of their own. As far as the Buddhist philosophical schools are concerned; for almost all of them the latter is of utmost importance. In this connection the observations of Guenther are worth noticing: "The importance of *citta*-attitude—whether it tends to become involved in *saṁsāra* or whether it tends to find its fulfilment and expression in *nirvāṇa*, is the key to Buddhist philosophy and psychology. Although the various schools of thought in Buddhism wrangled about the logical nature of the substantive *citta*, whether it is existent or substituent, none of them ever challenged the primacy of *citta*."[13] Thus we see that this power of producing a new consciousness (*citta*) is what we call a *bīja*. It is not an independent entity but only a nominal thing. So when the Sautrāntikas advocated the *bīja* theory, the purpose of this theory was to reconcile the abiding nature of the *santati* (continuity) with the momentary flashes of *dharmas*. According to Edward Conze[14] a seed is defined as the psychophysical organism or the complex of the five *skandhas*, in so far as it is capable of producing a fruit, either mediately or immediately, by the culmination of the evolution of the mental continuity.

Nāgārjuna, once having established a parallelism between

consciousness (*citta*) and the seed (*bīja*), tries to show that neither are tenable as far as the extinction (*uccheda*) and continuity (*śāśvata*) are concerned. In order to avoid this paradox the opponent introduces a new concept of *avipraṇāśa* (non-perishing) which is always associated with *karma* (action).[15] He says that *avipraṇāśa* is like a *ṛṇapattra* (signed note for the loan) and the *karma* is like a *ṛṇa* (loan). This *avipraṇāśa* (non-perishing nature of *karma*) is not necessarily destroyed even when the retribution gets its maturity. At this juncture Nāgārjuna tries to bring in the concept of *śūnyatā* in the domain of *karmaphala*. He says that there is *śūnyatā*, there is no extinction, there is no continuity and there is no world also. The action (*karma*) has *avipraṇāśa* (non-perishing) as its characteristic and this has been taught by the Buddha.[16] On this Candrakīrti comments: "Because an action done is obstructed, it does not exist by virtue of its self-being (*svabhāva*); thus on account of non-existence of self-being (*svabhāva*) of *karma*, *śūnyatā* occurs. And due to non-existence of *karma* there is no possibility of extinction of *karma* even, and due to the non-perishing nature of *karma*, there is fruition of *karma*. In the case of absence of fruition of *karma*, there arises the extinction of *karma*."[17] Here Nāgārjuna again says that according to his standpoint only *kalpanā* is justified. He further says: "If the *karma* is born in its form, due to its existence up to the time of its fruit, it becomes eternal (*nitya*); and due to its destruction its extinction is also there. When the *karma* is not born due to its nature being that of *śūnyatā*, then there is its existence, wherever is its destruction."[18] Following his famous method of dialectics Nāgārjuna seems to refute the existence and destruction or the non-existence of *karma*. Then he finally says that *karma* is not born because of its having no self-being (*svabhāva*) of its own; because it is not born, therefore, it is not destroyed.[19] Moreover he proposes that if the *karma* has any nature of its own, then it becomes definitely eternal; if the *karma* is *akṛta* (non-done), then no eternal *karma* is performed by anybody.[20] On this Candrakīrti comments that the action done by the doer, and accepted in the grammatical sense of the term (doer being independent), is not to be accepted as such; because the action is performed by anybody; this is not eternal. An eternal action is not done. An eternal thing is that whose existence is accepted as such.[21] After this Nāgārjuna tries to link *karma* with *kleśa* and says that if *karma* has any connection with *kleśa*, we say that *kleśas* also do not exist in principle. When the *kleśas* do not exist, where there can be (any existence) of *karma*.[22] Nāgārjuna also discusses whether there can be any doer and enjoyer of fruits of some action. He says that the *karma* is not born out of any cause (*pratyaya*); nor it is unborn out of any cause. Since the *karma* itself does not exist, the doer also does not exist in principle. When the doer is not there, the *karma* is also not there, how can there be any fruit born out of such a *karma*.[23] Candrakīrti expresses almost a similar opinion upon it.[24]

In order to fully comprehend the concept of *karma* (action) *phala* (fruit) and its *sambandha* (relation) it would not be out of place to refer to the *Gatāgataparīkṣā* (Motion and Rest) chapter of Nāgārjuna. When we contemplate any *karma* (action), it is always in relation to motion (*gati*). In other words we might say that any action always entails some motion. When we perceive any action in terms of motion, we also perceive some mover (*gantṛ*) and the space traversed (*gantavya*). Nāgārjuna in the *Gatāgataparīkṣā* says that if the movement itself were the very mover, it would follow that doer and the deed were one thing.[25] Here Nāgārjuna means to say that mover (*gantṛ*), *gamana* (movement) are totally different entities. He denies the existence of a mover, non-existence of a mover and both existence and non-existence of a mover.[26] Therefore, he finally declares (as I translate), "There is no motion, no moving and no space traversed."[27] Here also the commentator Candrakīrti says that if the seed itself passes over into the sprout, the sprout would be the seed and not the sprout, which entails the fallacy of eternalism. If the sprout arises from something other than the seed, that would entail the fallacy of causelessness. But nothing can arise uncaused, for example the horns of a donkey.[28] Following this example of seed and sprout it can be concluded that *karma* (action) and *phala* (fruit) are the two distinct entities and there is no relation between the two. If the *karma* (action) itself passes into *phala* (fruit), the *phala* (fruit) would be *karma* (action) and not the *phala* (fruit).

The preceding analysis shows that according to Nāgārjuna, *karmaphala* and its relation are not possible. All these are mere concepts and since concepts are always subjective, they are bound to lead us to conflicting descriptions of facts or a reality.

So all concepts or views are called *śūnyatā* by Nāgārjuna (*sarva-dṛṣṭiśūnyatā*).

References

1. Thomas L. Dowling, Karma and Sectarian Development; in *Studies in Pali and Buddhism*, p. 81, Delhi, 1979, ed. by A. K. Narain.
2. Iha santānavicchedakrameṇa janmamaraṇaparamparayā hetuphala-bhāvapravṛtyā saṁskārāṇāmātmano vā saṅsaraṇaṃ syāt, syāttadānim karma-phalasaṁbandhaḥ. Candrakīrti, *Prasannapadā* on Karmaphalaparīkṣā, Varanasi, p. 131, 1983.
3. Yathāvarṇite saṁsārābhave tu utpatyanantaravināśitvāc cittasya karmā-kṣepakāle ca vipākasyāsadbhavāt karmaphalasaṁbandhabhāva eva syāt. *Ibid.*, p. 131.
4. Ātmasamyamakaṃ cetaḥ parānugrahakaṃ ca yat/
Maitraṃ sa dharmas tadbījaṃ phalasya pretya ceha ca//
—*Madhyamakaśāstra*, 17.1 p. 131
5. Cinoti upacinoti śubhāśubhaṃ karma vipākadānasāmarthye niyamayatīti cetaḥ. Cittam manaḥ vijñānaṃ iti tasyaiva paryāyāḥ. Ibid. p. 131.
6. Herbert Guenther, *Philosophy and Psychology of Abhidhamma* p. 15, Delhi, 1957.
7. *Madhyamakaśāstra*, 17.6, p. 133.
8. Atha utpādānantravināśitvaṃ eva karmāṇāṃ abhyupetaṃ, nanu evaṃ sati, abhāvivhūtaṃ sat karma....avidyānasvabhāvatvāt naiva phalaṃ janayiṣyatity abhiprāyaḥ. Candrakīrti on Ibid. pp. 133-34.
9. Kiṃ punar idaṃ bīja nāma? Yan nāmarūpaṃ phalotpatau samarthaṃ sākṣāt pāramparyeṇa vā, santatipariṇāmaviseṣāt. Bhāṣyasphutārtha on *Abhidharmakośa* 2.36 p. 217, Varanasi, 1971 ed. D.D. Sastri.
10. Edward Conze, *Buddhist Thoughts in India*, p. 142, The University of Michigan Press, 1982.
11. Yo'ankuraprabhṛtir bījāt santāno' bhipravartate/
Tataḥ phalaṃ ṛte bījāt sa ca nābhipravartate//
Bījāc ca yasmāt santānaḥ santanāc ca phalodgamaḥ/
Bījapurvaṃ phalaṃ tasmānnocchinnaṃ nāpi śāsvataṃ//
—*Madhyamakaśāstra*, 17-7.8 p. 134
12. Jaini, P.S., 'The Sautrāntika Theory of Bīja', *Bulletin of the School of Oriental and African Studies*, Vol. 21, pt. I, p. 244.
13. Herbert V. Guenther, *Philosophy and Psychology in Abhidhamma*, p. 15.
14. Edward Conze, *Buddhist Thought in India*, p. 142.
15. Patraṃ yathāvipraṇāśas tatharṇim iva karma ca.
—*Madhyamakaśāstra*, 17.14 p. 136
16. Śūnyatā ca na cocchedaḥ saṁsāra ca na śāśvataṃ/
Karmaṇo' vipraṇās ca dharmo buddhena deśitaḥ//
—Ibid. 17.20 p. 118
17. Yasmāt karma kṛtam sat nirudhyate, na svabhāvena tiṣṭhate, tasmāt

karmaṇaḥ svabhāvenāvasthanāt śūnyatā copapadyate. Na caivaṃ karmaṇānavasthānad ucchedadarśanaprasangaḥ, avipraṇāśaparigraheṇa karmavipākasadbhāvāt. Vipākabhāve hi karmaṇaḥ ucchedadarśanaṃ syāt.

—Candrakīrti on Ibid. p. 138

18. Yadi hi karmaṇaḥ svarūpeṇotpādaḥ syat, tasya avipākaṃ avasthānānnityatvaṃ syāt vināśocchedaḥ syāt. Yadu tu karma naivotpadyate svabhāvaśūnyatvāt tadā tasya kuto' vasthānaṃ vināśo vā. Ibid. p. 138.

19. Karma notpadyate kasmāt niḥsvabhāvaṃ yatas tataḥ/
Yasmāc ca tadanutpannaṃ na tasmāt vipraṇaśyati//

—*Madhyamakaśāstra* 17.21 pp. 138-39

20. Karma svabhāvataś ceta syāc chāśāśvataṃ syād asaṁśayaṃ/
Akṛtaṃ ca bhavet karma kriyate na hi śāśvataṃ//

—Ibid. 17.22 p. 139

21. Kartuḥ svatantrasya kriyayā yadīpsitatamaṃ tatkarma. etac ca na yujyate. Kiṃ kāraṇaṃ ? Yasmāt kriyate na hi śāśvataṃ. Śāśvataṃ hi nāma tad yadvidyamānasattākaṃ.—

Candrakīrti on *Madhyamakaśāstra* 17.22 p. 139

22. Karma kleśātmakaṃ cedaṃ te ca kleśa na tatvataḥ/
Na cete tatvataḥ kleśāḥ karma syāt tatvataḥ kathaṃ//

—*Madhyamakaśāstra* 17.26 p. 140

23. Ibid. 17.29-30 p. 141.

24. Yataś caivaṃ pratyayasamutpanna vā apratyayasamutpanna vā karmedaṃ na saṁbhavati. Tasmād asya karmaṇaḥ kartāpi na saṁbhavati/ Yadā caivaṃ karma ca kartā ca nāsti tadā nirhetukaṃ karmajaṃ phalaṃ kuto bhaviṣyatīti.

—Candrakīrti on Ibid., p. 141

25. Yadeva gamanaṃ gantā sa eva hi bhaved yadi/
Ekibhāvaḥ prasajyeta kartuḥ karmaṇaḥ eva ca//

—*Madhyamakaśāstra* 2.19 p. 41

26. Ibid. 2.24-25 pp. 42-43.

27. Tasmāt gatiś ca gantā ca gantavyaṃ ca na vidyate. Ibid. p. 43.

28. Yadi bījaṃ evāṅkure saṅkramati, bījaṃ eva tat syān na yadankuraḥ, śāśvatadoṣaprasangaśca. Athānkuro' nyata āgacchati, ahetukadoṣaprasangaḥ. syāt. Na cāhetukasyotpattiḥ kharaviṣaṇāsyeva.

—Candrakīrti on Ibid., p. 43

8 THE RELATIONSHIP BETWEEN *PAṬICCASAMUPPĀDA* AND *DHĀTU*

AKIRA HIRAKAWA
Professor Emeritus, Tokyo University

1. *Varieties of Dhātu*

Dhātu has been used as a technical term from the earliest period of Buddhism onward. In the āgamas, the three doctrines of the five aggregates (*pañca khandhā*), the twelve sense spheres (*dvādasāyatanāni*), and the eighteen *dhātus* (*aṭṭhādasadhātuyo*) are taken as fundamental and as the basis for the exposition of various other doctrines, and therefore, are all clearly significant for early Buddhism.

The āgamas list these eighteen *dhātus* as follows: the *dhātu* of the eye (*cakkhudhātu*), visual material form (*rūpadhātu*), visual perceptual consciousness (*cakkhuviññāṇadhātu*), the ear (*sotadhātu*), sound (*saddhadhātu*), auditory perceptual consciousness (*sotaviññāṇadhātu*), the nose (*ghānadhātu*), odors (*gandhadhātu*), olfactory perceptual consciousness (*ghānaviññāṇadhātu*), the tongue (*jivhādhātu*), tastes (*rasadhātu*), gustatory perceptual consciousness (*jivhāviññāṇadhātu*), the body (*kāyadhātu*), tangibles (*poṭṭhabhadhātu*), perceptual consciousness of tangibles (*kāyaviññāṇadhātu*), the mind (*manodhātu*), mental factors (*dhammadhātu*), and the *dhātu* of mental perceptual consciousness (*manoviññāṇadhātu*).[1] These eighteen *dhātus* are mentioned at appropriate places in the āgamas, but virtually without conflicting views concerning their content and their order of presentation. This suggests that the teaching of these eighteen *dhātus* had been established early in the initial period of Buddhism. Moreover, the āgamas list these eighteen *dhātus* without further explaining their meaning, and in particular, without specifying the meaning of *dhātu* itself. Probably the meaning of *dhātu* was still clear in that period and required no special explanation. But now, for precisely that reason, it has become unclear how the initial period of Buddhism understood the term *dhātu*.

Though the āgamas do not explain the term *dhātu* itself, they do contain, in addition to the eighteen, many teachings involving *dhātus*. In particular, collected in the *Dhātusaṃyutta* of the *Saṃyuttanikāya* (14) are thirty-nine *suttas* relating to *dhātus* and giving various teachings involving *dhātu*.[2] In these there is a discussion of twenty-one types of *dhātu*: a group of seven *dhātus* including light (*ābhādhātu*), purity (*subhadhātu*), the sphere of space (*ākāsānañcāyatanadhātu*), the sphere of perceptual consciousness (*viññāṇānañcāyatanadhātu*), the sphere of nothing at all (*ākiñcaññāyatanadhātu*), the sphere of neither conception nor non-conception (*nevasaññānāsaññāyatanadhātu*), and the sphere of the cessation of conception and feelings (*saññāvedayitanirodhadhātu*),[3] a group of six *dhātus* including desire (*kāmadhātu*), ill-will (*vyāpādadhātu*), injury (*vihiṃsādhātu*), renunciation (*nekkhammadhātu*), absence of ill-will (*avyāpādadhātu*), and non-injury (*avihimsādhātu*),[4] a group of four *dhātus* including ignorance (*avijjādhātu*), the lowly (*hīnadhātu*), the mediocre (*majjhimadhātu*), and the elevated (*paṇītadhātu*),[5] and another group of four *dhātus* including earth (*paṭhavīdhātu*), water (*āpodhātu*), fire (*tejodhātu*), and wind (*vāyodhātu*).[6] Since a number of explanations are given of these types of *dhātu*, we are furnished with some clues for inferring the meaning of *dhātu* in these teachings.

In addition, the *Bahudhātukasutta* of the *Majjhimanikāya* (115) discusses various types of *dhātu*, beginning with the eighteen *dhātus* listed previously.[7] There, altogether, forty-one types of *dhātus* are discussed. In addition to the eighteen types of *dhātus* beginning with the *dhātus* of the eye (*cakkhudhātu*), visual material form (*rūpadhātu*), and visual perceptual consciousness (*cakkhuviññāṇadhātu*), these forty-one types include: the six *dhātus* of earth (*paṭhavīdhātu*), water (*āpodhātu*), wind (*vāyodhātu*), fire (*tejodhātu*), space (*ākāsadhātu*), and perceptual consciousness (*viññāṇadhātu*); the six *dhātus* of happiness (*sukhadhātu*), suffering (*dukkhadhātu*), joy (*somanassadhātu*), dejection (*domanassadhātu*), equanimity (*upekhādhātu*), and ignorance (*avijjādhātu*); the six *dhātus* of desire (*kāmadhātu*), renunciation (*nekkhammadhātu*), ill-will (*vyāpādadhātu*), absence of ill-will (*avyāpādadhātu*), injury (*vihesādhātu*), and non-injury (*avihesādhātu*); the three *dhātus* of desire (*kāmadhātu*), form (*rūpadhātu*), and the formless (*arūpadhātu*); and the two *dhātus* of constructed (*saṃkhatadhātu*) and unconstructed (*asaṃkhatadhātu*).[8] A *sūtra*[9] within the Chinese translation of the *Madhyamāgama* (47), the *Bahudhātukasūtra*.[10] which corresponds to the *Bahudhātukasutta*, gives a total of 62 types of *dhātu*. Suggesting various meanings for the term *dhātu*, these types include: the four *dhātus* of feelings (*vedanādhātu*), conception (*saṃjñādhātu*), formations (*saṃskāra-dhātu*), and perceptual consciousness (*vijñānadhātu*), the three *dhātus* of form (*rūpadhātu*), the formless (*ārūpyadhātu*), and cessation (*nirodhadhātu*); the three *dhātus* of the past (*atītadhātu*), the future (*anāgatadhātu*), and the present (*pratyutpannadhātu*); the three *dhātus* of the elevated (*praṇītadhātu*), the non-elevated (*apraṇītadhātu*), and the mediocre (*madhyamadhātu*); the three *dhātus* of the virtuous (*kuśaladhātu*), the unvirtuous (*akuśala-dhātu*), and the indeterminate (*avyākṛtadhātu*); the three *dhātus* of being in training (*śaikṣadhātu*), being beyond training (*aśaikṣa-dhātu*), and being neither in nor beyond training (*naivaśaikṣānāśai-kṣadhātu*); and the two *dhātus* of tending toward the fluxes (*sāsravadhātu*) and not tending toward the fluxes (*anāsrava-dhātu*).[11] In addition to these types, the āgamas also refer to *dhammadhātu*,[12] *nibbānadhātu*,[13] *lokadhātu*,[14] and so on. Although numerous types of *dhātu* are mentioned, the meaning of *dhātu* itself is not specified, and thus it is difficult to settle on a single meaning that would be common to all these specific cases.

In the *Visuddhimagga* (15), Buddhaghosa includes a section, the 'Exposition of *Dhātu*',[15] where he collects all the varieties of *dhātu* mentioned in the āgamas and enumerates thirty-five types. He next specifies to which of the eighteen *dhātus* of the eye, and so on, these thirty-five types of *dhātu* belong. Therefore, Buddha-ghosa sees the set of eighteen *dhātus* as the basis of all varieties of *dhātus*.

2. *Paṭiccasamuppāda as Dhātu*

Throughout the āgamas we find many teachings on dependent origination (*paṭiccasamuppāda*). Among these, the most impor-tant is considered to be the doctrine of dependent origination in twelve members (*dvādasaṅgapaṭiccasamuppāda*). And among those teachings that discuss dependent origination in twelve members, one teaching presented in the *Paccayasutta* of the *Saṃyuttani-kāya* (12.20)[16] declares dependent origination (*paṭiccasamuppāda*) to be *dhātu*. Dependent origination, this text states, is identical with *dhātu*:

Oh monks, what is dependent origination (*paṭiccasamuppāda*)?

> Oh monks, there is old age and death (*jarāmaraṇam*) in dependence upon the condition of birth (*jātipaccayā*). Whether Tathāgatas appear [in the world], or do not appear, this *dhātu* is established. It is established as *dhamma*. It is fixed as *dhamma*. [That is to say, it is] the state of taking 'this' as its condition (*idappaccayatā*).[17]

This passage presents dependent origination as that in which 'there is old age and death [aging and dying] in dependence upon the condition of birth [being born]'. In this case, birth is the condition (*paccaya*), and old age and death are what has been produced (*uppāda*). That is to say, this passage suggests that dependent origination is established in the relation between birth (or being born) and old age and death (or aging and dying). This dependent origination is then referred to equivalently as 'this *dhātu*'. The passage also claims that *dhātu* as dependent origination is established as truth (*dhamma*) whether or not Tathāgatas appear in the world.

Here, in the relation of dependent origination (*paṭiccasamuppāda*) the condition (*paccaya*) is more significant than that which has been produced (*uppāda*). What has been produced (*uppāda*) is the result and is a distinct existent (*bhāva*). This result is referred to as a *dhamma*: specifically, that *dhamma* that is produced in dependence upon conditions or *paṭiccasamuppannadhamma*. However, unlike the single resultant *dhamma* that it establishes, the condition is not singular, but multiple. Moreover, since the world is impermanent, even the resultant '*dhamma*' itself must constantly change. Now in this impermanent world, while a *dhamma* is said to be that which maintains (*dharati*) the same state, precisely because the existence of the world is impermanent, that *dhamma* does not have a fixed existence. A *dhamma* is that which can be recognized as an 'existent' in the midst of a manner of existing that is constantly changing. This recognition is possible because *dhammas* are endowed with a common character.[18] In this case in particular, a *dhamma* is called a 'dependently originated *dhamma*' (*paṭiccasamuppanno dhammo*) because it is the *dhamma* that is constructed through dependent origination.[19]

Although the previous teaching of dependent origination states that 'there is old age and death [aging and dying] in dependence upon the condition of birth [being born]', it is not the case that old age and death occur with birth alone as their condition. If old age and death occurred through birth alone, old age and death should occur immediately after birth. Since that is not the case, 'old age' occurs when many other conditions in addition to birth are assembled, and 'death' arises when yet other conditions join in. In this way, though the assembling of numerous conditions is necessary for old age and death, because 'being born' is the most significant among these conditions, it is picked out in particular and specified as the condition.

The 'condition' has the power to give rise to a *dhamma*, which is the effect, and in this case, birth is the condition whose power results in old age and death. Of course, it is not the case that 'being born' alone has this power; only one part of this power to give rise to an effect resides within birth. However, because that power of birth, if combined with other conditions, necessarily gives rise to both old age and death, it has regularity. We can understand the reference to *dhātu* in the previous *sutta* passage as making this point that 'there is regularity' in the efficacy of conditions. The third fascicle of the **Vijñaptimātratā-siddhiśāstra* gives the following explanation of *dhātu*: '*dhātu* has the meaning of cause'.[20] Now we see points of agreement between this explanation of *dhātu* and that presented in the previously cited *sutta* passage: namely, that a condition has 'the power to give rise to an effect'. *Dhātu* is then used in reference to 'this power, which is endowed with regularity'.

The conditioning relationship indicated in the previously cited statement, 'there is old age and death in dependence upon the condition of birth', is the final member (*aṅga*) of the teaching of dependent origination in twelve members. According to this teaching, after discovering birth as the condition for old age and death, one inquires into the condition in dependence upon which birth arises. And pursuing this condition through which birth occurs, one concludes that action (*karman*) from the previous lifetime becomes the condition for being born in this world. Observing that action in the previous lifetime is different for each person, one concludes that it is for this reason that each person has a different birth in this world. This action of the previous lifetime is called 'existence' (*bhava*), and this 'existence' is 'existence as action'. This passage next states that 'there is birth in dependence upon existence' (*bhavapaccayā jati*). However, birth in this world does not occur solely through action of the previous lifetime. In order to be born in this world, first both a father and mother must act as conditions. Then, besides them, many other conditions are required including food and air, and further, shelter and a country as a place of birth. Nonetheless, assuming that within the life of one person the most important condition for birth in this world is action of the previous lifetime, it is said that 'there is birth in dependence upon existence'.

Next, one discovers in the teaching of dependent origination in twelve members, that 'grasping' (*upādāna*) is the condition for the occurrence of 'existence', that 'craving' (*taṇhā*) is the condition for 'grasping', and so on, in order, 'feelings' (*vedanā*), 'contact' (*phassa*), the 'six sense spheres' (*saḷāyatana*), 'name and form' (*nāmarūpa*), 'perceptual consciousness' (*viññāṇa*), 'formations' (*saṃkhāra*), and 'ignorance' (*avijjā*). Here, the term *saṃkhāra* is the same as *saṃkhāra* in the phrase 'all *saṃkhāras* are impermanent', and refers to the 'power of forming' or constructing. The relationship between ignorance and formations is described as follows:

> Oh monks, there are formations in dependence upon ignorance (*avijjāpaccayā saṃkhārā*). Whether Tathāgatas appear [in the world], or do not appear, this *dhātu* is established. It is established as *dhamma*. It is fixed as *dhamma*. [That is to say, it is] the state of taking 'this' as its condition (*idappaccayatā*).[21]
>
> And then, following this:
>
> Oh monks, there are formations (*saṃkhārā*) in dependence upon ignorance. Here, that which is endowed with the nature of truth (*tathatā*), with a nature that is not false (*avitathatā*), with a nature that is without change (*anañña-thatā*), with the state of taking 'this' as its condition (*idappaccayatā*), that, Oh monks, is referred to as dependent origination (*paṭiccasamuppāda*).[22]

This passage suggests that the conditioning relationship, 'there are formations in dependence upon ignorance', is dependent origination. Moreover, it declares that this dependent origination is endowed with the nature of truth (*tathatā*). That is to say, this nature of truth inherent in dependent origination is understood to reside in both sides of the relationship between the formations that arise in dependence and ignorance that is the condition. This nature of truth is not only in the relationship between ignorance and formations; it also resides in the relationship between perceptual consciousness that arises with formations as its condition, between perceptual consciousness and name and form, and so on throughout the list of twelve members, concluding with the relationship between birth and old age and death.

However, even though it is said that 'there are formations in dependence upon ignorance', these formations are not produced with ignorance alone as their condition, but rather are produced when many conditions in addition to ignorance are assembled. Since ignorance is a type of defilement, it exists within the mind and operates together with other psychological operations. Moreover, when the mind exists, the body also exists. Consequently, as soon as these various conditions assemble and operate and their powers fuse into one, the effect, 'formations', is produced. Therefore, formations, though the composite of all these causes, when compared with 'each individual cause', are not the same as any one of them. Furthermore, since this 'composite of conditions' is in the state of being the cause and 'formations' are in the state of being the effect, the two cannot directly be said to be identical.

Since formations in the phrase 'there are formations in dependence upon ignorance' are *dhammas* produced through the assembly of the various conditions of ignorance, and so on, they are called 'dependently originated *dhammas*' (*paṭiccasamuppanno dhammo*).[23] However, in this discussion of dependent origination, even ignorance, and so on, which have become conditions, are also *dhammas*: namely, *dhammas* that have been produced in dependence upon other conditions. Therefore, a *dhamma* does not become a condition as one *dhamma* alone, but produces its power as a condition and gives rise to a new *dhamma* through its combination with many other *dhammas*. As soon as many *dhammas* assemble, this 'power of the condition' arises, and this power is then given the name '*dhātu*'. When *dhammas* assemble and become conditions, they become *dhātus*; the term *dhātu* refers to the 'power of becoming a cause and producing another *dhamma*'. As noted in the previously cited passage, this *dhātu* is endowed with *tathatā, avitathatā, anaññathatā* and *idappaccayatā*. This means that when ignorance becomes a condition in combination with other specified *dhammas*, they will necessarily produce 'formations' and not some other *dhamma*; this relationship is established and manifests regularity.

Since formations are produced as soon as the conditions of ignorance, and so on, assemble, these conditions of ignorance, and so on, and formations that are their result, can be said to be 'connected'. However, precisely for that reason, one cannot say that the 'composite of the conditions' of ignorance, and so on, and 'formations', are identical. For there is as yet no operation of formations in the composite of these conditions. Only with the emergence of the *dhamma* called formations is this power of formations exhibited for the first time. Consequently, it must be said that there is a 'break' between the conditions of ignorance, and so on, and formations as their effect. For example, children are born from their two parents, and yet the parents and children have a separate existence.

In this way, it is explained that the relationship between the various *dhammas* that are conditions and the *dhamma* that is the effect cannot be said to be one either of continuity or of rupture.[24] The changes in the phenomenal world occur through this relation between the condition and effect and, for that reason, it is said that 'all formations are impermanent' (*sabbe saṃkhārā aniccā*).

3. *Paṭiccasamuppāda and Paṭiccasamuppannadhamma*

According to the teaching of dependent origination (*paṭicca-samuppāda*), that which will become the condition is said to be the '*dhamma*', but when the *dhamma* exhibits its power as a condition, it is called '*dhātu*'. That is to say, the 'condition' is precisely the *dhātu*, but that which is the '*dhamma*' is not said to be *dhātu*. In other words, the *dhamma* that is produced in dependence upon conditions is referred to as *paṭiccasamuppanno dhammo* and this 'dependently originated *dhamma*' is said to be a *dhamma*, but not *dhātu*. In the previously cited *sutta* from the *Saṃyuttanikāya* (12.20), it is said:

> Oh monks, What are dependently originated *dhammas* (*paṭiccasamuppannā dhammā*)? Oh monks, old age and death (*jarāmaraṇa*) are impermanent, are constructed (*saṃkhata*), are produced in dependence upon conditions, are destroyed (*khayadhamma*), are perishing (*vayadhamma*), are separated from passion (*virāgadhamma*), and are extinguished (*nirodhadhamma*).[25]

Here, the term *dhātu* does not appear. Further, regarding the 'dependently originated *dhamma*', the same statements used here with regard to 'old age and death' are applied to the other members of 'birth' (*jāti*), 'existence' (*bhava*), 'grasping' (*upādāna*), 'craving' (*taṇhā*), 'feelings' (*vedanā*), 'contact' (*phassa*), the 'six sense spheres' (*saḷāyatana*), 'name and form' (*nāmarūpa*), 'perceptual consciousness' (*viññāṇa*), and 'formations' (*saṃkhāra*). About the last member, 'ignorance' (*avijjā*), it is said:

> Oh monks, ignorance is impermanent, is constructed, is dependently originated, is destroyed, is perishing, is separated from passion (*virāgadhamma*), and is extinguished. Oh monks, these are said to be *dhammas* that are produced in dependence upon conditions.[26]

That is to say, 'being born' is the 'condition' for 'aging and dying', and 'aging and dying' are 'dependently originated *dhammas*'; specifically, they depend upon the condition of 'being born'. In the same way, 'being born' is a 'dependently originated *dhamma*' from the perspective of the prior member, 'existence', and 'existence' is its condition. Consequently, 'being born' is both the 'condition' and the *dhātu* for 'aging and dying'. However, from the perspective of 'existence', it is nothing more than a 'dependently originated *dhamma*', and not, in that phase, a *dhātu*.

When a *dhamma* is isolated and does not cooperate with other *dhammas*, it is nothing more than a 'dependently originated *dhamma*'. The power with which that *dhamma* is endowed is not yet exhibited. For example, in the case of the phrase 'there is birth in dependence upon the condition of existence', this 'being born' is a '*dhamma*' produced in dependence upon various conditions, but because it has not yet become a 'condition' that produces another *dhamma*, it is not a '*dhātu*'. When this 'being born' cooperates with various other *dhammas* and serves as the condition that produces 'aging and dying', it then becomes a '*dhātu*'. '*Dhātu*' in this case means the 'power to produce' another *dhamma*.

According to the teaching of dependent origination in twelve members, since 'aging and dying' is the final member among the twelve, it is only understood as 'a dependently originated *dhamma*'. For the teaching of dependent origination in twelve members acknowledges the fact that actual human existence is suffering and this 'existence as suffering' is specified as 'aging and dying'. Then, this suffering is taken as the starting point for inquiring into dependent origination. Therefore, pursuing the condition by which 'aging and dying' originate, one discovers 'being born'. Since discovering the origin of suffering is the point of this inquiry, one does not consider here that aging and dying are the condition for the arising of another *dhamma*. Although aging and dying can indeed become the condition for the arising of another *dhamma*, its efficacy as a condition is simply not included within the principle of dependent origination in twelve members.

In the same way, though it is said that ignorance becomes the condition for the arising of formations (*saṃkhāra*), the condition through which ignorance itself arises is not specified here. However, as noted previously, ignorance also is impermanent, constructed, and a dependently originated *dhamma*.[27] Ignorance is mental delusion and a *dhamma* that is difficult to extinguish. However, because ignorance is also produced through dependent origination and is impermanent, it is a *dhamma* that can be extinguished. Specifically, ignorance can be extinguished by knowing completely its fundamental nature. We are deluded by ignorance precisely because we are not aware of it. Precisely those are deceived who are not aware that they are deceived, and for that reason, cannot escape deception. However, if one becomes aware of being deceived, one can at once escape deception. Similarly, those who are sleeping are not aware that they are sleeping, but if they become aware that they are sleeping, they have already escaped sleep.

Ignorance is the same. Ordinary people are deluded by ignorance precisely because they do not know its true nature. So once they gain insight into the true nature of ignorance, it disappears and they escape its shackles. According to the teaching of dependent origination in twelve members, to pursue the condition by which formations (*saṃkhāra*) are produced and to discover ignorance is to become aware of one's delusion, previously unrecognized; precisely this is attaining 'clear sight' (*vijjā*), meaning that one has acquired correct insight. Consequently, the teaching of dependent origination in twelve members suggests that one pursues the condition underlying the arising of suffering in human life and discovers that the fundamental condition is ignorance. Furthermore, since ignorance is 'something that disappears upon being discovered', the pursuit of the conditions within the teaching of dependent origination in twelve members ends with this ignorance.

In this way, viewed from the perspective of the formations, ignorance is the cause and the *dhātu*, but from the opposite perspective, ignorance is only a dependently originated *dhamma*. Consequently, in Buddhism, the meaning of '*dhātu*' should be understood in relation to the idea of dependent origination.

The previously cited *sutta* passage, *Saṃyuttanikāya* (12.20), which explains 'dependent origination' (*paṭiccasamuppāda*) and 'dependently originated *dhammas*' (*paṭiccasamuppanno dhammo*), was considered very important within the Buddhist tradition. When Buddhaghosa explains dependent origination in the *Visuddhimagga* (17), he bases his explanation on this *sutta* passage,[28] thereby suggesting that he considered it the most significant in the collection of *suttas* that discuss dependent origination. A *sūtra* corresponding to this Pāli *sutta* in the *Saṃyuttanikāya* (12.20) is also found in the Chinese translation, the *Tsa-a-han ching* (fasc. 13), of the *Saṃyuktāgama*.[29] Furthermore, among the twenty-five *sūtras* of the *Nidānasaṃyukta* found among the Sanskrit fragments of the *Saṃyuktāgama* discovered in Central Asia and published by Tripāṭhī, two *sūtras* (*sūtra* 14 *Pratītya*; *sūtra* 17 *Bhikṣu*) in this same way identify dependent origination with *dhātu*.[30] Thus, these texts, preserved in both the northern and southern traditions, are indispensable for understanding the early Buddhist teaching of dependent origination in twelve members.

4. *Remaining Issues*

In the previous section we examined certain *suttas* that consider dependent origination to be *dhātu*. In the Pāli *Aṅguttaranikāya* there is also a *sutta* that explains the threefold formula 'all formations are impermanent (*sabbe saṃkhārā aniccā*), all formations are suffering (*sabbe saṃkhārā*), all *dhammas* are non-self (*sabbe dhammā anattā*)', as '*dhātu*':

> Oh monks, whether Tathāgatas appear [in the world], or do not appear, this *dhātu* is established. It is established as *dhamma*. It is fixed as *dhamma*. That is to say, all formations are impermanent (*sabbe saṃkhārā aniccā*). This the Tathāgatas intuitively understand (*abhisambujjhati*), this they intuitively comprehend (*abhisameti*). Having intuitively understood and intuitively comprehended that all formations are impermanent, they relate it, explain it, make it known, establish it, reveal it, analyze it, and clarify it [for the people].[31]

Next, the same explanation is given for the phrases 'all formations are suffering (*sabbe saṃkhārā*)', and 'all *dhammas* are non-self (*sabbe dhammā anattā*)'.

Clearly, the phrase 'this *dhātu*' (*sā dhātu*) is mentioned in the doctrinal explanation of this threefold formula; however, what the *sutta* passage cited here intends by the term '*dhātu*' is not clear. Though it is probable that *dhātu* is interpreted as the fact that 'all formations are impermanent, all formations are suffering, all *dhammas* are non-self', and that this *dhātu* is understood as the regularity that obtains in that threefold characterization, we still cannot be certain of the import. For that reason, it is not possible to determine the meaning of *dhātu* from this *sutta* passage alone. Moreover, this *sutta* is found only in the Pāli *Aṅguttaranikāya*; no corresponding *sūtra* is extant in Chinese translation. And since the import of this *sutta* cannot be investigated by comparing it with a Chinese translation, nothing more can be said.

The term *dhātu* has other meanings in addition to that examined above: namely, as the 'power of bringing forth an effect' included within the condition (*paccaya*) aspect of dependent origination. For example, in giving various meanings explaining '*dhātu*', the Pāli *Visuddhimagga* (15) states: 'it is *dhātu* because it arranges; it is *dhātu* because it maintains'; and so on.[32] The *Mahāvibhāṣā* (fasc. 71) gives a total of eight meanings for *dhātu* and explains their import: that is, the meaning of *dhātu* is 'the meaning of species, of section, of part, of component, of distinction, of dissimilarity, of uniformity, of various causes'.[33] It next offers the theory of the Śābdikas, who give three meanings for *dhātu*: 'because it permeates it is called *dhātu*; because it supports it is called *dhātu*; because it fosters it is called *dhātu*'.[34] The *Mahāvibhāṣā* (fasc. 71) then offers lengthy interpretations of these various theories.[35] The *Abhidharmakośabhāṣya* (chap. 1), in an explanation of the meanings of aggregate (*skandha*), sense sphere (*āyatana*), and *dhātu*, limits the meaning of *dhātu* to species (*gotra*): 'the meaning of species is the meaning of *dhātu*' (*gotrārtho dhātvarthaḥ*)'.[36] Finally, the *Abhidharmasamuccaya* (chap. 1) suggests that *dhātu* has four meanings: 'the meaning of *dhātu* is the meaning of the seeds of all *dharmas* (*sarvadharmabījārtha*); the meaning of supporting its own particular characteristic (*svalakṣaṇadhāraṇārtha*); the meaning of supporting the cause and effect relation (*kāryakāraṇabhāvadhāraṇārtha*); the meaning of encompassing *dharmas* of all varieties (*sarvaprakāradharmasaṃgrahaṇa*)'.[37]

Thus, several types of texts that indicate meanings for *dhātu* have been cited here. But if we look closely, we find still other texts that suggest meanings for *dhātu*. So in order to correctly understand the meanings of *dhātu* indicated in the passages cited above further detailed study is necessary. Since an investigation of these points has already been published,[38] I have limited my remarks here to clarifying the relationship between 'dependent origination and *dhātu*'.

(English translation by Collett Cox.)

References

1. *Saṃyuttanikāya*, *Dhātusaṃyutta* no. 1, vol. II p. 140; *Saṃyuktāgama* [*Tsa-a-han ching*] T.2 (99) 16 p. 116a.
2. *Saṃyuttanikāya*, *Dhātusaṃyutta* vol. II pp. 140-77.
3. *Saṃyuttanikāya*, *Dhātusaṃyutta* no. 11, vol. II p. 150.
4. *Saṃyuttanikāya*, *Dhātusaṃyutta* no. 12, vol. II p. 151.
5. *Saṃyuttanikāya*, *Dhātusaṃyutta* no. 13, vol. II p. 153-54.
6. *Saṃyuttanikāya*, *Dhātusaṃyutta* no. 30, vol. II p. 169.
7. *Majjhimanikāya* no. 115 vol. III p. 61-67.
8. *Majjhimanikāya* no. 115 vol. III p. 62-63.
9. *Madhyamāgama* [*Chung-a-han ching*] T.1 (26) 47 p. 723a-c.
10. Cf. P. Pradhan, ed., *Abhidharmakośabhāṣya* (Patna: K. P. Jayaswal

Research Institute, 1975), 18.8; G. Nagao, ed., *Madhyāntavibhāgabhāṣya* (Tokyo: Suzuki Research Foundation, 1964), 46.

11. *Madhyamāgama* [*Chung-a-han ching*] T.1 (26) 47 p. 723a-c.

12. *dhammadhātu*, cf. *Majjhimanikāya* vol. I p. 395; *Dīghanikāya* vol. I p. 8; *Saṃyuttanikāya* vol. II p. 56, etc.

13. *nibbānadhātu*, *Itivuttaka* p. 38; *Saṃyuttanikāya* vol. V p. 8; AN vol. II p. 20, etc.

14. *lokadhātu*, *Saṃyuttanikāya* vol. I p. 26, vol. V p. 424.

15. Warren, H. C. ed., *Visuddhimagga of Buddhaghosācariya* XV, 25ff. HOS vol. 41, (Cambridge, Massachusetts: Harvard University Press, 1950), pp. 412-15

16. *Saṃyuttanikāya* 12.20 vol. II p. 25.

17. Ibid.

18. V. infra note 22. That dependent origination indicated by the phrase, 'there are formations (*saṃkhāra*) in dependence upon the condition of ignorance', is said to have *tathatā*, *avitathatā*, *anaññathatā*, and *idappaccayatā*. These terms suggest that dependent origination is endowed with the nature of truth.

19. V. infra note 25.

20. **Vijñaptimātratāsiddhiśāstra* [*Ch'eng-wei-shih lun*] T. 31 (1585) 3 p. 14a17.

21. *Saṃyuttanikāya* 12.20 vol. II p. 25.

22. *Saṃyuttanikāya* 12.20 vol. II p. 26.

23. V. infra note 25.

24. V., for example, *Saṃyuttanikāya* 12.24 vol. II, p. 33ff, where this way of thinking is indicated in the statement that suffering is 'not something caused by oneself, nor is it caused by another', and in the statements that claim that suffering is dependently originated (*paṭiccasamuppanna*) and thereby deny that it is made by oneself (*sayaṃkata*), by another (*paraṃkata*), by both (*sayaṃkatañca paraṃkatañca*), or is without a cause (*asayaṃkatañca aparaṃkatam adhiccasamuppannam*).

25. *Saṃyuttanikāya* 12.20 vol. II p. 26.

26. Ibid.

27. V. supra note 26.

28. Warren, *Visuddhimagga*, 440ff.

29. *Saṃyuktāgama* [*Tsa-a-han ching*] T.2 (99) 13 p. 85b and p. 84b.

30. Ch. Tripāthī, *Fünfundzwanzig Sūtras des Nidānasaṃyukta*, Berlin: Akademie-Verlag, 1962, 147-49, 164-65.

31. *Aṅguttaranikāya* III, no. 134, vol. I p. 286.

32. Warren, *Visuddhimagga*, 411ff.

33. *Mahāvibhāṣā* [*Ta-p'i-p'o-sha lun*] T.27 (1545) 71 p. 367c22-24.

34. *Mahāvibhāṣā* [*Ta-p'i-p'o-sha lun*] T.27 (1545) 71 p. 367c24-25.

35. V. A. Hirakawa, "Hō to engi", in *Hirakawa Akira chosaku shū* (Tokyo: Shunjū-sha, 1988) 1: 572-73.

36. Pradhan, *Abhidharmakośabhāṣya*, 13. *Abhidharmakośabhāṣya* [*A-p'i-ta-mo chü-she lun*] T.29 (1558) 1 p. 5a4; T. 29 (1559) 1 p. 165b11. Hirakawa, "Hō to engi", 1: 574.

37. *Abhidharmasamuccaya* [*Ta-ch'eng a-p'i-ta-mo chi lun*] T. 31 (1605) 1 p. 666c27-28; *Abhidharmasamuccayavyākhyā* [*Ta-ch'eng a-p'i-ta-mo tsa chi lun*] T. 31 (1606) 2 p. 704b25-c2. N. Tatiya, ed., *Abhidharmasamuccayabhāṣya* (Patna: K. P. Jayaswal Research Institute, 1976), 19.

38. V. Hirakawa, "Hō to engi", 1: 570ff.

9 DEPENDENT ORIGINATION: ITS ELABORATION IN EARLY SARVĀSTIVĀDIN ABHIDHARMA TEXTS

COLLETT COX
University of Washington

1. INTRODUCTION

Perhaps no aspect of early Buddhist teaching has been the object of greater scholarly attention than dependent origination (Skt. *pratītyasamutpāda*; Pali. *paṭiccasamuppāda*). And given its key role in certain early *sūtras* and the reverential characterizations of later traditional interpreters, this scholarly attention is not unjustified. Among his wide-ranging studies of early Indian Buddhist doctrine, Professor Alex Wayman has devoted several major articles to the topic of dependent origination.[1] However, as he warns us, we should not consider dependent origination 'as something before [our] eyes to see in clear relief, as one might see a book.'[2] Instead, we should be alert to the possibility of multiple meanings and purposes that must be extracted from the traditional accounts. Professor Wayman has himself suggested several different interpretative models for dependent origination, models which view variation in the elaboration of the dependent origination formula as reflecting different geographical traditions or different ways in which the formula could be used. Following the lead of Professor Wayman, whose life has been devoted to investigating many areas of Buddhist doctrine, this paper will explore one facet of the complicated evolution of the doctrine of dependent origination.

Indeed, our understanding of the function and significance of all aspects of early Buddhist doctrine, including dependent origination, can be clouded by a variety of different factors. For example, our own distance from traditional sources and scholarly predispositions toward certain interpretative models can result in a failure to recognize the determining role of particular historical and cultural contexts in the development of the systems of Buddhist teaching and practice. Interpretation of Buddhist doctrine can also, however, be complicated by a failure to take into account the natural growth of the tradition.[3] This growth has been guided by Buddhist interpreters whose primary interests were not presenting historical events accurately, but rather representing preserving, and clarifying a valued message. The contributions of these interpreters complemented and often superseded one another in the ever continuing construction of the Buddha's message that came to constitute the tradition. The textual and precedent mediated horizon of the monastic transmission and elaboration of the Buddhist tradition has been formed through the accumulation of successive layers of interpretative commentary; each commentary became the point of departure and determining focus for further layers of supercommentary, which were themselves potential authoritative bases for future interpretation. Relying upon this stream of traditional interpretation without first clarifying, as best we can, its compositional strata results in an interpretative stance that mirrors the ahistoricist perspective of the tradition itself and ignores the particular context for each stage or particular contribution. Instead, one must remain sensitive to the transformation by interpretation within the tradition and to the likelihood that later traditional interpretation, more often than not, obscures rather than clarifies earlier positions. Therefore, it remains a task for continuing textual and historical research to become conscious of this process by which the tradition grew, to isolate the significant contexts that constitute its various components and stages, and to arrest the collapsing of these contexts through ahistoricist interpretative models.

This sensitivity to context must also direct our attempts to understand specific doctrinal issues. That is to say, we must be attentive to the particular traditional context in which a doctrinal issue was elaborated and be open to the possibility that this context may have changed over time; a difference or change in context of exposition would then, in all probability, reflect a difference or change in function or purpose. In the case of dependent origination, this contextual sensitivity is particularly important in determining its relation to causation. For in the later Buddhist tradition, examination of dependent origination occurs in a context determined by philosophical and doctrinal discussions concerning the broader topic of causation, a context that is assumed to be original. Yet, despite later explicit connections drawn by the tradition between dependent origination and causation, or our own efforts to find in dependent origination a context for the development of the Buddhist theory of causation, we cannot assume that the early theory of dependent origination functions as an abstract causal principle or is even initially or intrinsically related to causal functioning. Instead, we must allow for the possibility that causation and dependent origination have quite different origins and different contexts of development.

The need to attend to origin and context is hindered by the structure and style of early texts, which often contain only essential characterizations of topics such as dependent origination, and thus make inferring the underlying purpose and interpretative context of these topics difficult. Sometimes we are limited to noting the bare occurrence of an item or topic in a text. Further, the omission or inclusion of a topic within a text may have been determined by the particular purposes of that text and cannot be taken as an indication of the relative importance or priority of that topic within the Buddhist tradition as a whole. Thus, contextual sensitivity demands that we not assume the function of dependent origination as a causal principle. Instead, we must examine the role of dependent origination from its earliest appearance within Buddhist teaching and its relation at each stage to other aspects of earlier and later Buddhist doctrine. Moreover, we must trace the process through which dependent origination came to be recognized as the central teaching of the Buddha and was reformulated in accordance with the changing interpretations of this teaching.

To date, the majority of the scholarly investigations of dependent origination have focused either on its presentation in early Buddhist *sūtras* or on its more detailed elaboration in the late scholastic Abhidharma and Mahāyāna treatises. These studies often assume the centrality of dependent origination and of its twelve member formulaic expression even within the earliest stratum of Buddhist teaching. They also frequently adopt one of two interpretative approaches, each of which implicitly assumes the importance of its own perspective within the earlier materials. These two approaches emphasize either the role of dependent origination as a generalized and logical principle of abstract conditioning applicable to all phenomena, or its role as the descriptive model for the operation of action (*karman*) and the process of rebirth. Though these assumptions of the centrality of dependent origination in general and of each of these interpretative approaches find support within both the early *sūtras* and later Abhidharma and Mahāyāna treatises, they have also not remained unchallenged by yet other historical and textual scholarly studies. For example, Ernst Waldschmidt, after examining accounts of the Buddha's enlightenment experience, questions the priority of those passages that identify dependent origination as the culmination of that experience.[4] Franz Bernhard pursues a structural and historical study of the twelve member formula of dependent origination and concludes that it is a compilation of earlier partial formulae.[5] Both Waldschmidt and Bernhard's research would, therefore, challenge the assumption that the later standardized doctrine of dependent origination actually constituted one of the core teachings of the Buddha. Studies adopting either of the two interpretative approaches—affirming either the role of dependent origination as an abstract principle of causation, or its function as a descriptive model for action—present an implicit challenge to those adopting the other. As an example of these conflicting interpretative approaches, Taiken Kimura in 1927 records a disagreement concerning the original meaning of dependent origination among four of Japan's eminent earlier Buddhist scholars: Chizen Akanuma, Hakuju Ui, Tetsurō Watsuji and himself.[6] The disagreement among these scholars is three-sided: Akanuma claims that dependent origination describes the temporal relation over several lifetimes as evidenced in the process of rebirth; Ui and Watsuji claims that it refers to the non-temporal logical or abstract relation among those factors constituting a given life; and Kimura himself suggests that it explains the course of the development of animate and, in particular, psychological activity.

Each of these scholars presents convincing arguments for his position and there is no doubt that each approach is solidly supported by one of the several interpretations of dependent origination offered by later Abhidharma literature. As with all questions of doctrinal development, the character of historical evidence available from the Indian Buddhist tradition precludes sure and clear reconstructions. Thus, sorting out the role of the dependent origination within the earliest Buddhist tradition, weighing the evidence for its centrality to the enlightenment experience of the Buddha, and assessing its later doctrinal development will require extensive and prolonged future research. Nevertheless, in this paper I hope to contribute, however provisionally, to this project by considering the presentations of dependent origination and their relation to theories either of causality or of *karman* and rebirth in the early Abhidharma literature, material that perhaps has not been examined as carefully in previous discussions of this issue. These texts provide the crucial transition between the earlier *sūtras* and the later Abhidharma texts and should be able to clarify the contexts from which the independently defined doctrine of dependent origination emerged and the process by which it was crystallized or transformed and finally incorporated into the stable doctrinal edifice of the later tradition. In particular, these transitional texts will be examined for the evidence they provide concerning the relation of dependent origination to abstract causal functioning.

2. The Characterization of Dependent Origination in the Sūtra Literature

In order to appreciate the interpretative transformation that the doctrine of dependent origination underwent within the early Abhidharma treatises, we must first briefly review the varying descriptions and purposes of dependent origination as presented in the early *sūtras*. Unfortunately, the character of the *sūtra* collection as an open-ended body of anonymous texts precludes our establishing a single universally applicable interpretation of dependent origination and presents certain difficulties to any attempt to trace the development of the doctrine of dependent origination and its historical importance through the various textual strata. Nonetheless, it is clear that within at least certain segments of the *sūtra* collection, dependent origination is accorded a very important role. For example, formulaic descriptions of dependent origination in the *sūtras* state that one who sees dependent origination, sees the teaching;[7] or, whether or not Buddhas appear in the world, dependent origination is established as a fact, and it is this that the Buddhas comprehend.[8] And at least one version of the Buddha's enlightenment and its subsequent lineage of interpretation sees dependent origination as the very culmination of that formative experience.[9]

These formulaic descriptions of dependent origination in the *sūtras* often include two parts. First, an abstract statement of dependency or conditionality takes the form: 'When this is, that is, from the arising of this, that arises; when this is not, that is not, from the cessation of this, that ceases.'[10] This twofold abstract statement is usually coupled with a specific list of conditioned and conditioning factors.[11] The variety in the early descriptions of dependent origination becomes apparent in these lists of factors, which also provide clues for the history of the development of what was to become the standard characterization of dependent origination in twelve members. The *Nidāna* book of the *Saṃyuttanikāya* offers ample evidence of this variety in its lists of conditioning factors. For example, in certain texts the principle of dependent origination is illustrated through the conditioning activity of the five appropriating aggregates (*upādānakkhandha*).[12] Other texts describe a series of conditioning relations that begins with perceptual consciousness (*viññāṇa*), which is established upon an object-support (*ārammaṇa*) by means of volition, intention, and being occupied; this series of conditioning relations concludes with the consequent future rebirth (*punabbhava*), birth (*jāti*), old age and death (*jarāmaraṇa*), and indeed the origin of the entire aggregation of grief, lamentation, suffering, and so on.[13]

The more frequent lists of conditioning factors include some factors that form part of a standard listing of twelve members. For example, the *Suttanipāta*, in explaining the origin of quarrels, disputes, lamentation, grief, selfishness, pride, arrogance, and calumny, traces a series of factors, including affection (*piyā*), inclinations (*chanda*), determination of something as pleasant (*sāta*) or unpleasant (*asāta*), contact (*phassa*), name and form (*nāmarūpa*), and concept (*saññā*).[14] The *Suttanipāta* also offers a listing of twelve factors that explain the origin of suffering: these include the substratum or seizing (*upadhi*), ignorance (*avijjā*), motivations (*saṅkhāra*), perceptual consciousness (*viññāṇa*), contact (*phassa*), feelings (*vedanā*), craving (*taṇhā*), grasping (*upādāna*), undertaking (*ārambha*), sustenance (*āhāra*), and instigation (*iñjita*).[15] In the *Saṃyuttanikāya*, certain texts, adopting what would appear to be an epistemological perspective, trace the origin of suffering to contact (*phassa*) and attribute the cessation of this contact to the cessation of the six sense spheres (*saḷāyatana*), which in turn conditions the cessation of feelings (*vedanā*), craving (*taṇhā*), grasping (*upādāna*), becoming (*bhava*), birth (*jāti*), old age and death (*jarāmaraṇa*), and indeed all forms of suffering.[16] This explanation of the origin of suffering is contrasted with four other causal theories according to which suffering depends upon oneself, another, both onself and another, or occurs by chance without a cause.[17] Other texts in the *Saṃyuttanikāya* adopt the perspective of the dynamic of action and rebirth. For example, in one case, the origin of birth (*jāti*) is traced through becoming (*bhava*), grasping (*upādāna*), and craving (*taṇhā*), and ultimately to feelings (*vedanā*). These feelings, in all three modes as pleasant, unpleasant, and neutral, are impermanent and, thereby, are attended with suffering. The destruction of birth then is said to result from the destruction of all grasping.[18] Another text emphasizes equally the roles of both ignorance (*avijjā*) and craving (*taṇhā*) as the foundation of a collocation of factors including the body (*kāya*), name and form (*nāmarūpa*), contact (*phassa*), and the six sense spheres (*saḷāyatana*), all of which produce happiness and suffering (*sukhadukkha*) and ultimately rebirth, birth, old age and death, and so on.[19] Several texts appeal to the 'descent' or 'entry' (*avakkanti*)—presumably into a rebirth state or womb, or possibly into some post-meditative form of embodiment—of name and form (*nāmarūpa*) or of perceptual consciousness (*viññāṇa*).[20] Still others ground the series of conditions culminating in suffering in a relation of reciprocal conditioning between name and form and perceptual consciousness.[21]

Despite this variation in the scriptural accounts of dependent origination, the later Abhidharma and Mahāyāna treatises most frequently standardize their presentation of dependent origination in a twelve member formula.[22] Though a doctrinal and textual history of the process by which the members came to be standardized at twelve lies outside the scope of this paper, two interpretative options have dominated scholarly explanations: the twelve member formula is original and is abbreviated in the various partial series of conditioning factors; or the twelve member formula is the product of combining earlier partial formulae.

Regardless of its ultimate origin, this twelve member formulation finds support in the *sūtras*.[23] One representative example, again from the *Nidāna* book of the *Saṃyuttanikāya* is as follows:

> Now, in this case, oh monks, the learned noble disciple thoroughly directs correct attention precisely toward dependent origination: when this is, that is, from the arising of this, that arises; when this is not, that is not, from the cessation of this, that ceases. Which is to say, there are motivations in dependence upon ignorance, there is perceptual consciousness in dependence upon motivations [and so on . . . up to old age and death]. In this way, there is the origin of this entire aggregation of suffering. But from the complete turning away from, the complete cessation of ignorance, there is the cessation of motivations, and from the cessation of motivations, there is the cessation of perceptual consciousness [and so on . . . up to old age and death]. In this way, there is the cessation of this entire aggregation of suffering.[24]

In this passage, the abstract statement defining dependent origination—'when this is, that is', and so on—is applied to the conditioning relation between successive pairs in a list of twelve factors, including ignorance (*avijjā*), motivations (*saṅkhāra*), perceptual consciousness (*viññāṇa*), name and form (*nāmarūpa*), six sense spheres (*saḷāyatana*), contact (*phassa*), feelings (*vedanā*), craving (*taṇhā*), grasping (*upādāna*), becoming (*bhava*), birth (*jāti*), and old age and death (*jarāmaraṇa*). This list detailing conditioned arising is referred to in the tradition as the 'emanation' series (*anuloma*). However, this series of twelve-fold conditioned arising is also followed by an analogous series representing the conditioned cessation of each factor and, consequently, of all suffering. This list detailing conditioned cessation is referred to as the 'extirpation' series (*paṭiloma*).[25] The twelve member formulation thus offers a specific program through which the religious objective of the cessation of suffering can be effected. By understanding that suffering arises through the mutual conditioning of certain specific factors, one is freed from the delusion that suffering is caused by oneself, another, both oneself and another, or is without a cause. Furthermore, through correct insight into this process of dependent origination (*paṭiccasamuppāda*) and into those things that have originated dependently (*paṭiccasamuppanna*) one is freed from the mistaken perspective of self expressed through such concerns as: 'Did I exist in the past? What was I in the past? Will I exist in the future? What will I be in the future? And, do I or do I not exist in the present? What am I at present?' and so on.[26] Therefore, it would appear that in these early accounts, conditioning or causation, as such, is important neither as an abstract descriptive principle nor as an explanation for the process of rebirth, but rather insofar as it explains the presence of suffering and thereby makes possible its termination.[27]

3. Dependent Origination in Early Sarvāstivādin Abhidharma Texts

3.1 *The Earliest Abhidharma Texts*

It is against this backdrop of the various descriptions of dependent origination presented in the *sūtras* that one should examine its treatment in the early Abhidharma texts. Among the earliest northern Indian Abhidharma texts, the *Saṅgītiparyāya* merely uses the terms 'dependent origination' and 'dependently originated factors' as categories in its classification of other factors.[28] Though this practice is attested in the *Dharmaskandha*,[29] both the *Dharmaskandha* and the *Śāriputrābhidharmaśāstra* also devote long independent sections to the topic of dependent origination.[30] The structural similarity between the *Dharmaskandha* and the *Śāriputrābhidharmaśāstra*, and between both and the Theravādin Abhidhamma text, the *Vibhaṅga*, has long been noted.[31] This similarity suggests a possible historical affinity among these texts and, as will be discussed, provides possible clues as to the development of the Abhidharma exposition of dependent origination.

In its exposition of dependent origination, the *Dharmaskandha* follows its normal pattern of first citing at length an appropriate *sūtra* passage, which is then elaborated by a detailed commentary.[32] In the passage cited here, the Buddha announces that he will expound both the process of dependent origination (*pratītyasamutpāda*) as well as those factors that have originated dependently (*pratītyasamutpanna*). In defining the process of dependent origination, he first offers the abstract statement of conditioning —'when this is, that is', and so on—and next lists the twelve factors in their presentation order from ignorance to old age and death. The Buddha then notes that the conditioning relations among these factors are established whether or not Buddhas appear to realize them. Indeed, the principle of dependent origination is comprehended, expounded, established, and clarified by all Tathāgatas; it is fixed, regular, true, and so on. In defining the second component of dependently originated factors, the Buddha explains each of the twelve members as impermanent, conditioned, constructed, dependently originated, being destroyed, passing away, fading, and ceasing. The Buddha concludes his discussion of dependent origination and dependently originated factors with the observation that correctly understanding both components prevents self-centered inquiry into the past, present, and future, inquiry which characterizes those holding the view of the persistence of self, the persistence of beings, the persistence of life, or the persistence of merit or demerit. All such views of persistence produce suffering; only through the view of dependent origination can this suffering and, in the end, rebirth be terminated.

In its subsequent comments on this passage, the *Dharmaskandha* presents an extensive analysis of both the general definition of dependent origination and the conditioning relation between each of the individual members constituting dependently originated factors.[33] First, it notes that dependent origination and dependently originated factors are identical in their intrinsic nature, but differ in specific instances: that is to say, the same factor can be considered either conducive to 'dependent origination' or 'dependently originated.'[34] This dual character of all factors can be further clarified through an analytical matrix of four categories (*catuṣkoṭi*): namely, factors that are dependently originating and not dependently originated—a null category; factors that are dependently originated and not dependently originating—the twelve members of dependent origination, presumably considered solely as effects of conditioning; factors that are both—the twelve members considered both as conditions and as effects of conditioning; and, finally, factors that are neither—factors, here unspecified, other than those listed above.[35] Without mentioning the abstract statement of conditioning, 'when this is, that is', and so on, the *Dharmaskandha* next examines the regular and established character of both the principle of dependent origination and of the individual conditioning relations. These individual conditioning relations are declared to be established for factors in the three time periods of past, present, and future, whether Buddhas appear or do not appear in the world; the principle of conditioning is declared unwavering as the natural and unchanging character of all factors and will be constant in its truth for all past and future sages.

In a subsequent section, the *Dharmaskandha* details the conditioning relations between pairs of members constituting the twelve member formulation.[36] The treatments of each of the individual relations utilize a limited range of topics and reveal a set of expository patterns that would, upon closer examination, provide internal textual criteria upon which to suggest possible origins of or connections among certain groups of members. The effort to unravel these topics and expository patterns is aided by a comparison of comparable discussions in structurally similar and possibly historically related texts: in this case, the *Dharmaskandha*, the *Śāriputrābhidharmaśāstra*, and the *Vibhaṅga*. Though the antecedents of the exposition of both dependent origination and its individual members and the process of its development cannot be unequivocally determined from internal textual grounds alone, at the very least, the recurrent topics and patterns testify to the composite character of the exposition—especially that of the *Dharmaskandha*—and suggest certain concerns that directed it at this comparatively early stage of doctrinal development.

Whereas the enumeration of the individual conditioning relations in both the *Śāriputrābhidharmaśāstra* and the *Vibhaṅga* includes only the twelve members of the standard formulation, the exposition of the *Dharmaskandha* is distinctive in several of the specific relationships it isolates. The three initial relations accord with those of the standard formula: namely, ignorance—motivations, motivations—perceptual consciousness, and perceptual consciousness—name and form. The *Dharmaskandha* next includes the relation, name and form—perceptual consciousness, which suggests a reciprocal relationship between name and form and perceptual consciousness as is attested in those *sūtra* passages that begin the conditioning series from this reciprocal relation.[37] The *Dharmaskandha* then follows the remainder of the standard formulation with one exception: between the two relations of the standard formulation, name and form—six sense spheres and six sense spheres—contact, the *Dharmaskandha* includes the relation, name and form—contact. This particular relationship is once again reminiscent of a *sūtra* passage, specifically the *Mahānidānasūtra,* which includes only nine members in a ten stage series that begins with a reciprocal relationship between name and form—perceptual consciousness and omits the six sense spheres.[38] Though it is not possible to trace unequivocally the source for the *Dharmaskandha's* unique enumeration of the individual conditioning relations, the similarity of the *Dharmaskandha* to the *Mahānidānasūtra* is striking. Indeed, the *Dharmaskandha* quotes the *Mahānidānasūtra* as a source for its elaboration of those members that are included in the ninefold enumeration of the *Mahānidānasūtra*. This would suggest that the *Mahānidānasūtra* was an important source for the composite exposition of the *Dharmaskandha*.

In its elaboration of these individual factors, the *Dharmaskandha* interweaves definitions and variant interpretations with quotations from the *sūtras,* certain of which are cited repeatedly in association with several different members. For example, in commenting on the first relationship, ignorance—motivations, the *Dharmaskandha* initially offers a definition of the first member, ignorance, through a list of synonyms. Next, the ignorance—motivations relation is explained as signifying the arising of lust, hatred, and delusion, all in dependence upon ignorance. Several illustrative quotations from the *sūtras* are then added, the last of which describes the arising of three varieties of motivations in dependence upon ignorance: namely, meritorious, demeritorious, and non-instigated motivations.[39] This final quotation then serves as the basis for a lengthy discussion of those circumstances, specifically those rebirth or meditative states in which ignorance gives rise to each of the three varieties of motivations.

A comparison of this exposition of the ignorance—motivations relation in the *Dharmaskandha* with that of the *Śāriputrābhidharmaśāstra* and the *Vibhaṅga* reveals certain basic similarities. All three begin their exposition with a definition of ignorance and explain the ignorance—motivations relation through the threefold categorization of motivations as meritorious, demeritorious, and non-instigated.[40] The *Śāriputrābhidharma-śāstra* and the *Vibhaṅga* then expand these three categories through the three varieties of motivations or actions arising from the body, speech, or mind. The *Dharmaskandha,* however, uses the characteristically Abhidharma categories of corporeal or verbal action, thought and thought concomitants, and dissociated factors.[41] For all three texts, the subsequent elaboration of the ignorance—motivations relationship focuses on the enumeration of those states in which ignorance gives rise to various types of motivations or action.

Aside from these structural similarities in exposition among the three texts, several basic concerns underlie and connect their discussions of certain individual members or conditioning relations. For example, in the *Dharmaskandha*, the concern with the effect of conditions upon meditative or rebirth states evident in the exposition of the initial ignorance—motivations conditioning relation also characterizes the exposition of virtually all other members and their conditioning relations. Some of these conditioning relations also mention explicitly the process of transit at death and the subsequent descent into the womb: the reciprocal relationship between perceptual consciousness and name and form; name and form—six sense spheres; name and form—contact; and grasping—existence. By contrast, the explanations of certain relations include a reference to what might be termed 'epistemological concern', which recounts the conditions upon which consciousness and experience occur: motivations—perceptual consciousness, name and form—perceptual consciousness, name and form—contact. Other relations focus exclusively on this epistemological concern: six sense spheres—contact: contact—feelings. And finally, still other relations combine this epistemological concern with discussion of the arising of defilements: feelings—craving; and craving—grasping.

The exposition of the twelve individual conditioning relations in the *Śāriputrābhidharmaśāstra* falls into two patterns. The exposition of those relations from ignorance—motivations to name and form—six sense spheres focus on the rebirth or meditative state in which these conditioning relations occur, with special attention given to the temporal status as present or future of the effect produced. The remaining conditioning relations, from the six sense spheres—contact to birth—old age and death, show a typological emphasis, listing the varieties of effects produced in dependence upon each type of condition. The *Vibhaṅga* differs from the other two texts in its use of a bi-level analysis that divides its discussion into two sections: namely, analysis in accordance with the *sutta* (*suttabhājanīya*), a relatively straightforward exegesis of a passage from the *sutta* through simple questions and definitions; and analysis in accordance with the *abhidhamma* (*abhidhammabhājinīya*), which further explains the passage through the application of various matrices and further questions. The underlying concern of the *Vibhaṅga's* exposition of dependent origination is set by the *sutta* passage selected for comment, a passage addressed explicitly to the conditions for the arising of virtuous (*kusala*) factors. The subsequent *abhidhamma* exegesis then details the conditions for the arising of virtuous, unvirtuous, and indeterminate factors in various cosmic realms and meditative states.

Of the three texts, the *Dharmaskandha* shows the greatest evidence of compilation and variation in its exposition of the relations among the individual members of dependent origination. However, in the absence of external evidence, a relative dating of these three texts is only possible through internal structural comparisons. Determining the relations among the texts is complicated by their independent historical contexts and the probability of multiple recensions. Despite the difficulty of determining their precise historical relations, the three texts give little if any consideration of causal theories and no explicit linking of causation and dependent origination. There is no dependent discussion of causation in the *Dharmaskandha* or the *Vibhaṅga*. Only the *Śāriputrābhidharmaśāstra* refers to a causal model: in its exposition of the conditioning relation between the motivations and perceptual consciousness members of dependent origination, it refers to eight within its own distinctive enumeration of ten conditions (**pratyaya*).[42] However, these ten conditions are not discussed again in the context of dependent origination, but serve as the subject of a separate detailed exposition in a later section.[43]

3.2 The Middle Abhidharma Texts and the Emergence of Causal Theory

It is precisely on these points of the emergence of causal

theory as a separate topic, the exposition of dependent origination and its individual members in terms of causal theory, and the relative importance given to each that the subsequent early Sarvāstivādin Abhidharma texts differ from those of the earliest period. In the *Vijñānakāya*, dependent origination and its individual members do not constitute the subject of a separate section, but instead are mentioned within a section devoted to the topic of 'causes and conditions'.[44] As would be expected from the *Vijñānakāya*, whose focus is the description of perceptual consciousness, the section on causes and conditions presents a detailed analysis of the range of conditions that give rise to consciousness analyzed from a variety of perspectives. The result is a complex matrix of varieties of consciousness that are dependent upon specific types of generative conditions in specific circumstances. For example, consciousness is itself analyzed: according to six varieties (i.e. visual, auditory, olfactory, gustatory, tactile, and mental); according to ten varieties (i.e. virtuous, unvirtuous, and either obscured or unobscured indeterminate within the realm of desire, and virtuous and either obscured or unobscured indeterminate within the realms of form and the formless realm); or according to fifteen varieties (i.e. five varieties —to be abandoned through the vision of the four noble truths or through cultivation—associated with each of the three realms). Consciousness is further specified according to time period, moral quality, association with certain types of defilements, and status as abandoned or not yet abandoned. These varieties of consciousness are then correlated to generative conditions themselves similarly analyzed according to the same varieties.

To begin this section detailing 'causes and conditions', the *Vijñānakāya* appeals to the twelve member formulation of dependent origination but with a noteworthy innovation. Without taking any specific *sūtra* passage as a point of departure, the *Vijñānakāya* offers two accounts of the twelve individual conditioning relations constituting the standard formulation: one reflects a simultaneous and the other a sequential temporal model. According to the simultaneous model, all twelve members function within a single moment and account for the arising of ordinary experience. For example, in the case of the arising of lust toward a desirable object in dependence upon lack of knowledge, this 'motivation' of lust is conditioned by the eleven remaining members: the lack of knowledge is ignorance; present cognition is perceptual consciousness; the collection of five aggregates is name and form; the organ bases of those aggregates are the six sense spheres; the composite of those six spheres is contact; sensation within that composite is feelings; pleasure produced by those feelings is craving; the extension of this craving is grasping; action that is able to produce the subsequent lifetime is existence; the present state of the aggregates is birth; the maturation of these aggregates is old age; and the passing of these aggregates is death. By contrast, in the sequential model, each of the twelve members, beginning with ignorance, serves as the condition for the arising of the subsequent member. The explanations of several of the individual members emphasize their role in the operation of *karman* and rebirth: for example, ignorance serves as the cause and condition for the arising of three varieties of motivations as meritorious, demeritorious, and non-instigated; these motivations condition the arising of perceptual consciousness, which constitutes passage either to a favorable or unfavorable destiny; this perceptual consciousness conditions the arising of name and form either in this lifetime or the next; name and form conditions the arising of the six sense spheres that are either complete or incomplete; and so on. The question of the temporal relation among the individual members is not addressed in the *sūtras*; thus, the important innovation of the *Vijñānakāya* consists in the suggestion that this conditioning process operates through both a simultaneous and successive temporal model.

Before proceeding with its matrix of varieties of consciousness and their respective 'causes and conditions', the *Vijñānakāya* presents a list of fourteen conditions for the arising of thought (*citta*) and then isolates from among them four conditions (*pratyaya*) that function to produce perceptual consciousness.[45] These four conditions constitute a significant component of later Sarvāstivādin causal theory. Thus, it is clear that in the *Vijñānakāya* abstract causal relations are beginning to be considered for their own sake, and not merely as a part of discussions of dependent origination. Indeed, consideration of dependent origination occupies the subordinate role of introducing an independent consideration of causal operations.

In the *Prakaraṇapāda*, as in the *Saṅgītiparyāya*, the terms 'dependent origination' and 'dependently originated factors' occur only as categories in its classification of other factors; dependent origination in its traditional twelve member formulation is not discussed.[46] However, the category of 'dependently originated factors' (*pratītyasamutpanna*) is declared to constitute the totality of conditioned factors.[47] This abstract redefinition and radical extension of the meaning of dependent originated factors to include all conditioned factors plays a key role in later Abhidharma texts. Though the four conditions presented in the *Vijñānakāya* are mentioned also in the *Prakaraṇapāda*, they are not discussed in detail as a separate topic.[48] Instead, the issue of causal relations is addressed only implicitly in the catechetical examination and elaboration of other factors.[49]

The **Āryavasumitrabodhisattvasaṅgītiśāstra* also devotes much more attention to the contextual operation of causes and conditions and restricts its discussion of dependent origination.[50] It raises the issue of and offers several explanations for a distinction between causes (*hetu*) and conditions (*pratyaya*).[51] It also refers to the four conditions as the basis for the arising of all moments of thought,[52] and discusses the operation of each condition in appropriate contexts. The issue of simultaneous conditions, so important to later Abhidharma analyses of causal operations, is also raised in discussions of the functioning of mental factors and the relationship of association proposed among these factors.[53] The twelve member dependent origination formula is accorded a certain measure of abstract importance: personal realization of the twelve causes and conditions and of the twelve dependently originated factors constitutes the essence of the Abhidharma;[54] the twelve causes and conditions are declared to be the deep meaning of the *sūtras* and *śāstras* and the silence of the sages;[55] and knowledge of the twelve causes and conditions distinguishes the person of knowledge from the fool.[56] Nonetheless, dependent origination and the individual conditioning relations do not serve as the topic of a separate lengthy section. Instead, discussion is limited to certain of the individual relations—in particular that between feelings and craving[57]—and to certain aspects of the traditional *sūtra* passage referring to dependent origination. Specifically, discussion of the traditional *sūtra* passage is restricted to the Buddha's declaration that to see dependent origination is to see the teaching,[58] and to various points of distinction between dependent origination and dependently originated factors.[59]

Finally, in the most recent of the early Sarvāstivādin Abhidharma texts, the *Jñānaprasthāna*, which became the central Abhidharma text for at least one branch of the Sarvāstivādin school,[60] conditioning relations are examined not in the context of dependent origination, but rather in relation to specific causal operations and, in particular, a newly elaborated theory of six causes.[61] The path of religious practice through which defilements are abandoned, the four noble truths are realized, and suffering is terminated is explained in terms of the operation of these six causes, and not in terms of dependent origination as such. However, unlike the *Prakaraṇapāda*, the *Jñānaprasthāna* does not completely ignore the traditional twelve member formulation of dependent origination,[62] but instead offers an unprecedented reinterpretation. The twelve members, the *Jñānaprasthāna* claims, are to be interpreted as extending over three lifetimes: the first two members operate in the previous lifetime to produce the middle eight members in the present lifetime; these present members then produce the last two members in the subsequent lifetime.

4. Conclusion

Thus, by the time of the *Jñānaprasthāna*, the Sarvāstivādin development of a separate theory of causal relations was extended through the theory of the six causes, which, from the *Mahāvibhāṣā* onward, was combined with the theory of four conditions as the two major components of the Sarvāstivādin causal model. The *Mahāvibhāṣā* also marks the beginning of abstract considerations of the process of causation and various specific causal models. With the emergence of an independent and abstract causal theory, dependent origination and its twelve member formulation, which had remained a stable but not doctrinally evolving teaching throughout the early Sarvāstivādin texts, was activated, as it were, through reinterpretation: it received its own particularized role, as an explanation of the process of rebirth, completely divorced from general causal theory.

The later Sarvāstivādin Abhidharma texts retain the advances in causal theory as well as the new interpretation of dependent origination evident in the *Jñānaprasthāna*. However, they also appear to innovate by connecting dependent origination to causality such that dependent origination becomes the conditioning principle underlying all specific causal interaction. As a general conditioning principle, dependent origination is then applied to all conditioned phenomena in either successive or simultaneous form through the specific causal theories of the six causes and four conditions. The twelve member formulation is reserved for a detailed explanation of the operation of action and the process of rebirth. This later twofold reinterpretation of dependent origination as a general conditioning principle and as providing the specific conditions for rebirth is achieved through a complex and extensive exegesis of the original *sūtra* passage—an exegesis that is claimed, of course, to represent its implicit original meaning.

References

1. Alex Wayman, "Buddhist Dependent Origination and the Sāṃkhya Guṇas", *Ethnos* (1962): 14-22; "Buddhist Dependent Origination", *History of Religions* 10 (1971): 185-203; "Dependent Origination: the Indo-Tibetan Tradition", in *Buddhist Insight, Essays by Alex Wayman*, edited by George Elder (Delhi: Motilal Banarsidass, 1984), 163-92 (first published in *Journal of Chinese Philosophy* 7 (1980): 275-300). Professor Wayman's "Notes on the Sanskrit term *Jñāna*", *Journal of the American Oriental Society* 75 (1955): 253-68, also investigates the first few members of the twelve member formula of dependent origination.

2. Wayman, "Dependent Origination: the Indo-Tibetan Tradition", 163.

3. For the necessity of giving due consideration to cultural context in the discussion of apparently neutral ahistorical philosophical issues, V. Madeleine Biardeau, "Jāti et lakṣaṇa", in *Beiträge zur Geistesgeschichte Indiens: Festschrift für Erich Frauwallner, Wiener Zeitschrift für die Kunde Süd- und Ostasiens* 12-13 (1968-69): 75-83.

4. Ernst Waldschmidt, "Die Erleuchtung des Buddha (1960)", in *Von Ceylon bis Turfan. Schriften zur Geschichte, Literatur, Religion und Kunst des indischen Kulturraumes* (Göttingen: Vandenhoeck & Ruprecht, 1967) 396-411.

5. Franz Bernhard, "Zur Interpretation der Pratītyasamutpāda-Formel" in *Beiträge zur Geistesgeschichte Indiens: Festschrift für Erich Frauwallner, Wiener Zeitschrift für die Kunde Süd- und Ostasiens* 12-13 (1968-69): 53-63.

6. This disagreement was occasioned by the interpretation of dependent origination presented in Kimura's book, *Genshi Bukkyō shisō ron*, completed in 1921. Articles published by Akanuma, Ui, and Watsuji then prompted a response by Kimura now included as an appendix to *Genshi Bukkyō shisō ron*, in *Kimura Taiken zenshū* 3 (1923; reprint, Tokyo: Daihōrinkaku, 1968), 363ff.

7. V. Trenckner, et al., eds., *The Majjhima-Nikāya*, 3 vols. (London: The Pali Text Society, 1896-99) [MN] # 28. *Mahāhatthipadopamasutta* 1: 191 *yo paṭiccasamuppādaṃ passati, so dhammaṃ passati. yo dhammaṃ passati, so paṭiccasamuppādaṃ passati.* V also *Madhyamāgama* [MA] T.1 (26) 7 # 30 p. 467a18. Cf. **Vinayamātṛkā* T.24 (1463) 4 p. 820b13ff.

8. Leon Feer, ed., *The Saṃyutta-Nikāya*, 5 vols. (London: The Pali Text Society, 1884-1898) [SN] 12.20 *Paccayasutta* 2: 25 *uppādā vā tathāgatānaṃ anuppādā vā tathāgatānaṃ ṭhitā va sā dhātu dhammaṭṭhitatā dhammaniyāmatā idappaccayatā. taṃ tathāgato abhidambujjhati abhisameti.* V. also *Saṃyuktāgama* [SA] T.2 (99) 12 # 296 p. 84b19-21.

9. Hermann Oldenberg, ed., *Vinaya Piṭakaṃ*, vol. 1 *The Mahāvagga* (London: Williams and Norgate, 1879), 1; SN 12.10 *Gotamasutta* 2: 10-11. SA.13 # 285 p. 79c27. V. also SA12 # 287 p. 80b24ff; *Ekottarāgama* [EA] T.2 (125) 31 # 4 p. 718a13. For accounts of the enlightenment that do not mention dependent origination, v. MN # 26 *Ariyapariyesanasutta* 1: 167; MN#36 *Mahāsaccakasutta* 1: 248-49; MN#4 *Bhayabheravasutta* 1: 23.

10. Though this phrase usually accompanies lists of specific conditioning factors, it also occurs alone: v. MN#79. *Cūḷasakuludāyisutta* 2: 32. *dhammaṃ te desessāmi: imasmiṃ sati idaṃ hoti, imassu' ppādā, idaṃ uppajjati; imasmiṃ asati idaṃ na hoti, imassa nirodhā idaṃ nirujjhati.* V. also EA. 32 # 9 p. 724b 16-17. Mitsuyoshi Saigusa reviews various patterns for this phrase in the *sūtra* collection: v. Mitsuyoshi Saigusa, "Shoki bukkyō no 'kore ga aru o tki kare ga aru", *Indogaku Bukkyōgaku kenkyū* 28 (1979): 38-44.

11. An interpretation defending the historical priority of this twofold abstract statement—"when this is, that is, from the arising of this..."—would argue that dependent origination begins as an abstract causal principle and the varying lists of factors reflect later and often conflicting elaborative material.

12. MN#28 *Mahāhattipadopamasutta* 1: 190-91. Cf. SN 12.21 *Dasabalasutta* 2: 27ff.

13. SN 12.38 *Cetanāsutta* 2: 65ff. Cf. SN 12.39 *Dutiyacetanāsutta* 2: 66ff, for a series incorporating the standard listing of factors from perceptual consciousness through old age and death.

14. Dines Andersen and Helmer Smith, eds., *Sutta-Nipāta* (London: The Pali Text Society, 1913), # 862ff, p. 169ff.

15. Andersen and Smith, *Sutta-Nipāta*, # 728ff, p. 141ff.

16. SN 12.24 *Aññatitthiyasutta* 2: 33ff. V. also SN 12.25 *Bhūmijasutta* 2: 37ff; 12.26 *Upavāṇasutta* 2: 41ff. For other texts with this apparent epistemological perspective, v. SN 12.43 *Dukkhasutta* 2: 72, which traces the arising of suffering to the initial contact that arises among the sense organ, the object-field, and the appropriate perceptual consciousness; contact in turn gives rise to feelings and then to craving as the origin of suffering. Suffering ceases through the cessation of craving, which in turn undermines grasping, existence, birth, old age and death, and so on.

17. For other *suttas* that counter these four views, v. SN 12.17 *Acelakassapasutta* and SN 12.18 *Timbarukasutta* 2: 19ff; SA. 12 # 302 p. 86a4ff, # 303 p. 86b24ff.

18. SN 12.32 *Kaḷārasutta* 2: 50ff. Cf. SN 12.52 *Upādānasutta*, 12.53-54 *Saṃyojanasutta* 2: 84ff, which trace the origin of suffering to craving.

19. SN 12.19 *Bālapaṇḍitasutta* 2: 24ff.

20. SN 12.58 *Nāmarūpasutta* 2: 90ff; SN 12.59 *Viññāṇasutta* 2: 91ff; SN 12.64 *Atthirāgasutta* 2: 101.

21. SN 12.65 *Nagarasutta* 2: 104ff; SN 12.67 *Naḷakasutta* 2: 112. V. also *Jen Pen yü-sheng ching* T.1 (14) p. 243b5ff; T. W. Rhys Davids and J. E. Carpenter, eds., *The Dīghanikāya*, 3 vols. (London: The Pali Text Society, 1890-1911) [DN] 15 *Mahānidānasutta* 2: 55ff, 62, which omits the six sense spheres and, therefore, lists only nine factors. Cf. SN 12.28 *Bhikkhusutta* 2: 43ff; SN 12.33 *Ñāṇavatthusutta* 2:56ff, where the series begins with motivations (*saṅkhāra*).

22. The variation in the enumerations of the members of dependent origination presented in the *sūtras* is duly noted in later Abhidharma texts: v. *Mahāvibhāṣāśāstra* T.27 (1545) [MVB] 24. p. 122a9ff; *Nyāyānusāraśāstra* T.29 (1562) [NAS] 25 p. 480c8ff.

23. It is important to keep in mind that it is possible, if not probable, that the *sūtra* canon was influenced in both style and content by an emerging Abhidharma corpus. Therefore, the priority of references in *sūtra* cannot be assumed. V. Bronkhorst, "Dharma and Abhidharma", 316ff.

24. SN 12.37 *Natumhasutta* 2: 65. *tatra kho bhikkhave sutavā ariyasāvako paṭiccasamuppādañ ñeva sādhukaṃ yoniso manasi karoti. iti imasmiṃ sati idaṃ hoti, imassu 'ppādā idaṃ uppajjati. imasmiṃ asati idaṃ na hoti. imassa nirodhā idaṃ nirujjhati. yad idaṃ avijjāpaccayā saṅkhārā. saṅkhārapaccayā viññāṇaṃ. . . .evam etassa kevalassa dukkhakkhandhassa samudayo hoti. avijjāya tv eva asesavirāganirodhā saṅkhāranirodho. saṅkhāranirodhā viññāṇanirodho. . . .evam etassa kevalassa dukkhakkhandhassa nirodho hoti.* V. also SN 12.20 *Paccayasutta* 2: 25; SA 11 #296 p. 84b14ff; MN #38 *Mahātaṇhāsaṅkhayasutta* 1: 261ff; MA 54 # 201 p. 768a13ff; *Yüan-ch'i ching* T.2 (124) p. 547b17ff.

25. It should also be noted that these twelve factors between ignorance and old age and death are listed in two different orders: one from old age and death to ignorance, which reflects the order in which these factors were discovered by the Buddha; and the other from ignorance to old age and death, which reflects the order in which the members were presented by the Buddha and observed by others. Though the 'presentation' order from ignorance to old age and death is more common in the later sources, Hakuju Ui suggests that the 'discovery' order from old age and death to ignorance is earlier. V. Hakuju Ui, "Jūni enga no kaishaku—engisetsu no igi", in *Indo tetsugaku kenkyū* (Tokyo: Iwanami shoten, 1965), 2: 303ff. For a review of the various orders in which the dependent origination formula is presented, v. Isshi Yamada, "Premises and Implications of 'Interdependence' (Pratityasamutpada)", in *Studies in History of Buddhism*, edited by A. K. Narain, (Delhi: B. R. Publishing Corporation, 1980), 373ff, and for Japanese scholarship on this issue, nt. 8 p. 388. Cf. Wayman, "Dependent Origination: the Indo-Tibetan Tradition", 163ff.

26. SN 12.20 *Paccayasutta* 2: 25-27; SA 11 # 296 p. 84b26ff; MN # 38

Mahātaṇhāsaṅkhayasutta 1: 265; MA 54 # 201 p. 769a9ff. Cf. also NAS 27. p. 496b17ff; AKB 3. 25c-d p. 133.20ff.

27. As an example of this common interpretation, v. I. Yamada, "Premises and Implications", 375.

28. *Saṅgītiparyāya* T.26 (1536) 1 p. 367c22ff, 1 p. 369a3ff, 12 p. 419a20ff.

29. V. *Dharmaskandha* T.26 (1537) [DS] 8 p. 491c18ff, 8 p. 492b4ff, where the category of dependently originated factors is listed as one category of factors to be observed within the investigation limb (*dharmapravicayasaṃbodhyaṅga*) among the seven limbs of enlightenment.

30. DS 11 p. 505a9—12 p. 513c10; for the section from 11 p. 505c26—12 p. 513c10, cf. Siglinde Dietz, ed., *Fragmente des Dharmaskandha, Ein Abhidharma-Text in Sanskrit aus Gilgit*, Abhandlungen der Akademie der Wissenschaften in Göttingen, Philologisch-historische Klasse 3, 142 (Göttingen: Vandenhoeck & Ruprecht), 25-70; *Śāriputrābhidharmaśāstra* T.28 (1548) [ŚAŚ] 12 p. 606b17—612b12. For the dating of these northern Indian Abhidharma texts see Hajime Sakurabe, *Kusharon no kenkyū*, (Kyoto: Hōzōkan, 1969), 41ff, and Baiyū Watanabe, *Ubu Abidatsumaron no kenkyū*, (Tokyo: Heibonsha, 1954), 135.

31. V. Taiken Kimura, *Abidatsuma ron no kenkyū, Kimura Taiken zenshū* 6 (Tokyo: Meiji shoin, 1937), 67ff; Ryūjō Yamada, *Daijō Bukkyō seiritsuron josetsu* (Kyoto: Heirakuji shoten, 1959), 70ff.

32. Though this *sūtra* passage is not identified in the *Dharmaskandha*, it closely resembles SA 11 # 296 p. 84b12ff; cf. SN 12.20 *Paccayasutta* 2: 25ff.

33. DS 11 p. 505b14ff.

34. In the *Prakaraṇapāda* (T.26 (1542) [PP] 6 p. 715c4) dependent origination (*pratītyasamutpāda*) is mentioned only in conjunction with dependently originated factors (*pratītyasamutpanna*) and both are defined simply as comprising conditioned factors. Cf. also the *Prakaraṇapāda* T.26 (1541) 6 p. 656a16ff, where the contents of 'dependent origination' and "dependently originated factors' are spelled out as those factors included within the eighteen elements, the twelve sense spheres, the five aggregates, the nine varieties of knowledge, and so on. For a later discussion of this and other interpretations of the relationship between dependent origination and dependently originated factors, v. MVB 23 p. 118a25ff.

35. The *Mahāvibhāṣā* (MVB 23 p. 118b15ff) attributes to the master Pūrṇāśa a different fourfold analytical matrix, which reflects the more developed doctrinal analysis and categorization characteristic of later Abhidharma texts: namely, factors that are dependent originating and not dependently originated are future factors; factors that are dependently originated and not dependent originating are the past and present five aggregates constituting *arhats* in the last moment prior to the termination of their life-streams; factors that are both include all past and present factors other than those of the previous categories; and, finally, factors that are neither are the unconditioned factors.

36. DS 11 p. 505c13ff; for the section from DS 11 p. 505c26ff, cf. Dietz, *Fragmente des Dharmaskandha*, 25ff.

37. V. *supra* nt. 21.

38. DN *Mahānidānasutta* 2: 55ff, 62; MA 24 # 97 p. 579c13ff; *Jen Pen yü-sheng*

ching T.1 (14) p. 243b5ff. Cf. *Dīrghāgama* # 13. [DA] 10 p. 60b8ff, which lists the twelve members of the standard formulation, including the six sense spheres.

39. SA 12 # 292 p. 83a27ff; SN 12.51 *Parivīmaṃsanasutta* 2: 82.

40. ŚAŚ 12 p. 606b28ff; *Vibhaṅga* p. 135; DS 11 p. 505c13ff.

41. DS 11 p. 506a15ff. Cf. Dietz, *Fragmente des Dharmaskandha*, 26ff.

42. ŚAŚ 12 p. 608a9.

43. ŚAŚ 15 p. 628c10ff, 25 p. 679b7ff.

44. *Vijñānakāya* [VK] T. 26. (1539) 3 p. 547a3ff.

45. VK. 3 p. 547b22ff. The *Mahāvibhāṣā* (MVB 21 p. 108c21ff) cites the *Prajñaptiśāstra* as the source for this theory of four conditions, though they do not appear in the sections of the *Prajñaptiśāstra* extant in Chinese translation (T.26 (1538)). For further application of the four conditions to an analysis of thought, v. VK 11 p. 548a29ff.

46. *Prakaraṇapāda* [PP]. T.26 (1542) 5 p. 711c6, 8 p. 725b16ff. Cf. similar use in the *Saṅgītiparyāya*, *supra* nt. 28.

47. PP. 6 p. 715c4.

48. PP. 5 p. 712b12ff, 7 p. 719a13ff.

49. For example, v. PP 10 p. 733c17ff.

50. On the character and possible sectarian affiliation of the **Āryavasumitrabodhisattvasaṅgītiśāstra* as connected with a possibly non-Kāśmīra lineage of the Sarvāstivādin sect, v. Watanabe, *Ubu Abidatsumaron*, 186ff, 248ff; R. Yamada, *Daijō Bukkyō seiritsu*, 401ff, 413ff; Sakurabe, *Kusharon*, 54, 87ff. For its dating as contemporaneous with or slightly later than the *Jñānaprasthāna*, v. Chizen Akanuma, (1934). *Sonbasumitsubosatsushoshūron*, Kokuyaku issaikyō indo senjutsubu, Bidonbu 6 (Tokyo: Daitō shuppansha), 62ff; Watanabe, *Ubu Abidatsumaron*, 195ff; Sakurabe, *Kusharon*, 54ff.

51. **Āryavasumitrabodhisattvasaṅgītiśāstra* [VSŚ] T. 28 (1549) 1 p. 724c20ff. This topic is raised again in Saṅghabhadra's *Nyāyānusāra*, NAS 20 p. 449b21ff.

52. VSŚ 3 p. 739c7.

53. VSŚ 2 p. 734b13ff, 3 p. 738c2ff.

54. VSŚ 2 p. 733a20ff.

55. VSŚ 4 p. 745c18ff.

56. VSŚ 10 p. 802b27ff.

57. VSŚ 2 p. 734a23ff.

58. VSŚ 2 p. 735a27ff. Noteworthy in this discussion is a distinction between seeing the *dharma* and seeing the individual (*pudgala*), and a reference to the voidness and the signless gates of liberation (*vimokṣamukha*).

59. VSŚ 2 p. 736a18ff. For a similar treatment, v. MVB 23 p. 118a25ff.

60. Giyū Nishi, "Ubushūnai ni okeru hotchi hi-hotchi kei nado no shoshu no gakusetsu oyobi gakutō no kenkyū", in *Abidatsuma Bukkyō no kenkyū*, by Giyū Nishi, 73-108. Tokyo: Kokusho kankō kai.

61. *Jñānaprasthāna* [JP] T.26 (1544) 1 p. 920c5ff. The *Mahāvibhāṣā* (MVB 21 p. 108c20ff) adds a discussion of the four conditions in its commentary on this passage.

62. JP. 1 p. 921b16ff. The *Mahāvibhāṣā* (MVB. 21 p. 109b21ff; cf. also NAS 25 p. 481a9) claims that the *sūtra* passage interpreted here is the *Mahānidānasūtra*. V. *supra* nt. 38.

10 DEPENDENT ORIGINATION IN BUDDHIST TANTRA

GEORGE R. ELDER
Hunter College, City University of New York

Dependent Origination has been judged, since ancient times, to be one of the most important of Buddhist doctrines, second only in significance to the Four Noble Truths. Yet it could be said that the four Āryasatyāni have a more strictly religious quality to them, beginning as they do with the reality of 'suffering'. By contrast, the twelvefold formula of Pratītyasamutpāda seems more philosophical in character, beginning as it does with the reality of 'nescience'—the problem of knowledge really; further, since Dependent Origination answers questions about the nature of existence and gives the classic Buddhist answer to the persistent Indian question about causation, it is this doctrine alone which is often called the 'key concept' for understanding Buddhism. We are reminded by the literature, both ancient and modern, that the one who 'sees' Dependent Origination is the one who is able to see the Dharma or see Thusness or see the Tathāgata himself (i.e. the Dharmakāya).[1] Yet sometimes it is said that to see Dependent Origination is to see the Four Noble Truths, a fact which returns the philosophical doctrine to the religious arena, a not uncommon feature of Indian thought.[2] But it could not be otherwise, since Gautama Buddha began his religious quest after seeing the Four Visions, the first three of which were old age, disease, and death. He would end his quest at the 'dawn' of his Enlightenment upon seeing 'old age and death' (*jarā-maraṇa*) in a new way, as the twelfth member of the chain of Pratītyasamutpāda. Occasionally, this last member of the formula is expanded to include *vyādhi*, 'disease', as well.[3]

Traditionally important, the doctrine of Dependent Origination has also been judged exceptionally difficult to understand. That judgment begins, of course, with Gautama's famous reproof of Ānanda who thought he grasped the meaning pretty well: the Buddha replied, 'Dependent Origination not only looks deep, it is deep'.[4] Accordingly, through the centuries, any

Buddhist worthy of respect has felt obliged to present his interpretation of the twelve-fold formula; and the same can be said for modern scholars who have expanded the literature on this topic to a vast extent. Professor Alex Wayman, to whom this volume is dedicated, has made significant contributions to the interpretation of Pratītyasamutpāda. While he discusses the doctrine throughout his many full-length books on various topics, there are three articles published which focus upon the formula: 'Buddhist Dependent Origination and the Sāṃkhya guṇas' (1962) which is an early effort to establish a correlation between Buddhist and Hindu thought by way of the *Kālacakratantra*; 'Buddhist Dependent Origination' (1971) which shows us the distinction between 'Eastern' and 'Western' Indian interpretations of the doctrine and—characteristic of Wayman's scholarship—distinctions within the distinctions; and finally 'Dependent Origination—the Indo-Tibetan Tradition" (1980 and reprinted in a my collection of Professor Wayman's essays, 1984) which introduces such subtleties as *pratītyasamutapāda* without persons necessarily implied and also the surprising interpretation of 'nescience' as sometimes with and sometimes without 'defilement'.[5] Indeed, the quality of these contributions is so exceptional that one is tempted to say that they 'not only look deep, they are deep'.

It will not be my purpose here, however, to review the vast literature on Dependent Origination nor even to analyze the topic from Wayman's particular point of view. Instead, I wish merely to provide some new materials as they have emerged from my current work on a translation of the *Saṃpuṭa Tantra* and especially as they emerge from the text's Sanskrit and native Tibetan commentaries. In doing so, I hope—in lieu of advancing very much our understanding of Buddhist Dependent Origination—to show more clearly what constitutes a Tantra and to what extent ancient tantric commentators can be considered as well-read and as sophisticated intellectually as their better-known non-tantric colleagues. I will make a point of using Dr. Wayman's translation and his works to demonstrate their usefulness and also to do honor, in part, to a remarkable scholar who has been my very generous mentor for many years.

THE SAṂPUṬA TRADITION

The *Saṁpuṭanāmamahātantra* was probably composed in the mid-6th century CE if we accept Wayman's argument for the composition of the seminal *Guhyasamājatantra* as early as the 4th century.[6] The *Saṃpuṭa* names the *Guhyasamāja* which must be antecedent enough to have gained fame.[7] Eventually becoming famous itself, the *Saṃpuṭa* was described by Mkhas-grub-rje in his *Fundamentals of the Buddhist Tantras* as a *tantra* in the Anuttarayoga class, of the Mother type, and 'explanatory' of both the *Hevajra Tantra* and the *Cakrasaṃvara Tantra*.[8] The commentarial tradition surrounding the text is truly impressive. At its head is a long meandering commentary by Indrabhuti who may well be Indrabhūti the Elder, *guru* of Padmasambhava, and writing in the late 7th or early 8th century. But the commentary by Abhayākaragupta—his *Āmnāya-mañjarī*—is superior and is considered by Tsoṅ-kha-pa, who quotes from it often, to be the main commentary on the *Saṃpuṭa*. It dates from the 12th century. From the same century is a short work by one Śuravajra; and then there is Bu-ston's 14th-century commentary as the major native Tibetan contribution. In what follows, I will refer to these various works but rely heavily upon the exceptional qualities of the *Āmnāya-mañjarī*.[9]

The doctrine of Dependent Origination in the *Saṃpuṭa* text is something of a needle in a haystack. It occurs first at the beginning of the fourth chapter of the first section (of ten sections for the whole work). There we find the following Sanskrit, as I have edited:

> buddhatvaṃ (nānyair) yad prāptaṃ kalpāsaṃkheya-koṭibhir yāvat/
> asminn api janmani tvaṃ prāpnoṣi sat-sukhenaiva//
> athavā vajradhara-tvam athavā cakravartitvam/
> aṣṭa-mahāsiddhiṃ vā anyāṃ manasīpsitāṃ vāpi//
> moho rāgo dveṣo mānas tv īrṣyā ca pañcasaṃkleśāḥ/
> sattvās tu pratibaddhā yena jayanti svāṅga-kenaiva//
> ebhir baddhāḥ sattvāḥ ṣaḍgati-saṃsāra-vartino jātāḥ/
> kurvanty aneka-pāpaṃ kleśair vimohitāḥ santaḥ//
> [there follow here six lines on esoteric yoga practices irrelevant to our purposes] . . . .
> taṃ hanti samartho bhūtvā śatruḥ samartho yathā śatruṃ/

mohaṃ moha-viśuddhyā dveṣa-viśuddhyā tathā dveṣaṃ//
rāgaṃ rāga-viśuddhyā māna-viśuddhyā mahāmānaṃ/
īrṣyām īrṣyā-viśuddhyā sarva-viśuddhas tu vajradhṛk//
tad-rūpa-viśuddhyā pañcakleśāḥ samaṃ yānti/
etāni pañcakulāni pañcajñānāni pañcabuddhāḥ//

I translate:

Whatever Buddhahood is to be attained in (nothing less than) an incalculable number of tens of millions of aeons, you will attain in this birth along with Sublime Bliss. Either as Vajradhara or as a Cakravartin, [you will attain] the Eight Great Siddhis or anything else you desire. Delusion, lust, hatred, pride, and jealousy are the Five Defilements; yet by their very own members (*svāṅga*), the ones by which sentient beings are bound, they conquer. By them, sentient beings are bound to births, circling in Saṃsāra according to the Six Destinies; they are confused by the Defilements and commit much sin. . . . Just as a powerful enemy can destroy someone, so someone being powerful can destroy that enemy: Delusion [is destroyed] by the purification of delusion, hatred by the purification of hatred, lust by the purification of lust, great pride by the purification of pride, jealousy by the purification of jealousy. Indeed, the purification of each wields a *vajra*. Given the pure form of these, the Five Defilements are the same: they are the Five Families, the Five knowledges, and the Five Buddhas.

On the face of it, these lines do not appear to be very tantric. The goal is still 'Buddhahood'; and while 'Sublime Bliss' (*satsukha*) seems a bit strong, it is still *sukha* that the yogin seeks in order to counteract the *duḥkha* with which Buddhism got its start. 'Vajradhara' is admittedly a new name for the rank of one who reaches the goal. Vajradhara is a tantric synthesis of the standard Five Supramundane Buddhas of non-tantric Mahāyāna. As for becoming a 'Cakravartin', the Hīnayāna Gautama Buddha says that he is one—not of the secular sort, of course, but one who 'turns the wheel' to destroy ignorance. The tantric 'accomplishment' called '*siddhis*' include such feats as the ability to fly, to become invisible, and are not very different in kind from the earliest *ṛddhis* of Buddhist tradition; and it has always been the case that one should 'destroy' defilement—the five listed here are standard. Granted, there are so many more deities in Buddhist Tantra that our text had to designate 'Families' to organize them all, but the process was really begun in the 'orthodox' Mahāyāna expansion of the pantheon. The 'Five Knowledges' are the usual non-tantric Mahāyāna 'Pure Dharmadhātu knowledge', etc.

There are, of course, obvious tantric nuances right at the surface of this text. Reference is made to the well-known 'quick path' of the Mantrayāna that one can achieve in 'one life' what takes other Buddhists a very long time. As well, one begins to feel that the Defilements are not just being eliminated but somehow being used to eliminate themselves, strangely being equated to positive realities like the Five Buddhas.

All of this can be seen without the commentaries and actually without very much knowledge of Buddhist Tantra. Yet when we do consult the *Saṃpuṭa*'s commentarial tradition, it becomes clear why it is that Professor Wayman has so often cautioned that it is 'hazardous' to try to understand a *tantra* 'just from reading it'.[10] It is particularly clear when one consults someone of the stature of Abhayākaragupta (PTT, Vol. 55, pp. 126-28 for this section). He tells us first of all that the 'Buddhahood' that could be attained by the Path of the Prajñāparamitā would be no more than the 'Īśvara' (*dbaṅ-phyug*) of the '10th Stage'—where one is still a Bodhisattva but tantamount to a Buddha—while 'Vibuddhahood' (*rnam saṅs rgyas ñid*) or complete Buddhahood is the state of 'Vajradhara' on the '11th Stage' attainable only by the 'Extraordinary Path' (*khyad par gyi lam*). An Eleventh Stage is nothing new to Buddhism, as Har Dayal points out, but there is a claim here in Mantrayāna to superiority not only of speed but also of the range of tantric practice.[11] It is apparently the 'yoga of *mudrās*' which makes it all possible by generating the 'Satsukha'—glossed as the more usual 'Mahāsukha'—which is 'of the nature of Vajradhara'. It would appear that the Great Bliss is, among other things, the feelingful side of the goal to accompany the more noetic side of Vajradharahood. Accordingly, Abhayākaragupta glosses '*vajra*' as 'Voidness' which, we could say, is apprehended by the mind rather than the heart and therefore needs a companion term. The title 'Cakravartin' is strictly tantric, says the commentary, since it refers to the yogin at the center of the *maṇḍala*: 'the Lord who manifests the unfathomable circle of the *maṇḍala*' or the circle of the deities who make up the *Saṃpuṭa* Maṇḍala.

After telling us that all sentient beings are 'completely defiled', Abhayākaragupta treats us to traditional definitions of the 'Defilements'. He is careful to begin the list with 'delusion'—and not 'lust' as is often the case—to equate the term with Dependent Origination's first member, 'nescience'. This anticipates a quotation from Nāgārjuna. The commentary continues: "Delusion as *avidyā* is that superimposition (*sgro 'dogs pa*) of nonexistent entities, the *dharmas* of *pudgala* and 'actuality' (*raṅ bzin*) . . . and is the opposite of *vidyā* which knows the Two Truths. Vidyā is also the knowledege of *anāsrava* having as object the Dharmatā'. There is just a hint here, by no means explicit, that 'superimpositions' are caused by the 'outflows' (*āsravas*) of the ignorant mind; and this combination of terms comes close to the modern psychological notion of the unconscious mind's projecting alien contents onto external reality.[12] Indeed, all of the 'Defilements' can be looked upon as 'superimpositions' or projections since they are so much 'dirt' that needs to be 'washed away'. Abhayākaragupta defines 'hatred' as a mental attitude that is hostile and angry but also one that is itself 'tortured' (*mnar sems pa*). 'Lust' is the expected equivalent of 'craving' (*sred pa*), the eighth member of Dependent Origination. 'Pride' is the 'conceited attitude of one who thinks himself superior to others whether or not this is realistic'; while 'jealousy' is being 'oppressed by the good qualities of others'. Bu-ston follows, nearly copies, Abhayākaragupta on all this; and he adds that after the Defilements comes *karma* and after that *karma* comes the maturation of *karma* and after that come the Defilements again. This is the 'firewheel' of repeated births (CW, Part 8 (na), pp. 314-20 for this section of the *Saṃpuṭa*).

Finally, in this general commentarial review of the *Saṃpuṭa* text, it is Bu-ston who notices the danger of misinterpreting the statement that sentient beings can 'conquer' with the very thing by which they are 'bound'. It does not mean, he says, that one should 'increase lust, etc'. (*'dod chags sogs 'phel bar 'gyur bas*); that interpretation would be 'wrong' (*mi 'thad*). The 'destruction of delusion by the purification of delusion, etc'.

means instead the usual nontantric formulae for 'purification': eliminating the two obscurations of defilement and the knowable, achieving Voidness (presumably of discursive thought), attaining the Five knowledges. And then suddenly the Tibetan commentator follows his Indian predecessor Abhayākaragupta with a set of distinctly tantric correspondences: the five *skandhas* are said to correspond to the Five Defilements which in turn correspond to the Five Buddhas. Nothing more is said about those equivalents, but Śuravajra states that they are to be contemplated on the Stage of Generation and then realized on the Stage of Completion by way of the winds and *cakras* (PTT, Vol. 55, pp. 258-59 for the section). In an essay entitled, 'Purification of Sin in Buddhism by Vision and Confession', Wayman writes:

> There is no doubt of the Buddhist theory that the dark forces of the mind must be brought into the light and there examined and that the evil withers when so exposed. But it must not be concluded that defilements cease merely by being seen: indeed, the theory demands that the seeing of them take place under controlled, or yoga, circumstances .... Māra was not vanquished simply by being seen; rather, vanquished because Gautama (his left hand in the *samāpatti* gesture) was unmoved by the spectacle, and because (his right hand in the earth-touching gesture) mythologically the earth goddess appeared.[13]

Now, without discussing the richness of the imagery of the Earth Goddess here and her crucial role in the man Gautama's Enlightenment, I think it is possible that tantric Buddhists—and perhaps all Buddhists—are trying to tell us that the awakened person can 'see' the Defilements in a new light. The defiled *skandhas* can be seen in the light of Vairocana, etc. Wayman suggests that Māra does not even go away but that the Siddha is simply able to observe him without being 'moved'. If the Defilements are not destroyed in any ordinary moral sense but are 'purified' in the extraordinary sense that they are now made conscious—and with that much objectivity one is no longer 'moved' by them or tempted to act them out—and if further those Defilements which never go away are understood to be manifestations of the divine powers of Vairocana, etc., then Tantra which comes closest to stating such a position for Buddhism is ethically radical. And one need not look around in the tradition for possible sex-yogas any more, for there is enough profound controversy in place already! Let us remember that Padmasambhava does not destroy the 'demons'; he converts them in such a way that they no longer trouble the religion.

Dependent Origination

In the *Saṃpuṭa* text, we read 'by their own members (*sva-aṅga*; *raṅ gi yan lag*).' Abhayākaragupta says first that this must mean the list of the Five Defilements; and so it appears from just reading the scripture. But then the commentator suggests that the members are the members of one's 'own body' and offers the obscure phrase, 'one in the lineage' (*rigs la gcig*)—by which he might mean the continuity of defilement by way of *karma*. A third meaning occurs to him: our 'members' by which we are bound yet by which we conquer are the 'twelve members of Dependent Origination.' That is an entirely unexpected meaning, it seems to me, but Abhayākaragupta has already drawn our attention to the equation of a few members of the *nidāna* chain with some of the Defilements; and he must also have in mind the peculiar fact that this chain which has us 'bound' in the forward direction (from members one through twelve) must be understood link by link in the reverse direction (from twelve through one) to be 'conquered'. True to form, Abhayākaragupta states first the earlier tradition, in this case the Vaibhāṣika position of Vasubandhu's *Abhidharmakośa*—what Dr. Wayman calls one of the 'Western' positions.[14] The twelve-fold formula represents 'three lives': the first two members represent the 'past life,' the third to the tenth the 'present life', and the final two members the 'future life'. Each of the members are defined almost as one would expect: (1) 'nescience' is 'delusion'; (2) 'motivations' are acts with 'outflows' coursing in desires; (3) 'perception' belongs to the five *skandhas* but is also the *citta* (*sems*) at the moment of transmigration (these two meanings will be sorted out eventually by Tsoṅ-kha-pa, as Wayman points out[15]); (4) 'name and form' are 'gestation' (*srid pa*) in the womb with the four stages of the embryo *rūpa* listed by the commentator; (5) 'the six sense bases' are merely referred to as 'the eye, etc.'; but then (6) 'contact' occurs with the 'combination of the sense organ, object, and perception'; (7) 'feeling' has the nature of pleasure, pain, and neutrality (*btaṅ sñoms*); while 8. 'craving' is the desire not to lose the feeling of pleasure, the desire to be free of the feeling of pain, or the desire for neither pleasure nor pain; (9) 'indulgence'—a translation which Wayman has had to defend—is here recognized as problematic. Abhayākaragupta asks if there is any difference between craving and indulgence and answers that 'indulgence' is 'enjoying what is craved' (*sred la mṅon par dga' ba*) and states further that 'craving is caused by what is at a distance while indulgence is caused by what is nearby' (*riṅ ba'i rgyu sred pa daṅ ñe ba'i rgyu len pa*). While I sense that '*upadāna*' is better translated 'attachment' when dealing with the Four Noble Truths, here 'indulgence' (supported by the Tibetan Bhavacakra picture of 'a person picking fruit') seems the right term. (10) 'gestation'—also a problematic or at least an unusual translation—is said by the commentary to be "birth equivalent to the sequence from 'name-and-form' to 'feeling' " (*srid pa las skyes pa ni miṅ daṅ gzugs kyi rim pas tshor ba ji srid pa'o*). Since '*srid pa*' was also referred to at member 4. where the embryo forms, surely 'gestation' is a likely translation for member 10. Since member (11) 'birth' is equivalent to the 'sequence from name-and-form to feeling' there is evidence in Abhayākaragupta of a different 'Western' expression of Dependent Origination, closer to that of Asaṅga where the first three members are those that 'cast down' into Saṃsāra while the members that are 'cast down' begin with 'name-and-form'.[16] All of this happens 'conditionally', of course, as Abhayākaragupta makes clear; and finally there is (12) 'old age and death' about which, soberly enough, nothing is said.

But, we are told, 'one should know these twelve members of Dependent Origination as the Three Paths': Bu-ston adds that the long formula is 'condensed' by these Three Paths. They happen to be (1) The Path of Defilement comprised of members 'nescience', 'craving', and 'indulgence' (2) The Path of Karma comprised of 'motivation and gestation' while (3) the Path of Maturation (*rnam par smin pa'i lam*) is composed of the members that remain. Nāgārjuna is quoted from his *Pratītyasamutpādahṛdayakarikā*: "The Wheel of Saṃsāra has Three Paths, without beginning, middle, or end. Like a firewheel, their circling is mutually caused'.[17] And so a commentary on a Tantra contains a commentary on the 'orthodox' Nāgārjuna: following the master, Abhayākaragupta says that the first path, the one of Defilement, precedes the others. And thus we have arrived at a logical reason for an extended discussion of Dependent Origination in the context of an extended discussion of Defilements.

The mood now turns—having given both the Abhidharma and nontantric Mahāyāna tradition their say—to something more tantric. Abhayākaragupta quotes from what he calls the '*Mañjuśrītantra*', probably the *Mañjuśrīmūlatantra* mentioned by Mkhas-grub-rje: 'Besides, one may well understand that Dependent Origination applies to all of the *dharmas* along with knowledge of the various deities and all the *mantras*'.[18] It is an interesting statement, for the point is that the tantric ritual procedures are not exempt from the general Buddhist position on the Path that all realities are relativized. The quotation continues:

> As to these *dharmas*, this occurs with regard to them: they move like void and illusion. There arises this 'heap of suffering' to the extent there is born 'motivations' having 'nescience' as condition. To the extent that one knows the 'birth' of these, know their 'staying' and their 'destruction.' For this reason, the learned person (*mkhas pa'i rigs can*) will endeavor to get rid of 'nescience.' With the cessation of *avidyā*, the *dharmas* based on ignorance (*ajñāna*) will cease. By abandoning ignorance, the Defilements will not wander from place to place; by the cessation of the causes for Saṃsāra, there will be no destinies. Nirvāṇa will become evident. By the explanation of 'birth and death' which comprehends the nature of Saṃsāra, one enters into the accomplishment of all the *mantras* without any effort.

On second thought, this tantric mood of the *Mañjuśrīmūlatantra* seems rather orthodox.

Dependent Origination and Time

In his essay, 'Buddhist Dependent Origination and the Sāṃkhya guṇas', 'Alex Wayman refers to the correspondences found in the *Kālacakratantra* between the twelve signs of the zodiac, the twelve members of Dependent Origination, and the three *guṇas* of the Hindu Sāṃkhya system. Actually, we are told, the correspondences come not from the *mūla tantra* itself but from a commentary, the *Vimalaprabhā*.[19] The focus is upon what might be called the 'three strands' of Prakṛti—e.g., 'nescience' is *tamas*, 'motivations' is *rajas*, 'perception' is *sattva*—and it is only in a footnote that we learn, by way of an example of additional materials, that 'Makara' (Capricorn) corresponds to the first member of Dependent Origination. What tantalizes in that essay is found more fully presented in an article by Biswanath Banerjee, 'Pratītyasamutpāda as Viewed by the Kālacakra school'.[20] There we learn that a tantric Buddhist system devoted to 'time' (*kāla*) cannot avoid references to the calendar; and so it is that the Buddhist Bhavacakra is equivalent to Kālacakra. Since the outer 'ring' of the Bhavacakra symbol is devoted to the twelve members of Dependent Origination, the twelve signs of the zodiac which correspond to the twelve lunar months are said to correspond to Pratītyasamutpāda. In tabular form, the results appear as follows:

Zodiac House	*Solar Month*	*Dependent Origination*
Makara (Capricorn)	Puṣya (Dec.-Jan.)	1. Nescience
Kumbha (Aquarius)	Māgha (Jan.-Feb.)	2. Motivations
Mīna (Pisces)	Phālguna (Feb.-Mar.)	3. Perception
Meṣa (Aries)	Caitra (March-April)	4. Name and Form
Vṛṣabha (Taurus)	Vaiśākha (April-May)	5. Six Sense Bases
Mithuna (Gemini)	Jyaiṣṭha (May-June)	6. Sense Contact
Karkaṭa (Cancer)	Aṣāḍha (June-July)	7. Feeling
Siṃha (Leo)	Śrāvaṇa (July-Aug.)	8. Craving
Kanyā (Virgo)	Bhādrapada (Aug.-Sept)	9. Indulgence
Tulā (Libra)	Aśvina (Sept.-Oct.)	10. Gestation
Vṛścika (Scorpio)	Kārttika (Oct.-Nov.)	11. Birth
Dhanus (Sagittarius)	Mārgaśīrṣa (Nov.-Dec.)	12. Old Age and Death

As a further refinement on the material, we are told that each fortnight or half lunar month corresponds to the entire chain of Pratītyasamutapāda: but the 'waxing' half of the month has to do with the 'order of creation' while the 'waning' half corresponds to the 'order of destruction'. Banerjee suggests, no doubt correctly, that these orders refer to the 'forward and backward' understanding of the formula, its *anuloma* and *pratiloma* forms.

To facilitate our appreciation of these correspondences, let us note Professor Wayman's citation of Tsoṅ-kha-pa's discussion of the *Kālacakratantra* with regard to the two times, 'basic' (*gzi dus*) and 'fruitional' (*'bras dus*). This comes from an essay entitled, 'Female Energy and Symbolism in the Buddhist Tantras':

> The twelve [members of Dependent Origination, viz.] unwisdom (*avidyā*) and so on, are the twelve transits of the wind. The twelve members of the fruitional time are [stoppage of Dependent Origination, viz.] stoppage of unwisdom, and so on, and the stoppage of the twelve transits.[21]

This is a clue to the fact that the tantric yogin is supposed to perform meditational acts with regard to the members of Dependent Origination during the 'bright' and 'dark' halves of the month. These acts have to do with the transfer or 'transit' of wind through nine orifices, namely, forehead, navel, crown of head, nostrils, ears, eyes, mouth, urethra, anus, that make it possible to go meditatively to various 'destinies' which correspond to this or that orifice. When the holes are stopped up by *mantra* syllables or by letters, it is possible to force the 'wind' out through the crown of the head—part of the procedure of developing what is called the 'Illusory Body'.

Further, we might notice that the *Kālacakra* correspondences are not entirely arbitrary, although the precise system, if any, is obscure. For example, 'Makara' in this system is the beginning of the solar year, so it is appropriate that it correspond to the first member of Dependent Origination. That this 'Water Monster' be equivalent to 'nescience' might be inferred from the monster who holds the Tibetan wheel of life. The second house is 'Kumbha', whose sign is the Jar—and yet 'motivations' to which it corresponds is depicted in the Tibetan pictures of the Bhavacakra as a potter making pots or jars. Even the third sign of the zodiac, 'Mīna' or Pisces has something to do with the third member of Dependent Origination, 'perception', since the Illusory Body is said to emerge in yoga from the Clear Light like a 'fish'—and that mysterious Body is sometimes said to be composed of 'wind and perception'. The sixth sign 'Mithuna', which can have a sexual nuance, is equivalent to 'sense contact'—usually depicted by the Tibetans as a pair of lovers kissing. The others do not as easily correspond.

New materials, related to 'time,' emerge as one explores the commentaries at the end of chapter two (part one) for the *Saṃpuṭatantra*.

> Vajragarbha asked: 'What are the Channels (*nāḍi*) in the body?' The Bhagavat responded: 'According to the variety of four Cakras, there are one hundred and twenty. According to the nature of the Bodhicitta, thirty-two are said to be most important'.

Abhayākaragupta informs us that the four Cakras or centers in the subtle body are located at the navel, heart, throat, and forehead; they correspond in order to various Bodies of the Buddha, viz., Nirmāṇa, Dharma, Saṃbhoga, and Mahāsukha (PTT, Vol. 55, p. 121 for the relevant section). Since the Channels cluster at each center to form what looks like a 'lotus', there are 'petals' assigned to the Cakras, in order: 64, 8, 16, 32—which together equal 'one hundred and twenty' Channels. From this it would seem that the reason why 'thirty two' Channels are 'most important' has to do with their location at the forehead Cakra from which at a certain point in the yoga the 'Bodhicitta' must descend to transform the yogin. Now, it so happens that these lines in the *Saṃpuṭa*, are very close to the ones found near the opening of the *Hevajratantra*; D.L. Snellgrove translates:

> Then Vajragarbha said: 'How many veins are there, Lord, in the *vajra*-body?' There are thirty-two veins, he replied, 'thirty-two that bear *bodhicitta*, and flow into the place of great bliss'. (I.1.13)[23]

Neither the *Saṃpuṭa* nor its commentaries tell us that there is a parallel to the *Hevajra*—perhaps we are supposed to know already. But surely this is one of the reasons that the *Saṃpuṭa* was judged eventually to be an 'explanatory' Tantra within the *Hevajra* lineage. But I would like to reverse the 'explanatory' direction here since one Vṛddhakāyastha, who has written a commentary on the *Hevajratantra*, announces that the verses cited have to do with the doctrine of Dependent Origination (PTT, Vol. 54, p. 160).[24] He makes the same observations that Abhayākaragupta does with regard to the Channels and the Cakras but then engages in an unexplained play of numbers—such that the number 'thirty-two' leads to 'sixty' which when divided by 'Means and Insight' yields the number 'thirty'. Now he is prepared to tell us that there are thirty 'lunar days' (*tshes gcig*) to the month, with 'fifteen' days for each of the phases of the moon, its bright ascent from the new moon and its dark descent from the full: these fifteen days correspond, says Vṛddhakāyastha, to the twelve members of Pratītyasamutpāda.

Of course, there are three 'extra' days in the correspondence, but the commentary simply says that 'three days are included in twelve days' (*tshes graṅs gsum tshes graṅs bcu gñis kyi naṅ du 'dus pa yin no*). What he seems to mean is that the objects of Buddhist meditation mentioned for the thirteenth, fourteenth, and fifteenth days of each phase of the moon have already been mentioned in the analysis of the first twelve days. I use the term 'meditation' with hesitation, since no explicit reference is made to a contemplative exercise; but we have already seen that such an exercise is in place for the 'bright fortnight' and the 'dark fortnight' of the *Kālacakra*. Should this be correct, then one is to meditate on the 'first day' on the object of 'the knowledge of nonduality'—which corresponds to 'nescience.' The materials can be tabulated as follows:

Dependent Origination	*Day*	*Object of meditation*
1. nescience	1.	Knowledge of Nonduality
2. motivations	2.	Means and Insight
3. perception	3.	Body, Speech, and Mind
4. name and form	4.	Four Great Elements
5. six sense bases	5.	Five Knowledges
6. sense contact	6.	Vajradhara who is inseparable from the Five Knowledges
7. feelings	7.	(Five Knowledges) with Means and Insight
8. craving	8.	'That' (*de ñid*) (probably Five Knowledges again) with Body, Speech, and Mind

9. indulgence	9. Five Knowledges and Four Great Elements
10. gestation	10. Twice five (probably two times the Five Knowledges)
11. birth	11. Twice the Five Knowledges plus the nature of Nonduality
12. old age and death	12. 'That' (twice Five Knowledges) plus the nature of Means and Insight
	13. 'That' plus Body, Speech and Mind
	14. 'That' plus the Four Great Elements
	15. Three times five (Knowledges) which are the Yoginīs

We can see how the 'extra' days in the correspondence do not bring in new Buddhist topics, just as the commentator indicated; we see too a certain 'logic' in the choice of topics—two-fold topics for the second day, four-fold elements for the fourth day, etc. There may even be an allusion to the 'antidote' theory of Early Buddhism whereby one meditates upon the opposite of a fault to correct it: 'Knowledge of Nonduality' would be the logical antidote to 'nescience'; 'Means and Insight' might be the perfect foil for the 'duplicity' of good and bad *karma* instigated by the 'motivations'. Other connections may be possible, but one feels a great deal of arbitrariness in the list—it would not be hard to come up with topics for many more days!

But the antidote solution falls upon the discovery that the *anuloma* or 'forward' review of Dependent Origination corresponds to the waxing phase of the moon while the 'backward' or *pratiloma* review corresponds to the waning phase wherein alone the chain is 'destroyed'. And yet one wonders if the chain is ever really destroyed. For it is also said that the waxing phase has to do with nothing less than 'Vajradhara' while the waning half of the month is equivalent to 'Nairātmyā'. One is given the impression that both directions of the chain are meaningful just as both phases of the moon make up a whole month.

GENERAL OBSERVATIONS

In closing, I think it might be useful—in the face of so many details—to say a few general things about the formula of Pratītyasamutpāda in Buddhism. First of all, let us be clear about the fact that in India the formula is always 'negative', i.e. a 'heap of suffering' for the Abhidharma, the nontantric Mahāyāna, and for the Tantric tradition as well. It could not be otherwise for a chain that 'binds' with such links as 'nescience', 'craving', 'indulgence', 'old age and death'. The 'relativity' announced by the formula is also supposed to be taken as a negative characteristic of Saṃsāra wherein there is nothing to depend upon absolutely. Even to state, as the Mādhyamika does, that there is 'no difference' between Saṃsāra and Nirvāṇa is not to do away with the unattractive features of the formula. It seems to me, however, that I hear rather often in scholarly meetings—but not actually in scholarly writing where one is more cautious—an appreciation for the 'relativity' of Dependent Origination as a revelation from Buddhism about how everything is so beautifully connected. This has to do with an Allen Watts sort of perception and may even be wise in its own right; but it has little to do with the Indian tradition.[25] The point is so obvious to me that I have had to ask myself why it is that I hear the 'positive' evaluation of Dependent Origination so often. I think one of the reasons is that Gautama is supposed to have discovered the chain in reverse order, to have turned 'nescience' into 'wisdom' and thereby caused the chain to collapse: and yet this Conqueror remained somehow subject at least to 'old age and death', as we know from accounts of his demise at the ripe old age of eighty. True, the traditions have tried to solve the problem by the notion of a *nirvāṇa* distinct from a more complete *parinirvāṇa* or by a 'Nirvāṇa with Remainder' distinct from 'Nirvāṇa without Remainder'. Tantra, however, seems to have something else in mind. If we bring to our aid what has already been suggested concerning the tantric attitude toward 'Defilement', then it would be possible for a yogin to 'see' Dependent Origination and become 'free' from it in the sense of no longer being 'moved' by its members—even though actually the chain of 'relativity' did not go away. This interpretation would make sense of the early biographical detail that Gautama Buddha contemplated the twelve-fold formula backwards and forwards, over and over, as if in doing so he was achieving a more 'conscious' relationship to its members, seeing them in a new 'light', but no longer 'moved' by them as at age twenty-nine. In his younger years, Gautama had reacted to the twelfth member of Dependent Origination thus:

> I too am subject to old age, not beyond the sphere of old age, and should I, who am subject to old age, not beyond the sphere of old age, on seeing an old man be troubled, ashamed, and disgusted?' This seemed to me not fitting.[26]

Six difficult years later, this same person was able to see the matter differently—or so it seems to me—not 'positively' really, but as something unavoidable toward which one could take up an objective attitude of acceptance. That could be said to 'conquer' the chain as something that binds; and yet it is by those 'very own members' that one becomes free. As the tantric materials put it, it is possible to unite Vajradhara and Nairātmyā, the bright and the dark phases of the Moon.

References

1. Alex Wayman, 'Buddhism', in *Historia Religionum*, vol. 2, Religions of the Present (ed. by C. J. Bleeker and Geo Widengren) (E. J. Brill, Leiden, 1971), p. 389.

2. Wayman, 'Buddhism', p. 424.

3. Har Dayal, *The Bodhisattva Doctrine in Buddhist Sanskrit Literature* (Motilal Banarsidass, Delhi, 1970 reprint of 1932), p. 242.

4. See the relevant section from the *Mahānidāna Sūtra*, translated by A. K. Warder in his *Indian Buddhism* (Motilal Banarsidass, Delhi, 1970), pp. 107ff.

5. Alex Wayman, 'Buddhist Dependent Origination and the Sāṃkhya guṇas,' *Ethnos* (1962), pp. 14-22; 'Buddhist Dependent Origination,' *History of Religions*, 10:3, pp. 185-203; 'Dependent Origination—the Indo-Tibetan Tradition', *Journal of Chinese Philosophy*, 7 (1980), pp. 275-300 and also in *Buddhist Insight*: *Essays by Alex Wayman*, ed. by George R. Elder, Religions of Asia Series, No. 5 (eds. Lewis W. Lancaster and J. L. Shastri) (Motilal Banarsidass, Delhi, 1984), chapter 8.

6. Alex Wayman, *The Buddhist Tantras*: *Light on Indo-Tibetan Esotericism* (Samuel Weiser, Inc., New York, 1973), chapter 2.

7. I am editing the *Saṃpuṭa* from Sanskrit manuscripts provided by Tokyo University and by the Institute for Advanced Study of World Religions, Stony Brook, New York. The Tibetan translation of the text comes primarily from the Japanese Photographic Edition of the Peking Edition of the Tibetan

Buddhist Canon designated in the notes as 'PTT'. The Derge edition, made available by Columbia University, New York, has also been consulted for questionable readings.

8. Alex Wayman with Ferdinand D. Lessing, *Mkhas grub rje's "Fundamentals of the Buddhist Tantras"*, (Mouton, The Hague, 1968), p. 253.

9. The Sanskrit commentaries, no longer extant, can be found in Tibetan translations in PTT, Vol. 55. Bu-ston's commentary comes from *The Collected Works of Bu-ston*, Part 8 (ña), (edited by Lokesh Chandra) (International Academy of Indian Culture, New Delhi, no date). Tsoṅ-kha-pa's preference can be determined from citations in Alex Wayman's, *Yoga of the Guhyasamājatantra*: *The Arcane Lore of Forty Verses* (Motilal Banarsidass, Delhi, 1977).

10. Wayman, *Yoga*, p. 102.

11. Dayal, *Bodhisattva Doctrine*, p. 282. See also Wayman, *Mkhas grub rje's*, p. 39.

12. The *āsravas*, I believe, deserve more attention in Buddhist scholarship; their elimination was, after all, originally the chief Buddhist attainment before being 'displaced' in the doctrine by the apparently more sophisticated formula of Dependent Origination. See Dayal, *Bodhisattva Doctrine*, pp. 116ff. Also hear my lecture, 'The Snake and the Rope: Projection Phenomena and Religion', C. G. Jung Foundation, 1986, available from the Foundation on audiotape.

13. Wayman, in *A Study of Kleśa* (ed. by Genjun H. Sasaki) (Shimizukobundo Ltd., Tokyo, 1975), pp. 511-512.

14. Wayman, 'Buddhist Dependent Origination', p. 187.

15. Wayman, 'Buddhist Dependent Origination', p. 189. For justification of the translation of 'perception', see Alex Wayman, 'Vijñāna' in *The Encyclopedia of Religion* (ed. Mircea Eliade) (Macmillan, New York, 1987).

16. Wayman, 'Buddhist Dependent Origination', p. 189.

17. The identification of the quotation is made by way of Wayman, 'Buddhist Dependent Origination', p. 188.

18. Wayman, *Mkhas grub rje's*, p. 344.

19. Wayman, p. 15.

20. Biswanath Banerjee, *Journal of the Ganganatha Jha Kendriya Sanskrit Vidyapeetha*, vol. 27, July-October, 1971, pp. 29-33. For helpful information on the ancient Indian calendar, consult A. L. Basham, *The Wonder that was India* (Grove Press, New York, 1954), pp. 492-93.

21. Wayman, *Buddhist Tantras*, p. 177. And see this work, pp. 141-3, for the orifice theory that follows below.

22. Wayman, *Yoga*, p. 284.

23. D. L. Snellgrove, *The Hevajra Tantra*, 2 volumes (Oxford University Press, London, 1959), Vol. 1, p. 49.

24. The Japanese Photographic Edition of the Peking Edition is difficult to read even though it was used for research purposes; there is an interlinear subcommentary that renders many of the main lines illegible. The Derge Edition (Volume 5 of the Tanjur, pp. 24-27) provided by Columbia University is a preferable source.

25. See Alan W. Watts, *Psychotherapy East and West* (Random House, New York, 1961), where he translates '*dharmadhatu*' as the 'field of related functions'. . . 'a vast network of jewels, like drops of dew upon a multi-dimensional spider web', p. 59. For a wiser and, I think, more accurate assessment, see C. G. Jung, 'On the Discourses of the Buddha', *Collected Works*, Vol. 18 (Princeton University Press, Princeton, 1950), par. 1575.

11 [*KEVALI*]*BHUKTIVICĀRA* OF BHĀVASENA: TEXT AND TRANSLATION

PADMANABH S. JAINI
University of California, Berkeley

INTRODUCTION

In my article on the *Muktivicāra* of the thirteenth century Digambara author Bhāvasena, a brief reference was made to its companion text, the *Bhuktivicāra*, by the same author.[1] Only a single palm-leaf manuscript of this work has survived and is part of Professor Ernst Leumann's library at the Bibliotheque Nationale, Strasbourg. As described by Chandrabhal Tripathi, the manuscript (no. 164) is complete and consists of no more than five folios inscribed in the Kannada script.[2] As I set out to transcribe the text, I found it to be in an extremely unsatisfactory condition, full of illegible words and repetitious sentences. Even so, the work seems to deserve attention as it deals with an ancient controversy over the nature of an Omniscient Being in the Jaina tradition. I therefore present here an abridged version (omissions indicated by. . .) which preserves all of the major arguments appearing in the original text.

'*Bhuktivicāra*' is, of course, the author's own abridgement for the full title, the *Kevali-bhuktivicāra*, an 'Investigation into the Eating of Food by a Kevalin'. The topic pertains to a controversy between the Digambaras and the Śvetāmbaras, the two ancient sects of Jainism, over the ability of an Omniscient Being (called Kevalin or Arhat in the Jaina tradition) to survive a lifetime without partaking of any food or water (kavala-āhāra, lit. food made into morsels). Both sects agree that the attainment of kevalajñāna (lit. knowledge isolated from karmic bonds, i.e. omniscience) is preceded by the total destruction of all forms of the desire-producing karma (called mohanīya), and also that such a person, subsequent to his becoming a Kevalin, leads the normal life of a Jaina mendicant (e.g. moving from place to place, preaching sermons, and so forth) for the duration of his life. They agree further that the Kevalin is still subject to the karmic force called *vedanīya*, which must at all times produce the experience of either physical pain (*asātā*) or pleasure (*sātā*), feelings inseparable from the state of embodiment. The Śvetāmbaras accordingly believe that a Kevalin, regardless of the absence of desire for food, must still feel the pain of hunger, and hence, like any ordinary human being, will not subsist without eating food. The Digambaras find this unacceptable, for they believe that eating as well as bodily functions such as answering the calls of nature, are incompatible with total freedom from desires as well as omniscient cognition which characterize a Kevalin. They have therefore asserted that in the absence of mohanīya-karma, the asātā-vedanīya of the Kevalin is incapable of yielding its karmic fruit and is, instead, transformed into the sātā variety, thus removing the very reason for eating food, namely, hunger and thirst.[3] The Digambaras don't deny that some form of āhāra or food is essential for keeping the body alive. They maintain, however, that this is accomplished by an involuntary intake (āhāra) of a subtle material substance called nokarma-vargaṇā, a process common to all embodied beings. In the case of ordinary beings, this nokarma-vargaṇā must be supplemented by some other form of food for the sustenance of their bodies. But, according to the Digambaras, the Kevalin's body undergoes such a transformation that his nokarma-vargaṇā also provides him with all necessary nourishment.[4] The Digambaras therefore describe the Kevalin's body as parama-audārika, an extremely pure body, a miraculous body as it were, free from all impurities and sustained by no other 'food' than the nokarma-vargaṇā. The Śvetāmbaras find no scriptural support for this theory of the parama-audārika body, and believe that a Kevalin, and even as exalted a person as the Jina Mahāvīra himself, must partake of food to assuage his hunger and to sustain his body. The debate between these two rival sects is thus an attempt to define the true nature of a Kevalin, to resolve the apparent conflict that exists between his Desirelessness (vītarāgatva) and his need to eat (bubhukṣā), between his Infinite Bliss (ananta-sukha) and the pain of hunger and thirst.

The beginnings of this debate are shrouded in mystery and probably are as old as the sects themselves, as is demonstrated by Dundas in his brilliant discussion in an article aptly entitled

'Food and Freedom'.[5] There is ground to believe that it was initiated by a second century Jaina mendicant sect called the Yāpanīya.[6] This sect is now extinct, but a major treatise (in 37 verses) entitled the *Kevalibhuktiprakaraṇa*, together with a prose *Svopajñaṭīkā* by the ninth century Yāpanīya author Śākaṭāyana has survived. A critical edition of this work, together with the *Strīnirvāṇa-prakaraṇa-Svopajñavṛtti* was published by Muni Jambūvijayajī in 1974.[7] This excellent edition also includes a most valuable appendix which reproduces discussions on this topic by later Śvetāmbara mendicant authors, notably, Śīlācārya's commentary on the *Sūtrakṛtāṅga*, Abhayadevasūri's *Sanmativṛtti*, and Vādi-Devasūri's *Syādvādaratnākara*. The appendix also contains the twelfth century Digambara author Prabhācandra's presentation of the Śvetāmbara arguments (the pūrvapakṣa) as found in his *Nyāyakumudacandra*, but unfortunately not his refutation of the Śvetāmbara position.[8] The dispute between the sects continues well beyond Prabhācandra's time, as can be seen in such Śvetāmbara works as the *Tarkarahasyaṭīkā* (on Haribhadra's *Ṣaḍdarśanasamuccaya*) of the fourteenth century Guṇaratnasūri,[9] the *Yuktiprabodha-Svopajñavṛtti* by the seventeenth century Meghavijaya[10] and the *Adhyātmamataparīkṣā* by the eighteenth century logician Yaśovijaya.[11] On the Digambara side, Prabhācandra probably had the last words on this debate, for no later work with the exception of the *Bhuktivicāra* of Bhāvasena (as produced here) has survived and the latter, as is clear from the text (#27), had access to it. The importance of this short work therefore lies not in any original contribution to the debate, for it makes none. Bhāvasena's work is nevertheless of significance for its display of open sectarian animosity toward the Śvetāmbaras, a hostility provoked by the dispute over the nature of the Kevalin, which leads him to regard his rival Jainas even lower than the heretic 'bhaktas' (see #29), evidently the devotees of Viṣṇu and Śiva.

Bhāvasenaviracitaḥ [Kevali]bhuktivicāraḥ

#1 Vīraṃ jineśvaraṃ natvā traividyaṃ vādivanditam /
Bhukti-Mukti-vicārārtham arthaśāstraṃ prakathyate //1//
anenaivārthaśāstreṇa svapakṣaḥ sādhyate 'dhunā /
vighaṭyate vipakṣo 'pi Śvetāmbaramatāgataḥ //2//. . .

#2 . . .iha hi bhagavadarhatparameśvarasyotpannakevalajñānasya bhuktiyuktiṃ kaścit Śvetāmbaravādī darśayann āha—

#3 "śarīram ādyaṃ khalu dharmasādhanam"/ tac ca śarīraṃ pañcamahābhūtātmakam āhārapūrvakam/ dehasthityartham āhāraḥ, āhārād ṛte dehasyāvasthānānupapatteḥ/ sthūlakṛśatvaṃ hi dehasyāhārānvayavyatirekānuvidhāyī, sati śarīre āhāraparihāro du[ṣka]raḥ syāt/ pakṣamāsaṣaṇmāsābdāvasāne 'py ekavāram āhāreṇa bhavitavyam /. . .

#4 dehasahāyaṃ vihāya sarvajñatvaṃ bhagavataḥ kathaṃ kathayanti tathyavādinaḥ, dehādhārāhāraṃ na mukhyakāraṇam [iti]/ āhārāt suprasannamanasi buddher āvirbhāvo bhavati, indriyapāṭavaṃ prakaṭatām aṭaty aṅgaṃ puṣṭāṅgatāṃ yāti/ no cel locanayor malinatvaṃ rasanajñāyāṃ nīrasatvaṃ nāsikāyām avyaktatā śrotrayor aspaṣṭatvaṃ kāyasya kṛśatvaṃ mater māndyaṃ gater jāḍyaṃ janair dṛśyate/ tasmād asmai dehaparigraham urarīkurvatā syādvādavādinā 'hāro py urarīkartavyaḥ /. . .

#5 . . .kevalinaḥ kavalaṃ bhuktiṃ pramāṇapañcakair prapañcyate/ kevalin dharmī bhuktimān bhavatīti sādhyo dharmaḥ/ dvividhavedanīyasya vidyamānatvāt/ yo ya īdṛśas sa tādṛśaḥ, yathā rathyāpuruṣaḥ/ dvividhavedanīyavidyamānaś cāyaṃ kevalī, tasmād bhuktimān bhavatīti/. . .

#6 tathā keval(l)ī bhuktimān, ṣaṭparyāptimatvāt, taijasā. . . bubhukṣāpakṣatvāt; dīrghāyuṣā vihāratvāt; sammatapuruṣavat /

#7 tat sarvaṃ krameṇa vicāryate/ dehāmukhyatāyām etad ayuktam/ nānāprakārāhāravaikalyadarśanāt/ pañcakṛtvā bhuñjānasya yādṛśī dehasthitir evaṃ catus trir dvir bhuñjānasya tādṛśaivaikabhojino hi tathā dināntaritabhojinām api/ tathā Bāhubaliprabhṛtīnāṃ prakṛṣṭayatīnāṃ pakṣamāsaṣaṇmāsasaṃvatsarapramitāhāravatāṃ prakṛṣṭaṃ dṛṣṭaṃ kāye kāntibalam/ tathā bahutarakleśāyāsaśīlavatī Sītā sattvasametā/ anaśanāditaponuṣṭhānaprakṛṣṭānāṃ yatīnāṃ doṣāvaraṇakṣayaḥ jñānātiśayaś ca dṛśyate/tathā cāyaṃ ślokaḥ—

doṣāvaraṇayor hānir niḥśeṣāsty atiśāyanāt /
kvacid yathā svahetubhyo bahirantarmal(l)akṣayaḥ //

[*Āptamīmāṃsā*, kārikā 4]

asyānaṅgīkāre svavyāghātaprasaṅgāt /

#8 . . .apramattād ūrdhvam āhāravyavahāravirahāt, sūkṣmasāmparāye kṣutpipāsādicaturdaśaparīṣahāṇāṃ vidyamānatvāt. . .

#9 . . .āhārapūrvikety atra āhāramātraṃ svīkriyate kavalāhāro vā? . . .prathamapakṣe siddhasādhyatā prasiddhā syāt/ sayogakevalini nokarmakarmāhāro 'smābhir abhidhīyate, tatra kavalāhārābhāvāt //

#10 athāhāro 'nnādilakṣaṇo lakṣyate tatreti cet /

#11 na, ṣaḍvidhāhārapāṭhāt/gāthāyāṃ tathoktam—"āhāro chabbidho ṇeyo"/ anyathaikendriyāṇḍajajīvānāṃ dehasthiter avakāśo na syāt/ tatra kavalāhāro na sambhavati/...tathā dvitīyapakṣe nākanikāyenānekāntāt/ teṣāṃ kavalāhārābhāve 'pi dehasthites sadbhāvāt /

#12 atha kavalāhārābhāve katipayadinair asmadādivad dehasthiter abhāvo vibhāvyate vidvadbhir bhāvaiḥ, tadvat kevalino 'py abhāva eva, iti cet /

#13 na, tatsādhakānām anumānādīnāṃ bahuśo darśanāt/ "yaḥ sarvāṇi carācarāṇi [as quoted in the *Viśvatattvaprakāśa*, p. 68]" ityādi svasaṃvedanasya...niratyaya ity āgamād avagamyate/...

#14 atha vedanīye vidyamāne "ekādaśa jine" [*Tattvārthasūtra*, ix, 11] santīti vacanāt kṣuttṛṣābubhukṣā tasmād bhaved iti/ tathā 'numānam—bhagavati vedanīyaṃ phaladāyi, karmatvāt, āyuḥkarmavat /

#15 naitat sādhvanumānam/ mohanīyasahāyaṃ vihāyāsātam api sātāyaiva/...tadatiśayajñānaviśeṣatvān [yathā] nakhakeśādivṛddhirāhityaṃ yathā caturāsyatvaṃ bhavati, bhavaty eva tathā kavalavikalatvaṃ tasmād asmin/ kavalāhāravyavahāraparihārāt parīṣahaparihāraḥ prabhavati /

#16 ...anantajñānaviśeṣād anantadarśanam anantavīryatvam anantasukhatvaṃ sukhena jāghaṭyate/ tathā coktaṃ ślokaḥ—

aiśvaryam apratihataṃ sahajo virāgaḥ /
tṛptir nisargajanitā vaśitendriyeṣu //
ātyantikaṃ sukham anāvaraṇā ca śaktiḥ /
jñānaṃ ca sarvaviṣayaṃ bhagavaṃs tavaiva // [?]

#17 viśiṣṭavedanīyodayabhogād bubhukṣābhuktiyuktir na bobhavīti/ tasminn arthe pramāṇaṃ pravartate/ vītarāgo bhagavān na kiñcid ādhātuṃ hātuṃ pravartate, pravṛttinivṛttiviṣayavidūratvāt, nivṛttavyāmohatvāt/ ya īdṛśas sa tādṛśaḥ, yathobhayasammataḥ paramayogī/tathā cāyaṃ tatas tathā /...

#18 api cālokasāmānyamanuṣyatvaṃ bhagavati parameśvare dṛśyate /

#19 manuṣyatvāviśeṣe 'pi...dīptataponidhīnāṃ paramayatīnāṃ tāratamyabhāvenāhāradūratvam/ ...ślokas tathā—

mānuṣīṃ prakṛtim abhyatītavān /

devatāsv api ca devatā yataḥ //
tena nātha paramāsi devatā /
śreyase jina Vṛṣa prasīda naḥ //
[*Bṛhatsvayambhūstotra*, kārikā 75]

ityāgamoktatvāt /...

#20 etena śarīratvavaktṛtvapuruṣatvādayo hetavo nirastā veditavyāḥ /

#21 kiñca dhyānaviśeṣād āvaraṇakṣayāt...svaparaprakāśajñānānandātmakasya nijaniranjananirupamasvarūpasya bhagavadarhatparameśvarasya kṣudhābubhukṣābhuktyā dainyāpādakaṃ Śvetāmbarācāryavacanam...acārutāyāḥ prathamaṃ prakaraṇam/ kṣudhātṛṣābhayadveṣetyādikarmārātijayān mārajij jina ity abhidhānāt, anekaviṣamabhavagahanavyasanaprāpaṇahetūn karmārātin jayantīti jinā iti vyutpatteś ca kṣudhādyanekadoṣaviṣayo na bhavatīti suniścitaṃ vipaścitām /

#22 ...atha kevalāvasthāyāṃ kavalāhāraparihāre samavasaraṇaviharaṇaṃ nopapadyate?

#23 maivaṃ vaktavyam/ tatpuṇyaprabhāvāc caturāsyatvādiguṇānāṃ niratiśayasvarūpāṇāṃ samavasṛtiprabhṛtivibhūtīnāṃ darśanāt /

#24 ...nanu ba[lava]tā vedanīyakarmaṇā nirmitapīḍāto bhuktibhāktvaṃ bhavatīti cet /

#25 na, agnir māṇavakaḥ, siṃho māṇavakaḥ, ity upamānāt; na hy agnisiṃhayoḥ māṇavakatvaṃ sambhavati/ vedanīyopamā saṃjñā vijñāyate tajjñaiḥ/ asahāyavedanīyaṃ kiñcit kartuṃ śaknoti? sahāyam antareṇa sphurati kiṃ pratāpaḥ, tejaḥprabhāvātigatabhasmavat? taddhy ekam api vedanīyaṃ vedanām utpādayitum akṣamam, yathaiko 'pi naṭabaṭuḥ svakīyaṃ skandham āruhya nārhati nartituṃ niḥsakhatvāt; niḥsahāyaḥ samartho 'py asamartha eva /...

#26 naitad bhuktiyuktir yauktikamatam avagāhate/ tat kathaṃ? kavalāhāratvāt kevalikāyasya malamūtrādyapavitratādoṣānuṣaṅgo...cāṅgīkartavyaḥ? tataś ca sarvavitvahānir ānīyate tasmai/ tasmād ekaṃ sandhitsor anyat pracyavate, ekaṃ kartum ārabdhasyānyathāgatam ityādi nyāyaparipāṭikoṭim āṭikate (?) teṣāṃ Dupaṭavādināṃ vacanam /...

#27 etāvatā kim uktaṃ bhavati?...ataḥ prakṣīṇamohe bhagavati na prabhavanti vedanīyaprabhāvāḥ/tasmād dagdharajjusvarūpavedanīyāt kṣutbubhukṣāpakṣaḥ kakṣīkriyate /

#28 parīkṣitam atra vicakṣaṇaiḥ—tarhi lalanālīḍhāliṅganacumbanariraṃsā 'pi kiṃ na syāt? tathā ca sarvaveditvaṃ samastavastuniḥspṛhavṛttivītarāgatvaṃ vaktuṃ na yuktaṃ yauktikavādibhir bhavadbhis tatra/...bhavaduktā yuktiḥ, sā ca parameśvarasya nidrātandrāvyādhi...bādhādurbodhatvam eva sandhāti/ tathā ca bhagavato jñānam indriyajam, jñānatvāt; asmadādijñāvad [iti] aniṣṭāpatteḥ /

#29 kiñca, kecid bhaktā bhagāder bhoktṛtvaṃ bhūyo bhāvayanti, te 'pi ṣoḍaśopacāreṇopacaranti, na hi sāttvikavṛttyā vartante/ tato mithyādṛṣṭibhyaḥ kaṣṭatarāḥ Pāṇḍupaṭāḥ/...kutaḥ? kṣudhādyaśeṣadoṣadūṣitaṃ devaṃ...kaṭhinamatiḥ smarati sutarāṃ vivekavikalatvāt/ svayaṃ kṣudhāgniduḥkhadaṃdahyamāno hi devo kathaṃ pareṣāṃ kṣudhāgniṃ vidhyāpayati? svayaṃ patan pumān patantaṃ katham uddharati? anyenānyasyānyakūpapatanam, na hy abhimatasthānaprāptiḥ/ tathā 'nekapātakapatitasya Śvetapaṭavādino nāsti paramā gatiḥ, yato 'tra kṣudhādidoṣaprakṣayopalakṣitavītarāgakevalini kavalagrasanavikasanakathanāt/ tathā pūrvācāryavacanam—"kevalikavalāhārābhyavaharaṇād avarṇavādo doṣaḥ darśnamohasya", saptatikoṭākoṭisāgaropamāyuṣasthiter bhājo bhavaṃ bhavaṃ virājante /...

#30 tasmād yato bhagavān bhuktiyukto na bhavati—anantacatuṣṭayasvarūpatvāt,...prakṣīṇamohavyūhatvāt, catustriṃśadatiśayasametatvāt, pañcamahākalyāṇavibhūtiviśiṣṭatvāt,...vyatireke rathyāpuruṣavat/ iti nirdiṣṭebhyo 'numānebhyo...iṣṭasiddhir abobhūyiṣṭa /...//

Translation:

#1 Having paid obeisance to Mahāvīra, the omniscient (traividya, i.e. the knower of the three times)[12] Lord of the Jinas, and one who is reverentially greeted by logicians (i.e. disputants in a debate), this meaningful treatise is expounded in order to investigate **Eating of Food** [**by a Kevalin (i.e. an Omniscient Being)**] and **Attainment of Mokṣa** [**by a Female**].[13] [1] By this meaningful treatise our own doctrine will be established, and the opposite view as held by the Śvetāmbaras will also be refuted. [2]. . .

#2 [Digambara:] Here a certain Śvetāmbara holds the view that the Lord Arhat, the highest Lord who has attained omniscience (kevala-jñāna)[14] eats food. In support of this view he says:

#3 'The body is indeed the foremost means of achieving

dharma"; and that body consists of the five great material elements supported by food. Food is for the sake of maintaining the body since without food the body cannot be sustained. This is proved by the fact that the thickness or thinness of the body invariably corresponds to the presence or absence of food. Hence as long as there is a body, the avoidance of food must be considered extremely difficult. [Even one who fasts] must eat at least once at the end of a fortnight, a month, six months, or a year...

#4 [Śvetāmbara:] How do those (i.e. the Digambaras) who claim to speak the truth assert even the endurance of omniscience in the Lord, without the assistance of his body? How can they maintain that the food that supports the body is not the chief cause [of sustaining his life]? Because of food the mind is at peace, intelligence appears, clarity of sense organs is produced, and the body is well nourished. Otherwise, the eyes become weak, the tongue ceases to taste flavour, the nose does not experience smell, the ears do not hear clearly, the body becomes thin, the mind becomes dull, and one's gait becomes laboured; all this is evident to everyone. Therefore, a follower of the doctrine of syādvāda (i.e. a Jaina), if he believes that the sustenance of the body is necessary for a Kevalin, must also admit food for such a person...

#5 [Śvetāmbara:]...Our view that a Kevalin takes food by morsels will be established by all five means of verification. [Here we present the following syllogism:] The point we seek to prove is that the Kevalin eats food. This is because there is in him the presence of the two-fold vedanīya-karma [which produces pleasure (*sātā*) and pain (*asātā*)]. Whosoever is like that must eat food, for example, a person on the street. The Kevalin has the two-fold vedanīya-karma. Therefore he must eat food.

#6 [Śvetāmbara:] Similarly, the Kevalin eats food because he has six paryāptis (a process by which a soul brings about the 'completion' of a new life).[15] He must have hunger (bubhukṣā, lit. "desire to eat") because of the 'heat body' (taijasa-śarīra, a body possessed by all embodied beings), and also because [even after attaining omniscience] he does move about for the duration of his long life, like any other human being...

#7 [Digambara:] All this will be examined in proper order.... Your statement is not correct, since the body is not the most important factor here. This is because the state of a body does not necessarily correspond to the number of days during which it remains devoid of food. For example, the condition of the body of one who takes food after skipping five meals, and of one who takes food after skipping four, three, or two meals, does not differ [proportionately]. Similarly, an extreme form of radiant energy is observed in the bodies of ascetics like Bāhubali who practice the highest form of control, and also in those who eat only once in a fortnight, a month, six months, or a year.[16] So was Sītā full of vigour, even after a great deal of suffering and exhaustion, while she kept her precepts.[17] In those mendicants who engage in austerities of fasting and so forth, there is also seen excellence of cognition as well as destruction of obscurations and passions, as has been said:

> The total destruction of defects (i.e. passions) and obscurations (of knowledge) must be possible in some person. Because these two admit of degrees [of absence in ordinary people]. For example, the internal and external dirt [in a piece of gold] which can be completely cleansed by proper means. [*Āpta-mīmāṃsā*, verse 4][18]

If you do not accept this, then you will be contradicting yourself.

#8 [Digambara:]...Moreover, all activities of eating cease beyond the [seventh spiritual] stage (guṇasthāna) called apramatta-virata (i.e. total renunciation free from all forms of carelessness).[19] As for the fourteen afflictions (parīṣaha, see below #14) beginning with hunger and thirst, these may exist only up to the [eleventh stage called] sūkṣma-sāmparāya (i.e. subtle desire) [and not beyond, in the thirteenth stage of the Kevalin].

#9 [Digambara:] Are you merely claiming some form of '*āhāra*' (food), or only that 'āhāra' which is eaten by morsels (kavala-āhāra)? In the first alternative there is no need for argumentation, because in the Kevalin with Activities (i.e. the thirteenth stage), we also admit the intake of *āhāra* in the form of the quasi-karmic molecules (called nokarma-vargaṇā) that a soul automatically takes in during the state of embodiment. The second alternative is not [applicable to this stage] since eating in the form of food made into morsels is not found there.

#10 [Śvetāmbara:] But 'āhāra' characterized as 'edible' is indicated [in the scriptures] for that stage.

*11 [Digambara:] No, because six kinds of āhāra are mentioned in the scripture, as is said in the verse: 'āhāra should be known as six-fold'.[20] Otherwise there would be no possibility of the sustenance of the bodies of beings with one sense (e.g. plants), or beings in eggs; for food by way of eating morsels is not possible for them....In the second alternative (of considering only the kavala-āhāra as food) there is the fault of inapplicability to those who live in the heavenly abodes. Their bodies are maintained even in the absence of food taken by morsels.

*12 [Śvetāmbara:] In the absence of food by morsels, within a few days, the sustanence of the body is in peril. The wise (i.e. the physicians) can figure from signs that our bodies may cease to exist. The same would be the case of a Kevalin who is like us.

*13 [Digambara:] No, [the case is not similar] because of the many inferences that support our contention. It is also known from the scriptures, as for example 'One who [knows] all sentient and insentient beings[21]...', and so forth, that the omniscient cognition [of the Kevalin] is free from all obstructions (i.e. it is not affected by the absence of kavala-āhāra)....

*14 [Śvetāmbara:] But surely as long as vedanīya-karma exists, the scriptural rule, namely, 'Eleven [afflictions are possible] in a Jina' (*Tattvārthasūtra*, ix, 11) would apply, and hence there would be thirst and hunger even for a Kevalin.[22] [We therefore offer the following] syllogism: The vedanīya-karma [even of a Kevalin] yields its fruit [in the form of hunger, etc.]. Because it is the nature of karma [to yield its fruit]. Similar to the āyu-karma (i.e. the karma which determines the duration of individual life) [which, you admit, yields its fruit even for a Kevalin].

*15 [Digambara:] This is not a proper argument, because, unassisted by mohanīya-karma (which produces passions such as desire and aversion), the pain-yielding (*asātā*) variety of vedanīya [undergoes transformation and] yields instead pleasure (*sātā*) only....[You admit that] due to the excellence of omniscient knowledge, the body of the Kevalin gains such transluscence that he can be seen as having four faces (i.e. can be seen from all four directions), and also that his nails and hair cease to grow.[23] For the same reason there is also the absence of eating food by morsels. The [argument based on the] scripture pertaining to the number of afflictions [considered possible for a Jina] is thus overcome.

*16 [Digambara:]. . .By the excellence of infinite knowledge, the presence also of infinite perception, infinite energy, and infinite bliss (ananta-sukha) [which would not be compatible with hunger and thirst] is easily established, as is said in the verse:

> Your glory is unobstructed and your freedom from passion is natural. So is your contentment, and the innate control over the senses. Oh Lord, only in you is to be found complete happiness, the totally unobstructed energy, and the cognition extending to all objects. [?]

#17 [Digambara:] The argument that the Kevalin is subject to the desire to eat (bubhukṣā) on account of the presence of the asātā-vedanīya-karma is rendered invalid by the following syllogism: The Lord being free from attachment, does not engage in receiving or forsaking something. Because of being free from delusion, he has departed from actions to be performed or to be given up. One who is like this must be of such a nature, as is the highest yogin acceptable to both [sides of the debate]. This person under discussion [i.e. the Kevalin] is like that and, therefore, he must conform to this description.. . .

#18 [Śvetāmbara:] But the Lord, the Highest Jina is [still a human being and is] seen to share conditions common to all human beings.

#19 [Digambara:] Notwithstanding his human condition [it can still be maintained that he does not eat]. [There is no single rule that uniformly applies to all human beings because] the periods of abstention from food can vary a great deal from one person to another, as is known from the examples of great mendicants, the veritable treasures of severe asceticism. . . .As is said.

> You have indeed transcended the human nature;
> and are a divine being even to the heavenly beings;
> Therefore, oh Lord, you are the highest divinity.
> Oh Jina Vṛṣabha, therefore, be gracious to us for our welfare.
>
> [*Bṛhatsvayambhū-stotra*, verse 75][24]

#20 [Digambara:] By the same [text] one should understand the refutation of arguments [for kavala-āhāra] based upon the Kevalin's corporeality, or his ability to speak, or upon his maleness, and so forth.

#21 [Digambara:] Moreover, by his pure meditation he has destroyed all obstructions to knowledge....He is endowed with that bliss which accompanies his omniscience. He has gained his own nature, which is immaculate and incomparable. Therefore, the words of the Śvetāmbara teachers implicating hunger and thirst in the Lord Arhat, the Highest Lord...are extremely disagreeable. He is called Jina precisely because he has overcome omit evil (māra) in the form of hunger, thirst, fear, hostility, and other similar karmic enemies. Moreover the word jina etymologically means one who has won a victory over enemies in the form of karmas that are instrumental in leading [beings] into a great many terrible calamities of rebirths. Thus it becomes well established for the learned that the Lord Jina is not subject to the defects of hunger and thirst, and so forth.

#22 [Śvetāmbara:] But in the absence of partaking of food, would it not be improper to say that the Kevalin moves about in the assembly hall [where he preaches]?

#23 [Digambara:] This should not be said. His moving about [even without food] is possible on account of his former meritorious acts, and is comparable to the various miraculous signs appearing in the assembly hall, such as his [being seen as having] four faces (i.e. his visibility from all four sides), and so forth.

#24 [Śvetāmbara:]...[We still submit that the Kevalin] may become an eater of food on account of the affliction [of hunger] produced by the powerful [pain yielding] vedanīya-karma.

#25 [Digambara:] Not so, because the learned speak of the presence of the pain-yielding vedanīya-karma in the state of a Kevalin in a [technical] sense comparable to the metaphorical usage such as 'This boy is fire (i.e. haughty)', or 'This boy is a lion (i.e. brave)'; surely, the fire and the lion do not become that boy. The asātā-vedanīya-karma [in a Kevalin] is incapable of producing its effect without the assistance [of the passion-producing mohanīya-karma]. Its existence there is comparable to a heap of ashes devoid of heat. Does fire blaze forth without the assistance [of fuel and wind]? The vedanīya-karma alone is incapable of producing any pain. It would be as absurd as a young juggler without an assistant climbing on his own shoulder and dancing; this is because truly even a capable person without help is incapable....

#26 [Digambara:] Moreover, your argument is not valid for

the following reason also. If you admit that the Kevalin eats food, then you may have to accept that his body is subject to the impurities of faeces and urine, etc. This would certainly lead to the loss of his omniscience. Thus, in joining at one spot you have broken at another. You started with one objective but it resulted in something quite different. Thus the words of the Śvetāmbaras (Dupaṭavādins, lit. those who wear clothes) cross the limits of logic.

#27 [Digambara:] What is the purport of all this? In the Lord, who has destroyed the mohanīya-karma, the painful effects arising from the presence of the asātā-vedanīya-karma do not prevail. The latter is comparable to a burnt piece of rope, from which you seek in vain to prove the presence of thirst and hunger [in a Kevalin].

#28 [Digambara:] This matter [namely, the presence of the desire to eat in the Kevalin] has been examined further by the learned [ācārya Prabhācandra:] 'Why should not there also be the [presence of the] desire for such carnal pleasures as embracing a woman and kissing [and so forth]?'[52] [Given your view of the presence in a Kevalin of the desire to eat] it is not proper for you, who profess to speak reasonably, to speak also of his omniscience and his total freedom from desire. Instead, your reasoning only links the defects of sleep, sluggishness, and disease (all proceeding from eating food) in the Highest Lord, the Kevalin. This will lead to the unwanted situation of admitting that the knowledge of the Lord is dependent on the senses, and therefore an ordinary knowledge, like the knowledge of people like us.

#29 [Digambara:] Certain [non-Jaina] devotees [of Viṣṇu or Śiva] believe [that their Deity] enjoys the pleasures of sex and so forth. They even worship [their Deity] with sixteen kinds of services, and also they do not behave in a wholesome manner. The Śvetāmbaras (called Pāṇḍupaṭāḥ, lit. wearers of white clothes) are worse than even these people who hold such wrong views....How? Totally devoid of discrimination, this unintelligent person thinks incessantly of the Deity who is afflicted by the defects of hunger and so forth. How can one who is himself burning with the pain of hunger, and so forth, be able to extinguish the fire of hunger in others? How can a falling man lift another falling person?...There is no arriving at the desired goal by this means. There is no attainment of the highest goal, namely mokṣa, for one who holds the view of the Śvetāmbara: the latter has fallen in manifold sins, since he speaks [blasphemously] of the eating of morsel food by a Kevalin who is free from desire and is characterized by the complete destruction of the defects of hunger, and so forth. This [is confirmed] by the words of ancient teachers: 'The sinful act of attributing faults [to the Kevalin] by saying that the omniscient eats morsels of food....[leads to the influx] of the faith-deluding variety of the mohanīya-karma'.[26] Such beings inherit karma that keeps them in transmigration for the long duration of seventy crores multiplied by seventy crores of the 'oceans' of time![27]

#30 [Digambara:] In conclusion, the Lord Kevalin does not eat food because he is of the nature of four infinities (of knowledge, perception, bliss and energy), because he has completely destroyed the mass of passion producing karma, because he is endowed with thirty-four miracles,[28] because he is distinguished by the majesty of five great auspicious events [viz. conception, birth, renunciation, enlightenment and nirvāṇa], all of which are not to be found in an ordinary person [lit. person on the street, i.e. one who eats food]. By these arguments well set forth, we have achieved our desired objective.

References

1. Padmanabh S. Jaini, "*Muktivicāra* of Bhāvasena: Text and Translation", *Indologica Taurinensia*, pp. 168-82, Vol., XIII, Torino, 1985-86. For a discussion on the date and works of Bhāvasena, known also as Bhāvasena Traividya, see the *Viśvatattvaprakāśa of Bhāvasena*, ed. V. P. Johrapurkar. Sholapur (Jīvarāja Jaina Granthamālā) 1964.
2. Chandrabhal Tripathi, *Catalogue of the Jaina Manuscripts at Strasbourg*, Leiden (E. J. Brill) 1975.
3. On the sātā and the asātā varieties of the vedanīya-karma, see Helmuth von Glasenapp, *The Doctrine of Karman in Jain Philosophy*, p. 80. Bombay (The Trustees, Bai Vijibhai J. P. Charity Fund) 1942. For rules pertaining to the transformation of one karman into another, see Nathmal Tatia, *Studies in Jaina Philosophy* (p. 255). Varanasi (Jaina Cultural Research Society) 1951.
4. For the functions of the nokarma-vargaṇā, see Balachandra Siddhānta-śāstrī, *Jaina Lakṣaṇāvalī*, Vol. II, p. 651. Delhi (Vīra Sevā Mandir) 1973.
5. Paul Dundas, "Food and Freedom: The Jaina sectarian debate on the nature of the Kevalin", *Religion*, XV, pp. 161-98. London (Academic Press Inc.) 1985.

6. For the history and literature of the Yāpanīya sect, see Padmanabh S. Jaini, *Gender and Salvation: Jaina Debates on the Spiritual Liberation of Women*, pp. 42-48. Berkeley (University of California Press) 1991.

7. *Strīnirvāṇa-Kevalibhuktiprakaraṇe* of Śākaṭāyana (with two *Svopajña-vṛttis*), Sanskrit text ed. Muni Jambūvijaya. Bhavanagar (Jaina Ātmānanda Sabhā) 1974.

8. *Nyāyakumudacandra* of Prabhācandra [Kevalikavalāhāravicāraḥ, vol. II, pp. 852-65] ed. Mahendra Kumar Jain. Bombay (Māṇikcandra Digambara Jaina Granthamālā) 1941. This topic is also discussed in the *Prameyakamalamārttaṇḍa* of Prabhācandra [pp. 299-307], ed. Mahendra Kumar Śāstrī. Bombay (Nirnayasagara Press) 1941.

9. *Ṣaḍdarśnasamuccaya* of Haribhadra with Guṇaratna's *Tarkarahasyadīpikā-vṛtti* [see pp. 203-10], Sanskrit text with Hindi tr. by Mahendra Kumar Jain. Varanasi (Bhāratīya Jñānapīṭha) 1969.

10. *Yuktiprabodha* of Meghavijaya with *Svopajñavṛtti* [see pp. 126-63], ed. Muni Ānandasāgara, Ratlam (Ṛṣabhadevajī Keśarīmalaji Śvetāmbara Saṃsthā) 1928.

11. *Adhyātmamataparikṣā* [see pp. 300-47] of Yaśovijaya, Sanskrit text with Gujarati tr. by Muni Bhuvanabhānusūri. Bombay (Divyadarśana Kāryālaya) 1986.

12. The ordinary meaning of the term *traividya* (proficient in three branches of classical learning, viz., Logic, Grammar and Philosophy) is not applicable here. A reference to the title of the author (see n. 1) is probably intended.

13. See P. S. Jaini (1985-86) in n. 1 and P. S. Jaini (1991) in n. 6.

14. For a discussion on the nature of omniscience in Jainism and Buddhism, see Padmanabh S. Jaini, "On the Sarvajñatva (Omniscience) of Mahāvīra and the Buddha", *Buddhist Studies in Honour of I. B. Horner*, ed. L. Cousins. Dordrecht (D. Reidel Pub. Co.) 1974.

15. The Jaina texts speak of six possible stages of completion of a new life (paryāpti) in the following order: food (āhāra), body (śarīra), breath (prāṇa), sense organs (indriya), speech (bhāṣā), and mind (manas). For full details, see Jinendra Varṇī, *Jainendra Siddhānta Kośa*, III, pp. 39-44. Varanasi, (Bhāratīya Jñānapīṭha) 1972.

16. For the legendary austerities of the Jaina mendicant hero Bāhubali, see Padmanabh S. Jaini, *The Jaina Path of Purification* [p. 205]. Berkeley (University of California Press) 1979.

17. In the Jaina version of the *Rāmāyaṇa*, Sītā, the wife of Rāma, eventually becomes a Jaina nun. See the *Triṣaṣṭiśalākāpuruṣacaritra* of Hemacandra, iv, 10, translated by Helen M. Johnson, *The Lives of Sixty-three Illustrious Persons*. 6 vols. Baroda (Oriental Institute) 1962.

18. *Āptamīmāṃsā of Samantabhadra*, Sanskrit text (with a Hindi commentary) in the *Āptamīmāṃsā-Tattvadīpikā*, ed. Udayachandra Jain. Varanasi (Shrī Ganeśa Varṇī Digambara Jain Saṃsthān) 1974.

19. For a description of the fourteen guṇasthānas, see Jaini: *The Jaina Path of Purification*, pp. 272-73.

20. Cf. ṣaḍvidho hy āhāraḥ: ṇokamma kammahāro kavalāhāro ya leppam āhāro; oja maṇo vi ya kamsaso āhāro chavviho ṇeyo. (Quoted in the *Prameyakamalamārttaṇḍa*, p. 300, see n. 8 above).

21. Verse quoted in the *Viśvatattvaprakāśa*, p. 68 (see n. 1 above).

22. The *Tattvārthasūtra* of Umāsvāti (albeit with several variant readings and sectarian commentaries) is probably the only scripture that is acceptable to both the Digambaras and the Śvetāmbaras. It describes (in sūtra ix, 9) twenty-two afflictions (parīṣahas), caused by various karmic forces, that a Jaina mendicant should patiently suffer as he progresses toward the goal of attaining the state of Kevalin. A question is raised about the number of afflictions that a Kevalin might suffer and the sūtra (ix, 11) answers that eleven afflictions—beginning with hunger, thirst, cold, heat (kṣut-pipāsā-śīta-uṣṇa)—which are produced by the vedanīya-karma are possible at this stage. This statement supports the Śvetāmbara position that the Kevalin eats food. The sixth century Digambara commentator Pūjyapāda in his *Sarvārthasiddhi* commentary, however, interprets this sūtra differently. He maintains that hunger and thirst at this stage are spoken of only conventionally (upacāra) since vedanīya-karma is unable to produce such pain in the absence of the mohanīya. Alternatively, he suggests that the sūtra should be supplemented with the words 'do not arise in the jina':...jine vedanīyasadbhāvāt tadāśrayā ekādaśaparīṣahāḥ santi...vedanābhāve 'pi dravyakarmasadbhāvāpekṣayā parīṣahopacāraḥ kriyate... athavā..., mohodayasahāyīkṛtakṣudhādivedanābhāvāt "na santi" iti vākyaśeṣaḥ. *Sarvārthasiddhi* [see ix, 11], ed. Phoolchandra Siddhāntaśāstrī. Varanasi (Bhāratīya Jñānapītha) 1971; translated by S. A. Jain, *Reality*, Calcutta (Vira Śāsana Sangha) 1960. For the Śvetāmbara commendaty (attributed to Umāsvāti), see *Sabhāṣyatattvārthādhigamasūtra*, ed. Khubchandra Siddhāntaśāstrī. Agas (Śrīmad Rājacandra Āśrama) 1932.

23. These are included in the thirty-four superhuman qualities (atiśayas) attributed to a Tīrthaṅkara Kevalin. For a full list, see Jinendra Varṇī, *Jainendra Siddhānta Kośa*, I, (arhanta, pp. 140-42).

24. *Bṛhatsvayambhū-stotra of Samantabhadra*, Sanskrit text included in the *Nityanaimittika-pāṭhāvalī*, Sanskrit and Prakrit Texts. Karanja (Kankubai Pāṭhyapustakamālā) 1956.

25. Cf. tathāhi—bubhukṣā mohanīyānapekṣasya vedanīyasya kāryaṃ na bhavati, icchātvāt, riraṃsāvat. bhoktum icchā hi bubhukṣā, sā kathaṃ vedanīyasyaiva kāryam? anyathā yonyādiṣu rantum icchā riraṃsāpi tatkāryaṃ syāt, tathā ca kavalāhāravat stryādāv api tatprasaṅgāt neśvarād asya viśeṣaḥ. *Nyāyakumudacandra*, II, p. 860; also *Prameyakamalamārttaṇḍa*, p. 304 (see n. 8 above).

26. This refers to the Digambara interpretation of the following sūtra: kevaliśrutasaṃghadharmadevāvarṇavādo darśanamohasya. *Tattvārthasūtra*, vi, 13. Commenting on the avarṇavāda of the Kevalin, Pūjyapāda says: nirāvaraṇajñānāḥ kevalinaḥ...kavalābhyavahārajīvinaḥ kevalina ity evam ādi vacanaṃ kevalinām avarṇavādaḥ. *Sarvārthasiddhi*, vi, 13. Examples of the avarṇavādas are not provided in the *Sabhāṣyatattvārthādhigamasūtra* (see n. 22 above).

27. This is the maximum period of duration of this variety karma:...mohanīyakarmaprakṛteḥ saptatiḥ sāgaropamakoṭīkoṭyaḥ parā sthitiḥ. *Sabhāṣyatattvārthādhigamasūtra*, viii, 16.

28. Seen n. 23 above.

12 THE EARLIEST PORTIONS OF *DAŚAVAIKĀLIKA-SŪTRA*

M.A. Dhaky

An ancient exegetical tradition[1] specifically ascribes the well-known *aṅga-bāhya* work, the *Daśavaikālika-sūtra*, to a single author, Ajja Sijjaṁbhava (Ārya Śayyambhava or Svāyaṁbhūva[2]), the third patriarch (*c* .B.C. 370-340) in the hagiological progression of what later was to emerge as the Śvetāmbara *saṁpradāya* or the Śvetapaṭṭa *āmnāya* of the Northern Nirgrantha Church.[3] The brief anecdotal details recorded in those notices (and dependent as well as derivative accounts in subsequent literature) report about the circumstances under which the author Śayyaṁbhava composed this famous and doubtless one of the few surviving more ancient and revered works of the Ardhamāgadhī canon. The tradition holds that Ārya Śayyaṁbhava composed it for the benefit of Managa (Manaka), a boy-friar who happened to be the patriarch's own son before ordination, and whose imminent death he is said to have foreseen.[4] That this tradition for its central fact must be fairly ancient and, to all seeming, accurate is proven by a pointed, and indeed significant reference in the earlier portion (*c*. A.D. 100) of the 'Sthavirāvali' or pontifical succession-list of the *Paryuṣaṇā-kalpa* (compiled *c*. A.D. 503/516).[5] Therein, Ajja Sijjaṁbhava is called 'Managa-pitā', father of Manaka.[6] To recall and intersperse an eminent and very ancient patriarch's worldly relationship in a hagiological list of holymen ordinarily would seem as irrelevant and queer as unneeded and irreverent. Apparently, then, the compiler of this part of the 'Sthavirāvali' knew the special bearing of what he was incorporating, and its significance is independently clarified by later exegetical records. After all, no personal matter pertaining to any other patriarch or pontiff—be he figuring in this or in an other ancient hagiological list like the 'Sthavirāvali' of the *Nandi-Sūtra* of Deva vācaka (*c*. mid 5th cent. A.D.)[7], or for that matter in any medieval or late medieval preceptoral list—has been noted or noticed. The Manaka anecdote therefore is of ancient origin and thus is of historical value. It is, in point of fact, singularly serviceable as a lamplight in tracing out and in determining the genuinely older portions that may be ascribed to the intentions and style of Ārya Śayyaṁbhava. Because the doctrinal and disciplinary passages and verses, if composed for a very young friar, a minor, have to be what is needed for him, and what he can comprehend.

Traditionally,—as a pious, just as an explicit, faith of the commentators from the sixth century A.D. onward, and also as a fond belief of the most current writers,—the entire *Daśavaikālika-sūtra* has been taken as of single authorship and hence, by implication, of the same period.[8] However, the assumption runs into serious difficulties when analytical tools are applied. Whatever the meaning of the title 'Daśavaikālika' may be,—it has been variously explained by the early and medieval commentators,—the fact remains that it contains *daśa* or 10 chapters, of varying lengths, differing styles and of different decades, and also of differing degrees of seriousness as well as of treatment of the primary matters which a Nirgrantha ascetic ought to know for monastic observances. Keeping 'Manaka', the boy-friar, as our quid, the orientation of the peculiar style, phraseology, and the manner of organization adopted by Ārya Śayyaṁbhava can at once be perceived. The factors of language, metre, and the nature of content involved also help detect what was germane to the original author's style, his thinking and preferences, and what indeed was consistent with the most ancient times and climes in which the author and his young friar-son lived. It would then be possible to separate the earliest strata inside the text which, with some confidence, can be ascribed to Ārya Śayyaṁbhava.

The history of the continual existence of the *Daśavaikālika-sūtra* helps take certain primary decisions. That it existed in the eighth, seventh as well as in the sixth century A.D. in the shape much as we today see it, is proven by the exegesis on the work—the Sanskrit *vṛtti* of Yakinīsūnu Haribhadra Sūri (*c.* mid 8th cent. A.D.), a *cūrṇi* styled as the *Vṛddha-vivaraṇa* (*c.* last quarter of the 7th cent. A.D.) in the *vṛtti* by Haribhadra (which is today available), the *cūrṇi* of Agastyasiṁha (*c.* A.D. 600) and of course the *niryukti* (*c.* A.D. 525).[9] The overall text may have been in this shape before the Valabhī Synod II (*c.* A.D. 503/516), and possibly Valabhī Synod I (*c.* mid 4th cent. A.D.) as well as the contemporaneous Mathurā Synod since hardly anything of the Gupta-Vākāṭaka-Maitraka period is seen anywhere inside the fabric of the text. Since the Yāpanīya sect of the Nirgranthas recognized and owed allegience to the Ardhamāgadhī canon of the Northern Church, the quotations from this *sūtra* are found in the Yāpanīya pontiff Aparājita Sūri's commentary (*c.* late 8th and early 9th cent. A.D.) on the *Ārādhanā* of (the Yāpanīya pontiff) Śivārya (*c.* 6th cent. A.D.). In point of fact, prior to that commentary, Aparājita Sūri had written a commentary on the *Daśavaikālika-sūtra* itself, currently though unavailable. The commentator, moreover, in his *Ārādhanā*-commentary, quoted from the *Daśa-vaikālika*. Since the Yāpanīyas had branched off from the main stream of Northern Church some time early in the third century A.D.,[10] it is clear that the *Daśavaikālika* seemingly had existed before the Kuṣāṇa period, though it may not then have had quite the same shape we today encounter, in spite of the relative over all high antiquity of its language and content. As will be shown, a greater part of Śayyaṁbhava's text is lost (if it originally had contained 10 chapters) and was substituted by chapters containing relatively earlier material that belonged to a few other cognate āgamic disciplinary works of the periods posterior to Śayyaṁbhava's. However, as will be shown, some four verses from the *Daśavaikālika's* second chapter (2.7-10) are incorporated in the 'Rathanemīya' chapter of the *Uttarādhyayana Sūtra* (22.42-44, 46), the chapter being dateable to *c.* 1st or 2nd century A.D. So the *Daśavaikālika-sūtra*, arguably, was known before the beginning of the Christian (or Common) Era.

The following chapterwise analytical survey, though of necessity brief, of the work can reveal the original portions of the work on the grounds of the general principles laid down in the foregoing discussion.

1. Draumapuṣpīya

The famous opening verse beginning with the propitious phrase *Dhammo maṅgala mukaṭṭhaṁ* of this first and very short chapter, which contains only five verses, undoubtedly is the most ancient and oft-quoted. A portion of its lower hemistisch '*devā vi taṁ namaṁsaṁti*' is imitated in the *Ṛṣibhāṣitāni*[11] and in the *Uttarādhyayana-sūtra*.[12] The next four verses in the simplest but effective style with the aid of the metaphor of the 'flower and the black-bee' tells about how, delicately and with discretion and care, to beg the food. As is clear from their spirit, style and content, the verses are meant for a very young monk who has been recently admitted to the order; hence these doubtless were meant for Manaka; and so the whole chapter is originally of Śayyaṁbhava.

2. Śrāmaṇyapūrvika

A close correspondence in the wording as well as meaning of the verse 2 of this chapter with the *Saṁyukta-nikāya* (1.2-7) of the Pali canon has been suggested:[13]

कतिऽहं कुज्जा सामण्णं जो कामे न निवारए।
पदे पदे विसीदंतो संकप्पस्स वसं गतो ।।

—दशवैकालिक सूत्र २-१

कतिहं चरेय्य सामज्ज चितं चे न निवारेय्य
पदे पदे विसीहेय्य संकप्पानं वसानुगो ।।

—संयुक्तनिकाय १-२-७

This upholds the suggestion of the high antiquity of the *Daśavaikālika* verse, which, if anything, is less sophisticated and more archaic in form as compared to the Pali parallel verse. Since the entire chapter is looked upon as homogenous in style and consistent in content, it may suggest that nothing has been added to or taken away from the original. At least at first sight it may seem so. However, the three verses following the first one, rendered though in the Anuṣṭūbh metre like the preceding, do not quite seem consistent with the first verse nor with the central fact of the text of this chapter, as will be shortly observed. Of this the first foot of the verse 2 (*Vattha-gandha-malaṁkāraṁ ithīo sayanāni ca*) is exactly paralleled in the *Sūtrakṛtāṅga* (I.3.2.17) whose first book is in general not later than *c*. B.C. 300-200.[14] While it cannot positively be proved that an interpolator has borrowed from the *Sūtrakṛtaṅga*, at least the partial irrelevance of the verse to our text can be sensed and established. There is, for instance, no reference in the main text to either clothing (*vastra*), perfume (*gandha*), or ornament (*alaṁkāra*), although there may be an illustration (*dṛṣṭānta*) of lying sexually with a woman (*itthio sayanāni ca*) indirectly covered by verses 6-10.

The next two verses[15] (numbered 4 and 5 in all printed texts) are, besides being in Indravajrā, seriously complex and definitely cannot have been meant for a boy-monk. The interpolation—as I theorize—may have been prompted with the motive of stressing the impropriety for a recluse to be passionate. These verses, of course, look ancient, as though belonging to the period not later than *c*. 2nd-1st century B.C. They, however, are not in the style, nor do they accord with the spirit, of Śayyaṁbhava's modulations.

The rest of the chapters, excepting for the two verses in chapter 4 (30-31), are not at all in Śayyaṁbhava's style, motive, or genius of his writing. In point of fact, they are in differing styles, of different periods, not always homogenous, though a general relevance for articulating them here may be sensed by the nature of topics they cover and their over all delineation. (And this possibly had led to the supposition that the entire work is from the pen of Śayyaṁbhava.) A few chapters even reveal layers or laminae in the make up of their strata.

3. KṢUĪLIKĀCĀRA

Verses 1 and 10-15 are reminiscent of the style of the early chapters in the *Uttarādhyayana* and hence may be of the Mauryan period; while vs. 2-9, being more in the enumerative vein of the later *āgamas, niryuktis*, and *saṁgrahaṇīs*, and definitely much later than the forenoted seven verses.

4. ṢAṬJĪVANIKĀYA

The chapter consists of at least five major components of differing compositions. The *sūtras* 1-9, in prose, recall Śramaṇa Bhagvat Kāśyapa Mahāvīra's exposition of the six classes of souls. Sūtra 10, likewise in prose, is in the style of the *Pratikramaṇa-sūtra*, one of the six *Āvaśyakas*. Next follow 12 verses on *Ṣaṭjīvanikāya* (six classes of beings) regarded with uncertainty (or dubiousness as to their originality?) by the two *cūrṇis* on the *Daśavaikālika*. The verses of course are not late and at some date prior to the seventh or sixth century A.D. were extracted from some early source (*saṁgrahaṇī*?) and introduced here in view of their topical relevance to the prose part. Next, the *sūtras* 11-17 relate to the *pañca-mahāvratas* or five great vows of the friar and are met with in the selfsame style within the 'Śramaṇa-sūtra' part of the *Pratikramaṇa-sūtra*. *Sūtras* 18-23, in prose, are in the general style of the *Ācārāṅga* Book II (*c.* 1st cent. B.C.-A.D.), each *sūtra* likewise beginning with the phrase *Se bhikkhū vā bhikkhūṇī vā*. This is followed by a versified portion covering some 28 verses (24-51) of which, as earlier noted, only vs. 30 and 31 could be of Śayyaṁbhava's selection. In point of fact, the verses in this portion of the chapter reveals at least five laminae and each lamina is rendered in a different metre and reflects a different style. The first five verses (24-29) are uniform in style and begin with the word '*Ajayaṁ*', and each ends with *hoti kaḍuyaṁ phalaṁ* which thus forms the refrain. The second lamina contains the earlier noted two verses (30, 31) of Śayyaṁbhava's original chapter. These are as follows:

> **कतं चरे कतं चिट्ठे कतमासे कतं सए।**
> **कतं भुंजतो पावं कम्मं न बंधती ।।**
> **जतं चरे जतं चिट्ठे जतमासे जतं सए।**
> **जतं भुंजंतो भासंतो पावं कम्मं न बंधती ।।**
>
> —दशवैकालिक-सूत्र ४-३०-३१

Of these the second is paralleled, with a slight linguistic difference, in the *Suttapiṭaka*, *Khudaka-nikāya*, 'Itivṛtta' of the Buddhist canon:

> **यतं चरे यतं तिट्ठे यतं अच्छे यतं सये।**
> **यतं समिञ्जये भिक्खु यतमेतं पसारये ।।**

The next five verses (32-36) forming the third lamina are in fairly early style (*c.* 1st cent. B.C.), followed by 12 verses in a uniform style with the rhyming words *jayā* and *tayā* in the endings of the first and second hemistich. The verses 45-46 mention the term *kevali* which otherwise rarely figures in the earliest parts of the oldest Ardhamāgadhī canonical books. The fourth lamina covering the last three verses is again in different, indeed in heavy early style.

The chapter thus has an exceedingly small portion of the 4th century B.C., just two verses to be precise, the rest seemingly dating within the larger bracket of *c.* 2nd-1st century B.C.-A.D., the four versified laminae may have been taken from what are known in the Nirgrantha parlance as *saṁgrahiṇīs* or collections of floating verses.

5. PIṆḌAIṢAṆĀ

The chapter, entirely in verse, consists of two *uddeśas* or lessons, of which the first contains as many as 131 verses that are obviously not uniform in style. The opening verse has its peculiar style. But verses 2-30 seem consistently from the same hand: However, those from 31 to 49, with a refrain *na me kappati tārisaṁ*, are from a still different hand. Vs. 50-55 do not betray this refrain nor are they in the same style, but are taken from some other source. Verses 56, 58, 59, 61, 63, 65, 67, 69, 73, 75, 77, 79, 81, 83, 85, 87, 89, 91, 93 and 95, however, show the forenoted refrain, these verses in most cases alternate with a verse each without the refrain. This group is followed by another group (vs. 96-131) differing in style from the foregoing two. It is this section in which the controversial verses 104, 115 occur, which may lead to infer that the Nirgrantha mendicants used to eat non-vegetarian food, and on which the two *Ācārāṅga* prose passages in Book II (*cū*. 1/10—403-04) are based. Stylistically, almost the entire *uddeśa* I, despite differing hands, could be as early as *c*. 2nd cent.-1st B.C., but positively not of Śayyaṁbhava's time. It is clear that the controversial verses are the handiwork either of some Buddhist monk turned Nirgrantha friar, or by some influential *kṣatriya* pontiff having a strong following, who could not give up his pre-ordination non-vegetarian habits in eating. For these rules violate the fundamental doctrine of non-violence and compassion for all beings upheld and rigorously adhered to by Mahāvīra himself as is clear from the archaic passages in the *Ācārāṅga* (I-1.6.49-55) and also from the work's following early statements:

सव्वेपाणा पिआतगा सुखसाता वुक्खपतिकूला अप्पियवधा
पियजीविनो जीवितुकामा । सव्वेंसि जीवितं पियं ।

—आचारांग-सूत्र १-२.४.७८

से नातिते नाती आवते न समनुजानते
सव्वामगंधं परिन्नाते निरामगंधे परिव्वते ।

—आचारांग-सूत्र १-२.५.८८

A very early patriarch, as Śayyaṁbhava (*c*. B.C. 350-330) was, could not have transgressed this fundamental tenet. Even Ārya Bhadrabāhu (*c*. B.C. 325-290) and Ārya Sthūlabhadra (*c*. B.C. 300-275) could not have approved of a monastic begging rule which exceptionally, but also flagrantly, goes against a principle which is the very backbone of the Nirgrantha creed. As is shown, the verses in question are a part of the third constituent of *uddeśa* 1. Structurally, the *uddeśa* 1 of the chapter for certain has a topical, though not stylistic, consistency.

Uddeśa 2 of this chapter contains 50 verses; and not only is a stylistic uniformity perceived, but their over-all cadence betrays a character slightly earlier than that of *uddeśa* 1. And yet the *uddeśa* cannot belong to the time of, or be by Śayyaṁbhava; its rules are addressed to friars (and nuns) fairly advanced in the monastic set up and hence in age. These could not have been meant for Manaka.

6. Dharmārthakāma

The entire versified chapter, despite small divergencies in style and metre at places, seems consistent in its matter as well as its general style. In its corpus it alludes to Mahāvīra as Nātaputta, and, in verses 19-20, a defence is built for allowing some minimal possessions to a recluse.[16] The basic doctrines of the Nirgrantha religion, including emphasis on non-violence, are repeatedly stressed in this chapter. The general style of the verses, as I comprehend them, reflects 2nd-1st century B.C. and hence the verses are not of Śayyaṁbhava's making. And they do not look like being composed for Manaka.

7. Vākyaśuddhi

This chapter, consisting as it does of 57 verses, though early, say of *c*. 2nd century B.C., has a style of phrasing and articulation which differs from those of the foregoing chapters. In itself it is fairly uniform, dealing as it does with the need of reticence and discretion in speech and its motivations and innate emotions. Stylistically, however, it does not sound or seem to be the handiwork of Ārya Śayyaṁbhava.

8. Ācārapraṇidhi

It is close in style to the preceding chapter even when the material constitution occasionally differs. In verse 49 it refers to *Ācāraprajñapti* (possibly the *Ācārāṅga* Book I; alternatively, just a code of monastic discipline) and the *Dṛṣṭivāda* (the doctrines and beliefs of other religious systems, *dṛṣtis*, usually looked upon as 'false' [*mithyā*]). In verse 50 it enjoins friars to refrain from making predictions on the basis of astrology (*nakhatta*), (prognosticative) interpretation of dreams (*sumina*), omenology (*joga*), incantations (*manta*) and medical practice (*bhesaja*). In v. 51 it refers to *leṇa* (*layana*, a rock-cut cave), the monks being advised not to do preachings with the motive of getting it (from the worldly followers.) Although the material for some of the verses may have come from sources *c*. 3rd century B.C., the general impression of the style is of 2nd-1st century B.C. And indeed the injunctions of this chapter can hardly be said to apply to a friar of a very minor age.

9. VIṆAYA-SAMĀDHI

The chapter in general refers to the principles and rules of monastic conduct and discipline and within its parameters also to what the attitude of the disciples should be toward their teachers. The first *uddeśa* of the chapter is in 17 Triṣṭubh stanzas, thus by its content not contradicting the suggested temporal bracket, i.e. not later than the Mauryan period. The first, and the last two verses (22, 23), of the second *uddeśa*, are likewise in the Triṣṭubh, the rest are in Anuṣṭubh or Śloka. Its verses 10 and 11 refer to *devas, yakṣas*, and *guhyakas*, the latter term not figuring in the classification of demi-gods of the later *āgamas*. Like the *Uddeśa* 1 (5, 10) the term *mokṣa* also figures here (v. 2). The third *uddeśa* is in prose where ślokas are also interspersed, in some cases apparently as citations. In the verse 12, the term *jina-vacana* occurs. The chapter, stylistically of the 3rd-1st century B.C., by virtue of its content and at places a heavy style, was meant for grown-up friars.

10. SABHIKṢU

The 21 verses of this chapter, in general, talks about the undesirable activities and practices a true recluse must avoid. Here the terms such as Nātaputta (for Mahāvīra), *buddhavacana* (word of the Buddha, i.e. Jina), and also *bhaya-bhairava*—a term fairly common in early Buddhist texts—occur. All in all, the chapter is meant for a disciple who has already spent some years in monastic discipline, and indeed thus was not addressed to Manaka, even when it is sufficiently ancient, its antiquity plausibly going back to the Mauryan period.

The *Daśavaikālika* also possesses two *cūlikās* or appendices which the tradition ascribes not to Śayyaṁbhava but to the nun Dakṣā, the biological sister of Ārya Sthūlabhadra.[17] The introductory initial *sūtras* of the first of what is styled *Rativākya-cūlikā* is in prose. Next follow verses in Śloka forming one group which in style resembles several other Anuṣṭubh verse-groups in the main body of the *Daśavaikālika*. The subsequent eight verses are in Triṣṭubh and in different style. This appended chapter, too, is quite ancient. The second *cūlikā,* titled *Vivikta-caryā,* admonishes the friar of what he must not eat and drink and how he must devote his time to introspection, meditation and self-disciplinary practices. The inaugural verse in Śloka is of later origin; so are the next three verses in Āryā metre. Verses 5-16 are in an ancient metre, the Triṣṭubh. The bulk of this chapter (except for the initial four verses) is fairly ancient and can go to the period B.C. 250-150.[18]

This brief, and of necessity a preliminary, survey indicates what the original parts composed by Ārya Śayyaṁbhava were. The rest represent substitutions made at a later date perhaps for the lost original, or the original chapters were deliberately replaced by chapters containing material of sufficiently venerable age with a bearing on the code of conduct, admonitions and red signals to the dangers which lay in the path, which the friars must avoid in monastic life. Seemingly, for the later pontiffs, the didactic aphorisms for a boy-friar were not useful for the grown up in the clergy and this obsolescence may have prompted their substitution by more pertinent verse collections.

As a sequel, the text of Chapter 1 and those verses from Chapter 2, which can be ascribed to Ārya Śayyaṁbhava, are appended. The original Ardhamāgadhī forms of the words of the text have been restored by removing in later Mahārāṣṭra Prakrit affectations, a procedure adopted here as well in the *āgamic* quotations cited elsewhere in this paper.[19]

References

1. *Cf.* the *Bṛhat-kalpa-niryukti* (*c.* A.D. 525) and the *Bṛhat-kalpa-bhāṣya* (*c.* mid 6th cent. A.D.).

2. *Cf.* Walther Schubring, *The Doctrine of the Jainas*, reprint, Delhi 1978, p. 44, *infra* 3.

3. The 'Sthavirāvali' of the *Paryuṣaṇā-kalpa* (earliest part *c.* A.D. 100), as well as the 'Sthavirāvali' of the *Nandisūtra* (*c.* mid 5th cent. A.D.), the

two being the earliest sources, lay down the following order of succession of the patriarchs of the Northern Church:

Arhat Vardhamāna (Jina Mahāvīra)
(Preaching period B.C. 507-477)

- *Gaṇadhara* Gautama
- *Gaṇadhara* Sudharamā
  - (1) Ārya Jambū
  - (2) Ārya Prabhava
  - (3) Ārya Śayyaṁbhūva (or Śvāyambhūva)
  - (4) Ārya Yaśobhadra
    - (6) Ārya Bhadrabāhu (contemporary of Candragupta Maurya, *c.* B.C. 320-290)
      - Ārya Godāsa (and others)
      - (8) Ārya Mahāgiri
    - (5) Ārya Sambhūta
      - (7) Ārya Sthūlabhadra
      - (9) Ārya Suhasti (contemporary of Maurya Samprati: *c.* B.C. 235-215)

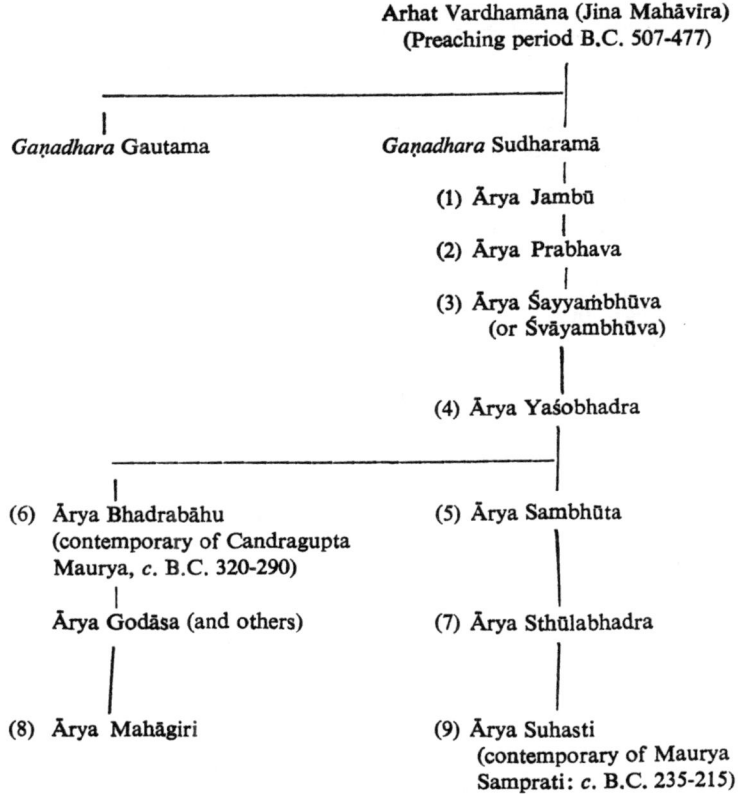

The date of Ārya Śayyaṁbhava depends on the date of the *nirvāṇa* of Jina Mahāvīra at one end, and of Ārya Bhadrabāhu as well as of Ārya Suhasti at the other. The recent recomputation (or rethinking) tends to bring down the *nirvāṇa* of Gautama Buddha from B.C. 483 to *c.* B.C. 383; if this is proven valid, it would seriously affect the date of Mahāvīra who was contemporary of Buddha. (I am still not in favour of a late date for the two great teachers.) At the opposite end, Ārya Bhadrabāhu was contemporary of Candragupta Maurya and Ārya Suhasti was of Maurya Aśoka's grandson Samprati who, in Aśoka's life time, and in emperor's late years, apparently had governed the Mālavadeśa and adjoining Western territories. This would make Ārya Bhadrabāhu a junior contemporary of Candragupta Maurya. The practical time-bracket emerging for Bhadrabāhu's grand-preceptor Ārya Śayyaṁbhava would then be *c.* B.C. 375-345. Since the apostles Gautama and Sudharmā were the direct disciples of the Jina and, according to the tradition, had survived the Jina by some years, the sequential computation is best begun with the first patriarch, Ārya Jambū.

4. This is recorded in the medieval sources which may have some earlier tradition, written or oral, before them.

5. This is the date given at the end of the 'Jinacaritra' portion inside that *āgama*.

6. थेरस्स नं अज्जपभवस्स कच्चायनसगुत्तस्स अज्ज सिज्जंभवे थेरे अंतेवासी मनगपिता वच्छसगुत्ते ।।
थेरस्स नं अज्जसिज्जंभवस्स मनगपितुनो वच्छसगुत्तस्स अज्ज जसभद्दे थेरे अंतेवासी तुंगियायनसगुत्ते ।।

7. Deva Vācaka's preceptor Duṣya gaṇi was the great grand-preceptor of Devarddhi gaṇi, this latter pontiff had presided over the Valabhī Synod II in either A.D. 503 or 516 in the time of the Maitraka ruler Dhruvasena I. Hence Deva Vācaka could have flourished between *c*. A.D. 435 and 475 and the central date for his *Nandi-sūtra* has been suggested here *c*. A.D. 450. The concerned hagiological succession is in the following order:

Duṣya gaṇi
- Deva Vācaka (*c*. A.D. 435-475)
- Sthiragupta
  - Kumāradharma
    - Devarddhi gaṇi (A.D. 503/516)

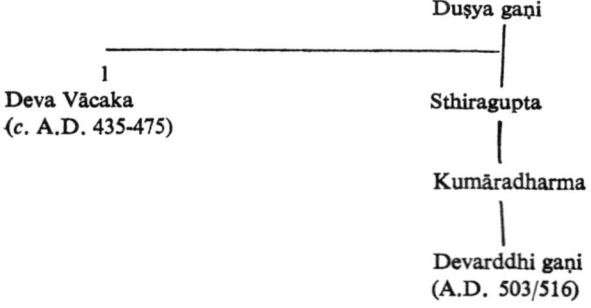

8. This, regrettably, includes even the greatest German stalwarts of Nirgranthology!

9. The available *niryuktis*, as judged by their metre (Āryā), language (largely Mahārāṣṭra Prākṛta), content (much advanced dogmas and doctrinal notions), more relaxed disciplinary rules, mention therein of relatively later historical personages, the later word-forms and the cultural data involved and many other concommittant details which relate to younger ages), appear in general to be of the late Gupta-Vākāṭaka period. Traditionally, of course, Ārya Bhadrabāhu is believed to be the author of the *niryuktis*, a myth proved improbable by Muni Punjavijaya, who propounded a second Bhadrabāhu, brother of the astronomer Varāhamihira (6th cent. A.D.). This alternative supposition, however, is equally erroneous, the author of the *niryuktis* is still unknown. For the *niryuktis*, a date after the Valabhī Synod II as propounded by Muni Punyavijaya, however, seems valid though it cannot be *c*. A.D. 460-470 since this date is based on a computation of the date of the *nirvāṇa*

of Mahāvīra as B.C. 527, which goes against all historical synchronism.

10. Ārya Śivabhuti, disciple of Ārya Dhanagiri and confrère of Ārya Kṛṣṇa, was the progenitor of the Boṭika sect, identified with what was to be known in Southern India as 'Yāpanīya Saṅgha', palpably from the 5th century onwards. 'Kaṇha Samaṇa' depicted on an inscribed tablet from Mathurā, dated to K.E. 95 (*c.* A.D. 239), has been identified with the Ārya Kṛṣṇa figuring briefly in the Boṭika anecdote of the *Uttarādhyana-niryukti* (*c.* A.D. 525), the *Āvaśyaka-mūla-bhāṣya* (*c.* A.D. 550), and more elaborately in the *Viśeṣ=Āvaśyaka-bhāṣya* of Jinabhadra gaṇi kṣamāśramaṇa (*c.* A.D. 585), the Āvaśyaka-*cūrṇi* (*c.* A.D. 600-650) and in the subsequent *Āvaśyaka* literature. I have discussed this issue elsewhere and hence will not enlarge upon it in the present context.

11. जे इमं पावकं कम्मं नवे कुज्जा न कारवे ।
देवापि तं नमंसन्ति धितिमं हिततेजसं ।।
—इसिभासियाइ ३६.१

12. देव दानव गंधव्वा जक्ख खखस किन्नरा ।
षमेथारिं नमंसंति कुक्करं जे करंति तं ।।
—उत्तराध्ययन-सूत्र १६.१८

13. I am grateful to Shri C.S. Upasak for drawing my attention to the Pāli verse under reference.

14. वन्थगंधमलंकारं इन्थीओ सयनानि च ।
भूंजाहिमाति भोगाति आउसो पूजयामु तं ।।
—सूत्रकृतांग-सूत्र १-३.२.१६८

15. The two *sūtra*-verses in question are cited below for comparing:

समाए पेहाए परिव्वयंतो, सिया मणो निस्सरई बहिद्धा ।
न सा महं नो वि अहं पि तीसे, इच्चेव ताओ बिणएज्ज रागं ।।
आयावयाही चय सोगुमल्लं, कामे कमाही कमियं खु दुक्खं ।
छिंदाहि दोसं विणएज्ज रागं, एवं सुही होहिसि संपराए ।।
—दशवैकालिक-सूत्र २.४-५

16. In this verse, it is stated that an object is not *parigraha* or possession but *murcchā* or attachment toward it is in a real sense the possession:

न सो परिग्गहो पुत्तो नातपुत्तेन तातिना ।
"मुच्छा परिग्गहो पुत्तो" इति पुत्तं महेसिन ।।
—दशवैकालिक-सूत्र ६.२०

This ancient clarification is the basis for the famous *sūtra* inside the *Tattvārthādhigama-sūtra* of Vācaka Umāsvāti (*c.* A.D. 375), namely *Murcchāḥ parigraha* (7.12).

17. This myth is today known from a reference in the *Pariśiṣṭa-parva* of Hemacandra (*c.* A.D. 1166).

18. The style, leaving aside the initial few later verses, is quite archaic.

19. The original Ardhamāgadhī forms of the words in the most ancient canonical works can be largely traced in the *cūrṇis* as well as sometimes in the citations figuring in the older Sanskrit commentaries. Dr. K. R. Chandra has been for some years working on the restoration of the Ardhamāgadhi forms, as I am working in my own way on the basis of the principles formulated by me. The editors of the *āgamas* know the meaning, but not the linguistic correctness or otherwise of the word-forms, the correct Ardhamāgadhi more often figuring in the assembly of the variant readings which they show in the footnotes, and accept the later Mahārāṣṭra Prākṛta forms for the text! In the Mahārāṣṭra Prākṛta, '*ṇa*' most often replaces '*na*', '*ya*' replaces several consonants like '*ta*', '*da*', etc., '*ha*' figures for '*tha*' and '*dha*', '*da*' for '*ta*' and so on. The Mahārāṣṭra Prākṛta has ruined the original look as well as in part damaged the antiquity of the Nirgrantha canon. The Western Nirgranthologists have done very little on the score of restoring the original Ardhamāgadhī word-forms of the texts they edit. They are concerned largely with the metres used and the meaning of the Prākṛta words employed. (And there of course figures scores of jolting abbreviations and countless footnotes, several of which refer only to old writers and writings in German whose works are neither available, nor understood in the original, in India.)

ORIGINAL SOURCES

1. *Āyārāṅga-suttam, Ed.* Muni Jambūvijaya, JAS/2(I), Bombay 1977.
2. *Sūyagaḍaṁgasuttaṁ, Ed.* Muni Jambūvijaya, JAS/2(2), Bombay 1978.
3. *Dasaveyāliyasuttaṁ Uttarajhayaṇāṁ and Āvassayasuttam, Eds.* Late Muni Puṇyavijayaji and Pt. A.M. Bhojak, JAS No. 15, Bombay 1977.
4. *Isibhāsiyāiṁ, Ed.* Walther Schubring, L. D. Series 45, Ahmedabad 1974.
5. 'Therāvalī (Śri Kalpasūtra sthavirāvalī)', *Śri Paṭṭāvalī Samuccaya, Ed.* Muni Darśanavijaya SCSG, 22, Viramagam 1933, 1-11.
6. *Tattvārthasūtra, Dis.* Pt. Sukhlalji, SPJG 17, 4th Ed., Ahmedabad 1977.
7. *Śri Pariśiṣṭhaparva Ed.* Śubhaṅkaravijaya, SNVG 24, Bombay, Ahmedabad, Bhavnagar 1956.

(१)

द्रुमपुष्पितम्

धम्मो मंगलमुक्कट्ठं अहिंसा संजमो तपो ।
देवावि तं नमंसंति जस्स धम्मे सदा मनो ।। १ ।।
जथा दुमस्स पुप्फेहि भमरो आविचती रसं ।
न च पुप्फं किलामेति सो य पीणेति अप्पगं ।।२।।
एमेए समणा मुत्ता जे लोगे संत्ति साधुनो ।
विहंगमा व पुप्फेहि दानभत्तेसने रता ।।३।।
वयं च विंत्ति लब्भामो न च कोई उवहम्मती ।
अहाकडेहि रीयंते पुप्फेहि भमरा जथा ।।४।।
मधुकार समा बुध्धा जे भवंति अणिस्सिता ।
नानापिंडरता दंता तेन चुच्चंति साधुनो ।।५।।

(२)
श्रामण्यपूर्विकम्

कतिऽहं कुज्जा सामण्णं जो कामे न निवारए।
पदे पदे विसीदंतो संकप्पस्स वसं गतो ? ॥१॥
वत्थ गंधमलंकारं इत्थीओ सयनानि च।
अच्छंदा जे न भुजंति न से चागि त्ति वुच्चति ॥२॥
पक्खंदे जलितं जोति धूमकेतुं दुरासदं।
नेच्छंति वंतयं भोत्तुं कुले जाता अगंधने ॥६॥
धिगत्थु ते जसोकामी जो तं जीवितकारणा।
वंतं इच्छसि आवेतुं सेतं ते मरणं भवे ॥७॥
अहं च भोगरायस्स तं चऽसि अंधगविण्हिनो।
मा कुले गंधना होमो संजमं निहुतो चर ॥८॥
जदि तं काहिसि भावं जा जा दिच्छिसि नारिओ।
वाताविध्धो व्व हडो अट्ठियप्पा भविस्ससि ॥९॥
तीसे सो वचनं सोच्चा संजताए सुभासितं।
अंकुसेन जथा नागो धम्मे संपतिपातओ ॥१०॥
एवं करेति संबुध्धा पंडिता पवितक्खणा।
विनियंहंति भोगेहि जथा से पुरिसोत्तमो ॥११॥
ति बेमि ॥

13 BUDDHIST AND MĪMĀMSĀ VIEWS ON LAKṢAṆĀ

K. KUNJUNNI RAJA

Though the Mīmāṃsakas and the Buddhist logicians were opposed to each other on various topics, there is a remarkable similarity on their views on some aspects of metaphoric transfer (*lakṣaṇā, upacāra, gauṇī vṛtti*). According to the Mīmāṃsakas the primary meaning of a word like 'cow' is the universal which is the essential quality common to the particular instances of the class. Both Jaimini and Śabara use the term *ākṛti* to refer to the universal. Kumārila Bhaṭṭa says in his *Ślokavārttika* that the term *ākṛti* is used in the sense of *jāti* or the universal. *jātim evākṛtim prāhur vyaktir ākriyate yayā* (Ākṛti section, verse 3). Patañjali also used the term *ākṛti* in the sense of the universal. Later writers in the field of Mīmāṃsā use the term *jāti* itself. The primary meaning of a word is something permanent, and cannot be the particular instances of the class. It was, however, admitted that in a sentence it is the particulars (*vyakti*) that enter into syntactic relationship.

Regarding the question as to how the particular is cognized from the universal, there are different views. According to the Prābhākara School of Mīmāṃsā the particular is known from the universal because of the invariable connection between the two, and since the same cognition comprehends both the universal and the particular *jātisamānasaṃvitsaṃvedyatvād vyakteḥ*. According to the Bhāṭṭa Mīmāṃsā, the particular is obtained from the universal through *lakṣaṇā* or secondary significance. It is accepted that *lakṣaṇā* requires the incompatibility of the primary meaning in the context, and some relationship between the primary and the actual meanings. If each word in a sentence gives its own isolated meaning which is in the form of a universal, it is not possible to have any syntactic relationship among the word-meanings and a connected, unitary sentence-meaning cannot be obtained. But we know from the context that the utterance of the sentence is for the purpose of conveying a connected meaning. Hence on the basis of the discrepancy of the literal word-meanings (which are isolated universals) with the intended purport (*tātparyānupapatti*), *lakṣaṇā* is resorted to get at the particulars.

Kumārila Bhaṭṭa says in the *Ślokavārttika*:

जातेरस्तित्वनास्तित्वे न हि कश्चिद् विवक्षति ।
नित्यत्वाल्लक्ष्यमाणाया व्यक्तेस्ते हि विशेषणे ॥

(Ākṛti section, p. 932, Chowkhamba ed.)

(Nobody wants to speak about the existence or nonexistence of the universal which is eternal; these two (existence and non-existence) apply to the particulars which are got through *lakṣaṇā*).

The Bhāṭṭas are definite that the apprehension of the particular from the universal is through *lakṣaṇā*.

Lakṣaṇā is possible only when there is discrepancy. The significative power of the word (*padaśakti*) is only for the universal; the particular (*vyakti*) is got from the universal by resorting to *lakṣaṇā* because of the discrepancy (*anupapatti*). *Nyāyaratnamālā* (*Vākyārthanirṇaya*, Varanasi ed. 1972) says:

तस्माज्जात्यभिधायित्वात् शब्दस्तामेव बोधयेत् ।
सा तु शब्देन विज्ञाता पश्चाद् व्यक्ति प्रबोधयेत् ॥ (v. 42)

Sometimes the term *ākṣepa* 'implication' is also used instead of *lakṣaṇā*, and this is identified with *arthāpatti* (Presumption).

व्यक्तिप्रतीतिरस्माकं जातिरेव तु शब्दतः ।
प्रथमावगता पश्चाद् व्यक्ति यां कांचिदाक्षिपेत् ॥ (ibid. v. 39)

There has been some confusion regarding *lakṣaṇā* and *ākṣepa* while dealing with the Mīmāṃsā position by the Navya Nyāya scholars beginning from Gaṅgeśopādhyāya down to the modern times. Explaining the Mīmāṃsā views Gaṅgeśa gives three different theories—*lakṣaṇā, ākṣepa* and *tulyasaṃvitti* (simultaneous cognition of the universal and the particular). *Maṇikaṇa* sums it up: गवादिपदानां जातिरेव शक्या; व्यक्तिः आक्षेपात्, लक्षणया तुल्यवित्तिवेद्यतया वा लभ्या इत्येके । (p. 80 Adyar Library edition)

The third view is that of the Prābhākaras; the other two are said to be held by Bhaṭṭa Mīmāṃsakas—Gaṅgeśa seems to consider *ākṣepa* as the view of Kumārila Bhāṭṭa and *lakṣāṇā* as the view of Maṇḍanamiśra.

Strictly speaking, there is no difference between the two views. In a paper presented to the International Congress of Orientalists at Delhi in 1964, I had pointed out that the verse quoted by Gaṅgeśa as from Maṇḍana is found in Kumārila Bhaṭṭa's *Ślokavārttika* itself (Ākṛti section, p. 932 quoted above) and that there is no authority for ascribing it to Maṇḍana. This verse wrongly attributed to Maṇḍana by Gaṅgeśa (*Tattvacintāmaṇi*, Śaktivāda, p. 587) and his followers (cf. Jagadīśa's *Śabdaśaktiprakāśikā*, p. 87) is actually Kumārila's own verse.[1] Authorities on Bhāṭṭa Mīmāṃsā have taken *lakṣaṇā* as responsible for obtaining the notion of the particular from the universal. Pārthasārathi Miśra says in the *Śāstradīpikā*.

लक्षणा वाभ्युपेतव्या जातेस्तेनाभिधेयता । (1.3.10)

Some commentators have tried to distinguish the two by saying that *ākṣepa* means *arthāpatti*, and that from the invariable concomitance between *vyakti* and *jāti* the *vyakti* is obtained after getting the *jāti*.

आक्षेपः—व्यक्तेर्जात्यविनाभूतत्वात् शब्दाद् जातिबुद्ध्यनन्तरं क्रमेण व्यप्त्याद्यनुसंधानेन व्यक्तिबुद्धिरित्यर्थः ।

(*Tarkatāṇḍava*, vol. II, p. 230 Ed. Mysore University, 1935)

We cannot accept the view that in *ākṣepa* or *arthāpatti* no special function of the word is involved, for *lakṣaṇā* itself works on the principle of *arthāpatti*.[2]

The Buddhist logicians do not accept the view of the Mīmāṃsakas and the Naiyāyikas about the existence of a positive entity called the universal (*jāti* or *sāmānya*). To them only the particular at a time-point (*svalakṣaṇa*) is ultimately real. The so-called objective world is made up of a succession of such momentary particulars, like the still pictures of a cinema. To the Buddhists real perception is the unerring knowledge of the unique particular that is taken by the senses; the concepts produced in the mind are not part of perception, but only a kind of sign for inference. Words deal directly with conceptual images which are purely subjective constructions of the mind (*vikalpas*). The meaning of a word is the conceptual image whose essence is the negation of all its counter-correlates (*anyāpoha*); words deal directly with the concepts. Diṅnāga says:

विकल्पयोनयः शब्दाः विकल्पाः शब्दयोनयः ।
तेषामन्योन्यसंबन्धो नार्थान् शब्दाः स्पृशन्त्यमी ।।४।।

(Partly quoted by Stcherbatsky, *Buddhist Logic* II, p. 405n, and fully but anonymously quoted in *Uṃveka's* commentary on *Ślokavārttika*, Madras University edn. p. 61)

While the Mīmāṃsakas accept the reality of the universal, the Buddhists consider it as the preclusion of its counter-correlates. Nārāyaṇa quotes Kumārila Bhaṭṭa to show that practically the Buddhist *vikalpa*, in the form of *anyāpoha*, is the same as the *jāti* of the Mīmāṃsakas:

अगोनिवृत्तिसामान्यं वाच्यं यैः परिकल्पितम् ।
गोत्ववस्त्वेव तैरुक्तमगोऽपोहगिरा स्फुटम् ॥

(*Mānameyodaya* p. 237)

According to the Buddhist logicians there is no primary referent for a word, for the essential nature of an object transcends the pale of all forms of knowledge and expression. So each word which refers directly to the *vikalpa*, or the mental construct can be applied to the object only *indirectly* by a sort of transfer or *upacāra*. In the *Vijñaptimātratāsiddhi* commentary by Sthiramati on Vasubandhu's *Triṃśikā* it is stated thus:

मुख्यपदार्थो नास्ति तस्य सर्वज्ञानाभिधानविषयातिक्रान्तत्वात् ।
.... अपि च सर्व एवायं गौण एव, न मुख्योऽस्ति ।

(ed. Sylvain Levi, Paris 1925, p. 17)

Thus it is clear that there is similarity between the Buddhist logicians and the Bhāṭṭa Mīmāṃsakas in considering the understanding of particulars as based on metaphoric transfer.

Mrs. Radhika Herzberger says in her book on *Bhartrhari and the Buddhists*, D. Reidel Publishing Co. 1988, that Diṅnāga's Apoha doctrine was meant to ensure that names apply to the perceptual objects. It is true that the Apoha doctrine was meant to bridge the gap between the perceptual and the conceptual, and that the world of precepts and the world of concepts are not totally exclusive of each other. But in the face of Diṅnāga's statement *nārthān śabdāḥ spṛśanty amī*, it is difficult to accept the view that words apply 'directly' to objects. As Matilal has observed, "The names cannot 'express' the particulars 'directly', but the only way a name can identify or refer to a particular is through negation and elimination of other concepts" according to Diṅnāga. (*Epistemology, Logic and Grammar, Indian Philosophical Analysis*. Mouton, 1971, p. 41)

The Bhāṭṭa Mīmāṃsakas who advocate the theory of Abhihitānvayavāda of verbal comprehension resort to *lakṣaṇā* for conveying the syntactic relation among the word-meanings. The words in a sentence convey their individual meanings and stop with that; then the word-meanings convey the syntactically connected sentence-meaning. All the authorities on Bhāṭṭa Mīmāṃsā have stated that it is through *lakṣaṇā* that the sentence-meaning is comprehended.

वाक्यार्थो लक्ष्यमाणो हि सर्वत्रैवेति नः स्थितिः ।

(Kumārila Bhaṭṭa, Quoted in *Tattvabindu*, p. 153)

पदस्वरूपाभिहितैः पदार्थैः संलक्ष्यतेऽसाविति सिद्धमेतत्

(Pārthasārathi Miśra, *Nyāyaratnamālā*, p. 125)

पदाभिहितैः पदार्थैः लक्षणया वाक्यार्थः प्रतिपाद्यते ।

(*Śāstradīpikā*, p. 154)

लभ्यते च समभिव्याहारान्यथानुपपत्त्या पदानामन्वितार्थपराणां स्वाभि-धेयार्थरूप समवेतान्वितावस्थाप्रत्यायनं लक्षणया ।

(Vācaspati Miśra, *Tattvabindu*, p. 131)

पदार्था एव वाक्यार्थं लक्षयन्ति ।

(Cidānanda, *Nītitattvāvirbhāva*, p. 232)

वयं तु पदार्थाः लक्षणयैव वाक्यार्थं बोधयन्तीति ब्रूमः ।

(*Mānameyodaya*, p. 94)

Thus it seems that the Bhāṭṭa Mīmāṃsakas resort to *lakṣaṇā* for getting the notion of the particular from the universal, and also for getting the syntactic relationship among the word-meanings. Now the problem is (1) Should we resort to two *lakṣaṇās* for the two purposes or (2) can the same *lakṣaṇā* effect both?

The problem has not been raised seriously by earlier writers. If an operation can effect only one result, we may have to accept two *lakṣaṇās*. But nobody has spoken about two *lakṣaṇās* while explaining verbal comprehension of the sentence-meaning, and the law of parsimony (*lāghava*) requires the simpler approach in solving the problem. Hence it seems preferable to assume that only one *lakṣaṇā* is needed to explain the two effects—*vyaktilakṣaṇā* and *anvayalakṣaṇā*. The incompatibility in the context (*tātparyānupapatti*) is the lack of a unified connected sentence meaning; this can be solved only by resorting to both the operations—*jāti* to *vyakti*, and the addition of *anvaya* (syntactic relationship). The process of *lakṣaṇā* can be completed only by removing the contextual incompatibility, and it is only proper that both the operations are to be considered as effected by the same *lakṣaṇā vyāpāra*. Even the Buddhist logicians accept that a positive sentence meaning is got on the basis of the word-meanings which are mere mental constructs (*vikalpa*) without any reality in them except the preclusion of all their counter-correlates.

Nārāyaṇa Bhaṭṭa, author of the *Mānameyodaya*, seems to support the view of a single *lakṣaṇā* effecting both the results in the comprehension of the sentence-meaning. He says that the word-meanings, which are basically universals, convey the sentence-meaning through *lakṣaṇā*. He seems to hold the view that there is no need to have two *lakṣaṇās*, one to get the particulars from the universals, and the other to convey the syntactic relation.

वयं तु पदार्थाः लक्षणयैव वाक्यार्थं बोधयन्तीति ब्रूमः। वाच्यार्थानुपपत्त्या हि लक्षणा भवति। अत्र च पदैः स्मार्यमाणा गवादिपदार्थाः यद्यन्योन्यान्वयं विना सामान्यरूपा एवावतिष्ठेरन् तर्हि पदानां व्युत्पत्तिसमयावधृतमेकविशिष्टार्थबोधतात्पर्यं विरुध्येत इति सामान्यरूपस्य वाच्यस्यानुपपत्तेरन्योन्यान्वयरूपे विशेषे एव पदार्थाः पर्यवस्यन्ति ॥

"But we say that the sense of the words conveys the meaning of the sentence only by secondary implication. Indeed secondary implication comes in through the nonintelligibility of the expressed meaning. And here senses like 'cow' etc. recollected by the words, if they should remain in their generic form without mutual syntactical relation, then there would be contradiction of the purport of the words to indicate a unitary qualified object as determined at the time of learning. And so since the generic form signified is unintelligible the meaning of words leads up to the particulars consisting in mutual syntactical relation."

(Adyar Library ed. p. 96)

Ānandavardhana argues in his *Dhvanyāloka* that in an example like *Gaṅgāyām ghoṣaḥ*, 'the village on the Ganges', the discrepancy of the primary meaning in the context is removed by resorting to the meaning of 'the bank of the Ganges'; the scope of *lakṣaṇā* stops with that. The further meanings of coolness and sanctity do not come from the transferred meaning of 'the bank' but directly from the primary meaning of 'the Ganges'. They are therefore assigned to the power of suggestion. If the power of *lakṣaṇā* is exhausted when the discrepancy is removed, it also follows that the power of *lakṣaṇā* continues till the discrepancy is fully removed; the transfer of *jāti* to *vyakti*, by itself, will not remove the discrepancy; hence adding of the syntactic element has also to be taken as part of the same *lakṣaṇā*, getting all the unified sentence-meaning.

References

1. 'A so-called view of Maṇḍana on word-meaning', *Proceedings of the International Congress of Orientalists*, Poona, 1969.

2. D. M. Datta, *The Six Ways of Knowing*, p. 284; Mukulabhaṭṭa in his *Vākyārthamātṛkā* gives the example of *pīno devadattaḥ divā na bhuṅkte* as an example of *lakṣaṇā*.

14 GRAMMARIANS AND PHILOSOPHERS

On the *anuśāsana: na karmadhārayān matvarthīyo bahuvrīhiś cet tadarthapratipattikaraḥ*

KAMALESWAR BHATTACHARYA, *Paris*

Under this form, the *anuśāsana* is cited by late authors.[1] The idea, however, goes back to Kātyāyana, *Vārttikas* 4-5 on Pāṇini II, 1, 69, and was developed by Patañjali in his *Mahābhāṣya*, and, later, by authors such as Vāmana in his *Kāvyālaṃkārasūtravṛtti*,[2] Puṇyarāja in his comment on Bhartṛhari's *Vākyapadīya* II, 86, the commentators on the *Mahābhāṣya*, Kaiyaṭa and Nāgeśa (Nāgoji) bhaṭṭa, and Śaraṇadeva in his *Durghaṭavṛtti*.[3]

Mathurānātha Tarkavāgīśa, who cites the *anuśāsana* in connection with the interpretation given by the 'Ancients' (*prāñcaḥ*) of the expression *sādhyābhāvavadavṛttitvam* in the *Vyāptipañcaka* section of the *Anumānakhaṇḍa* of Gaṅgeśa Upādhyāya's *Tattvacintāmaṇi*, says that he has developed the point in his *Guṇaprakāśarahasya* and (*Guṇa*)*dīdhitirahasya*. The relevant passages are quoted by Paṇḍita Śivadatta Miśra in his edition of the *Vyāptipañcakarahasya*.[4]

The basic point was already discussed by Vardhamāna Upādhyāya, while dealing with Udayana's explanation of the form *aguṇavattvam* in the *Padārthadharmasaṃgraha* (=*Praśastapādabhāṣya*): *guṇā yeṣu vartante te guṇavantaḥ, na guṇavanto 'guṇavantaḥ, teṣāṃ bhāvas tattvam*. Vardhamāna writes: *nanu na vidyante guṇā yasyeti bahuvrīhiṇaiva vivakṣitārthalābhe nañtatpuruṣān matub vyarthaḥ, karmadhārayamatvarthīyād bahuvrīhir eveṣṭo lāghavād iti nyāyāt, pratyuta paryudāsanañā guṇetaravattvaṃ* (so read) *tatra pratīyeta, tac ca vivakṣitaṃ nety ata āha*: guṇā yeṣv *iti*.[5]

The question naturally received the attention of late grammarians such as Bhaṭṭoji Dīkṣita and Nāgeśa. The latter writes that a possessive-making suffix is not added to a karmadhāraya or a nañtatpuruṣa compound, nor are these compounds made with a word ending in a possessive-making suffix; as there is 'heaviness' (*gaurava*) in a double word-formation (*vṛtti*), a bahuvrīhi alone is correct in these cases. Violations of this principle are observed, however; and Nāgeśa says that, in view of the usage of the 'cultured' (*śiṣṭa*), the principle of parsimony (*lāghava*) is ignored here.[6]

One of the most illustrious violations is that cited by Paṇḍita Śivadatta Miśra:[7] the form *asubvataḥ*, used by the author of the *Mahābhāṣya* himself, instead of analysing *asupaḥ*, in Pāṇini VII, 3, 44, as a bahuvrīhi. As Kaiyaṭa observes, the author of the *Bhāṣya* does not resort to the principle of parsimony; for, in virtue of this principle, the bahuvrīhi alone is correct.[8]

Śaraṇadeva, in the *Durghaṭavṛtti*, cites other violations from Jinendrabuddhi's *Nyāsa* as well as from literary works of Kālidāsa, and he solves the problem with the statement that the principle in question only represents the opinion of some and, therefore, is not binding.[9] This view is also cited, as an alternative explanation, by Cāritravardhana, while commenting upon *Kumārasaṃbhava* V, 16: *tvaguttarāsaṅgavatī*, the other explanation being that the compound in question is a tṛtīyātatpuruṣa (*tvacā uttarāsaṅgavatīti tṛtīyāsamāsaḥ*).[10] Both these explanations are to be found in Vallabhadeva's commentary on *Meghadūta* 12 (11): *bisakisalayacchedapātheyavantaḥ*,[11] and perhaps also in his commentary on *Kumārasaṃbhava* V, 16.[12]

The logician Mathurānātha Tarkavāgīśa evinces better sensibility when he explains Meghadūta *bisakisalayacchedapātheyavantaḥ*. He says: The excellence, abundance, etc., of the provisions (*pātheya*), which are intended to be expressed, cannot be expressed by the bahuvrīhi: *bisakisalayacchedapātheyāḥ*; therefore, the possessive-making suffix is added to a karmadhāraya.[13] It is, indeed, when we have to deal with cases like this that we understand the meaning of the principle: 'A possessive-making suffix should not be appended after a karmadhāraya when a bahuvrīhi serves to express the meaning' (*na karmadhārayān matvarthīyo bahuvrīhiś cet tadarthapratipattikaraḥ*). Needless to say, a similar explanation can be extended to Kumārasaṃbhava *tvaguttarāsaṅgavant-* and to *Raghuvaṃśa* IV, 44: *phalavatpūgamālin-*.[14]

In the same vein, Vācaspatimiśra, in the *Sāṃkhyatattvakaumudī*, observes, while commenting upon *Sāṃkhyakārikā* 11, that, while the bahuvrīhi *prasavadharman* ought to have been employed, the Manifest (*vyakta*) is called *prasavadharmin*, the possessive-making suffix *-in-* being appended to the karmadhāraya *prasavadharma*, in order to express the idea that the property of production is constantly associated with the Manifest (*prasavadharmeti vaktavye matvarthīyaḥ prasavadharmasya nityayogam ākhyātum*).[15]

References

1. See, e.g., Gopendra-Tippabhūpāla, *Kāmadhenu* on Vāmana's *Kāvyālaṃkārasūtravṛtti* V, 2, 58 (Srirangam: Sri Vani Vilas Press, 1909); Mathurānātha Tarkavāgīśa, *Vyāptipañcakarahasya* (Daniel H. H. Ingalls, *Materials for the Study of Navya-Nyāya Logic*, Cambridge, Mass. 1951: *Harvard Oriental Series* 40, pp. 90 and 91); Nāgeśa, *Uddyota* on Kaiyaṭa's *Pradīpa* on Patañjali's *Mahābhāṣya* on Kātyāyana's *Vārttika* 5 on Pāṇini II, 1, 69 (Nirnaya-Sagar Press edition, Vol. II, p. 410b).

2. *Loc. cit.*

3. On Pāṇini V, 2, 118 (in L. Renou's edition: *La Durghaṭavṛtti de Śaraṇadeva: Traité grammatical en sanskrit du XIIe siècle*, Paris, 1940-56).

4. Benares, 1928 (*Kashi Sanskrit Series* 64, Nyāya Section No. 8), pp. 14-15. The *Guṇaprakāśarahasya*, recently edited in Varanasi, has not yet been available to me.

5. *Kiraṇāvalī* and *Prakāśa*, Vol. II, ed. Narendra Chandra Vedantatirtha, Calcutta, Asiatic Society (*Bibliotheca Indica*), 1956, p. 405.

6. *karmadhārayān nañtatpuruṣāc ca na matvarthīyaḥ. matvarthīyāntena ca na tau. vṛttidvayakalpane gauraveṇa tatra bahuvrīher eva sādhutvāt. kvacit tu śiṣṭaprayogānurodhena lāghavānādarād bhavaty eva yathādaṇḍī apucchī avāggmī ekadeśina ityādi. Vaiyākaraṇasiddhāntalaghumañjūṣā* (ed. Mādhava Śāstrī Bhandari, Benares, Chowkhamba, 1925), p. 1448.—In the *Bṛhacchabdenduśekhara*, on *Siddhāntakaumudī* 712 (Pāṇini II, 2, 1), Nāgeśa follows Kaiyaṭa (*Pradīpa* on *Mahābhāṣya* on Pāṇini V, 2, 94) in justifying compounds such as *adaṇḍin-*, *avāggmin-*: the meanings intended to be expressed cannot be obtained from bahuvrīhis. *yatrāpi matvarthīyenārthaviśeṣapratītis tatrāpi tadantena nañsamāsaḥ, yathā—adaṇḍī apucchī avāggmī iti. daṇḍapucchasaṃyoganiṣedhasya samyagbhāṣitvaniṣedhasya ca bahuvrīher anavagamāt*, Kaiyaṭa, *Pradīpa* (Nirnaya-Sagar Press edition, Vol. IV, p. 348); *adaṇḍī avāggmītyādau matvarthīyāntenaiva nañsamāsaḥ, na tu tatra bahuvrīhiṇā gatārthatvam. daṇḍasaṃyoganiṣedhasya samyagbahubhāṣitvaniṣedhasya ca tato 'navagamāt*, Nāgeśa, *Bṛhacchabdenduśekhara* (ed. Sītārāma Śāstrī, Varanasi, 1960: *Sarasvatībhavana-Granthamālā* 87, Vol. II, p. 1016).

See also *Uddyota*, loc. cit.—Patañjali speaks only of *laghutva*: . . .*tatra karmadhārayaprakṛtibhir matvarthīyair abhidhānam astu bahuvrīhiṇeti bahuvrīhiṇā bhaviṣyati, laghutvāt*. (*Mahābhāṣya* on *Vārttika* 5 on Pāṇini II, 1, 69: Kielhorn's edition, Vol. I, p. 404, 15-16). Kaiyaṭa explains this as *pratipattilāghava* 'economy of understanding' as opposed to *pratipattigaurava* 'heaviness of understanding'. And he refers to the view of 'others' (*anye*) who explain this as *śabdalāghava* 'economy of expression' as opposed to *śabda-*

gaurava 'heaviness of expression'. Nāgeśa thinks that it is the latter explanation which Patañjali had in mind: *idam eva Bhāṣyasvarasasiddhaṃ matam.* And he explains *śabdalāghava* and *śabdagaurava* as referring, respectively, to a single and to a double word-formation: *ekasyaivārthasya pratipādanāya vṛttidvayāpekṣāyāṃ garīyān śabdo bodhako bahuvrīhau tv alpa iti bhāvaḥ.*

Nāgeśa further points out that by *karmadhāraya* is also indicated *nañsamāsa,* and that this is suggested by Patañjali himself in *Mahābhāṣya* on Pāṇini VI, 4, 161.

7. *Op. cit.*, p. 17.

8. *na subvad asubvad iti nañsamāso 'supa ity asya bahuvrīhitvapradarśanāya. Bhāṣyakāreṇa lāghavaṃ nāśritam. tadāśrayaṇe hi bahuvrīhir eva nyāyyo na tu matubantaḥ samāsaḥ. Pradīpa* on *Mahābhāṣya* on Pāṇini VII, 3, 44 (Nirnaya-Sagar edition, Vol. VI, p. 205). See also Nāgeśa, *Bṛhacchabdenduśekhara,* loc. cit.

9. *ekīyamatam etat. ye tu lāghavārthaṃ nānumanyante tanmatenaite prayogāḥ. Durghaṭavṛtti* on Pāṇini V, 2, 118 (L. Renou's edition).—Śaraṇadeva cites the opinion of Maitreyarakṣita, according to whom the suffix *-in-* is added to the bahuvrīhi *ekadeśa* to form *ekadeśin* (*bahuvrīher ekadeśaśabdād iniḥ*). The Western grammarians (Whitney, Wackernagel, Renou), who regard this type of compounds as pleonastically enlarged bahuvrīhis, are, therefore, not isolated.

Śaṅkara, in his commentary on *Bhagavadgītā* XIII, 12, cites the opinion of some (*kecit*) who regarded *anādimat* as formed with the suffix *-mant-* added to the bahuvrīhi *anādi,* but who, considering this formation to be illicit, as it involved a repetition, proposed to read in the *Gītā* verse *anādi matparaṃ brahma* (this is also the reading adopted by Rāmānuja) instead of *anādimat paraṃ brahma.* Śaṅkara analyses *anādimat* as Udayana analyses *aguṇavattvam* (see above) or as Kaiyaṭa analyses *asubvat* (see preceding note): *ādir asyāstīty ādimat. na ādimad anādimat,* but, at the end, says that, although the suffix *-mant-* has the same meaning as the bahuvrīhi, it has been used for metrical reasons (*matupo bahuvrīhiṇā samānārthatve 'pi prayogaḥ ślokapūraṇārthaḥ*). Śrīdhara follows Śaṅkara; but Nīlakaṇṭha and Madhusūdana Sarasvatī interpret differently. The latter explains the suffix as implying excellence (*atiśāyana*) or constant association (*nityayoga*)—two of the meanings in which the possessive-making suffixes are employed (see *Ślokavārttika* in *Mahābhāṣya* on Pāṇini V, 2, 94: Kielhorn's edition, Vol. II, p. 393; Madhusūdana's idea is technically explained by Dharmadatta (Bacca) Jha in his *Gūḍhārthatattvāloka*). (*Bhagavadgītā* with the *Śāṅkarabhāṣya* with Ānandagiri, *Nīlakaṇṭhī, Bhāṣyotkarṣadīpikā* of Dhanapati, *Śrīdharī, Gītārthasaṃgraha* of Abhinavagupta, and *Gūḍhārthadīpikā* of Madhusūdana with *Gūḍhārthatattvāloka* of Dharmadattaśarmā [Baccāśarmā]. Edited by Wasudev Laxman Shastri Pansikar, Bombay: Nirnaya-Sagar Press, 1912.)

10. See M. R. Kale's Notes in his edition and translation of the *Kumārasaṃbhava* (reprint Delhi: Motilal Banarsidass, 1967), p. 86.

11. Ed. E. Hultzsch, London, 1911.

12. See Gautam Patel's edition, Ahmedabad, 1986, p. 141 (read [Note] *vidyate* for *vidhate*).

13. *tatra pātheyaniṣṭhotkarṣabhūyastvādilakṣaṇasya vivakṣitārthasya tadar-*

thakamatuppratyayaṃ vinā bahuvrīhito lābhāsaṃbhavāt: Śivadatta Miśra, *op. cit.*, p. 15.—Mathurānātha also recognizes that there is *śabdagaurava* 'heaviness of expression' in *aguṇavattvam*, even when analysed in the way in which Udayana analyses it, viz., as a nañtatpuruṣa formed with a word ending in a possessive-making suffix (see Nāgeśa, above). But he says that the meaning intended to be conveyed, viz., 'difference from things having qualities' (*guṇavadbhinnatva*)—as the common property (*sādharmya*) of qualities (*guṇa*)—cannot be expressed by a bahuvrīhi. *na ca śabdalāghavādare matuppratyayottaraṃ nañtatpuruṣo 'pi mūloktaviruddho bahuvrīhiṇaiva tallabhyārthasya lābhasaṃbhavena śabdagauravād iti vācyam. matuppratyayānantaraṃ nañtatpuruṣalabhyasyārthasya guṇavadbhinnatvarūpasya bahuvrīhiṇā lābhāsaṃbhavāt.* (*Ibid.*)

14. Mallinātha explains as tṛtīyātatpuruṣa (see above) both Meghadūta *bisakisalayacchedapātheyavant*—and Kumārasaṃbhava *tvaguttarāsaṅgavant*—. For Raghuvaṃśa *phalavatpūgamālin-* he adopts a type of interpretation that was rejected by Vāmana (*loc. cit.*), although in *Kumārasaṃbhava* I, 32 he interprets *caturasraśobhi* in the same fashion as Vāmana (see also Vallabhadeva: Patel's edition).

15. In writing this article—at a moment when no public library possessing the texts I needed was accessible to me—I had to rely often upon my notes. I am, therefore, conscious of its imperfections, which will be remedied, I hope, in future.

Mr. François Grimal calls my attention to Vīrarāghava's explanations of *mahāpātakin* in Bhavabhūti's *Mahāvīracarita* (III, p. 96 in the 4th edition from the Nirnaya-Sagar Press, 1926). Both these explanations are supported by tradition: (1) the karmadhāraya *mahāpātaka* has acquired the conventional meaning of murder of a Brahmin, etc.; therefore, the possessive-making suffix is added (as, e.g., in *kṛṣṇasarpavān* [*valmīkaḥ*]: *Mahābhāṣya* on *Vārttika* 5 on Pāṇini II, 1, 69); (2) the idea of excess, which is intended to be conveyed, cannot be obtained from the bahuvrīhi *mahāpātaka*. In these circumstances, the prohibition *na karmadhārayāt . . .*does not apply. *mahāpātakaśabdo brahmahatyādiṣu yogarūḍhaḥ. tasmād iniḥ. yad vā mahāpātakaṃ brahmahatyadirūpam atiśayenāstīty atiśayavivakṣāyāṃ karmadhārayād iniḥ. atiśayo hi na bahuvrīhilabhyaḥ. nātaḥ* na karmadhārayād *iti niṣedhaḥ.*

ADDITION

In *Kumārasaṃbhava* I, 37, Mallinātha explains *anumeyaśobhi* in the same way as Vāmana; but Vallabhadeva apparently reads *anumeyaśobham.*

POSTSCRIPT

This paper does not seem to be in the right place, in a volume entitled "Buddhist Philosophical Researches". But I was asked to "write on Hindu Philosophy rather than on a Buddhist topic" (letter dated 27th November, (1989).

15 KASHMIR ŚAIVISM (KS) AND THE VEDĀNTA OF ŚAṄKARA

PROFESSOR R.C. DWIVEDI

Dean, Faculty of Arts, University of Rajasthan, Jaipur

There is no direct reference to the Brahmasūtra or to the works of Ādi Śaṅkara in the literature that constitutes the backbone of Kashmir Śaivism.[1] Somānanda (end of the 9th century A.D.), Utpala (beginning of the 10th century A.D.), and Abhinavagupta (middle of the 10th century A.D. to beginning of the 11th century A.D.) who followed Śaṅkara (820 A.D.) chronologically and who may be considered the trinity of Śaiva monism make numerous references to Veda, Upaniṣads, Gītā and the Vedānta[2] but none to the Brahmasūtra or its celebrated Bhāṣya by Śaṅkara. In fact, the Bhagavadgītā is classed as an Āgama[3] and is continuously commented upon by Śaiva thinkers including Vasugupta, Abhinavagupta and Rāma Kaṇṭha and is extensively quoted in commentaries on the Īśvarapratyabhijñākārikā by Abhinavagupta. Upaniṣadic sentences have been quoted with approval[5] and in support of the basic doctrines of KS. Somānanda who systematised the monistic school of Śaivism refers to many views of Vedānta in his *Vision of Śiva* (Ch. VI.2-15), *Śivadṛṣṭi*. Amongst them are those who held that Brahman assumed diverse forms (*Citrabrahmavāda*), others believed in the plurality of the self (*nānātmavāda*). Another Vedantic opinion considered Brahman as the material cause (*upādāna*) of the universe. The *ātmavādins* amongst them held the individual soul to be the absolute. The *netivādins* denied any positive sense to Self or Brahman. Others held that the selves are like sparks of the fire-like *Brahman* (*sphuliṅgātmavādins*), the *pratibimbavādins* regarded the Self as a reflection of Brahman, another opinion believed in the plurality of selves in different bodies with inherent duality of the world, still others held that the individual souls are mutually different but they are essentially one with the Brahman, just like various streams and the sun. Some Vedāntins maintained that the knowledge, freedom, and bondage are within the sphere of *avidyā* itself. References and allusions to Vedānta and its various philosophical opinions recur in the works of Utpala and Abhinavagupta as well.

Many of these opinions, more particularly in Somānanda, can be traced in the pre-Śaṅkara Vedānta but Abhinavagupta,[6] if not Utpala, seems to show awareness of the Vedānta as advocated by Śaṅkara. Yet it is a moot question whether these *ācāryas* had any direct knowledge of the Vedānta of Śaṅkara or they were simply referring to the tradition of Vedānta as found in the Upaniṣads and the Gītā and also Gauḍapāda. Modern writers on KS have assumed without any clear and conclusive evidence that the Śivasūtras were inspired by Śaṅkara; that he visited Kashmir in the beginning of the 9th century A.D. as per the doubtful description found in the Śaṅkara-digvijaya; that the works like the Dakṣiṇāmūrti-stotra, the Saundaryalaharī, and the Prapañcasāra are from the pen of Śaṅkara whose Tantric monism or Śakta following is reflected in KS; that the life of Śaṅkara as Śakta-Śaiva and his thought should not be split in interpreting his philosophy. This has led many scholars like Bühler, Chatterji, Dasgupta, K.C. Pandey, B.N. Pandit and others to think that KS or the Śaiva monism of Kashmir is an application of Śaṇkara's principles to the Śaiva philosophy. This is not true or complimentary to either of these two systems of thought. These do share many common ideas, forms and arguments mutually and also implicitly with the idealistic schools of Buddhism. A correct view could be that Śaṅkara and KS proposed two alternative models of nature of reality in reaction to the rise of subjective idealism of the Yogācāra and the Śunyavāda of the Mādhyamikas in keeping with their tradition (Saṁpradāya) of interpreting authority of the Śruti (mainly Upaniṣads) on the one hand and the Āgamas on the other. The Vākyapadīya of Bhartṛhari, the Bhagavadgītā and the Upaniṣads including the Māṇḍūkyakārika were common sources for the growth of idealism in orthodox non-Buddhist circles. However, to begin with Somānanda did not agree with any of these sources and the Śaiva thinkers do not show any respect for the Brahmasūtra and make no direct reference to Śaṅkara. The Nyāya, Vaiśeṣika, Yoga, Buddhism and Jainism do not claim to present interpretative study of the scriptures or the revealed texts. As against this, Mīmāṁsā, Vedānta and Śaivism (both northern and southern) claim to be rooted in their traditional scriptures. The first amongst these is diametrically opposed to the Vedānta of any sort. The Upaniṣads are variously interpreted by a great line of philosophers foremost amongst whom is Śaṅkara. Both KS and Śaṅkara give importance to spiritual experience (*anubhava and Svasaṁvedana*) and accept the significance of reasoning (*tarka or sattarka*) as an aid to the understanding of the Vedānta or the Śaivāgamas. Just like the Upaniṣads, the Āgamas present diverse traditions of dualistic, dualistic-cum-non-dualistic and non-dualistic thoughts, spiritual pathways, rites and rituals. Abhinavagupta was the Śaṅkara of Kashmir who strengthened Śaiva monism and integrated and syncretised diverse ritualistic traditions into the theology of oneness with Śiva known as Śivādvaita or Śiva-advaya. Contemporary writers describe KS as realistic idealism, idealistic monism (K.C. Pandey), monistic idealism (J. Rudrappa), concrete monism (R.K. Kaw), theistic monism (B.N. Pandit) and so on. Mālinīvijayavārtika, which is regarded as a basic Āgama of the KS, described it as *Parādvaita* and *advaya* where dualism and non-dualism (realism and idealism by implication) are on equal terms (I.262), where distinctions are neither accepted nor rejected (*Idam hi tat porāduaitam bhedatyāgagrahu na yat*), no division can split the *advaya* nature of reality (Ibid. I.261). Apparent opposites like pleasure and pain, freedom and bondage, sentiency and insentiency are synonyms like pot and jar and these cannot touch the integral nature of reality, declares Abhinavagupta in his *Tantrāloka* (II.19).

According to Kashmir Śaivism the ultimate reality, spoken of as Maheśvara, Anuttara, Parama Śiva, Bhairava, etc., is *cit, caitanya* or consciousness. It is *cetana* or conscious, as it is invariably related to or is inseparable from the power or action of consciousness that is *citikriyā*. Consciousness has two important characteristics, namely, self-luminosity (*svaprākaśatā*) and self-consciousness (*Vimarśa*). While *prakāśa* or luminosity is a transcendental and static aspect of the self, the self-critical consciousness (*Vimarśa*) implies a universal and dynamic aspect of the self. A stir or *spanda* in the consciousness like a ripple in the still water, represents the Śakti aspect of Śiva. The self-luminous consciousness manifests itself first as Śakti where everything is one complete whole without any distinction or manifestation of subject and object. Through its second manifestation the consciousness reveals complete unity of the objective universe with the subject, the self. At this stage, which is known as Vidyā, thisness is identical with the I-ness. At the third stage of Māyā the subject and object, the whole universe, appear as mutually distinct and separate elements. Advaita Vedānta denied the reality of matter in order to preserve the transcendental integrity of Brahman. Change and activity belong to the sphere of nature which may be practically real but is finally unreal. There can be no real relationship between the transcendental being and Nature. The self is one only and it is none other than the Brahman: *Ātmā ca Brahma*. It is beyond all change, transformation, mutability and specifications and hence nothing can distinguish one self from the other. This implies that the one reality can be known only by negation and that any change or modification is apparent and not real. Any identification of the absolute with the universe or of the universe with the absolute is false superimposition. This is brought about by the inexplicable nature of ignorance, Māyā and/or Avidyā at macrocosmic and microcosmic levels, KS and Vedānta agree that the absoluteness is not qualified or predicated by anything standing outside or external to it. The absolute is pure in both the systems. According to the Vedānta it is only in the secondary sense that the Brahman can be defined; otherwise it is beyond all descriptions and characterisations. It cannot be grasped by speech or mind. *Anuttara* of Śaivism is of the same nature. The autonomy of consciousness or independence of eternal reality from the body and mind is accepted both by Vedānta and Śaṅkara. However the Brahman of Vedānta is self-luminous but it is not self-conscious. It is, therefore, spoken of as *Śānta*, i.e. without any activity. The manifestation of the universe is in spite of him. The consciousness or Brahman undergoes no change. The ultimate metaphysical principle of Kashmir Śaivism, Maheśvara, manifests Himself through three important stages of Śakti, Vidyā and Māyā out of His own free will (*svātantrya*). He is a free agent eternally associated with manifold powers to imagine the world in his own image through his critical consciousness or Vimarśa Śakti. Utpala offers two analogies to explain the nature of consciousness according to his system. The reality is like a mirror with one important difference. The ordinary mirror can and does receive reflections of external objects without in any way being affected by the objects which are reflected in it. It does not, however, create them. It lacks free will for creativity. The consciousness first creates or imagines the universe of subjects and objects through its power of imagination. These objects so manifested remain one with the consciousness as the objects reflected in the mirror. The universe is, thus, a reflection in a universal mirror. What is reflected in the mirror of consciousness is its own creation and imagination externally manifested. The consciousness can also be spoken of as universal mind. Just as an individual mind is capable, in its creativity, in imagining or dreaming the subject-object universe and just as this universe is in no way different from the individual mind, and it is in fact identical with it, similarly the whole universe is identical with the nature of consciousness. The distinctions of subject and object, the duality of body and mind, the difference of internal and external proceed from the free activity of self-luminous consciousness. It is not fettered by any external affections. There is in fact nothing extrinsic or external to it. The consciousness can be spoken of as complete I-ness, Pūrṇa-Ahaṁtā, or pure subjectivity free to manifest the universe of limited subjects and objects. But nothing is really different from the universal mind, the consciousness or *citi*. The individual mind has certain limitations, the universal mind has none. It is free and does not depend on any external thing either to bring the whole universe into being or to maintain it separately as it were, or to merge it in its own identity. The universe is like the thought or idea of the universal mind which is neither exhausted nor affected by its manifestation. The self-luminous, self-critical and free consciousness is the source of all thoughts and actions. This view of consciousness establishes an omniscient and omnipotent permanent reality which is both transcendental and immanent and is able to create, sustain and merge the universe and also obscure and reveal itself at will. While Vedānta accepts Brahman to be the cause of creation, sustanance and dissolution, it does not accept its freedom of obscuring and revealing Itself which is the real form of play as well.

The Kashmir Śaivism and the Vedānta were aware of the Buddhist view of the soul. According to this view the conception of an abiding entity called soul, self or God is an illegitimate abstraction. It does not believe in the existence of soul which is nothing but a stream of ideas. The self is nothing but a flux of cognitions which belongs to no permanent subject. Such a subject is not a fact of experience. The Śaiva and Vedānta consider this view untenable. They assert that synthesis of various cognitions and experiences cannot be adequately explained without assuming a priori entity of permanent self. But this consciousness according to KS is not a passive witness. The consciousness is dynamic. This dynamism is spoken of as Spanda, 'vibration'; Svātantrya, 'freedom'; and Aiśvarya 'lordship'. The reality which is devoid of this freedom of action and knowledge would be inactive like the Brahman of Vedānta. The omniscience and omnipotence of Brahman are really due to the contingency of nescience (Śaṅkarabhāṣya). Brahman is not a creator God (*Īśvara*), for creation is unreal according to the Vedānta. In KS, Śiva is real ground of all things, their very essence and substance. Brahman of the Vedānta is the basis (*adhiṣṭhāna*) of an unreal world. According to KS the consciousness and its contents are identical and equally real. This is absolute idealism because, according to this, nothing exists independently of Śiva.

The external objective world is the manifestation of what is really internal and remains reflected within the integral unity of consciousness. Śiva is both a witnessing self and a perceived object. The KS understands the world as a symbol of the absolute which is always in the state of becoming, appearing in diverse forms through its power of freedom. Creation is conceived here in aesthetic and Yogic terms and as a spontaneous play of the Lord. It is both real and delightful. Rippling of the ocean, externalisation by a yogin of essentially internal thought, the art-object of an artist and images reflected in the mirror, are generally cited as examples to illustrate the externalisation of inward reality eternally manifesting itself in diverse forms and still maintaining its integral unity. In this view the world is nothing but externalisation of the consciousness and is not in any way different from it, and it is so because it is real creation of consciousness. The world is not a snake in the rope or the second moon or the silver in the conch-shell. It is free expression of the power of the Lord Śiva. In brief, Vedānta and KS are opposed to the realism positing independence of the subject and object but both present different models of the nature of consciousness. According to the Vedāntin, change, predication, or mutability will defile the purity of consciousness, but according to the KS consciousness is all, full and comprehensive, hence duality and diversity also do not exist beyond it. Consciousness is not contentless. In fact, the consciousness and its contents are identical both in manifest and unmanifested forms. The consciousness is dynamic and not quiet. It is self-resplendent like a gem and, unlike it, it is also self-reflective which is the very characteristic of the consciousness. Vedānta in essence is the criticism of the Sāṁkhya by way of denying ontological status to the Prakṛti and rendering it as an inexplicable illusory experience, *avidyā*. The KS is the critique of the Vedānta by way of establishing the integral unity and dynamism of the consciousness.

Both succeeded in successfully challenging the Buddhist view that changing consciousness of changing objects will never posit any coherence and unity and will be devoid of an abiding and permanent Self. Vedānta and KS thus represent sister thoughts and two facets of idealism to meet the Buddhist challenge in India of 8th to 10th centuries A.D.

References

1. The term Kashmir Śaivism refers to the monastic Śaivism developed in Kashmir on the basis of the Āgamas, mainly by Somānanda, the author of *Śiva-dṛṣṭi*; his disciple, Utpala, who wrote a number of works including his most celebrated Īśvarapratyabhijñākārikā; and the most brilliant and encyclopaedic writer Abhinavagupta whose works include two commentaries on the former work, a brief comment on the Bhagavadgītā, Bhagavadgītārthasaṁgraha and the Tantrāloka. The Śivasūtras revealed to Vasugupta and the Spandakārikā of Kallaṭa, younger contemporary of Somānanda, also helped the development of monism in Kashmir.

2. For references to Veda (Śruti), Brāhmaṇa, Upaniṣads, Gītā and the various philosophical schools and opinions see Śivadṛṣṭi, VI Ahnika, Appendices to the Doctrine of Divine Recognitions Vol. 1-2, R. C. Dwivedi General Editor MLBD Delhi, 1986; Appendix B of Abhinavagupta: An Historical and Philosophical Study, K. C. Pandeya, Chowkhamba Sanskrit series office, Varanasi, 1963.

3. According to the Harivaṁśa Kṛṣṇa was taught sixty-four Āgamas by Durvāsas in Kali age and according to the Mokṣaparvan of Mahābhārata Kṛṣṇa was taught dualistic, non-dualistic and dualistic-cum-nondualistic Āgamas, Commentaries on the Bhagavadgītā by a number of Śaiva ācāryas and the legend of initiation of Kṛṣṇa into Śaiva Āgamas attests to the popularity of the Gītā and its closeness to Śaiva tradition, which was primarily based

on the Āgamas and manifested its occasional hostility to and reconciliation with the Vedic tradition.

4. See IPVV Vol. I, pp. 28, 29, 65, 92, 297, Vol. II, pp. 48, 73, 74, 206, 210, 298, 354, Vol. III, pp. 142, 279, 298, 328, 393.

5. For example: *Tameva bhāntamanubhāti Sarvaṁ* (Kaṭha Upaniṣad, 5-15) quoted in Īśvara-pratyabhijñāvivṛtivimarśinī (IPVV in short) KSTS Vol. II, p. 339; Sadeva somya idamagra āsīt (Chāndogya upaniṣad VI.2.1) Ibid., p. 203; Vijñātāramare kena vijānīyad (Bṛhadāraṇyaka, II.5.19) Ibid in Vol. I, **p. 72.**

(i) **अन्तर्गतविश्ववीर्यसमुच्छलत्सत्तात्मकविसतवश्त्वाषानन्दशक्त्यैकघनं ब्रह्म बृहद व्यापकं बृहितं च न तु वेदान्तपाठकांगीकृतेकेवलशून्यवादाविदूरवर्ति ब्रह्मदर्शन-मिदम्**

—**परात्रीशिकाविवृति, पृ०** 229

(ii) **चिद्रूपस्यैकत्वं यदि वास्तवं भेदः पुनरयमविद्योपप्लवादित्युच्यते तदा कस्याय मविद्योपप्लव इति न संगच्छते। ब्रह्मणो हि विद्यैकरूपस्य कथमविद्यारूपता। न चान्यः कश्चिदीस्ति वस्तुतो जीवादिर्यास्य अविद्या भवेत्।**

—**ईश्वरप्रत्यभिज्ञाविमर्शिनी** 2-4-20

(iii) **अतएव भेदाभेदयोर्विरोधं दुःसमर्थमभिमन्यमानै रेकैरविद्यात्वेनानिवच्यित्वं मपरैश्चाभाभसलग्नतया सांवृतत्वदमभिदधद्भिरात्मा परश्च वञ्चितः।**

—**वही** 2-3-14

(iv) **ननु वेदान्तिभिरुभयात्मकत्वेऽपि अनुर्यात्तकतारूपमनिर्वायच्त्वमत्र स्फुटं विरोधात्।**

—**वही** 2-4-3

(v) **बाधके च प्रमाणे सति नेदं रजतं नेदं रजतं शुक्तिका इति निषेधनिष्ठतया प्रतीतौ मिथ्यात्वं स्यात्। तेन बाधकेन प्रमाणेन मिथ्यात्वं कार्यम्। तत्कस्य क्रियते, तत्र किं यस्मिन्काले तद्रजतता भवेत। स काल एव न भवतीति मिथ्या-त्वमभ्यु पगमः। तन्न, नैव हि अकाले कालाभावे कस्यचियज्जननं नाम किंचित्काल-रहितायाः क्रियाया अयोगादित्यर्थ :। जनिक्रिया वा बाध्यते? तन्न, रजतादिकार्यं कृत्वा क्रिया समाप्ता। तस्या असत्या को बाधार्थः स्वमेव तस्या अभावात्। इदानीं च बाधविषयत्वाभावात् को बाधः।** **शिवदृष्टिवृत्ति,** 4.15-16

16 SIDDHI-S IN THE BHĀGAVATA PURĀṆA AND IN THE YOGASŪTRA-S OF PATAÑJALI—A COMPARISON

DR. T.S. RUKMANI

The *Bhāgavata Purāṇa,* along with the other *Purāṇas,* are all considered to be the works of the great Vyāsa. Traditionally he is also the author of the commentary on the *Yogasūtra*-s of Patañjali. It will thus be interesting to study the *siddhi*-s as described in these two works.

The *Bhāgavata Purāṇa* is acknowledged as a book of synthesis and a narrow, sectarian spirit is absent here. In a book which has *bhakti-yoga* as its supreme message, *mokṣa* can only be *sālokya, sārṣṭi, sāmīpya, sārūpya* and *sāyujya,* as described in many places in the *Bhāgavata Purāṇa.*[1] The synthetic character of the *Bhāgavata Purāṇa,* on the other hand, comes out clearly in many passages which are close to *Sāṅkhya, Yoga* and *Vedānta* including *Advaita Vedānta.*[2]

That *Yoga* has been given an important place in the *Bhāgavata Purāṇa* is brought out clearly when Śuka, at the beginning of the second skandha, in answer to Parīkṣit's question as to what a man who is about to die is to do, states that he should give up all his possessions and make for himself an *āsana* in a solitary place. Then he should meditate on the three-lettered *Oṃ* with perseverance disregarding the distractions caused by the qualities of *rajas* and *tamas.*[3]

Various meditations on both gross and subtle aspects of *Bhagavān* are described in the second skandha of the *Purāṇa*[4] which remind one of the different *sthitibandhinī*-s in the *Yogasūtras* of Patañjali.[5] In the description of death of a *yogī* in the *Purāṇa* the various *cakras* and the *Brahmarandhra* are mentioned. In place of the attainment of *kaivalya, mokṣa* is the state of Viṣṇu in the *Purāṇa.*[6]

The *Bhāgavata Purāṇa* is also an important text of the *Bhāgavata* school or the *Pāñcarātra* cult and *ekatva* or *sāyujya* is an important conception of *mokṣa* in this literature. *Ekatva* means 'the cessation of all worldly existence and a sense of identification with the Supreme Being'. It is also described as 'the return of *Brahman* into His own true nature'.[7] There are many verses in the *Purāṇa* which proclaim the return of the individual soul to the Absolute and its merging into the Absolute.[8] The advaitic trend of these passages is unmistakable. But the *Purāṇa* takes care to mention, even in such passages, that the object of concentration is always *Bhagavān* thus preserving its overall character as a book of *bhakti*.

The *Bhāgavata* emphasizes *yoga* as *bhakti* and it is in the method of realisation of its spiritual goal that *Yoga* becomes important. Just as *Nyāya* with its stress on correct reasoning became indispensable for epistemological enquiries in every school of philosophical thought, so also *Yoga* with its tools of *yama, niyama, āsana, prāṇāyāma, pratyāhāra, dhāraṇā, dhyāna* and *samādhi* was generally accepted as the means to reach the ultimate ontological truth in each system, which may vary according to its own beliefs. As a result *yoga* became an indispensable part of the spiritual quest in many of the systems both orthodox and heterodox. It is therefore not surprising to find such a large number of yogic passages in the *Bhāgavata Purāṇa.*

The *siddhi*-s are an integral part of the *Yoga* philosophy, and it is interesting to note that the *Bhāgavata Purāṇa* describes them in many places. But in this paper the *siddhi*-s as described in the tenth chapter of the eleventh skandha have been taken up for comparison with the *siddhi*-s mentioned in the *Vibhūtipāda* of the *Yogasūtra*-s.

The very first verse in this chapter of the *Purāṇa* states that to the *yogī* who has controlled his senses and *prāṇa*-s and concentrates his mind on *Bhagavān* various *siddhi*-s come.[9] In the *Yogasūtras* we are told by Patañjali that the *siddhi*-s are obstacles in the realisation of the ultimate goal, but are powers in the state of activity in the world.[10]

Thus, on the face of it, while it appears that the *siddhi*-s will come to any one practising *samādhi*, not all are agreed on that. For instance, Vijñānabhikṣu very clearly mentions that 'those respective *saṃyama*-s are to be practised only by *yogī*-s who desire these respective powers'.[11] And those desiring liberation should practise *saṃyama* only on knowledge in the form of distinction between the *sattva*-intellect and *puruṣa*.[12] The same idea is reiterated by Vijñānabhikṣu again when he repeats that only the *siddhi* of insight into the distinction between *sattva* and *puruṣa* will ensure liberation.[13]

Thus, from the above, it appears that one is free to choose the *siddhi* and strive for it through the appropriate *saṃyama*. Calling the *siddhi*-s obstacles by Patañjali also then makes sense. For if *siddhi*-s come any way, irrespective of desiring them or not, there seems to be an inevitability to the whole process over which one has no control. But the *Yogasūtra-s* lay a lot of emphasis on self-effort and on the choice of the object for *samādhi* (*saṃyama*). The connection between the object of *saṃyama* and the *siddhi* attained seems to be inherent and if the choice of *siddhi* were not there then it would have been sufficient to indicate any one *samādhi* which, when done to pefection, will not only give rise to *kaivalya* in due course but will also give rise to the various *siddhi*-s, on the way. It is perhaps this logic that has made later commentators remark, as already mentioned, that the kind of *saṃyama* determines the kind of *siddhi* that will come about.

In the context of the *siddhi*-s the *Yogasūtra*-s insist on the practice of *saṃyama*, while the *Bhāgavata Purāṇa* is content to limit itself to *dhāraṇā* or *dhyāna*. *Saṃyama* is a technical word referring to *dhāraṇā*, *dhyāna* and *samādhi* practised with reference to the same object.[14] Instead of repeating the three—*dhāraṇā*, *dhyāna* and *samādhi* every time, the purpose is achieved by using the word *saṃyama*. Later commentators see *saṃyama* as a device or formula for the sake of brevity.[15]

The next question then is whether there is any difference between what is said by the *Purāṇa* and by the *Yogasūtra-s* in this regard. The *Purāṇa* uses the words *dhāraṇā*, *yogadhāraṇā*, *dhāraṇāvidaḥ*, *dhāraṇāyogapāragaḥ*, *yoga* and various forms of the root √*dhyai* in place of *samādhi* or *saṃyama*.[16] Even though the word *samādhi* is not specifically used, the sense conveyed by all these words is *samādhi*. It is only in *samādhi* that the mind becomes one with the object of meditation. It has to be preceded by *dhāraṇā* and *dhyāna* for the mind by its very nature cannot attain *samādhi*, at least initially, without going through *dhāraṇā* and *dhyāna*. Thus Patañjali defines *dhāraṇā* as fixing the mind on one object[17] and *dhyāna* as the continuous flow of thoughts pertaining to the same object.[18] And when the same *dhyāna* shines as the object alone (in the mind), appearing to have lost its reflective nature, it is *samādhi*.[19] Thus it can be seen that both *samādhi* and *saṃyama*, in the context of *siddhi*-s can only mean the same thing. Therefore both the *Bhāgavata Purāṇa* and the *Yogasūtra-s* mean the same thing while using the words *dhāraṇā* (*dhyāna*) and *saṃyama* respectively.

The *Bhāgavata Purāṇa* first mentions the eighteen *siddhi*-s collectively as a result of *yogadhāraṇā*,[20] and then goes on to describe their connection individually with the kind of concentration practised. All the *siddhi*-s here are the results of *samādhi* on different aspects of *Bhagavān* Himself. Depending on the specific aspect of *Bhagavān* taken up for *samādhi*, a particular *siddhi* comes into being which is in congruence with that *samādhi*. Thus the *siddhi* of omniscience comes to the *yogī* whose mind is purified by *bhakti* towards *Bhagavān* and who knows how to concentrate on God.[21] Such a one is also unaffected by birth and death says the *Purāṇa*.

Again, in the *Purāṇa* the eight common *siddhi*-s—*aṇimā*, *mahimā*, *laghimā*, *prāptiḥ*, *prākāmyam*, *īśitvam*, *vaśitā* and *kāmāvasāyitā* are all obtained by *dhāraṇā* on *Bhagavān* in his various representations, as having those properties. Thus in the case of *mahimā* and *vaśitā* the *Purāṇa* says—'Fixing one's mind, having a similar attribute, on Me as possessing the adjunct of the cosmic intelligent mind, one attains the power of immensity. Concentrating on Me as possessed of the adjunct of ether and the other elements one attains the respective immensities of those elements.'[22] 'Fixing the mind on Nārāyaṇa, the Transcendent One, called also *Bhagavān*, the *yogī* like Me, attains the power of self-control.'[23]

Thus in the *Bhāgavata Purāṇa* all *siddhi*-s are already there in *Bhagavān* in an infinite form and are conferred on *yogī*-s, in varying degrees, depending on their devotion.

In the *Yogasūtra*-s there is an intimate connection between *saṃyama* on an object and the *siddhi* which comes into being as already mentioned. Thus *siddhi*-s like *aṇimā*, *mahimā* etc., come to one practising *saṃyama* on the different aspects like grossness, subtlety, essential nature and so on of the elements.[24] The *siddhi* of knowledge of the sounds of all living beings comes to one practising *saṃyama* separately on a word, its intended object and the idea conveyed.[25] This is echoed in the *Bhāgavata Purāṇa* when it says that 'by meditating on *Bhagavān* with ether as an adjunct and listening to the subtle sound through one's mind he hears the varied speeches of living beings manifested in that ether.'[26]

Entering another's mind, another's body,[27] giving up one's body at will,[28] assuming any form that one desires,[29] going anywhere one wants to go,[30] are all mentioned in the *Bhāgavata* and they can all be achieved by meditation on *Bhagavān* Himself. Thus it says 'Using the mind as material, whatever forms the *yogī* wishes to assume, he assumes those desired forms, by resorting to the power of concentration on Me'.[31] As a *Purāṇa* advocating *bhakti* as a supreme means to liberation and with *Bhagavān* being the repository of all the powers, meditating on *Bhagavān* is enough to achieve all the *siddhi*-s as well as *mokṣa* in the *Purāṇa*.

But when we look at these very *siddhi*-s in the *Yogasūtra*-s we find that there is a conscious effort to match the particular *siddhi* with the object of *saṃyama*. Knowledge of other people's minds for instance comes by *saṃyama* on ideas.[32] The *Yogasūtra* seems to say that by *saṃyama* on the phenomenon of ideas, as represented by a single idea, there can be a transcendence into the realm of ideas per se—almost like the archetypal Idea in Plato and then it is easy to know all ideas including ideas in other people's minds.

As for entering another's body the *Yogasūtra* mentions it as due to the loosening of the *karmabandha* through the power of *samādhi*. 'He then removes the *citta* from his own body and places it in another's body.'[33] Vyāsa goes on to say that the sense organs follow the mind which is thus placed in another body. The simile he uses is of the bees following the king bee: 'Similar to the bees following the king bee the sense organs follow the mind when it enters the body of another person'. The *Bhāgavata Purāṇa* also uses the same simile but worded differently. It says that leaving the gross body and taking on the subtle body, 'he should pass through the external air like a bee (to another body)'.[34]

There seems to be a logical connection between *saṃyama* on a particular object and the resulting *siddhi* in the *Yogasūtra-s*. Thus, in connection with the *siddhi* of hearing divine sounds it is said that practising *saṃyama* on the relationship between *ākāśa* and the organ of hearing results in this *siddhi*.[35] *Ākāśa* in

Indian philosophy has always been connected with the property of sound (*śabda*). Thus *saṃyama* on the connection between the two is spoken of as resulting in divine hearing.

Again in the *siddhi* of 'movement in space' Patañjali mentions that by practising *saṃyama* on the relationship between the body and *ākāśa* or by *samāpatti* on lightness such as that of cotton fibre, there follows movement in space.[36] Vyāsa by way of explaining the relationship between the *saṃyama* and this *siddhi* says 'wherever there is the body there is *ākāśa* since it makes room for it; therefore the body has an invariable relationship to it (*ākāśa*). The *yogī* who practises *saṃyama* on that relationship conquers that relationship and becomes light.'[37] As a result of this *siddhi* he can move anywhere he wants including space. The second alternative, i.e. *saṃyama* on objects like cotton fibre to attain this *siddhi*, is not difficult to follow. If oneness with light objects like cotton is achieved then the body can move over water, over spiders' webs and through air. Again while talking about the *siddhi* of being invisible to ordinary human beings Patañjali says, 'By practising *saṃyama* on the outer form of the body when its power to be seen is stopped, there being no contact with the light of the eye, there is disappearance of the yogī's body'.[38] It is the eye which sees outside objects; therefore when this power to be known is stopped by *saṃyama* on the outer form of the body, there being no contact with the eye, the person becomes invisible. In keeping with this logical connection with a particular *saṃyama* and its own *siddhi* the knowledge of death comes about by *saṃyama* on *karma*. 'Karma is either fast in fruition or slow in fruition; by practising *saṃyama* on them or on portents of death, there is knowledge of death.'[39] Believing in the concept of *jīvanmukti* which is tied up with *prārabdha karma*, *yoga* cannot logically advocate giving up the body at will. All the yogic methods can only achieve *jīvanmukti*. The *Bhāgavata Purāṇa*, on the other hand, mentions the giving up of one's body or death along with the other *siddhi*-s.[40]

The movement through space or being invisible to others is not mentioned as *siddhi*-s in the *Bhāgavata* section. It is also silent about the *siddhi* of knowledge of earlier births. But in Patañjali knowledge of earlier births comes through *saṃyama* on the *saṃskāra-s*.[41] Since birth, span of life and kind of experience are all connected with *karma* and *saṃskāra-s*, the relationship between *saṃskāra*-s and birth is logical.

Thus one can say that the close connection seen between a *saṃyama* and its *siddhi* in the *Yogasūtra*-s is its unique feature. It is also not arbitrary and links up with the metaphysical doctrines of the system. The *Bhāgavata Purāṇa*, on the other hand, dispenses with this logical connection and confers the various *siddhi*-s as rewards for devotion to *Bhagavān*.

There is also no gradation of the *siddhi*-s in the *Bhāgavata Purāṇa*. In the chapter under consideration *Bhagavān* states, at the beginning, that the *siddhi*-s are eighteen in number, eight pertaining to Himself and the remaining due to perfection in *sattva*. In passing, one also notices that the *siddhi*-s mentioned in this section are very few compared to as many as thirty described in the *Yogasūtra*-s. The *siddhi*-s in the *Yogasūtra*-s also cover a wide range of powers right from physical prowess[42] to the highest spiritual attainment.

After mentioning the eighteen *siddhi*-s generally, the *Bhāgavata Purāṇa* describes them one by one in the later verses. But even here there is no distinction drawn as to which is the higher and which is the lower *siddhi*. All the *siddhi*-s are acquired by meditating on the corresponding aspect of *Bhagavān*. It is therefore not possible to count some *siddhi*-s as higher than some other ones unless one says that certain aspects of *Bhagavān* are inferior to certain other aspects of Him. As that is not possible one has to draw the conclusion that there is no higher or lower *siddhi* in the *Bhāgavata Purāṇa*. Thus the *Purāṇa* makes a categorical statement that *Bhagavān* is the lord of all *siddhi*-s. 'He is their cause and is their maintainer.'[43]

In the *Yogasūtra*-s there is a clear cut division between the minor and the major *siddhi*-s. The most important *siddhi* is the insight into the difference between the *sattva*-intellect and *puruṣa*.[44] While all the other *siddhi*-s come about by the practice of *saṃyama* with reference to the sense-organs and objects of knowledge, this comes about by the practice of *saṃyama* with reference to the knower.[45] It can also come into being by *saṃyama* over the moments and their succession.[46] This is a state where one is omnipotent and omniscient. All the others are individual powers and are inferior in comparison to this last one. This is also the last stage of *saṃprajñāta samādhi* and the *Viṣṇu Purāṇa* describes all other knowledge (*siddhi*-s) as equal to light and this knowledge (*siddhi*) born of insight as equal to the light of the sun.[47]

In a work which deals with *Yoga* in detail this is as it should be. The *Bhāgavata Purāṇa* acknowledges these beliefs in society by finding a place for them. As a book of *bhakti*, with the belief in the supremacy of *Bhagavān*, *siddhi*-s in the *Purāṇa* can fit in only as blessings to the ardent devotee.

References

1. T. S. Rukmani. *A Critical Study of the Bhāgavata Purāṇa*. pp. 32, 132.
2. (a) *Bhāgavata Purāṇa* second skandha.
   (b) Bharatan Kumarappa. *The Hindu Conception of the Deity*. pp. 117-18, 120.
   (c) T. S. Rukmani, ibid pp. 25-26, 30, 133, 206.
3. Bhā. P. II.I.
4. ibid. II.1.22-23.
5. Patañjali-*Yogasūtra*-s I.34-39.
6. Bhā. P. II.2.21.
7. Bharatan Kumarappa. ibid. p. 117.
8. Bhā. P. III.27.6-11.
9. ibid. XI.10.1.
10. Patañjali. *YS*. III.35.
11. T. S. Rukmani. *Yogavārttika of Vijñānabhikṣu*. Vol. III p. 73.
12. ibid. p. 73.
13. ibid. pp. 184-85.
14. Patañjali. *YS*. III.4.
15. T. S. Rukmani. *Yogavārttika of Vijñānabhikṣu*. Vol. III p. 7.
16. Bhā. P. XI.10.2-36.
17. YS. III.1.
18. ibid. III.2.
19. ibid. III.3.
20. Bhā. P. XI.10.3.
21. ibid. XI.10.28.
22. ibid. XI.10.11.
23. ibid. XI.10.16.
24. Patañjali. *YS*. III.44-45.
25. ibid. III.17.
26. Bhā. P. XI.10.19.
27. ibid. XI.10.26.
28. ibid. XI.10.24.
29. ibid. XI.10.22.
30. ibid. XI.10.21.
31. ibid. XI.10.22.
32. Patañjali *YS*. III.19.

33. ibid. III.38.
34. Bhā. P. XI.10.23.
35. *YS*. III.41.
36. ibid. III.42.
37. Vyāsabhāṣya on III.42.
38. *YS*. III.21.
39. ibid. III.22.
40. Bhā. P. XI.10.24.
41. *YS*. III.18.
42. ibid. III.23-30.
43. Bhā. P. XI.10.35.
44. *YS*. III.49.
45. T. S. Rukmani. *Yogavārttika of Vijñānabhikṣu*. Vol. III p. 184.
46. *YS*. III.52.
47. *Viṣṇu Purāṇa* 6.5.62

17 LANGUAGE AND METAPHOR IN INDIAN STOTRA LITERATURE

With Special Reference to the Saundaryalaharī *and* Mahimnastava

R.K. SHARMA

INTRODUCTION

The oral tradition of devotional literature is very much alive in India even today. The devotional Sanskrit songs addressed to the Mother Goddess or other divine manifestations such as Śiva, Viṣṇu, Gaṇeśa, Kārtikeya, Sūrya, Hanūmān, Gaṅgā etc. are very popular and are recited or sung in temples and homes all over the country. The language and metaphor used in these stotras share quite a few common characteristics, depending, of course, on the God or Goddess addressed.[1]

The *Saundaryalaharī*[2] (generally ascribed to Śaṅkarācārya 800 A.D.) consisting of a hundred (or 103) Śikhariṇī stanzas represents an elegant poetic description of the Beauty of the Cosmic Mother. Apart from its devotional and tantric significance, the work excels in linguistic and imaginative exquisiteness.

Similarly the *Mahimnastava*[3] (or more popularly known as the *Mahimnastotra*) consisting of thirtyone Śikhariṇī stanzas represents the description of greatness of Lord Śiva. While SL is characterized by verbal, semantic and imaginative elegance conducive to the depiction of divine Beauty, M.S. is characterized by verbal and semantic depth conducive to the depiction of divine Greatness (mahiman).

The paper deals with the two stotra texts in particular presenting a sample survey of the passages marked by verbal or semantic and imaginative aesthetic elegance.

Gonda's views

As Gonda points out 'Hymns of praise and collection of more or less separate eulogistic stanzas have been composed in all the literary languages of India, whether modern or classical . . . The good and original specimens of this genre are products of earnest faith, pious enthusiasm, and real poetic vision and inspiration and as such indicative of the psychological mood with which Hindu worship is performed; expressive of misery of karman, and rebirth, as well as the hope for emancipation characterized by a felicitous harmony of rhythm, symmetry in form and harmony in expressions, by images and figurative expressions, pointing to a sphere or reality other than mundane existence, by the almost obligatory occurrence of symbols, metaphors, and references to myths which as a rule are liable to different and fresh interpretations. Although the devotional character is not always prominent and although their wordings often tend to be stereotyped, a modern reader, may, through the Sanskrit garb, often perceive true poetic thought and genuine religious feelings.'[4]

SAUNDARYALAHARĪ

Let us first have a look at 'the poetic thought' in *Saundarya-laharī* (SL).

Glance

The all-auspicious and all-embracive Divine Glance is depicted as an embodiment of all aesthetic sentiments (rasas), as follows:

'May your Glance be compassionate to me, O Mother,—the Glance that is sublime with erotic sentiment (Śṛṅgāra) in relation to Lord Śiva, full of disgust (bībhatsa) towards persons other than (opposed to) Lord Śiva, full of anger (raudra) for the Gaṅgā, amazed (adbhuta) at the heroic exploits of Lord Śiva, terrified (bhayānaka) at the sight of serpents (in the body) of Lord Śiva, excelling (vīra) the beauty of lotus and with smiles towards (hāsya) your girl companions.'[5]

This invocation itself provides a specimen of poetic excellence in stotra literature. All the eight major aesthetic sentiments (rasas) are metaphorically brought in to represent the various facets—the mutually contradictory ones—of Divine Glance. The quintessence of Indian aesthetics (rasa) is also introduced here in the garb of certain myths related to the Mother Goddess and to Lord Śiva.

Humbleness

Let us look at humbleness par excellence in the following metaphoric expressions in SL's concluding stanza:

'This invocation, O Mother, consisting of vocal expressions, constitutes nothing but your own vocables (this is just presentation of your own words to yourself; nothing is mine). This is like presentation of lamplight to the Sun, presentation of water oozing out of the moonstone to the Moon—the source of nectar, presentation of its own waters to the ocean.'[6]

Draviḍaśiśu

Thus it is difficult to determine whether SL represents excellence of aesthetic experience or of devotional sentiments or of Tantric mysticism or of all of them taken together. It is not yet clear either, who is that blessed 'Draviḍaśiśu' (referred to in verse 75) who had tasted 'an ocean of the milk of poesy flowing from the breasts of Mother Goddess and had become the poet laureate of the master poets (kavīnāṃ prauḍhānām ajani kamanīyaḥ kavayitā). But whosoever he may be (Śaṅkarācārya himself or Śrī Jñānasambandha—the illustrious Śaiva saint) the author of these poems excels in aesthetic expressions mingled with myths and metaphors with sublime sound-effects in the setting of words all throughout.

Poetic Siddhi

How expressive are the following three stanzas dealing exclusively with the siddhi of poetic intuition!

(i) Bright as the autumn moonlight, wearing a crest of plaited and coiled hair with moon on it,
with your (four) hands respectively bestowing gifts and granting freedom from fear, holding a crystal rosary and a book,
if to you, as such, the good should salute only once, how would they fail to have utterances laden with the sweetness of honey, milk and grapes?[7]

(ii) You Aruṇā (the glowing red), with the loveliness of the morning sun to [open] the lotus clusters of the minds of poets,
those few illustrious ones who worship you as such, with

utterances profound, and surgings of the ever youthful passion Viriñciś beloved (Goddess Sarasvatī), impart delight to the nobles.[8]

(iii) The inspirers of utterances, who are bright as a slate of moonstone,
Vaśinī and the others—whoever contemplates you with them, O Mother,
becomes a fashioner of exquisite poems, with aptly phrased—
expressions, sweet with fragrance from the lotus mouth of the Queen of Speech (Goddess Sarasvatī).[9]

The above verse themselves provide admirable specimens of poetry rich in alliterative, metaphoric and suggestive expressions, laden with poetic rhythm all around.

Aruṇā Karuṇā

Mother Goddess is eulogised, as 'Compassion deeply red (Aruṇā Karuṇā) of Lord Śiva', 'who is curly of hair, naturally straightforward in her gentle smile (arālā keśeṣu prakṛtisarlā mandahasite); [delicate] like the Śirīṣa in her mind, firm as a rock in the curves of her breasts (Śirīṣābhā citte dṛṣad iva kaṭhorā kucataṭe); inexpressibly slender in her waist, wide in the regions of her breasts and hips (bhṛśaṃ tanvī madhye pṛthur urasijā-rohaviṣaye). Her blessings are sought: "let her, the companion of Śambhu, the ineffable [Śakti] Aruṇā be victorious to save the world (jag t trātuṃ Śambhor jayati karuṇā kācid aruṇā). Vide SL 92.

The various parts of the body of Cosmic Mother are beautifully depicted in SL. Some specimens laden with metaphoric, aesthetic and mythical elegance are reproduced below:

1. *Forehead*

"Your Forehead which shines beautiful and pure in its brilliance,

I consider it to be a second half moon to the half moon in your crest;

if the two were transposed, put together and joined,

then cemented with nectar, as though with an unguent, they would become a [Soma-filled] full moon.'[10]

The minute poetic observation is, indeed, remarkable in this imaginative description of the crowned divine Forehead!

2. *Abdominal Hair*

"With his body burnt up by multitudes of flames from Hara's wrath,
the mind-born one (Kāma) entered the deep pool of your navel,
thence, O daughter of the mountain, there arose smoke like a creeper,[11]
this, O Mother, folk, know, as the line of your abdominal hair."

How subtle and mythically charged is this description of abdominal Hair! The elegance of Apahnuti (metaphor by suppression) is especially remarkable here.

3. *Feet*

'In the snow it perishes, [but] they are capable of treading upon the slopes of snowy peaks;
at night it folds in sleep [but] they are bright by night as well as by day;
it is only a vessel to receive Lakṣmī (Śrī, prosperity or beauty), [but] they shower prosperity (or beauty) in profusion upon your suppliant—
what wonder is there here, Mother, that your two feet surpass the lotus?'[12]

The metaphor used here is termed vyatireka (metaphor by reversion).

Glance revisited

Besides being an embodiment of all the eight aesthetic sentiments, the Glance Divine is also (depicted as) an embodiment of eight Indian cities through the play of double-meaning expressions (puns) in verse 49 as follows:

'Far extending (Viśālā), auspicious (Kalyāṇī), its sudden beauty uncontested (Ayodhyā) by blue lotuses;
a shower (Dhārā) of streams of compassion, honeyed (Madhurā) as it were, fortunate (Bhogavatikā), helpful (Avantī), Victorious (Vijayā), ever an array of many cities in your glance;
for ever does it prevail, conforming to the characteristic of each (separate) city name.'

Through the following reasoning by metaphor (kāvyaliṅga), SL seeks the compassionate look of the Goddess:

'With your long-extended eye, which is like a slightly opened blue lotus,

O wife of Śiva, in compassion, bathe, even me, distant and wretched,

by that (bathing), this person (I) becomes rich (blessed) and through such a [small] thing, there is no loss to you;

the cooling moon sheds its beams alike on grove and palace.'[13]

SL, a work of Beauty

Thus SL (The flood of Beauty) is immensely rich in metaphoric expressions, puns, aesthetic manipulations of myths, alliterative and expressive refinements conducive to the depiction of Beauty of the Mother Goddess. Even the line of vermillion placed on the dividing line of Mother's hairlock is considered as the 'imprisoned rising sun' in the custody of black hair symbolising the revengeful darkness (counter-attacking the Sun—the dispeller of darkness).[14] SL expresses wishes for all sense organs becoming the bees (ṣaṭcaraṇatām) on the divine feet-lotuses showering the pollens of Beauty.[15]

These semantically and verbally beautified genuinely aesthetic sublime poems are mostly free from stereotypes. Ever fresh imagery, elegant verbal and semantic symmetry, spontaneity in expressions and originality in linguistic and metaphoric aesthetics constitute what we call *Saundaryalaharī*.

MAHIMNASTAVA

The *Mahimnastava* (the praise of Lord Śiva) (MS) is equally rich in Metaphor and other elements of poetry. Its poetic elegance lies in verbal and imaginative depth. Even its myth-based metaphors are marked with depth and subtleties.

Gaṅgā on Śiva's head

Metaphoric description of Cosmic Greatness as against the Cosmic Beauty in SL is evident in MS's picturesque presentation of Gaṅgā on Śiva's head as follows:

'[The heavenly Ganges] filling the sky, splendid in the scattering of its foam, which is counted to be the host of stars

the flood of waters, which seems like a mere drop on your head,

makes the world seem only an island girdled by the ocean,
by that alone your divine body with its enduring greatness can be imagined.'[16]

How effective is the following Ocean-river imagery, in depicting the concept of 'unity in diversity':

'Since the way of religion is diverse including the triad of the Vedas, the Sāṃkhya, the yoga the doctrine of Paśupati, Vaiṣṇavism, one person considers this one best, and another that one suitable, due to the variety of preferences you are, for men who favour different paths—straight or winding the single goad, as the Ocean is of Waters.'[17]

Lotus imagery

The following are the two metaphoric representations of the heads and the eyes depicted as substitutes, for a real lotus in the context of Lord Śiva's worship respectively:

(i) 'The ten-headed Rāvaṇa reduced the three worlds, without effort, to a state where they no longer opposed him,
and still had his (twenty arms) dominated by the itch for war;
this because he had made an offering to your lotus feet consisting of (nine of) his heads like a row of lotus,
which was a consequence of unwavering devotion to you, O destroyer of the three cities.'[18]

(ii) 'When Hari who (daily) used to offer a thousand lotuses at your feet,
was (once) short by one, he extracted one of his lotus-like eyes;
that bit of excess devotion (his eye) underwent evolution, and in the form of his discus,
ever stays alert, O destroyer of the three cities, to protect the three worlds.'[19]

[A similar Lotus-eye-interchange motif manifests itself in Śrīkālahasti Suprabhātam (morning prayers in the Kālahastīśvara temple near the Śrivenkateśvara temple) in the context of a Śaiva Saint Kaṇṇappa (Kaṇṇappabhaktaśarabhah) of Śarabha clan who offers one of his eyes to Lord Śiva, in lieu of a lotus flower.]

Tārāmrga (star-antelope) imagery

The epic imagery 'Rudra chasing a star-antelope in the form

of a hunter' (*rudras tārāmṛgam yathā MBH*. 3.262.19; cf. ABHŚ. 1.6) finds, a place in the following verse in the form of an eternal ethical rod represented by the bow of Lord Śiva as a hunter:

'O Lord, the lord of creatures (Brahmā) who in a stag's form had been violently and lustfully pursuing his own daughter transferred into a doe, while he was obsessed with desire to enjoy her,

and who had fled from you with bow in your hand until he reached the sky—him yonder, pierced by your arrow up to the feathering, fearstricken as he is, your ardour for the chase does not release [him] even to this day.'[20]

This is, in fact, an allegorical representation of the constellation Ārdrā chasing the constellation Mṛgaśiras (Orion) in the firmament.

Unfathomability

Even though considered by Norman Brown as spurious, the following Mālinī stanza constitutes the last śloka of MS (excluding other descriptions and phalaśruti) in the oral tradition all over the country even today:

"Were there ink powder equal to Mount Asita (Black mountain) in an inkpot like the Ocean, the pen, a branch from the (five) best trees of the gods and the leaf (on which to write), the wide earth, if Śāradā (Goddess of learning) should take the pen and write for eternity.

Still O Lord, she would not encompass your qualities.'[21]

This traditional metaphoric depiction of the unfathomability of Lord Śiva's Greatness displays, in fact, the spirit of humility and unqualified devotion.

Reasoning by metaphor

A similar verse (even though not found in MS oral tradition) is found quoted in Appayyadīkṣita's *Kuvalayānanda* as an example of kāvyaliṅga (reasoning by metaphor) and is also referred to in Brown's edition (appendix). This too is nothing but subtle metaphoric symbolization of rationalistic sentiments of devotion, dedication, self confidence and humility as follows:

'Pardon my two sinful acts, O Maheśa, the destroyer of the Puras, because this body (of mine) has manifested itself (again in this birth), it is inferred that I did never offer my salutation to you in the previous birth;

as I am offering my salutation to you now, I am sure to be free from the bodily bondage and so I will not be able to offer my salutation to you even in future.'[22]

Thus the language and metaphor in MS are characterized by semantic and imaginative aesthetic depth conducive to the depiction of divine greatness. The hymn also abounds in mythical and philosophical imagery. Besides, scholastic temper is more prominent in the language and metaphor of MS which is universally acknowledged as one of the best specimens of the ancient Indian poetic art.

ORAL TRADITION

The above sample survey of the two most popular hymns of classical Sanskrit (SL and MS), addressed to the Mother Goddess and Lord Śiva respectively, confirms Gonda's concluding remarks to the effect that Indian Stotra literature is immensely rich in 'true poetic thought and genuine religious feelings". Unlike Vedic hymns of restricted distribution, the hymns preserved in classical Sanskrit had, moreover, all along an unrestricted (more or less) popular circulation to such an extent that the two hymns just surveyed are regularly sung and recited in temples and homes all over the country.

Of course, the oral tradition of Stotra literature has been undergoing a process of evolution. In that process it has been growing and/or transforming itself with regard to the objects of comparison (upamāna) as well as Tertia comparationis (upamānadharma), right from the Vedic age till today.

Father imagery

The simple Ṛgvedic prayer addressed to the fire god comparing the latter to a father and seeking his protection (sa naḥ pite'va sūnave Rg.1.1.9) is found almost repeated in the MBH. (cf. Bhagavadgītā 11.44) and is still alive in an expanded form in our oral tradition in Sanskrit (tvam eva mātā ca pitā tvam eva...) as well as in Hindi (tumhī ho mātā pitā tumhī ho. . .).

Even medieval and modern Indian languages abound in Stotra literature with true poetic fervour. Tulasīdāsa's (1600 A.D.)

Vinayapatrikā, for example, is exceedingly rich in metaphoric excellence and devotional fervour. Some of his metaphoric innovations deserve special mention.

(i) He compares the mind with a fish that does not want to part with water (mind inseparably attached to objects of enjoyment). So he requests Lord Rāma to catch the fish that is mind through the thread of his compassion, the hook of the Aṅkuśa sign of his feet and absolute love as a bait. So that the mind that is fish is hit and caught and the root cause of all the miseries is removed thereby.[23]

(ii) Tulasī laughs at the inexplicable nature of creation. The creation is nothing but a painting without colour on a vacuum canvas by a bodyless painter; it cannot be wiped out even through washing; it is also afraid of death and subjects itself to miseries through this body. In the mirage of this world there lives an extremely terrible crocodile which (even though) devoid of mouth, devours all those who approach the mirage in order to quench their thirst. Some say that all this is real; some describe it as unreal; according to some it is all real-unreal. Tulasī says that it is only the one free from all these three fallacious views of life, who can have a realisation of oneself.[24]

Innumerable folk songs still lie hidden among the various communities all over the country. They too abound in popular oral poetic devotional literature. For example, a Maithilī folk song (I am not yet aware of its original source) presents a dialogue between the Mother Goddess and Lord Śiva—the former requesting the latter for a dance performance and the latter refusing to do so (ahã kahai chī Gaurā nācailā ham konā nācab he). The style of the dialogue of the divine couple is altogether mundane but loving. Lord Śiva says that if He starts His dance-performance, the snakes will fall down from his body and will be devoured by Kārtikeya's peacock; drops of nectar will fall from the mooncrescent, and so the inmates of the cemetary will be revived; even the Goddess will get terrified at the terrific sight and will get away from the dancing ground and as such who will watch the dance performance (nāc ke dēkhat hē)?

If someone could collect just the benedictory verses from Sanskrit dramas and other texts on the various disciplines, that would make a distinct contribution to the study of devotional religious literature. For example, the benedictory, verse in the *Abhijñānaśākuntalam* identifies the eight perceptible parts of Śiva's body, viz. water, fire, yajamāna, the sun, the moon, space, the earth, and the air-representing a devotional identification of the object of worship (Śiva) with the cosmos. Similarly, very interesting from the point of view of metaphoric complexity and elegance is the benedictory verse in the *Muhūrtacintāmaṇi* (an astrological text by Rāma) depicting the elephant-faced Gaṇeśa's childish behaviour in snatching away the decorative ketaka leaves from his Mother's ears and placing them in his mouth and so forming, as it were, a second tooth for himself for a moment (gaurīśravaḥketakapatrabhaṅgam. . .muhūrtākalitadvitīyadaṇtapraroho. . .).

In any case, the vast amount of Stotra literature in Sanskrit, Pāli, Prākṛta, Apabhraṃśa and other Indian languages (including classical and modern Dravidian languages) has unfortunately missed the attention of scholars it deserves. Quite a lot is required to be done to promote such studies. It would be worth while compiling an encyclopaedia of similes and metaphors in Indian devotional literature in classical Sanskrit and other Indian languages. Unlike other kāvyas, the stotra literature still represents a living oral tradition throughout India. Thus a systematically organised study into this vast ocean of literature would open the door for diving deep into the great cultural heritage of India and would also stand us in good stead for further comparative study of the devotional/religious literature of the world.[25]

References

1. Bṛhat stotraratnākara, Bombay, 1963.
2. Saundaryalaharī (Flood of Beauty) ed. tr. W. Norman Brown, Harward Univ. Press, 1958. (S.L.)
3. Mahimnastava (Praise of Śiva's Greatness) ed. tr. W. Norman Brown, AIIS, Poona 1965. (M.S.)
4. Medieval Religious Literature in Sanskrit, Wiesbaden 1977 by Jan Gonda, Ch. XV Stotra Literature pp. 232-70.
5. SL 56.

śive śṛṅgārārdrā taditarajane kutsanparā
saroṣā gaṅgāyaṃ giriśacarite vismayavatī/
harāhibhyo bhītā sarasiruhasaubhāgyajayinī
sakhīṣu smerā te mayi janani dṛṣṭiḥ sakaruṇā //

6. id. 102
pradīpajvālābhir divasakaranīrājanavidhiḥ
sudhāsūteś candropalajalalavair arghyaracanā /
svakīyair ambhobhiḥ salilanidhisauhityakaraṇaṃ
tvadīyābhir vāgbhis tava janani vācāṃ stutir iyam //
7. id. 15.
śarajjyotsnāśubhrāṃ Śaśiyutajaṭājūṭamukuṭāṃ
varatrāsatrāṇasphaṭikaguṭikāpustakakarām /
sakṛn na tvā natvā kathamiva satāṃ sannidadhate
madhukṣīradrākṣāmadhurimadhurīṇā bhaṇitayaḥ //
[aesthetic symmetry in the setting up of sounds and words like
na tvā and natvā, madhurimadhurīṇā etc. may also be noted]
8. id. 16.
kavīndrāṇāṃ cetaḥ kamalavanabālātaparuciṃ
bhajante ye santaḥ katicid aruṇām eva bhavatīm /
vriñcipreyasyās taruṇataraśṛñgāra laharī
gabhīrābhir vāgbhir vidaddhati satāṃ rañjanam amī //
9. id. 17.
savitrībhir vācāṃ śaśimaṇiśilābhañgarucibhir
vaśinyādyābhis tvāṃ saha janani saṃcintayati yaḥ /
sa kartā kāvyānāṃ bhavati mahatāṃ bhañgisubhagair
vacobhir vāgdevīvadanakamalāmodamadhuraiḥ //
[Cf. commentaries thereon in Saundaryalaharī with nine commentaries and Eng. Hindi and Tamil tr. Tiruchirappali 1976]
10. id. 46.
lalāṭam lāvaṇyadyuti vimalam ābhāti tava yad
dvitīyaṃ tau manye mukuṭaghaṭitaṃ candraśakalam /
viparyāsanyāsād ubhayam api sambhūya ca mithaḥ
sudhālepasyūtiḥ pariṇamatī rākāhimakaraḥ //
11. id. 76.
harakrodhajvālāvalibhir avalīḍhena vapuṣā
gabhīre te nābhīsarasi kṛtasaṅgo manasijaḥ /
samuttasthau tasmād acalatanaye dhūmalatikā
janas tāṃ jānīte tava janani romāvalir iti //
12. id. 87.
himānīhantavyaṃ himagirinivāsaikacaturau
niśayāṃ nidrāṇaṃ niśi ca parabhāge ca viśadau /
paraṃ lakṣmīpātraṃ śriyam atisṛjantau samayināṃ
sarojaṃ tvātpādau janani jayataś citram iha kim //
13. id. 57.
dṛṣā drāghīyasyā daradalitanīlotpalarucā
davīyāṃsaṃ dīnaṃ snapaya kṛpayā mām api śive /
anenā 'yaṃ dhanyo bhavati na ca te hānir iyatā
vane vā harmye vā samakaranipāto himakaraḥ //
14. id. 44.
vahantī sindūraṃ prabalakabarībhāratimira-
dviṣāṃ vṛndaiḥ baṅdīkṛtam iva navīnārkakiraṇam /

tanotu kṣemaṃ nas tava vadanasaundaryalaharī-
parīvāhasrotaḥsaraṇir iva sīmantasaraṇiḥ //

15. id. 90

dadāne dīnebhyaḥ śriyam aniśam āśānusadṛśīm
amandaṃ saundaryaprakaramakarandaṃ vikirati /
tavā 'smin mandārastabakasubhage yātu caraṇe
nimajjan majjīvaḥ karaṇacaraṇaḥ ṣaṭcaraṇatām //

16. MS 17.

viyadvyāpī tārāgaṇaguṇitaphenodgamaruciḥ
pravāho vārāṃ yaḥ pṛṣatalaghudṛṣṭaḥ śirasi te /
jagad dvīpākāraṃ jaladhivalayaṃ tena kṛtam ity
anenai'vo'nneyaṃ dhṛtamahimadivyaṃ tava vapuḥ //

17. id.7.

trayī sāṃkhyaṃ yogaḥ paśupatimataṃ vaiṣṇavam iti
prabhinne prasthāne param idam adaḥ patthyamiti ca /
rucīnāṃ vaicitryād ṛjukuṭilanānāpathajuṣāṃ
nṛṇām eko gamyas tvam asi payasām arṇava iva //

18. id. 11.

ayatnād āpādya tribhuvanam avairavyatikaraṃ
daśāsyo yad bāhūn abhṛta raṇakaṇḍūparavaśān /
śiraḥpadmaśreṇīracitacaranāmbhoruhabaleḥ
sthirāyās tvadbhaktes tripurahara visphūrjitam idam //

19. id. 19.

haris te sāhasraṃ kamalavalim ādhāya padayor
yad ekone tasmin nijam udaharan netrakamalam /
gato bhaktyudrekaḥ pariṇatiṁ asau cakravapuṣā
trayāṇāṃ rakṣāyai tripurahara jāgarti jagatām //

20. id. 22.

prajānāthaṃ natha prasabham abhikaṃ svāṃ duhitaraṃ
gataṃ rohidbhūtaṃ riramayiṣum ṛśyasya vapuṣā //
dhanuṣpāṇir yātaṃ divam api sapatrākṛtam amuṃ
trasantaṃ te'dyā'pi tyajati na mṛgavyadharabhasaḥ //

21. id. Appendix 1.

asitagirisamaṃ syāt kajjalaṃ sindhupātre
surataruvaraśākhā lekhanī patram urvī /
likhati yadi gṛhītvā śāradā sarvakālam
tadapi tava guṇānām īśa pāraṃ na yāti //

22. id. Appendix. Cf. Kuvalayānanda.

vapuḥprādurbhāvād anumitam idaṃ janmani purā
purāre nai'vā'haṃ kvacidapi bhavantaṃ praṇatavān /
naman nucktaḥ sampraty aham atanur agre'py anatimān
maheśa kṣantavyaṃ tad idam aparādhadvayam api //

23. Tulasīdāsa: Vinayapatrikā, Gorakhpur, 1965; p. 175.

viṣaya vāri mana mīna bhinna nahī
hōta kabahū pala eka /
tā te sahaō bipati ati dāruṇa
janamata jōni aneka //
kṛpā ḍōri banasī pada ankuśa

parama prēma mṛdu cārō /
ehi bidhi bēdhi harahu mērō dukh
kautuka rāma tihāro //

24. id. p. 185.
sūnya bhīti para citra ranga nahī
tanu binau likhā citērē /
dhōē miṭai na, marai bhīti,
dukha pāīa ehi tanu hērē //
ravikara nīra basae ati dāruṇa
makara rūpa tehi mā hī̃ /
badan hīna so grasae carācara
pāna karana jé jā hī̃ //
kou kaha satya jhūṭha kaha kōu
jugala prabala kou māne //
tulasidāsa pariharae tīna bhrama
sō āpana pahicānē //

25. This paper is basically the same as it was read in the Department of Linguistics, University of Illinois at Urbanā-Champaign, U.S.A. on April 13, 1989.

P.S. Translations from SL and MS are mostly from W. Norman Brown's respective editions, with some modifications here and there.

18 *PITTA* VERSUS *AGNI*—AN AYURVEDIC PERSPECTIVE

According to Ayurveda, the individual is an epitome of the universe. All the material and spiritual phenomena of the universe are present in the individual and all those present in the individual are also contained in the universe.[1] The individual is the conglomeration of the factors derived from five *mahābhūtas* in which the *cetanā* or consciousness is manifested.[2] The five *mahābhūtas*, viz., *pṛthvī, ap, tejas, vāyu* and *ākāśa* are present in the body in the form of *doṣas*, viz., *vāyu, pitta* and *kapha*; *dhātus*, viz., *rasa, rakta, māṃsa, medas, asthi, majjā* and *śukra*; and *malas*, viz., urine, stool, sweat, etc. These *doṣas, dhātus* and *malas* constitute the foundation of the body.[3] The *doṣas* regulate all the physiological activities of the body, the *dhātus* constitute the body matrix and the *malas* are waste products which are eliminated from the body but partially utilised in the body structure.

Three Doṣas

These three *doṣas*, viz., *vāyu, pitta* and *kapha*, pervade the entire body. When in the state of equilibrium, they preserve and promote positive health of an individual, and if this equilibrium is disturbed, then this leads to disease and decay of the individual.[4] *Suśruta* has explained this with reference to the phenomena in the macrocosm. In the universe, *soma* (moon), *sūrya* (sun) and *anila* (wind) cause *visarga* (elimination of energy), *ādāna* (absorption of energy) and *vikṣepa* (dissipation of dynamic activities) respectively to sustain it. These three factors, viz., *soma, sūrya* and *anila* are represented in the body in the form of *kapha, pitta* and *vāyu* respectively and the latter, in a similar way, sustain the microcosm (body) through *visarga, ādāna* and *vikṣepa*.[5]

Agni

Generally, *agni* as an independent and separate entity is not taken into account while enumerating the composition of the body. According to Suśruta *agni* (*pitta*), *soma* (*kapha*), *vāyu* (*vāta*), *sattva*, *rajas*, *tamas*, five senses and *ātman* (soul) constitute *prāṇa* (life-force).[6] Here *agni* is used as a synonym of *pitta*. But, *Suśruta* while defining a '*svastha*' or a 'healthy person' has stated, "A person having equilibrium of *doṣas* (*vāyu*, *pitta* and *kapha*), *agnis*, *dhātus* and *malas*, and perspicuity of the soul, senses as well as mind should be called healthy."[7] Here he has made a clear distinction between *pitta* and *agni*. *Agni*, according to Caraka is the basis of strength, health, longevity and *elan vitae*.[8] Suppression of *agni* is the cause of all diseases.[9] Even alleviation or aggravation of *doṣas* is stated to be dependent upon the *agni*.[10] *Agni* causes digestion of food; in the absence of food, it digests the *doṣas*, viz., *vāyu*, *pitta* and *kapha*; when these *doṣas* are reduced, *agni* digests the *dhātus*; and thereafter it digests (anihilates) the *prāṇa* (*elan vitae*).[11] Thus, a clear distinction is made between *pitta* and *agni* in ayurvedic classics.

Caraka, while enumerating properties and functions of *pitta*, has not described its five divisions. On the other hand, he has detailed the thirteen groups of *agnis* which are responsible for the digestion and metabolism of food.[12] In this text Marīci is quoted according to whom *agni* of the macrocosm is represented in the form of *pitta* in the human beings (microcosm) and which performs all the activities relating to digestion, etc.[13]

Five divisions of *pitta* are enumerated in the *Suśruta Saṃhitā*. But in this text, the suffix *agni* is added to each division, viz., *pācakāgni*, *rañjakāgni*, *sādhakāgni*, *ālocakāgni* and *bhrājakāgni*.[14] Vāgbhaṭa, on the other hand, has clearly described five divisions of *pitta* as *pācaka pitta*, *rañjaka pitta*, *sādhaka pitta*, *ālocaka pitta* and *bhrājaka pitta*.[15]

Pitta

The term '*pitta*' is derived from the √*tap* which is included in the *divādi*, *eurādi* and *bhvādi* groups of verbs. Accordingly, it is interpreted to mean "a substance which endows auspiciousness (*tap aiśvarye*) or which causes combustion (*tap dāhe*) or which produces heat (*tap santāpe*). Combustion or digestion of food includes splitting of food ingredients into small and absorbable particles, making heterologcus products into homologous ones, and their absorption and assimilation into body system resulting in the synthesis of various categories of tissue elements. Simultaneously heat and energy are produced. Apart from digestion, metabolism and heat as well as energy production, (which are also the functions of *agni*) *pitta* has some unique features (which are different from those of *agni*) like imparting colour to red blood cells, complexion to the skin, strength to the sense organs and support to the intellectual faculties.

Relationship between Pitta and Agni

Sanskrit lexicons describe many synonyms common to both *pitta* and *agni*. Even though there are distinctive features, several properties are commonly shared by both the *pitta* and *agni*. There was, therefore, confusion in their identification. Suśruta has discussed this question. According to him, "It should be ascertained if *agni* is different from or it is the same as *pitta*. *Agni* has no existence independent of *pitta*. The latter has the attributes of *agni* because of which it causes combustion, digestion, etc., inside the body. Therefore, in a secondary sense, *pitta* itself is called *agni*. If the attributes of *agni* are reduced, then such drugs as are stimulants of *agni* are administered and when it is increased in excess, then cooling drugs are administered to alleviate *agni*." Therefore, Suśruta has concluded there is no separate existence of *agni* independent of *pitta*."[16] Dalhaṇa, the commentator has made efforts to justify the conclusion drawn by Suśruta. According to him, from the logical point of view, i.e. (1) *pratyakṣa* or direct observation, (2) *anumāna* (inference) and (3) *āgama* (authoritative scriptures), *agni* is the same as *pitta*.[17]

The following references in ayurvedic texts make a clear distinction between *pitta* and *agni*:

(1) Ghee alleviates *pitta* but stimulates *agni*.
(2) Goat's milk and fish cause aggravation of *pitta* but they do not stimulate *agni*.
(3) Sleep during the day time causes aggravation of *pitta* but it subdues *agni*.
(4) One of the varieties of *agnimāndya* (suppression [weakness] of the power of *agni*) is caused by aggravated *pitta*.
(5) While describing the cause of premature greying of hair it is stated that because of anger, grief and exhaustion, the bodily heat (*agni*) enters into the head in association with

pitta to cause such premature greying. In this reference both *pitta* and *agni* are treated as two different entities.

(6) While describing the characteristic features of a healthy person *pitta* and *agni* are described as two different entities.

In view of the above Dalhaṇa has made a distinction between *agni* and *pitta* inasmuch as the latter is endowed with taste (*rasa*), attributes (*guṇa*), potency (*vīrya*), etc., whereas the former, that is, *agni*, is devoid of all such qualities. According to him the treatment of morbidities in *agni* could be performed through *pitta*, because of which an effort has been made to show their identity.

Bhāvamiśra has given a clear solution to this knotty problem. According to him, it is the *uṣṇa* (heating) attribute of *pitta* which is responsible for its functions like *pācana* (digestion), *rañjana* (coloration of the blood) and *darśana* (vision). Therefore, *agni* does not exist independent of *pitta*. *Pitta* according to him (also according to Vāgbhata)[18] is composed of five *mahābhūtas*. When the *agni mahābhūta* in it becomes predominant, and when *pitta* becomes devoid of *ap mahābhūtas*, then only *pitta* performs such functions like digestion and heat production. It is this modified state of *pitta* which is called *agni*. *Pitta* is liquid, unctuous and *adhogāmī* (having the tendency to move downwards) whereas *agni* has opposite attributes. These are the distinguishing features between *pitta* and *agni*. But *agni* always remains in and constitutes a part of the total concept of *pitta*. *Pitta* is pervaded by *agni* and it is through this *agni* that all the functions of *pitta* are manifested. Thus, Bhāvamiśra has drawn the following conclusions:

(1) *Agni* does not exist independent of *pitta*. The latter, in addition, has other (*ap*) *mahābhautic* properties like liquidity, unctuousness and downward movement. Iron ball is not hot. But when it is heated, a distinction cannot be made between the iron ball and the heat that emanates from it. Similarly, *agni*, though possessed with different properties, in a strict sense cannot be differentiated from *pitta*.

(2) *Pitta* is composed of five *mahābhūtas*. But the predominance of *agni mahābhūta* and reduction or abscence of *ap mahābhūta* makes it to perform all the activities of *agni*.

(3) This *agni*, as an inseparable component of *pitta* circulates all over the body through different channels to sustain life because of which it is called *kāyāgni*, *kāyoṣmā*, *paktā* and *jīvana*.[19]

Conclusion

Pitta though composed of five *mahābhūtas* is dominated by *agni* and *ap* and bears the characteristic features of both these *mahābhūtas*.[20] It is the predominance of *agni* and reduction of *ap mahābhūta* which enables *pitta* to perform functions like digestion and metabolism. Though in reality *pitta* and *agni* are two different entities, because of their eternal association, in practice, these are treated as synonymous. In this context '*appittam*'[21] described in *Amarakośa* as a synonym of *agni* should be interpreted as *ap rahitaṃ pittaṃ*. By implication *pitta* free from *ap mahābhūta* should be equated to *agni*.

Notes

1. Caraka: Śārīra 5:3.
2. Caraka: Śārīra 6:4.
3. Suśruta: Sūtra 15:3; Aṣṭāṅga hṛdaya: Sūtra 11:1; Suśruta: Uttaratantra 66:6.
4. Caraka: Sūtra 12:13; Caraka: Sutra 20:9; Caraka: Vimāna 1:5; Caraka: Śārīra 12:13.
5. Suśruta: Sūtra 6:8; Suśruta: Sūtra 21:8.
6. Suśruta: Śārīra 4:3.
7. Suśruta: Sūtra 15:20.
8. Caraka: Sūtra 27-32.
9. Aṣṭāṅga hṛdaya: Nidāna 12:1.
10. Caraka: Cikitsā 5:136.
11. Kṣemakutūhala: Uttara: 3.
12. Caraka: Cikitsā 15:6-38.
13. Caraka: Sūtra 12:11.
14. Suśruta: Sūtra 21:10.
15. Aṣṭāṅga hṛdaya: Sūtra 12:10-14.
16. Suśruta: Sūtra 29:1.
17. Dalhaṇa on Suśruta: Sūtra 29:1.
18. Aṣṭāṅga hṛdaya: Sūtra 12:10-12.
19. Bhāvaprakāśa: Pūrvakhaṇḍa 3:10-18.
20. Caraka: Śārīra 7:16; Suśruta: Sūtra 42:5; Aṣṭāṅga Saṅgraha: Sūtra 20:1.
21. *Amarakośa*: Prathamakāṇḍa: Svargavarga 56.

19 THE DOCTRINE OF 'AHAM-ARTHA'

R. V. JOSHI, *Delhi*

The followers of Advaita and Vaiṣṇava Vedānta categorically differ on this doctrine. The Advaitin explains 'aham-artha' or 'I-sense' in five ways:

(i) that ego (ahaṁkāra) is 'I-sense'.
(ii) that consciousness reflected in conscience* is 'I-sense'.
(iii) that consciousness conditioned by conscience in the form of ego is 'I-sense'.
(iv) that the uniting element of animate and inanimate (cit-acit-granthi) is 'I-sense'. It amounts to that ego-consciousness (ahaṁkāra-caitanya) modified by identical superimposition (tādātmya-adhyāsa) is 'I-sense'.
(v) that pure consciousness is not 'I-sense'.

The Advaitin declares the ego of Sāṁkhya as 'I-sense' but rejects the Sāṁkhya theory of creation. This stand is not logical. Even if we accept for the sake of argument that the Advaitin does not disagree with the Sāṁkhya theory of creation, the ego as propounded in non-dualism does differ from the ego of Sāṁkhya, because the ego in non-dualism is different in each individual 'Self' while the ego in Sāṁkhya is not different in each individual 'Self'. The Sāṁkhya accepts a threefold ego of the nature of (i) a pure ego associated with goodness and virtue (sāttvika) (ii) a dynamic ego with passion and pride (rājasika) and (iii) an ego as experienced in ignorance and inertia (tāmasika).[1] Nevertheless, the ego in Sāṁkhya is not destroyed during profound repose or dreamless sleep of an individual, otherwise the ego of every individual will simultaneously be destroyed. Therefore, the ego of Sāṁkhya and the ego of Vedānta are not identical.

The Non-dualist accepts 'I-ness' (ahantva) in ego and not in

*In a later passage it appears that the author uses the word 'conscience' for the *antaḥkaraṇa* (Ed.).

'Self', otherwise on account of 'I-ness' the pure 'Self' will become qualified (saviśeṣa) and in that case the attribute 'I-ness' will have to be accepted in 'Self'. When 'I-ness' is accepted in 'Self', all individual 'Selves' will be understood as 'I' (aham) because—'Self' is one without a second. Our normal experience in life is however different. We understand individual 'Self' by 'This', 'That', 'You' and 'He' and not in the form of 'I'. The objection is untenable so far as Sāṁkhya is concerned because in Sāṁkhya all 'Puruṣa' are different from each other. 'Puruṣa' in Sāṁkhya is without any modification (nirvikāra) but not without attributes (nirdharmaka). As such there is no defect in Sāṁkhya in accepting 'I-ness' in 'self',[2] while the Non-dualist accepts 'I-ness' in ego and not in 'self'.[3]

Let us first examine the non-dualistic view that conscience is ego and ego is 'I-sense'. In non-dualism the sāttvika part of five elements as a result of nescience, produces conscience divided into (i) mind (manas), (ii) intellect (buddhi), (iii) ego (ahaṁkāra) and (iv) citta (mind stuff). A close perusal of the theory of creation in Vedic and Paurāṇic cosmology and the theory of creation in the Mokṣadharma parva of the Śānti parva of the Mahābhārata indicates that conscience of non-dualism and mind of the Upaniṣads are equivalent terms.[4] Mind is considered as endowed with several functions such as volition (saṁkalpa), determination (adhyavasāya), desire or feeling (abhimāna), thinking, contemplation, faith and knowing.[5]

The Paurāṇic point of view that mind and senses originate from pure egotism associated with goodness and virtue (sāttvika ahaṁkāra) does not agree with the non-dualistic view wherein mind originates from pure parts (sāttvika aṁśa) of five elements. We come across several non-dualistic Sanskrit texts saying that the principle of intelligence is the ego, or an ego-element originating from the principle of intelligence is the ego. The Non-dualist maintains that the conscience, originating from five elements, is ego.

The materialistic school of Cārvāka maintains the existence of 'I-sense' till death, while the Advaita Vedānta maintains that 'I-sense' is destroyed and produced in each sleep and awaking. 'I-sense' is different day by day in each individual. By the time one and the same 'I-sense' continues to exist in an individual 'Self' in Cārvāka system, thousands of 'I-sense' are produced in another individual 'Self' in non-dualism. Therefore the Non-dualist cannot maintain one and the same form of 'Self' till liberation.

The Non-dualist solves this problem stating that although the ego, a product of nescience, is destroyed during profound repose, it continues to exist in causal form.[6] The causal form of the ego, obviously, could not be nescience because nescience could never be the direct cause of conscience because Non-dualist accepts conscience as a product of five elements. This helps us to prove that either ego or five elements could be the causal form of ego. Nescience is certainly not the causal form of ego.

The destruction of 'I-sense' during profound repose creates another difficulty. In case in non-dualism 'I-sense' is destroyed in each profound repose of an individual 'Self' and a new 'I-sense' is produced, the Non-dualist should accept that all impressions of our experience stored in sub-conscious mind are also destroyed along with the destruction of the first 'I-sense' and the awakened man could not remember his past experience considering himself identical with the former 'I-sense'.

It may be argued that in the profound repose ego remains merged in the causal nescience and the ego—impression resides on the support of nescience. In the awaking state this very nescience transforms itself into conscience and the impressions remain in conscience on the support of nescience. Thus the newly created ego recalls the objects of experience of the former ego.

The reasoning is fallacious. We may agree that the second ego may recollect the objects of experience of the first ego but we cannot agree that both these egos are identical. We do experience the identity of the two egos of yesterday and today. This proves that 'I-sense' is not destroyed during profound repose. Secondly, when in non-dualism ego of all individual 'Selves' is destroyed in dreamless sleep and all impressions remain in causal nescience, naturally a question arises how these impressions reach a particular individual ego of a 'Self' from this causal nescience. To accept innumerable egos of innumerable 'Selves' as an entirely new creation from one causal nescience will create another difficulty. Impressions residing in a particular ego on the previous day would reach any ego the next morning, travelling through nescience during dreamless sleep. As a result

'X' should be able to remember the objects of the experience of 'Y' because when 'X' and 'Y' are awakened all new egos are similar before the multitude of impressions residing in causal nescience and there would be no regulator to carry a certain group of impressions to a particular ego where this group did reside on the previous day.

The Non-dualist may argue that in spite of the fact that nescience is one, there is some partial difference in nescience. Therefore, during dreamless sleep, ego at the time of merging itself in nescience, places its own impressions in a certain part of nescience. The next morning these very impressions automatically reach that very ego when the same ego is produced from that very part of nescience. To avoid this indirect process of merger and production, the Vaiṣṇava Vedānta proposes the identity of 'I-sense' and 'Self' in lieu of presumed innumerable parts of nescience. It is an easier [conception] than the merger and production of different egos in different parts of nescience due to which the relevant centres carry the impressions to their own receptacles.

It will not be correct to interpret the Upaniṣadic text: 'Then the father is no father, mother is no mother, the worlds no worlds and Gods no Gods'[7] in the sense of absolute negation of external world during profound repose because in reality the external world does continue to exist. The closing of the eyes of a pigeon towards an attacking cat does not negate the existence of cat. What the *Bṛhadāraṇyaka Upaniṣad* exactly means in this context is this that one becomes completely unaware of the external world in the state of profound repose. The negation is just in the figurative sense. Likewise, all Śruti texts appearing to interpret the merger of ego during profound repose should be taken in the figurative sense that therein ego continues to exist. During awaking, one experiences; 'I am fat'; 'I am a man'; 'I am a woman'. Such experience depends on the intellect arising from ego.

The Śāṅkara Bhāṣya on the Brahmasūtra indicates that intellect has the minutest size in the distinguishing property of 'Self'[8] and this limiting adjunct relation of 'Self' and intellect having no beginning exists till liberation.[9] Intellect as a potential exists in the states of profound repose and deluge.[10] Conscience, a limiting adjunct of 'Self' is designated by several terms such as mind, intellect, ego and mind stuff.[11] The testimony of the *Brahmasūtra Śāṅkara-Bhāṣya* postulates that only that could be accepted as a limiting adjunct of 'Self' which exists even in profound repose and deluge. It therefore becomes the demand of propriety that such a limiting adjunct is accepted as an object of 'I-Intellect' or the feeling of 'I' (aham-buddhi) because this limiting adjunct is nothing else but nescience. Consequently, conscience is 'I-sense'. The merger of ego during profound repose is the secondary meaning. In fact, only the operational function of ego ceases during profound repose and not ego itself. The negation is of functions such as volition, desire, feeling or determination. This proves that the acceptance of the merger of the distinguishing property of 'Self' during dreamless sleep is inconsistent with the viewpoint of the *Śāṅkara Bhāṣya*. Even if it be argued that all intellects in the form of the distinguishing property of 'Self' are not identical with nescience, we cannot afford not to accept that all conditioned intellects are different from each other and have no beginning at all. At the same time the Non-dualist will be forced to accept the destruction of these conditioned intellects at the time of the deluge. The non-dualistic view that the merger of the limiting adjunct of the 'Self' and the negation of 'I-sense' in the state of profound repose does not hold good.

The uniting element of animate and inanimate in not 'I-sense'

Madhusūdana Sarasvatī has explained in the 16th century in his *Advaita-Siddhi* that 'I-sense' means uniting the elements of animate and inanimate (cit-acit-granthi). This Sanskrit term has been interpreted as an intricate knot. It makes one commit errors after errors. The darkness extends. One thinks that he knows many things, while he remains most ignorant of what he is most assured of. The bondage and attraction of 'I-ness' and 'Mine-ness', and the repulsion of separateness or otherness, hostility, very curiously make him restless. He hangs oscillately between them.[12] The Sanskrit term includes animate or consciousness or the principle of universal intelligence by the word 'cit' and inanimate (conscience) by the word 'acit'. This very 'I-sense' is known as ego when we have the apprehension of 'I'. 'I-sense' of the nature of ego having the idea of the apprehension of 'I' or 'I experience' is the substratum of 'Self' (cit). From the apprehension 'I am the performer', 'I-sense' appears as the substratum of the state of being the performer (kartṛttva) etc. attributes residing in conscience (acit). This should not be understood as simple mutual relationship between animate and inanimate but there exists mutual identical superimposition (tādātmya-adhyāsa) between the two. This very uniting element of consciousness and conscience appearing identical due to misapprehension is known as 'I-sense'. Hence 'I-sense' and ego are identical.[13]

This interpretation of 'I-sense' is questionable. One may enquire what is exactly meant by 'uniting element'. Does it represent the nature of animate and inanimate? Or, does it represent the superiority of one over another? The second question is what is the cause of the activity of 'I' (pravṛtti-nimitta). Neither consciousness nor ego could be accepted as the cause of the activity of 'I' because we do not find usage of the word 'I' in this sense. Our normal experience is that everybody uses the word 'I' keeping in mind 'I-ness' as the cause of the activity of 'I'. The meaning of the word 'I' as either consciousness qualified by ego or ego qualified by consciousness does not appear appropriate because in that case we would be bound to accept the relation of qualification and qualified (viśeṣaṇaviśeṣya-bhāva saṁbandha). This sort of relation cannot be accepted simply because there does not exist the relation of difference or non-difference. In the former case the consciousness of difference will continue to exist and an identical super-imposition would be an impossibility. In the latter case it would be necessary to accept mutual super-imposition otherwise it would be going against the non-dualistic school of Vedānta. Truly, by accepting the relation of qualification and qualified through the relation of non-difference the consciousness can manifest ego but it must not be forgotten that an ego could never manifest consciousness according to non-dualism wherein consciousness is without any attribute (nirdharmaka). One might insist that an ego would appear to be associated with consciousness but in that case one would immediately differentiate ego from consciousness and super-imposition would be impossible. If the idea of the Non-dualist is to suggest the appearance of consciousness along with the attribute 'I-sense' of the ego, the Non-dualist indirectly agrees that 'I-ness', the cause of the activity of 'I', is a property of the ego and in that case 'You-sense' of an ego would not be acceptable in non-dualism. It is noteworthy that the meaning of an ego as 'You-sense' is also accepted in non-dualism because it is meant for another (parārtha). In fact, the ego accomplishes the purpose of consciousness. One will not fail to note that the attributes such as 'the state of being the performer and enjoyer' are admitted in an ego according to non-dualism and not in undifferentiated consciousness through an ego. It would therefore be against the non-dualistic view to hold that consciousness appears along 'I-ness' of ego. Ego is not meant for another and as such does not yield the idea of 'You-sense'. The idea of identical super-imposition of ego and consciousness is not correct because we all feel 'I, the sentient perform'. In such experience ego appears as the locus of consciousness and super-imposition of consciousness remains impossible. The difference between ego and consciousness is obviously proved on the basis of the relation of container and contained.

It would not be out of place to examine the meaning of two 'aham' words, viz. (i) aham, indeclinable ending in 'm' (ii) aham, declined from the noun 'asmat' or 'asmad' in nominative singular ending in 't' or 'd'. The primary sense of both these words has been accepted by Madhusūdana Sarasvatī in the Advaita-siddhi as ego. Neither of the two denotes the sense of 'Self' in the tradition of Advaita Vedānta. To determine the meaning we should take into account the authority of Sanskrit grammar. The *Kāśikā-Vṛtti* and the *Padamañjarī* on the aphorism of Pāṇini 'ahaṁ Śubhayor yus' (5.2.40) clearly indicate that one 'aham' is an indeclinable representing the inflection of nouns (vibhakti pratirūpaka avyaya), while the second 'aham' is declined from the noun 'asmad' by the substitute 'aha'. Both the words apparently appearing as identical are not identical so far as their meaning is concerned.[14] The indeclinable 'aham' denotes the sense of ego, and the declined 'aham' the sense of 'Self'. To take these two words as synonyms would mean to violate the rules of Pāṇini grammar. The non-dualist view is not correct because ego has nowhere been accepted in the sense of the uniting element of animate and inanimate.

I may refer to the *Śāṅkara Bhāṣya* that conscience, viz. mind, intellect, ego and ego stuff has four mental functions: doubt, right knowledge, slumber and remembrance respectively.[15] The evidence shows that ego going with egotism or pride is one of the four aspects of conscience. Ego cannot go with any other remaining three functions. To accept the identical sense of all the above-mentioned four words would mean that the word 'asmad' could be used with any of the four functions and ego could be applied to any of the four on the ground of the uniting element of animate and inanimate. Since such is not the position, the uniting element of animate and inanimate cannot be accepted as the meaning of 'I-sense'. To elaborate it further we may take an example of the statement, I am fat, there is an apprehension of the egoistic feeling of 'Self' on the inanimate substratum such as body but we do not have any idea of gross ego. Therefore the meaning of ego and the meaning of the declined 'Aham' word is not one and the same. The indeclinable 'aham' always remains in the same form, while the declined 'aham' has this form only in nominative singular. In accusative and genitive, the forms of 'asmad' are 'mām' and 'mama' respectively. There is no proof to establish the identical meaning of the two 'aham' words. On the other hand, we have authority of Sanskrit grammar and dictionary regarding the meaning of the indeclinable 'aham' in the sense of ego or egotism and the declined 'aham', 'mām' and 'mama' denote an altogether different sense and that sense is 'Self'. The non-dualistic view of the uniting element of animate and inanimate as 'I-sense' is not correct on the ground that all statements such as 'I, the sentient, perform the action and enjoy' prove an existence of consciousness in 'I-sense'.

Existence of 'I-sense' in Suṣupti

The Sanskrit word Suṣupti denotes the sense of profound repose or dreamless sleep. It has been explained by Śaṅkarācārya as spiritual ignorance.[16] It has already been observed that according to non-dualism 'I-sense' is different from 'Self'. Now, let me remind that 'I-sense' of the nature of 'I' does exist in the states of awaking and dream but does not exist in the states of profound repose and liberation, while the eternal 'Self' exists in all these three states. This is the contention of the Non-dualist. The Non-dualist argues that had there been 'I-sense' during profound repose, one would have had the idea of 'I'. Since we never have the idea of 'I' during profound repose, there is non-existence of 'I-sense'. Likewise, had 'I-sense' been existent in the state of liberation, ignorance would continue to exist. There is of course no possibility of ignorance in liberation. Therefore, non-existent 'I-sense', in the states of profound repose and liberation, is not the internal 'Self'. Consciousness existing in both these states is considered as 'Self' in Advaita Vedānta.

It has been made clear that according to Advaita Vedānta 'I-sense' is of the nature of 'I' i.e. the uniting element of animate and inanimate. The concept includes the sentient 'Self' as the insentient conscience of the nature of ego. There is mutual identical super-imposition between conscience and ego. During the apprehension of 'I' one has the idea of ego as identical with consciousness and of consciousness as identical with ego. This very uniting element of mutual identical super-imposition between consciousness and ego is accepted as 'I-sense' in Advaita Vedānta. It is noteworthy in this connection that in non-dualism the super-imposition of ego on consciousness is direct. It is only after this super-imposition that the attributes such as performer and enjoyer existing in conscience of the nature of ego become imposed. Nevertheless, this superimposition of ego on consciousness has no limiting adjunct while the super-imposition of the attributes on consciousness is limited by the adjuncts. Since ego by its very nature exists in the states of awaking and dream, we experience 'I' but in the state of profound repose it exists in the form of causal nescience and therefore we do not experience its existence. In the state of liberation, nescience, the material cause of the ego, is destroyed and the ego ceases to exist either by its own form or by causal form. Thus in liberation there is no possibility of existence of the ego at all.

The Viśiṣṭādvaita school of Rāmānuja maintains that 'I-sense' is 'Self'. Ego is not included in 'I-sense'. 'Self' without ego is 'I-sense'. 'I-sense' exists in the states of profound repose and liberation. In case 'I-sense' is non-existent during profound repose, Rāmānujist argues, one would be forced to accept two different 'I-sense' viz. (i) 'I-sense', existing in the awaking and dream states on the previous day (ii) 'I-sense' existing in awakening after sleep. This would amount to that the second 'I-sense' would not be able to remember the objects experienced by the first 'I-sense'. This is our normal experience that he who experiences certain things in life remembers them in the future. It is an absolute impossibility that the first 'I-sense' experiences and the second remembers. Otherwise, the experience of 'X' would be remembered by 'Y'. It is therefore more reasonable to accept only one 'I-sense'. We notice the common experience as follows: I, who performed certain actions, am now performing this action'. This recollection supports the identical characteristics of the two 'I-sense'. One and the same 'I-sense' exists in the dormant condition during profound sleep and continues to exist during sleep and after sleep.[17]

It may be questioned that if an 'I-sense' exists during profound repose, why do we not experience it and why does it not become as object of our experience. Since it is never experienced during profound repose, it would be more appropriate to accept its non-existence. The simple logic is that happiness, unhappiness and 'I-sense' manifest by the way of experience only so long they exist. It is self-contradictory to maintain that they exist but do not become the object of our experience. The view of Rāmānuja school finds strong support of Naiyāyika who declares that 'Self' of the nature of 'I-sense' remains unmanifest in dreamless sleep.

There is no such rule that all existing objects must become the object of our perception. There are several such objects which exist and are not perceived. 'I-sense' can also exist remaining unmanifest. The argument that by nature 'I-sense' should manifest so long it exists is untenable because according to Advaita Vedānta too 'I-sense' exists in the most subtle form and remains unmanifest. In fact, wherever there is some function of internal or external senses, we experience 'I-sense'. If it is argued that the first individual 'I-sense' is the substratum of the 'I-ness' of the second individual 'I-sense' and therefore the second individual 'I' understands the 'I' of the first individual, then the subtle form could also be accepted as the substratum of 'I-ness'. This would be an additional proof for the existence of 'I-sense' during profound repose.

The outstanding proof of the existence of 'I-sense' during profound repose is recollection. For instance, one recollects: 'I, who performed such and such actions yesterday, am now awakened after sound sleep'. This experience attests the identity of yesterday's and today's individual 'I-sense' and its existence during profound repose. Truly, there is no experience during the state of profound repose because the attributive consciousness is contracted. The profound repose can only become the object of inferential knowledge after awakening from sleep.

The contention of the Non-dualist is that 'I-sense' is destroyed during profound repose but consciousness and nescience however exist. Any one of these two could be the locus of the impressions which are in fact the cause of memory after dreamless sleep. It is not at all necessary to accept the existence of 'I-sense' during profound repose for the sake of remembering the previously experienced objects.

The argument is not a strong one. First, there is no proof to hold that consciousness of the nature of nescience exists during profound sleep. It cannot be proved that knowledge and ignorance coexist during profound repose. Both cannot coexist in the absence of the knower; it may be kept in mind that the Non-dualist further accepts the non-existence of the knower 'I-sense' in profound repose. Then how can knowledge and ignorance coexist in the absence of knower. Our common experience (i) 'I know' (ii) 'I do not know' prove that 'I-sense' is the substratum of knowledge and ignorance. Besides, consciousness and ignorance cannot be accepted as a receptacle of the impressions. It is only 'I-sense' which is the locus of the impressions. The other point is also refuted that 'I-sense-ego' is destroyed during dreamless sleep but it exists as causal nescience—the substratum of impressions, on the ground that when nescience is considered as locus of impressions, nescience would also become the knower. The Non-dualist will thus have no alternative but to accept nescience as a knower and the ego will not be reckoned as a knower because the ego cannot recall impressions belonging to nescience.

In this way on the basis of the experience of recollection the identity of the 'I-sense' of yesterday and the 'I-sense' of today is established beyond doubt. The existence of the 'I-sense' during profound repose is automatically proved. In the case when there is absence of an 'I-sense' during profound repose, the 'I-sense' —the locus of impressions is destroyed, one cannot recall any impressions at all. For want of proof, therefore, consciousness and nescience cannot be accepted as the substratum of impressions. Similarly, consciousness without any modification (nirvikāra) and without any special characteristic (nirviśeṣa) cannot become the locus of impressions. We have already noticed that nescience could neither become the locus of impressions otherwise it will be the knower. Therefore, the only plausible proposition is that of Vaiṣṇava Vedānta that the 'I-sense' exists during profound repose. Both the logicians and the followers of the qualified non-dualistic school of Vedānta (Rāmānuja) maintain this view. The only difference between these two philosophical traditions is that when the logician (Naiyāyika) does not accept the manifestation of the 'I-sense' during dreamless profound sleep but simply recognises its existence, the followers of the qualified non-dualism accept both the existence as well as the manifestation of 'I-sense' during profound repose.

Existence of 'I-sense' in the state of liberation

I now proceed to examine whether 'I-sense' exists in the state of liberation. It may be kept in mind that the school of Advaita Vedānta totally rejects the existence of 'I-sense' in liberation. The Viśiṣṭādvaita school of Vedānta, however, maintains the existence as well as the manifestation of 'I-sense' in the state of liberation on the basis of the authority of the Śruti texts;

(a) 'I shall obtain it after my transition from this world.'[18]

(b) 'Like unto the moon which escapes from the mouth of Rāhu, I shall purify myself, my body, and, become free (by the aid of meditation) verily, attain—the uncreated Brahmaloka.'[19]

The above cited quotations denote an intensive desire of one who is desirous of liberation. The quoted text proves that liberation is definitely related to 'I-sense' of one who desires liberation. The main purport of the text is that we are all an object of enjoyment of the 'Supreme Self' as an object of enjoyment.[20]

The Taittirīya Upaniṣad further states:

(i) 'Rasam hyevāyaṁ labdhvā ānandī bhavati' (for any one obtaining taste becomes delighted). II.7.1.

(ii) 'Eṣa hyeva ānadayati' (for it is He (the Supreme Self) that fills with bliss). Ibid.

The textual authority supports that blissful Supreme Self alone bestows bliss and one attains bliss by realising Supreme Self of the nature of sentiment (Rasa).

A large number of such Upaniṣadic texts teaches us that in the state of liberation one does attain the inexhaustible bliss and that one should not leave any stone unturned to get rid of the bondage of all the three miseries of the mundane world. It is only with this goal in mind that one adopts the listening, cognitive and repeated meditation etc. as means of realisation. Noteworthy is the fact that Non-dualist does also agree to the cessation of all the miseries and the attainment of unsurpassed bliss of the 'Supreme Self' in the state of liberation. Had such bliss been not manifest in liberation, its attaining had little sense. But in case such bliss becomes manifest to a liberated 'Self', he must experience as follows: 'I am enjoying the bliss', 'I am endowed with bliss'.

It may be argued that to accept the 'I-sense' and its manifestation in the state of liberation would amount to accept the 'Self' as ignorant and transmigratory in the state of liberation, on the simple logic that so long as there is the 'I-sense', the 'Self' is ignorant and transmigratory. Therefore, it would be more appropriate to accept, the Non-dualist says, ego as 'I-sense' which does not exist in liberation. Here an objection can be raised against the Non-dualist view which maintains the existence and manifestation of 'Cognition-Self' (saṁvid Ātman) in the state of liberation as that would likewise mean the coexistence of ignorance and transmigration in liberation if cognition continues to exist. The followers of non-dualism however advocate that only the incongruous manifestation of a 'cognition-Self' is pervaded by ignorance, and only in the state of transmigration does incongruous manifestation exist. Hence, there is ignorance only in transmigration, I may mention, in this connection, that both the existence and the manifestation of an 'I-sense' in liberation are not pervaded by ignorance and transmigration. It is only an incongruous manifestation opposed to the real nature of 'I-sense' which becomes pervaded by ignorance and transmigration. In fact, the false nature is not manifest in liberation. Only the real nature in the form of 'I-sense' becomes manifest.

The contention of Advaita Vedānta, that 'I-sense' is ego and that it ceases to exist in the state of liberation, while the 'attributeless Self' of the nature of consciouness continues to exist, does not hold good. It would be more rational to admit 'I-sense' as 'self' and its existence in liberation rather than accepting 'I-sense' as ego and negating its existence in liberation. Otherwise no sensible person would adopt to the austere means in order to attain liberation because the moment he understands that he is identical with that ego which will discontinue who would like to negate one's own existence. So long as the Non-dualist accepts the existence of a subtle ego in liberation, one may adopt the means in order to liberate oneself, but when the complete negation of an 'I-sense' in the state of liberation is accepted, who would give an ear to the scriptures blowing the trumpets of liberation.[21]

It may be advocated by the 'Non-dualist' at this stage that the 'I-sense' of the nature of ego does not distinguish between 'cognition-Self' and itself. It misapprehends itself as non-different from 'cognition-Self'. The answer is not satisfactory because the 'I-sense' of the nature of ego regards itself as non-different from the 'cognition-Self' on account of misapprehension. Then it certainly understands the reality of its existence in the state of liberation. As such it should further believe in discontinuation of cognition in liberation, i.e. the cognition with which it earlier felt its own identity. To say that by misapprehending the existence of 'I-sense' of the nature of ego one would believe one's own existence in liberation is not logical. The simple reason is that he who believes his existence in liberation by misapprehension has not in reality understood the real nature of liberation. Besides, in non-dualism the complete destruction of nescience and ego is the concept of liberation. Non-dualist argues that one activates oneself to the means of liberation on the misapprehension of the idea of the continuance of 'I-sense' in liberation but in fact in his view 'I-sense' is destroyed as soon as the knowledge of non-dualism appears. This would remind us of an analogy of a person desirous to attain final liberation of the nature of bliss suddenly finding his head cut into pieces. Therefore, this type of liberation of the nature of the destruction of ego could never be accepted as the goal of life.[22]

The Non-dualist further postulates that being afflicted by the threefold miseries of the mundane world to which all mortals are subject, the individual 'Self' might consider that so long as there exists the sense of 'I-ness', it is impossible to get rid of the miseries,[23] and therefore one must destroy oneself, i.e. with destruction of 'I-sense'. Thus considering one's own destruction one would adopt the means of liberation and the destruction of 'I-sense' thus desirable.

The above view is rejected on the basis of the following Śruti texts which declare that the knower of the 'Supreme Self' becomes 'Supreme Self' and that the liberated Self knows all knowable. The Upaniṣadic evidence proves the existence of 'I-sense' as of the nature of knower. The textual passages in support are as follows:

1. 'One passes beyond death only after realising Him. There is no other way to escape from the circle of birth and death.'[24]
2. 'Whoever knows the 'Supreme Brahman becomes even Brahman.'[25]
3. 'That man who knows this confronts not death nor disease nor does he meet with pain or suffering. He observes everything, and attains everything in every way' .... Truly the knower of 'Self' becomes 'Self'.[26]

The above cited Śruti text clearly declares that the direct knowledge of the Supreme Self is the best means to attain immortality. In case 'I-sense' is destroyed in the state of liberation as accepted in non-dualism, the direct knowledge of the Supreme Self will become the cause of death because the knower ego will perish. This will contradict the Śruti tradition. To avoid this inconsistency it is better to accept that the 'I-sense' exists in the state of liberation.

Furthermore in non-dualism the 'attributeless cognition' is regarded as the 'Self' and that in the states of knowing and thinking etc., attributes do not exist in 'attributeless cognition'. In addition to this, the 'Self' is regarded as eternally liberated. This is a self-contradictory view because in the absence of the states of the knowing and thinking etc. attributes, the 'Self' could not listen to the scriptures or contemplate upon 'Supreme Self'; and so why would the eternally liberated attributeless cognition-Self desire liberation at all. One may argue that in the states of knowing and thinking, etc. attributes are superimposed on the eternally liberated attributeless cognition-Self, and therefore one becomes desirous of liberation considering oneself unhappy due to misapprehension and likewise becomes a listener and thinker when there is super-imposition of the states of knowing and thinking.

I am inclined to mention that in the above discussion the standpoint of non-dualism is perhaps not correctly represented. In reality in non-dualism superimposition is a function (*vṛtti*)—

an attribute of conscience. Therefore, conscience may be deemed a listener, thinker, happy or unhappy and not the 'Self' of the nature of knower. It is not possible to prove that a 'Self' of the nature of cognition is entitled to liberation. It would be further incorrect to say that the knower 'I-sense' activates the 'cognition Self' to liberation on the simple ground that an 'I-sense' would not adopt any means of liberation as that would amount to its own destruction, and that such an activity of an 'I-sense' would be compared to the activity of a person who is desirous to cut off his own head in order to save the life of his beloved wife from death and who has been declared hopeless by the medical experts. Similarly, even if the 'Self' is liberated, the non-existent 'I-sense' in the state of liberation would not get any reward of his activity. It must, therefore, be admitted that the 'I-sense' does exist in the state of liberation and only then could there be some possibility of the right to liberation.

In order to justify the non-dualistic point of view it is generally explained that according to non-dualism conscience is four fold. The word 'I' does not simply mean conscience of the nature of ego but it stands for the consciousness conditioned by conscience. Therefore, consciousness conditioned by conscience is 'I-sense' (i.e. antaḥkaraṇāvacchinna caitanya is aham-artha). In the state of liberation in spite of the destruction of the attributive conscience or ego, the consciousness continues to exist. As such there is no inconsistency in non-dualism and with the desire 'I would like to be liberated' this very consciousness conditioned by conscience activates the means of liberation such as listening to the religious discourses and reading the religious scriptures. The reasoning of the Non-dualist does not remain good at the examination on the touchstone of the following argument. One may enquire who makes efforts for liberation with such a pre-desire, i.e. 'I-the bound, would like to be liberated by such and such actions'. Is it conscience or consciousness? In the former case it would be a fruitless effort so far as conscience is concerned because conscience would itself be destroyed in the state of liberation. In the latter case the consciousness cannot be regarded as the locus of activity since it is considered as attributeless in the tradition of Advaita Vedānta.

The Non-dualist further makes an attempt to support his point of view on the following three arguments:

(a) There is superimposition of the locus of the activity and conscience-identity on consciousness.

(b) Ego, by superimposing its identity on consciousness, regards itself as the substratum of activity.

(c) Ego, on account of its identical superimposition on the 'attributeless consciousness' regards consciousness as the 'substratum of the activity'—is erroneous knowledge. The object of this erroneous knowledge is consciousness. To be such an object is the bondage of consciousness, and in the state of liberation the consciousness becomes liberated from the activity of the false knowledge. The bondage and liberation in connection with consciousness are not inconsistent.

All these arguments can be easily refuted:

(a) According to the non-dualism superimposition is a function of conscience. Naturally its substratum will be conscience and not consciousness. Therefore, it would not be correct to maintain consciousness as the locus of the activity.

(b) The substratum of bondage is ego and not consciousness. As such bondage cannot be established in consciousness.

(c) Simply on account of the objectivity of the false knowledge, it would be incorrect to accept bondage in consciousness. This is ascertained by an illustration of our normal experience in daily life. For instance, when people regard 'Mahatma Gandhi' as a very kind-hearted and noble person, he would not become cruel due to falsity of experience or some wrong information about him. An atheist does not believe in the existence of God, but God does not become non-existent for a believer orthodox simply by this (non-belief). If a blind person cannot see the light of Sun, this is not the fault of Sun. It is the visionary defect of an eye. Likewise, it is true that on account of ego the 'attributeless consciousness' is regarded as the locus of the activity but there could not be any defect in the consciousness on account of erroneous knowledge or false understanding. In the absence of any defect, bondage in consciousness remains out of question and all efforts towards liberation would be entirely useless.

In this context the point of view of Sāṁkhya philosophy appears to be more reasonable. According to the Sāṁkhya system the Self (Puruṣa) is unattached, pure consciousness and the permanent changeless. Bondage and liberation are in relation with causal matter (Prakṛti). Both remain out of question so far as pure consciousness is concerned. The outlook of Sāṁkhya is justified by the reasoning that matter is bound and that intellect exists in the state of bondage by its very nature and in the state of liberation in the causal form.[27] Bondage means a false unification of consciousness with matter, and liberation means it dissociation in Sāṁkhya. To accept bondage and liberation in consciousness is not a very sound proposition because in non-dualism consciousness is regarded as 'attributeless'. Neither bondage nor liberation could exist in the ego because the ego has no causal form in the state of liberation.

Testimony of the Upaniṣads

I now examine the testimony of the Chāndogya and the Kaṭha Upaniṣads along with the Bhāṣyas of Śaṅkarācārya and Rāmānujācārya on the concept of 'I-sense-Self' theory. Taking into consideration the 'Science of Unconditioned Supreme Self' (Bhūmā-vidyā)[28] as propounded in the Chāndogya Upaniṣad, the Non-dualist establishes a difference between the 'I-sense' and the 'Self' and a non-difference between the 'I-sense' and the ego. The science has been explained in three stages in the Chāndogya Upaniṣad:

1. From 'sa eva adhastāt 7.25.1' to 'sa eva idaṁ sarvam', declaring the, unconditioned Supreme Self' as all pervading.
2. From 'atha ataḥ ahaṁkārādeśaḥ', to 'aham eva edaṁ sarvam' announcing the 'I-sense' of the nature of ego as all pervading. It is on this evidence that identity of 'I-sense' and ego has been interpreted by the followers of non-dualism.
3. From 'atha ataḥ Ātmādeśaḥ' to 'Ātvaiva adhastāt' to Ātmaiva idaṁ sarvam 7.25.2, stating 'Self' as all pervading.

The main argument of the Non-dualist against the 'I-sense-self' theory is that if 'I-sense' and 'Self' were identical the instruction of an ego (aham artha ādeśa) alone would be sufficient in the present context. The instruction of a 'Self' (Ātmādeśa) bears testimony to the fact that an 'I-sense' and a 'Self' are not identical.

Let us carefully examine this Upaniṣadic evidence. It is clear from the study of the Chāndogya Upaniṣad that the 'unconditioned Supreme Self', 'I-sense' and 'Self' all three have independently been spoken of as all pervading. It would therefore be not correct to consider them different; or else on the basis of the same Upaniṣadic testimony and same logic the 'unconditioned Supreme Self' and the 'Self' would also be regarded as different, while even in non-dualism they are both regarded as identical in essence. If the identity of the 'unconditioned Supreme Self' and 'Self' is accepted in spite of their separately being pointed out in the text, the identity of 'I-sense' and 'Self' could not be denied.

A comparison of the Śāṅkara Bhāṣya and the Rāmānuja Bhāṣya on the Chāndogya Upaniṣad quoted above clarifies a number of points. I present below a brief comparative study of the two bhāṣyas for the ready reference of the readers.

The Śāṅkara Bhāṣya interprets the passage in question as follows: 'Verily that extends below, it extends from above, it extends from behind, it extends from before, it extends from south, it extends from north,—of a truth it is all this.'[29]

Śaṅkarācārya clearly states in his bhāṣya that the 'unconditioned Supreme Self' is meant by the word 'That', therefore, one might be confused that the 'Self' is different from the 'unconditioned Supreme Self'.[30] To avoid this confusion the Chāndogya Upaniṣad imparts the instruction of ego defined as egoistically in the following way: 'Verily I extend from below, I extend from above, I extend from behind, I extend from before, I extend from south, I extend from north,—of a truth I am all this'.[31]

The purport of the Śāṅkara-bhāṣya is very clear that the teaching of the instruction of ego is meant to prove the identity of the 'perceiver individual Self' and the 'unconditioned Supreme Self'. One should not therefore confuse this instruction of ego to prove the identity of the 'unconditioned Supreme Self' and the multitude of the body, mind, senses and vital airs as an ordinary man takes this multitude as 'I', and thereupon for want of discrimination regards the multitude as 'I-sense'. To avoid this confusion the Chāndogya Upaniṣad finally imparts the instruction of 'Self' defined as psychically: 'Verily, the 'Self' extends from below, the Self extends from above, the Self extends from behind, the Self extends from before, the Self extends from south, the Self extends from north,—of a truth the Self is all this.'[32]

The final instruction obviously covers the pure and eternal 'Self'. The study of the Śāṅkara-bhāṣya reveals that the 'unconditioned Self' (Bhūman) indirectly described as 'That', the 'perceiver individual Self' or 'I-sense' directly described as 'I', and the 'Self' directly described as 'Self' all are one and the same. It is just to avoid any misunderstanding that the description is threefold. In no way can a difference between 'I-sense' and 'Self' be proved by an impartial review of the Chāndogya testimony. In the beginning of all these instructions we read, 'It extends below', 'I extend below', and 'The Self extends below'. Had the 'unconditioned Self', 'I-sense' and 'Self' been different, the all-pervasiveness of the three could not be rightly justified. The reasoning, that the separate instruction is to establish a difference between the 'I-sense' and the 'Self', is incongruous to the spirit of the Śāṅkara-bhāṣya.

According to the Rāmānuja-bhāṣya the 'unconditioned Supreme Self' is omniscient, and all the sentient and insentient objects of the universe exist in the form of the inner Self. One should meditate upon the 'unconditioned Supreme Inner Self' through the feeling of 'I', (aham buddhi), i.e. 'I am everywhere'. By meditating on the Supreme Self in this form of one's own individual inner Self through the feeling of 'I', one distinctly realises the difference between individual Self and the Supreme Self. The idea is elaborated by an illustration. When we say 'The jar is blue', we do not distinguish blue quality from the substance. The instruction of 'I-sense-ego' is thus to make an aspirant realize the separate existence of the 'Supreme Self' within himself. We should not forget that ego stands here for the feeling of 'I' and the instruction of ego means to denote that one should meditate upon the 'unconditioned Supreme Self' through the feeling of 'I'. The Sanskrit word 'ahaṁkāra' referred to in this context is derived from the root $\sqrt{}$Kṛ to do preceded by by the noun 'aham' with the suffix 'ghañ' in the sense of abstract idea, meaning the production of 'I-idea' known as ego.[33]

It may be recalled that the feeling of 'I' is produced only in relation to the individual Self. It is never produced in relation to the 'Supreme Self' because the 'Supreme Self' does not become the object of the feeling of 'I'. The testimony of the Chāndogya

Upaniṣad discussed above is a conclusive proof that the word 'aham' (I), denoting individual Self, stands for the individual inner Self. It is only through the individual inner Self that the Supreme Inner Self becomes realised. The 'Supreme Self' is thus the inner self of the individual self, and the 'Supreme Self' is meditated upon through the feeling of 'I' because He is the inner self of the individual Self. The instruction of the 'Self' is therefore meant to establish that the 'Supreme Self' is the inner Self of the individual Self, and that He becomes related through the feeling of 'I' alone. In this way according to Rāmānuja there is complete identification among the 'unconditioned Supreme Self', 'I-sense' and 'Self' and that all these three stand for one and the same Ultimate Reality.

The Kaṭha Upaniṣad states that 'Our senses have been created by God with a tendency to move outward. It is for this reason that man looks outside himself rather than inside. Rarely a wise man, who is desirous of immortal life, looks to his inner Self with his eye turned inwards'.[34] The Kaṭha Upaniṣad testifies that the realisation of the individual inner Self is the only means to attain liberation. This means is indirect while the realisation of the Supreme Self is the direct means of liberation.

Dr. S. Radhakrishnan has rightly concluded in the Principal Upaniṣads (London, 1933, pp. 93-94). 'There does not seem to be any suggestion that the individual egos are unreal. They all exist through the Self and have no reality apart from it. The insistence on the unity of the Supreme Self as the constituent reality of the world and of the individual souls does not negate the empirical reality of the latter.'

Meaning of Pratyak-Ātman and Parāk-Ātman

It would be most helpful to understand the doctrine of 'aham-artha' as identical with 'Self' if we interpret these two technical terms of Vedānta philosophy. Both these terms have been used by the followers of Advaita and Vaiṣṇava Vedānta alike. To begin with, let me recall that Pratyak-Ātman stands for Jīva-Ātman (individual Self) when we accept the compound 'karmadhāraya', while the same word stands for Paramātman (Supreme Self of the individual Self) if a 'tatpuruṣa' compound is accepted. Either compound interprets the word 'Pratyak' in the sense of the 'self'. Therefore, the 'pratyaktva' proves that 'Self' is 'I-sense'.

Pratyak means directed inwards. It stands for the individual inner 'Self'. Parāk means directed outwards or towards the outer world (as the senses). Pratyak is self-luminous and Parāk is illumined by another. The sense of Pratyak is obviously opposed to that of Parāk. In Advaita, cognition is regarded as self-luminous. Therefore, 'Self' of the nature of cognition is Pratyak Ātman. Parāk is explained as 'param prakāśakatayā añcati', signifying it as 'paraprakāśa', i.e. which is luminous by another. On the basis of this interpretation the Non-dualist again makes an attempt to deny the identity of 'I-sense' and 'Self'. It is therefore essential to re-examine the meaning of these two terms along the tradition of Vaiṣṇava Vedānta.

The Non-dualistic interpretation is rejected on the following grounds:

1. Pratyak would now be bracketed with pain, pleasure and desire because they are also self-luminous, so long they exist.
2. Cognition is regarded as a characteristic of 'I-sense'. As such, cognition is a 'dharma' (attribute or special characteristic mark) and 'I-sense' is a 'dharmin' (where the special characteristic or properties of having the nature reside). According to the above interpretation cognition is dependent. Therefore only the independent 'I-sense' would be regarded as the individual 'inner Self' and not the dependent cognition.
3. The Naiyāyika and the Vaiśeṣika totally reject any self-luminous entity. According to them 'Self' (Ātman) is known as 'inner Self' (Pratyak-Ātman). Neither of these sister schools of logic of Indian philosophy consider 'Self' as self-luminous.

The older Vaiṣṇava tradition interprets in the following way:

(a) Pratyak literally means going backwards or directed inwards (pratīpam añcati). It denotes the 'Self' existing inside the body, mind, intellect, ego and senses and controlling them together. Needless to say that all schools of Vedānta refer to 'Self' by the term 'Pratyak-Ātman'. Every human being has the mental perception of 'I' which denotes 'Self' and nothing else. The object of this shines of itself, i.e. illuminates itself and this very object is known as the 'Self'.[36] Furthermore, in case the

'I-sense' is different from 'Self', 'Self' will not be accepted as 'Pratyak' because it is only on account of Self arrogating thought that 'Pratyak' is distinguished from 'Parāk'.[37]

(b) 'Parāk' literally means directed towards the outer world as the senses. Any object, therefore, which attains another or is attained by another or illumines another is understood as 'Parāk' (Param añitca prāpnoti, parenopādīyate parasmai prakāśate). Parāk is therefore that which exists for another. All the objects of the universe such as jar etc. exist for 'I-sense'-Self' because their ultimate result goes to 'I-sense-Self'. Hence Parāk.[38]

Pratyagartha is obviously different from Parāgratha and Prayagartha and 'I' are identical, 'Jīva' is known as individual 'Self' or 'Ātman' when conditioned by a body, known as consciousness when it becomes a substratum of knowledge, and as Pratyak when there is feeling of 'I' due to attributive consciousness (dharmabhūta jñāna).[39] An individual inner Self marked as 'A' is not considered as Pratyak for another individual inner Self marked as 'B' because 'A' is not experienced as 'I' by 'B'. Therefore Pratyak is an object of the feeling of 'I'. This feeling of 'I' is not different from 'I-sense'.

This thesis of Vaiṣṇavism is fully supported by th. Vaiśeṣika school of Indian philosophy.[40] The Vaiśeṣika Sūtras of Kaṇāda clearly indicate that the apprehension of feeling of 'I' is related to one's own individual inner 'Self' and that 'I' is never considered as the 'Self' of another individual being. We comprehend the idea of 'I' as related to one's own 'Self'. If the body was 'Self' and the object of 'I-apprehension' was body, the body of another being would also have been apprehended as 'I'. Such is not our experience in life. Therefore, the object of our 'I-apprehension' is something different from the body and that is 'Self'. 'I-apprehension' is always in connection with one's own individual 'Self'. The nature of the individual inner 'Self' is an object of one's own perception but the nature of the 'Self' of another being is only an object of inferential knowledge. The distinction among different individual 'Selves' is thus obvious.

A comparative study of the commentary of Śaṅkara Miśra, the gloss of Jayanārāyaṇa and the bhāṣya of Chandrakānta on the above referred Vaiśeṣika Sūtras of Kaṇāda makes it quite clear that since the intuitional apprehension 'I' arises in respect of one's own 'Self' and since it does not exist in respect of other

'Self' it is proper to regard one's own individual inner 'Self' as the primary reference. In case the primary reference were to the body, the intuitional apprehension should have been produced by external senses because the body is not an object of mental perception. The apprehension 'This is 'I' is mental because it is produced without the operation of external senses. The apprehension is neither inferential for want of logical reason, nor verbally communicated for want of authoritative text. It is further noteworthy that it refers to one's own individual 'Self' and not to the 'Self' of another for the 'Self' of one man remains beyond the senses of another man.[41]

In the prima facie view an objection is raised by the Non-dualist against his own point of view that 'the objects and their relative peculiar characteristics are superimposed on the individual inner Self', the substratum, on the simple logic that the substratum is never accepted as an object of knowledge. Unless one acquires the knowledge of substratum, the superimposition remains out of question. It may thus be explained that it is only after the knowledge of substratum that superimposition of silver on the conch-shell is experienced.[42] The prima facie view is rejected in the Śaṅkara-bhāṣya, wherein the individual inner 'Self' (Pratyak-Ātman) is not accepted as an absolute non-object of knowledge. Accordingly the individual inner 'Self' does become the object of intuitional apprehension of 'I'[43]. One does experience the idea of 'I-ness' in relation to the individual inner 'Self'. In case 'Self' was not an object of the apprehension of 'I' and was simply an object of the apprehension of conscience, we would have called the 'Self' as 'This' and not as 'I' because conscience being inanimate could only be designated by 'This' or 'That'.

A study of the Śaṅkara-bhāṣya shows that Pratyagartha and Parāgartha are two entirely different philosophical notions. Pratyagartha denotes the idea of 'I-ness' going towards the knower, while Parāgartha is always an object of the apprehension of 'This' or 'That'. There is no objectivity of 'I-apprehension' in relation to 'Pratyak-Ātman' and it is further to be kept in mind that the objectivity of 'I-apprehension' is always related to the objectivity of perception. Therefore, Pratyak-Ātman is definitely an object of 'I-apprehension'. To make it more comprehensive it is stated that we do acquire the knowledge of substratum which is none else but Pratyak-Ātman and there should be no hindrance in accepting the superimposition of the objects and their special characteristic marks in Pratyak-Ātman. The Śāṅkara-Bhāṣya, on a close perusal, makes it clear that even Śaṅkarācārya has distinguished Parāgartha from Pratyagartha on the basis of 'I-intellect'. This attests that the idea of 'I-ness' is identical with the idea of individual inner 'Self' (i.e. Pratyak-Ātman).

Let us carefully examine the above-mentioned view of the non-dualism that not pure consciousness but consciousness conditioned by conscience is the object of 'I-apprehension'. Suffice to say that conscience as a limiting adjunct is an object of 'This-apprehension'. As such in the consciousness which is distinguished by the limiting adjunct, the 'I-apprehension' automatically steps in. If 'Self' is not accepted as an object of 'I-apprehension', the 'I-apprehension' would have no scope at all (nirviṣaya). It is needless to say that the objectivity of 'I-apprehension' is not acceptable even to Non-dualist. It is therefore a demand of propriety that the 'Self' of the nature of consciousness should be accepted as an object of 'I-apprehension' which is not different from the idea of 'I-ness'.

We have already seen that there is some basic difference between Non-dualist and Vaiṣṇava points of views. The Non-dualist maintains that the idea of 'Self' exists in 'I-apprehension' and it is only due to this fact that the 'Self' is recognised as perceptible, but the Non-dualist is not prepared to accept that in this 'I-apprehension' exists an imposition of 'I-ness' of conscience. Suffice to enquire that when the Non-dualist accepts the idea of 'Self' in 'I-apprehension', why not accept the 'Self' as the 'I-sense' instead of travelling through the imposition of 'I-sense' on 'Self'. Our experience becomes quite normal just by accepting the identity of 'I-sense' and 'Self'. Moreover, in the case of the imposition such as the crystal and the red flower, the redness of the flower is reflected on the crystal. The flower appears red apart from the crystal and the crystal appears red in the close proximity of the flower. It therefore becomes acceptable that the redness of the flower is reflected on the crystal. Such is not the condition between 'I-sense' of conscience and 'Self' because conscience never appears as 'I' apart from 'Self'. Hence the identity of the 'I-sense' and the 'Self'.

In case the 'I-sense' resides in the 'Self' as an attribute of ego, an aspect of consciousness as generally accepted by Non-dualist, one may question what is the locus of 'I-ness' in relation to God (Īśvara) as described in the Upaniṣadic tradition.[44] 'I-sense' could certainly be accepted as an attribute of conscience and ego when God is conceived as consciousness conditioned by conscience or as consciousness conditioned by an ego; but it is a known fact that in Advaita Vedānta God is regarded as consciousness conditioned by Māyā.[45] It may be kept in mind that there is no idea of 'I-ness' in the state of Māyā. Truly, ego remains non-existent prior to godly supreme determination such as 'I wish to be many' and ego is produced only after the creation of the principle of intelligence (mahat), the first evolution according to Sāṁkhya philosophy.[46]

We are now left with no other alternative but to accept that 'I-ness' in God is not to be imposed from outside but that it belongs to God from within. This enables us to maintain that ego, a modification of causal matter (Prakṛti) is not 'I-sense' but 'Self' is 'I-sense'. Besides, 'I-intellect' is God as evidenced by the Upaniṣadic tradition.[47] This very knowledge is regarded as the righ knowledge because misapprehension of any sort is impossible in omniscient God. Therefore, 'I-ness' as described in God could not be an imposed one. By accepting an imposition of the 'I-ness' on God, one indirectly accepts the existence of misapprehension in God. On account of the non-existence of ego at the time of godly supreme determination and on account of the non-existence of ego in God, the apparent 'I-ness' in God has got to be accepted as belonging to the misapprehension of God.

I should further elucidate the Advaita point of view. The Non-dualist explains that in the intuitional apprehension of 'I' the united ego and consciousness appear as the basis of the mutual identical superimposition. I have already explained in detail the notion of the uniting element of animate and inanimate accepted as the 'I-sense' in non-dualism. Now it would be interesting to examine the Cārvāka point of view in this regard. It is a well-known fact that all the six orthodox system of Indian philosophy refute the 'body-Self' concept of Cārvāka and all of them unanimously agree that body is neither 'I-sense' nor consciousness. Therefore, it is not very scholarly to declare the body as 'Self'. In the false identification of 'Self' with the body, as the Cārvāka maintains, he has to accept 'I-intellect' in the body and therein appears the identification of a body with the ego and consciousness. The 'Self' of the nature of consciousness appears identical with the body due to false knowledge.

The Non-dualist attacks against the Cārvāka on the ground that first and foremost we should not forget that the 'Self' of the nature of consciousness appears as 'I' due to false identity with conscience. Therefore, this very 'I' getting identical with the body appears as 'I am handsome', 'I am ugly', 'I am fat', 'I am of dark complexion'. This kind of apprehension is known as false identification with the body. To eradicate this wrong notion, the Non-dualist has first to establish difference between 'I-sense' and the body and then has to remove the misapprehension of non-difference between ego and consciousness and finally has to establish non-identity of 'Self' and ego.

It has already been observed that 'I-sense' does not mean the uniting element of animate and inanimate but it is 'Self' itself. The false identification with the body is not very different from the misapprehension of non-difference between 'I-sense' and 'non-Self' (anātman): No misapprehension can logically be established at the root of the false identification with the body as indirectly advocated by the Non-dualist in the form of misapprehension between consciousness and ego. Furthermore, the celebrated writer of the Iṣṭasiddhi accepts the object illuminating knowledge as objectless or having no scope and without any substratum. He declares that this very knowledge is the principal characteristic of the 'Self'. The object illuminating knowledge appears as an attribute of 'I-sense' on the basis of the apprehension, 'I know'. The difference between 'I-sense' and knowledge as characteristic (dharma) and as that which possess the characteristic (dharmin) is obvious. The misapprehension of non-difference between 'attributeless Self' and 'I-sense' is an impossibility.

I have already mentioned that the Non-dualist interprets the word 'aham' (I) as conscience when there is false identification with the ego and superimposition of the ego as consciousness conditoned by conscience when there is false identification with the body. This involves a defect, because there is only one meaning of 'I-sense' and that meaning is 'Self'.

Upavarṣa and Vedāntadeśika

Upavarṣa, a pre-Śaṅkara author of several writings on

Mīmāṁsā philosophy and his followers accept complete identity of 'I-sense' and 'Self'. They clearly propound that the 'Self' is an object of 'I-apprehension'. Jayanta Bhaṭṭa (9th century), one of the most celebrated logicians of the old school of Hindu logic clearly refers to the tradition of Upavarṣa in his Nyāya-mañjarī, and of the followers of Upavarṣa who directly realised the 'Self' as an object of the feeling of 'I-apprehension'. Some scholars hold that this Upavarṣa was none else but Baudhāyana. We are still not in a position to accept this view for want of valid evidence. In my opinion this Upavarṣa was the younger brother of Varṣa, the teacher of Pāṇini, the most celebrated Indian grammarian. Evidently by the time of Jayanta Bhaṭṭa the tradition of Upavarṣa occupied a prominent place in ancient Indian philosophical thought. Jayanta Bhaṭṭa clearly states that Upavarṣa and his followers of the Pūrva Mīmāṁsā accept complete identification of 'I-sense' and 'Self'.[48]

The 'I-sense-Self' theory has a support in the course of the long history of Indian philosophy. It has been supported by the Cārvāka, Bauddha,[49] Naiyāyika, Vaiśeṣika, Pūrva Mīmāṁsaka and Vaiṣṇava Ācāryas with special reference to Rāmānuja school of Vedānta. The evidences from Yāmunācārya and Vedānta-Deśika produce ample testimony in favour of this theory.

Yāmunācārya maintains that it is proved beyond doubt by logic and verbal testimony that 'Self' and 'I-sense' are identical and that the 'Self' is knower.[49] The two statements 'I know' and 'I do not know' indicate the existence of knowledge and ignorance in 'I-cognition' in relation to the difference of time. This is our normal experience that by the rise of a particular knowledge in 'I-cognition' the previous ignorance is dispelled. The 'Self' misapprehends itself as body in the apprehension, 'I am fat', 'I am weak'. This is certainly nescience in the form of false apprehension with the body. Nescience is possible only when we accept 'I-ness' and 'knowerness' (jñātṛttva) in the 'Self'. In the absence of 'I-ness' and 'knowerness' in the 'Self' the false identification with the body remains an impossibility. Hence knower Self-'I-sense'.[50]

In fine, I put forward the conclusive evidence from Vedānta-deśika, the well-known great Guru (mahādeśika) who has fully supported the 'I-sense-Self' theory on the basis of the following arguments:

प्रत्यक्त्वादुपलम्भतो मम सुखं भावीति मोक्षेच्छया
मुक्तब्रह्ममुमुक्षुवेदवचसा सुप्तोऽहमित्युक्तितः ।
मां नाज्ञासिषमित्यपि स्ववपुराद्यज्ञानमात्राश्रयात्
स्वापप्राच्यनिजक्रियास्मरणतोऽप्यात्माहमर्थः स्थिरः ॥

1. 'Self' (Ātman) is the individual inner Self (Pratyak) and non-Self is 'Parāk'. The nature of individual inner 'Self' is self-luminous, while 'Parāk' illumines another or illumines for another. Pratyak is connected with the idea of 'I' and Parāk to an object denoted by 'This' and 'That'. 'I-sense' exists for itself and the objects exist for the benefit of 'I-sense'. Therefore, 'I-sense' is 'Self'.
2. The 'Self' is regarded as eternal, animate and knower.[51] Our normal experience is as follows: 'I am the knower'.[52] This attests that wherever 'I-ness' and 'knowerness' exist, the conscious 'I-sense-Self' also exists.
3. The philosophical thinking maintains that the 'Self' experiences the miseries of the mundane world and desires to attain liberation in order to get rid of the cycle of birth and death. Such an intensive desire impels 'Self' to follow the means of liberation. The experience of miseries, the desire to get rid of them and the desire to enjoy the inexhaustible bliss in the state of liberation could belong to 'I-sense' alone.
4. Here are five questions from the Vedic literature. They are ascribed to liberated persons, the Supreme Self, and persons desirous of liberation. Vedāntadeśika attaches primary importance to the authority of the Vedic testimony in support of the theory of 'I-sense-Self'.

   (a) 'I am food (Taittirīya Upaniṣad III.13.6). This is a statement of a liberated person.
   (b) 'I became Manu' (Bṛhadāraṇyaka Upaniṣad 1.4.10). A statement of Vāmadeva who is regarded as a liberated person while alive.
   (c) 'I enter in all in the form of life.'[53] A statement of Supreme Self.
   (d) 'I go for refuge to all-Effulgent Self.'[54] A statement of one who is desirous of liberation.
   (e) 'I was alone in the beginning' (ahamekaḥ prathama-

māsam) Atharvaveda. Vedic testimony. All the above quoted citations testify identity of 'I-sense' and 'Self'.

5. We know by now that according to Advaita Vedanta the gross ego is the 'I-sense' and it is destroyed in the state of profound repose. Our experience is however different. It tells us when awaking from profound repose that one slept so long happily but did not know anything. Hence the existence of 'I-sense' in profound repose. Only 'I-sense' existent in profound repose could be Self and nothing else. According to non-dualism, conscience does exist in profound repose. In the case where conscience is the 'I-sense', one should have the apprehension 'I was non-existent during profound repose'. Since such is never our experience, it follows that 'I-sense' is 'Self'.
6. In the tradition of Advaita Vedānta, the 'Self' is regarded as self-luminous (svayaṁprakāśa) and eternal. As such, the 'Self' continues to illumine and exist in profound repose. In the case where the 'I-sense' is the 'Self' argues the Non-dualist, the 'I-sense' should have been existent in profound repose. Nevertheless, such is not the case because the 'Self' in profound repose does not remain aware of 'I'. Therefore, self-luminous 'Self' is not 'I-sense'. Besides, awaking from profound repose it tells us that one had no awareness even of oneself. Such an experience establishes negation of 'I-sense' in the state of profound repose. The non-existence of 'I-sense' and self-luminous Self in the state of profound repose are two entirely different concepts of Vedānta and they are not identical, maintains the Non-dualist.

The above view of Advaita Vedānta does not hold good on the following grounds: (1) The 'I-sense-Self' illumines itself in the states of awaking, dream, profound repose and swoon, on the basis of the attributes such as oneness, the state of individual inner 'Self' and concord. (2) The illumination pertains to the inherent nature of 'Self' or 'I-sense'. Thus the self-luminous 'I-sense-Self' illumines in the state of awaking, and dream on account of the qualities viz. knowledge, desire, happiness and unhappiness by attributive consciousness (dharma-bhūta jñāna). During the state of profound repose the 'Self' does not illumine by attributive consciousness but by its own nature. The attributive consciousness, over-powered by tamas, becomes contracted during profound repose. Truly, the 'I-sense-Self' being endowed with the attributes oneness, the state of individual inner 'Self' and concord illumines by its own nature during profound repose but does not remember the various attributes of name, form, varṇa and Āśrama such as a Brāhmaṇa, a Sannyāsin on the simple ground that the attributive consciousness remains hidden. The meaning of the statement 'I had no awareness even of myself' is as follows: I had no similar awareness of myself during profound repose as I always have during the state of awaking. As I understand myself as a brāhmaṇa, or as a sannyāsin or a Professor or an Ambassador during awaking on the basis of outer attributes. I had no memory of any such attribute during profound repose. In this way, the objection of the Non-dualist against the existence and illumination of 'I-sense' during profound repose and against the identity of 'I-sense' and 'Self' is clearly rejected.

I therefore conclude that the 'I-sense' and the 'Self' are identical. The 'I-sense' is not the non-self as maintained by the Non-dualist. The 'I-sense' exists in the dreamless profound sleep. In the state of liberation, the 'I-sense', abandoning all undesirable wordly forms, names, shapes and attributes exists in its pure form and as such 'I-sense' is properly entitled to study the scriptures, the best means of liberation. The identity of 'I-sense' and 'Self' may therefore be tacitily accepted.

References

1. Īśvarakṛṣṇa, Sāṁkhya-Kārikā, 25.

2. The Ātman-Puruṣa of Sāṁkhya is in reality 'Nirguṇa'. This view of Sāṁkhya is evident from the Mādhyamakāvatāra VI, 121 quoted in the Prasannapadā commentary of Chandrakīrti on Nāgārjuna's (Mūla) Mādhyamakakārikā; cf. Murti, T.R.V., The Central Philosophy of Buddhism, London, 1955, p. 203.

3. The problem of Self and non-Self in Hindu and Buddhist tradition has never ceased to interest researchers, cf. Guha Abhyankumar, 'Jīvātman in the Brahmasūtra', Calcutta, 1921; Mrs. Rhys Davids, 'The Birth of Indian Psychology and its Development in Buddhism', London, 1936; Narahari, H.G., 'Ātman in pre-Upaniṣadic Vedic Literature', Madras, 1944; Gonda, J. 'Notes on Brahman', Utrecht, 1950; Lacombe, O. 'La Direction Spirituelle selon les tradition indiennes, dans Direction spirituelle et Psychologie', (Etudes Carmilitaries) Bruges, 1951; Biardeau Madeline, 'La Philosophie de Maṇḍana

Miśra vue a partir de la Brahma-Siddhi, Paris, 1969; L'Ātman-Brahman dans le Buddhism Ancien, Bhaṭṭācharya Kamaleswar, Paris, 1973.

4. Sengupta Anima, 'The Evolution of the Sāṁkhya School of Thought', 1959, Patna, pp. 70-80.

5. Brahmasūtra 2.4.12 (ed) Sivanand Saraswati, Rishikesh, 1949, pp. 523-24.

6. Joshi Rasik Vihari, 'The Role of Indian Logic in the Doctrine of Causality', Melanges d'Indianisme a la Memoire de Louis Renou, Paris, 1968, pp. 403-08.

7. Bṛhadāraṇyaka Upaniṣad IV.3.22.

8. Śāṅkara Bhāṣya on the Brahmasūtra 11.2.29. (ed.) Saraswati Satyananda, Varanasi, Samvat 2028, pp. 508-10.

9. Ibid., II.3.30.

10. Ibid., II.3.31, p. 512.

11. Ibid., II.3.32. 'Nityopalabdyanupalabdhiprasaṅgaḥ anyataraniyamo vānyathā.'

12. Tripathi, Manassukharama Suryarama, 'A Sketch of the Vedanta Philosophy', Bombay, 1910, p. 140.

13. Lacombe, O. 'L' Absolu selon le Vedanta', Guenther, Paris, 1937, pp. 28-35; op. cit. Tripathi Manassukharama, Suryarama, 'Śāṅkara Vedanta interprets the Vedanta unity by harmony between Egotism and Altruism', pp. 126-32.

14. (a) La Kaśikā-Vṛtti, (ed.) Yutaka Ojihara et Louis Renou, Paris, 1960-67.
(b) Tattva-muktā-kalāpa of Vedāntadeśika, (Bhāvaprakāśa pp. 40-41) Vol. II. (ed.) S. Narasimhachar, Mysore, 1940.

15. Manobuddhirahaṁkāraścittam karaṇamantaram,
sanśayo niścayo garvaḥ smaraṇam viṣayā ime/
Śāṅkara-Bhāṣya on Brahmasūtra, Op.Cit. Satyanand Saraswati, p. 544.

16. avidyātmikā hi bījaśaktiḥ avyaktaśabdanirdeśyā
Parameśvarāśrayā māyāmayī mahāsuṣuptiḥ/
Śāṅkara Bhāṣya on the Brahmasūtra (ed.) Saraswati Satyanand, Varanasi, Samvat 2028, pp. 287-88.

17. 'Even in the state of dreamless sleep, though there is no consciousness of objects, still the sense of 'I' (ahamartha) persists.'
The Vedanta, Ghate, V.S., Poona, 1960, p. 25.

18. The Twelve Principal Upaniṣads (Chāndogya Upaniṣad (13.1) (ed.) Mitra and Cowell, Vol. III, p. 274.

19. Op. Cit., Ibid., p. 274.

20. Cf. Mitra and Cowell, Taittirīya Upaniṣad, 3.30, pp. 231-32; Ranade, R.D., A Constructive Survey of Upanisadic Philosophy, Bombay, 1967 p. 257.

21. ahamartha-vināśaścen mokṣa ityadhivasyati,
apasarpedasau mokṣakathāprastāvagandhataḥ/
Śrībhāṣya p. 67 (ed.) Annangaracharya, Kanchipuram, 1956.

22. 'ahamityeva hi tasya svarūpam' Śrī Yāmunāchārya's Siddhitraya (Ātmasiddhi p. 39) (ed.) Rāmānujāchārya, Madras, 1972.

23. "........the mundane is itself the transmundane and the transmundane

it itself the mundane." Venkata Ramanan, Nāgārjuna's Philosophy as Presented in the Mahā-Prajñā-Pāramitā-Śāstra, Tokyo, 1966, p. 122.

24. Tameva viditvātimṛtyumeti nānyaḥ panthāḥ vidyate 'nayāya/ Śvetāśvatara Upaniṣad, (ed.) Swami Tyagishvaranand, Madras, 1957, pp. 70-71.

25. Brahmavid Brahmaiva bhavati/Māṇḍūkya Upaniṣad 3.2.9.

26. Cf. op. cit., Mitra and Cowell, (Chāndogya Upaniṣad) Vol. III, pp. 247-48.

27. Sāṁkhya-Kārikā of Īśvarakṛṣṇa 62 and 63; cf. Mukerji, J.N., The Theory of Reality, Calcutta, 1930, pp. 60-64, 97-98; Sengupta Anima, 'The Evolution of the Sāṁkhya School of Thought', Patna, 1959, pp. 49-51.

28. 'It is Sanatkumāra who teaches the doctrine of Bhūman. Bhūman is that infinite happiness which arises by the vision of the divinity all around. A Constructive Survey of Upanishadic Philosophy, Ranade, R.D., Bombay, 1968, p. 37.

29. Chāndogya Upaniṣad VII.25.1, op. cit., The Twelve Principal Upaniṣads, (ed.) Rajendralal Mitra and E.B. Cowell, Madras, 1932, Vol. III, p. 245.

30. Chāndogya Upaniṣad, Śaṅkarāchārya-granthāvalī, Delhi, 1964, pp. 296-97. As regards the 'neti neti prakriyā' of Advaita Vedanta, Mrs. Rhys Davids has observed, 'this is as if one were to come abored asking for the captain and rejecting boatswain and purser as being 'not he' were to go away saying 'there is no captain'. 'The Self' : an over looked Buddhist Simile, JRAS, 1937, p. 260.

31. op. cit. Chāndogya...pp. 245-46; Cf. Tattva-muktākalāpa' of Vedāntadeśika (Bhāvaprakāśa pp. 230-31) (ed.) S. Narasimhachar, Mysore, Vol. II, 1940.

32. op. cit., Chāndogya... p. 246.

33. ahaṁkaraṇam ahamkāraḥ.

34. Kaṭha Upaniṣad II.4.1; cf. Ranade, A Constructive Survey of Upanisadic Philosophy, p. 247.

35. Finite Self (Ramanujist Idea of Self) (ed.) Bon Maharaj, Vrindaban, 1963, pp. 14-20.

36. 'svasmati prakāśamānatvarūpam pratyaktvam', Śrībhāṣya, Sūtraprakāśikā, p. 94; op.cit. Finite Self, pp. 14-15.

37. 'ahamartho na cedātma pratyaktvam nātmanām bhavet, ahambudhyā parāgarthāt pratyagartho hi bhidhyate/ Śrībhāṣya, p. 67 (ed.) Annangaracarya, Kancipuram, 1956. 'sa sādhanānuṣṭhānena yadyahameva na bhaviṣyāmi ityavagacchet, apasarpedevasau mokṣakathāprastāvāt; tataśca adhikāriviraḥādeva sarvam mokṣasāstram apramāṇam syāt/Ibid., p. 71.

Cf. Yāmunācārya's Siddhitraya (Ātmasiddhi, p. 39) (ed.) Ramanujacharya, Madras, 1972.

38. Tattavmuktākalāpa of Vedāntadeśika (Sarvārthasiddhi, Ānandadāyinī and Bhāvaprakāśa commentaries on verses Nos. 6 and 7 of the Jīvasara chapter) (ed.) S. Narasimhachar, Mysore, 1940, Vol. II, pp. 208-69.

39. Śārīraka-mīmāṅsā-bhāṣya, 1.1.1 (Rāmānujagranthamālā) (ed.) Annangaracharya, Kanchipuram, 1956, p. 67.

40. 'ahamiti pratyagātmani bhāvāt paratvābhāvāt arthāntarapratyakṣaḥ/

The Vaiśeṣika Sūtras of Kaṇāda, III.2.14 (ed.) Basu B.D. and Sinha Nandlal, Allahabad, 1923.

41. Ibid., Basu and Sinha, pp. 124-25.

42. Joshi, Rasik Vihari, Validity of Knowledge in Indian Logic, Dr. V. Raghavan Felicitation Volume, Delhi, 1975, pp. 180-86.

43. 'na tāvadayam ekāntena aviṣayaḥ, asmatpratītiviṣayatvāt aparoṣkatvācca pratyagātmasiddheḥ/

Brahmasūtra Bhāṣya (ed.) Mahamahopadhyaya Anantakrishna Shastri, Bombay, 1938.

44. 'He (the Supreme Soul) desired: Let me become many, let me be born.' Taittirīya Upaniṣad II.6.2.

45. 'It's infinitesimal part becomes the qualified Brahman, through its association with the unreal principle of Māyā.' Tripathi, Manassukhram Suryarama; 'A Sketch of the Philosophy of Vedanta', Bombay, 1901, p. 73.

46. Sāṁkhya-kārikā of Īśvarakṛṣṇa, 22.

47. Chāndogya Upaniṣad, VI.3.2; 'Eighteen Principal Upanishads', (ed.) Limaye V.P. and Vadekar R.D., Poona, 1968.

48. 'Tatra pratyakṣa-mātmānam Aupavarṣāḥ Prapedire,
aham-pratyayagamyattvāt svayūthya api kecana/

Nyāyamañjarī of Jayanta Bhaṭṭa, (ed.) Madhvacharya Adya, Varanasi, 1969, Vol. II, p. 3.

49. "....one can say that the one accepts or denies Ātman as much as the other, both the Mādhyamaka and the Advaita Vedanta deny Ātman as a separate substantial entity inhabiting the body of each individual, and both accept Ātman in the sense of essential nature of the individual as well as of all things..., ātman brahman means there is hardly any difference between the two." K. Venkata Ramanam, Nagarjuna's philosophy as presented in Mahā-Prajñā-Pāramitā-śāstra, Rutland-Tokyo, 1966, p. 320.

50. Ataḥ pratyakṣa-siddhattvāt ukta-nyāyāgamānvayāt, avidyāyogataścātmā jñātāhamiti bhāsate/ The Siddhitraya of Yāmunācārya, (ed.) Ramanujacharya, Madras, (Ātmasiddhi, pp. 41-44), 1972.

51. 'Vedānta-deśika very clearly accepts in the Adhikaraṇasārāvalī that the individual inner 'Self, (Pratyak) is 'I-sense'. (Pratyaṅṅātmāhamarthaḥ), Adhikaraṇasārāvalī, p. 240 (ed.) Annangaracharya, Kanchivaram, 1940; cf. atohamartho jñātaiva pratyagātmeti niścitam/, Śrībhāṣya, p. 67 (ed.) Op.Cit., 1956.

52. 'He is eternal among the eternals and intelligent among all that are intelligent.' Śvetāśvatara Upaniṣad. (ed.) Swami Tyagishwaranand, Madras, 1957 (II.6.13)

53. 'entering these objects in the form of life (Self) I shall be manifest in various names and forms.' Chāngogya Upaniṣad, VI.3.2.

54. '......seeking liberation I go for refuge to the Effulgent one, who turns the understanding Ātman.' Śvetāśvatara Upaniṣad, VI.18.

CONTRIBUTORS

Prof. ANDRE BAREAU who was born 1921 near Paris, retired as Professor of Study of Buddhism at the Collège de France. He has published several works and numerous articles and monographs on Indian Buddhism, especially on the Buddha's biography, the history and doctrines of the ancient schools of the so-called Hīnayāna (*Les sectes bouddhiques du Petit Véhicule*, etc.).

Prof. KAMALESWAR BHATTACHARYA Docteur ès Letters (Paris), Directeur de Recherche (1st class) at the Centre National de la Recherche Scientifique, Paris, was formerly Visiting Professor, University of Toronto (Canada), etc. He has published: *Les Religions brahmaniques dans l'ancien Cambodge* (1961); *Recherches sur le vocabulaire des inscriptions sanskrites du Cambodge* (1964; 2nd edn., 1991); *L'Ātman-Brahman dans le Bouddhisme ancien* (1973); *The Dialectical Method of Nāgārjuna* (Vigrahavyāvartanī) (1978; 3rd edn., 1990); *Le Siddhāntalakṣaṇaprakaraṇa du Tattvacintāmaṇi de Gaṅgeśa avec; Le Dīdhiti de Raghunātha Śiromaṇi et la Ṭīkā de Jagadīśa Tarkālaṃkāra* (*Journal Asiatique*, 1977—), and numerous articles on various topics of Indology, in French, English and Sanskrit.

DR. BHAGWAN DASH is holder of Post-graduate qualifications in Āyurveda and Sanskrit, and Doctorate degree in Tibetan Medicine. He was Deputy Adviser in Āyurveda to the Govt. of India in the Ministry of Health. In 1980, he took voluntary retirement from his Government job to pursue his Āyurvedic practice and carry out researches in Āyurveda and Tibetan medicine on both of which he has already written 45 books.

Prof. COLLETT COX is Associate Professor in the Department of Asian Languages and Literature at the University of Washington. Her field of research is Indian Buddhist Abhidharma and her recent work includes publications on Buddhist epistemology, religious praxis, soteriology, and hermeneutics. She is the author of *Disputed Dharmas: Early Buddhist Theories on Existence.*

Prof. M. A. DHAKY had been Research Professor of Indian art and architecture at the L. D. Institute of Indology and currently continues to work as the Associate Director (Research) of the American Institute of Indian Studies, Varanasi, on a project, the Encyclopaedia of Indian Temple Architecture. He does much research in Jaina Prakrit texts.

Prof. R. C. DWIVEDI, Professor of Sanskrit and Dean, Faculty of Sanskrit Studies, University of Rajasthan, Jaipur is the senior most professor of Sanskrit in the country. He is the author of a number of books and research papers covering various aspects of Sanskrit studies including *Alaṅkāraśāstra*, Buddhism Jainism and Kashmir Śaivism. He has visited a number of countries for academic programmes. Dr. Dwivedi is a member of the Central Sanskrit Board, Rashtriya Sanskrit Samsthan, Rashtriya Veda Vidya Pratisthan and also of the Executive Councils of a number of Universities. An astoundingly able administrator, Dr. Dwivedi has been awarded Certificate of Honour by the President of India in recognition of his contribution to Indological Studies.

DR. GEORGE R. ELDER received a Ph.D. from Columbia University in 1978 in Buddhist Studies under the guidance of Dr. Wayman. He edited Wayman's essays entitled *Buddhist Insight*. A tenured Associate Professor at Hunter College in New York for several years, he is currently National Editor of ARAS (Archive for Research in Archetypal Symbolism).

DR. MICHAEL HAHN, born in 1941, is Professor of Indian and Tibetan Studies at the University of Marburg, Germany. His published books (10) and papers (50) focus on the Buddhist contribution to classical Sanskrit literature. He has edited and translated works of Nāgārjuna, Āryaśūra III, Haribhaṭṭa, Candragomin, Gopadatta, Śivasvāmin, Jñānaśrīmitra and Ratnākaraśānti.

Prof. AKIRA HIRAKAWA is Professor Emeritus of Indian Philosophy at Tokyo University. He is the author of over two hundred and forty articles and twenty books including major studies of *Vinaya* and early Indian Buddhism and a three-volume Sanskrit-Chinese-Tibetan index to the *Abhidharmakośabhāṣya*. Currently, he is directing the publication of his own collected works.

Prof. R. V. JOSHI, (b. 1927) a versatile scholar has creative writings in Sanskrit (a Mahākāvya Mohabhaṅgam and Khaṇḍa, Kāvyas), Critical writings in English, French, Spanish, Sanskrit and Hindi in the field of Vedas, Navya Nyāya and Vaiṣṇavism. He was offered Professorship in Sanskrit at Jodhpur and Delhi Universities where he headed the department for 15 years. He was Visiting Professor of Sanskrit, Philosophy, Indic Studies at Columbia University, New York, El Colegio de Mexico, Mexico, Universities of Czechoslovakia' Poland, Hungary, Cambodia. He was known as 'Modern Bāṇabhaṭṭa' in Varanasi when he was 22, and is distinguished for ornate classical style of Sanskrit eloquence. He has traditional training in Navya Nyāya and Navya Vyākaraṇa at Varanasi and modern training with Louis Renou and Jean Filliozat at Paris. He is recipient of numerous Awards and Honours. He is Chief Editor, Pt. Rampratap Shastri Publications Series, Editor, Sofia Indological Series, Chief Editor, French Journal 'Renocontra Avec l'Inde', and Co-ordinator Director of UNESCO Spanish Translation Project of Sanskrit and Pali texts. Comparative Religion and Philosophy, Navya Nyāya, Vyākaraṇa Vedanta and Vaiṣṇavism are his forte.

Prof. PADMANABH S. JAINI is Professor of Buddhist Studies in the Department of South and Southeast Asian Studies at the University of California, Berkeley. He is the author of numerous works dealing with Sanskrit Abhidharma literature, including *Abhidharmadīpa with Vibhāṣāprabhāvṛtti*, and has published extensively on the Pali apocryphal *Jātakas* including an edition of the *Paññāsa-jātaka*, which he translated as *Apocryphal Birth-Stories.* He has authored a number of works on Jainism as well, notable among which are *The Jaina Path of Purification* (1979) and *Gender and Salvation: Jaina Debates on the Spiritual Liberation of Women* (1922).

Prof. K. KUNJUNNI RAJA, M.A., Ph.D (Madras), Ph.D (London) is Hon. Director, Adyar Library and Research Centre, Madras. He was formerly Professor and Head of the Department of Sanskrit University of Madras. His publications include *The Contribution of Kerala to Sanskrit Literature*, *Indian Theories of Meaning*, ed. *Naisadhānanda* (with A. K. Warder), *Encyclopaedia of Indian Philosophy*, Vol. V (with Harold Coward), *New Catalogus Catalogorum*, Vols III-V (with V. Raghavan), VI-XI, Prof. Kunjunni Raja is recipient of Certificate of Honour for Sanskrit from the President of India (1990).

Prof. SHINJO NOBUSADA KAWASAKI was born in December 1935. He is Professor, Institute of Philosophy, National University of Tsukuba, Japan. He studied in the Graduate School, Columbia University in the city of New York, under Prof. Alex Wayman, 1967-1969 and obtained his Ph.D. (Tokyo University in 1987). He has published *A Study of Sarvajña in Buddhism*, in February 1992, Tokyo.

Prof. HAJIME NAKAMURA was born in Matsue-City, Japan in 1912. He is Professor Emeritus at the University of Tokyo and a member of Japan Academy of Sciences. Currently, he is Director of The Eastern Institute, Tokyo. Recipient of the Imperial Prize by the Japan Academy of Sciences (1957) and Cultural Order by the Emperor of Japan (1977), Prof. Nakamura was awarded several honorary degrees, including Honorary D. Litt. from Govt. of India and Deshikottama from Visvabharati University. Among his works in the English Language are: *Ways of Thinking of Eastern Peoples*: India, Tibet, Japan (1964). *A Comparative History of Ideas* (1975), *Indian Buddhism* (1980), *A History of Early Vedanta Philosophy* (1983).

DR. HARI SHANKAR PRASAD (born 1953) holds M.A. degree from Banaras Hindu University and Ph.D. from The Australian National University. He a senior Reader in the Department of Philosophy at Delhi University where he teaches Indian Philosophy. His main area of specialization is Buddhist Philosophy. He has published a number of books and articles in national and international journals.

DR. T. S. RUKMANI, Principal, Miranda House, University of Delhi is the first D. Litt. awardee so far in the Sanskrit Department of Delhi University. Earlier, she was Director of Non-Collegiate Women's Educational Board and Fellow, Indian Institute of advanced study, Shimla. Her published books are *Critical Study of the Bhāgavata Purāṇa*, *Śaṅkara—His Life and Philosophy*, *Religious Consciousness and Life Worlds* (Ed.), *Yogavārttika of Vijñānabhikṣu*—critical annotated translation in English in four volumes, and more than 35 papers in research journals both in India and abroad.

Prof. N. H. SAMTANI, BJK Institute of Buddhist and Asian Studies, Sarnath, Varanasi, was Former Chairman, Department of Pali and Buddhist Studies, Banaras Hindu University, now retired. He was sometimes visiting Professor of Buddhist Studies, University of Wisconsin, U.S.A., McMaster University, Hamilton, Canada and ICCR Visiting Professor of Indian Studies, Chieng Mai University, Thailand. He major works are *Arthaviniścaya-sūtra* (Ed.) and its commentary (*Nibandhana*), Patna, 1971. The text was brought by Rahul Sankrityayan from Tibet.

Prof. R. K. SHARMA, born on March 20, 1927, was initiated to Vedic and Śāstraic Studies at Lokamanya Brahmacaryasrama, Muzaffarpur, and trained on modern lines at Patna University. As a Fulbright Scholar, he worked with Prof. M. B. Emeneau at University of California. He has all along been contributing to promotion of Sanskrit Studies in India and abroad as Founder Director Rashtriya Sanskrit Sansthan, Joint Educational Adviser, Govt. of India, Vice-Chancellor of the two Sanskrit Universities at Darbhanga and Varanasi, Visiting Professor at Columbia University of New York City, University of Bihar and Chicago, Organising Secretary of two world Sanskrit Conferences, etc. He is a recipient of Presidential Award of Honour in Sanskrit and a Fellow of the Royal Asiatic Society.

A poet, novelist and critic, he has more than a dozen publications (apart from more than one hundred research papers) to his credit, including six creative writings in Sanskrit two for which have earned Sahitya Akademi and Bharatiya Bhasha Parishad Calcutta respectively.

DR. T. R. SHARMA, Reader-in-Sanskrit, has been teaching Sanskrit in S.G.T.B. Khalsa College, Delhi University for more than three decades. He has four publications to his credit (two of them prize winning) along with more than 30 research papers read at various seminars, conferences in India and abroad. His specialisation is Upaniṣads, Indian Culture and Civilization and Buddhist Philosophy.